Organizational Behavior
in Education

SIXTH EDITION

Organizational Behavior in Education

Robert G. Owens

Distinguished Research Professor Emeritus
Hofstra University

ALLYN AND BACON
Boston ✦ *London* ✦ *Toronto* ✦ *Sydney* ✦ *Tokyo* ✦ *Singapore*

Senior Editor: *Ray Short*
Editorial Assistant: *Karin Huang*
Composition Buyer: *Linda Cox*
Manufacturing Buyer: *Suzanne Lareau*
Marketing Manager: *Kris Farnsworth*
Production Coordinator: *Deborah Brown*
Editorial-Production Service: *P. M. Gordon Associates*
Cover Administrator: *Linda Knowles*

The first and second editions were published as
Organizational Behavior in Schools.

Library of Congress Cataloging-in-Publication Data

Owens, Robert G.
    Organizational behavior in education / Robert G. Owens.—6th ed.
      p.   cm.
    Includes bibliographical references and index.
    ISBN 0–205–26909–5
      1. School management and organization—United States.
    2. Organizational behavior.   I. Title.
LB2806.09   1998
371.2—dc21   97–23120
                                                             CIP

Printed in the United States of America

10 9 8 7 6 5 4 3 2 1   02 01 00 99 98 97

To my wife, Barbara,
without whose love, help, and encouragement
this book would never have been

CONTENTS

CHAPTER 5
Growth-Enhancing Environments in Educational Organizations   159

CHAPTER 6
Leadership   199

CHAPTER 7
Conflict in Organizations   229

CHAPTER 8
Decision Making   251

CHAPTER 10
The Holographic Imperative and Qualitative Research   335

Today, teaching and learning organizational behavior in education can be especially confusing. On the one hand, postmodernists reject—often stridently—traditional organizational theory whereas, on the other hand, theoretical organizational concepts continue to be indispensable to understanding the complexities of the subject. In this sixth edition I have attempted to weave these two seemingly disparate views together to provide a balanced discussion so that students will have an understanding of both points of view, which they will find existing side by side in the real world of their professional practice.

A description of some of the major changes introduced in this edition may be in order. The Prospective is a brief statement of the intellectual heritage that is the underlying context of the exposition of organizational behavior in education presented in the following chapters. In Chapter 1, in response to many requests, I have returned a brief history of the mainstreams of organizational thought to a prominent place at the opening of the book. Chapter 2 reintroduces some of the organizational theory concepts, again in response to requests from instructors, that had been dropped from the fifth edition. Chapter 3 includes a new discussion of the concept of building human capital, which is the endgame of managing organizational behavior in education.

I am grateful for the many helpful comments that I have received from those who found earlier editions useful in their teaching.

Robert G. Owens
Fort Myers, Florida
May 16, 1997

A school is a world in which people live and work. Like any other social organization the world of the school has power, structure, logic, and values, which combine to exert strong influence on the ways in which individuals perceive the world, interpret it, and respond to it. In short, the behavior of people at work in an educational organization—individually as well as a group—is not merely a reflection of their idiosyncratic personalities but is influenced, if not defined, by the social norms and expectations of the culture that prevail in the organization. This interplay between individuals and the social environment of their world of work is powerful in giving rise to organizational behavior, which means the behavior of people in the school organization. Those who would be educational leaders will find a clear grasp of the essentials of organizational behavior helpful in deciding what to do as they engage in the practice of leadership. This simple statement sets forth the central assumptions underlying this book.

Because an understanding of organizational behavior cannot be handed to you in a neat package of rules, algorithms, and recipes, you have a very active role to play in reading this book and coming to an understanding of organizational behavior. By merely reading and remembering, much as countless students have read other texts before, you probably will learn a great deal that will be useful in your present work and will be even more useful as you increase your field of influence as a leader. But if you ponder what you read, question it, challenge it, and ask yourself—and discuss with other people—how it all fits into the practical realities of your work, your experience, and your personal view of the world, the book will be much more useful to you both now and in the future.

One reason for this is that you will encounter many people in your professional practice whose understanding of organizational behavior will be at a different stage of development from your own. Many people will be skeptical about some of the viewpoints that this book suggests. In this growing and developing field, it is important that you not merely understand and internalize your commitment to certain principles and practices of organizational behavior, but that you also understand why some may disagree with them and doubt their practical usefulness in the harsh realities of the embattled schools of America.

Moreover, as I have suggested, both our knowledge of organizational behavior and the culture in which the school exists will continue to evolve. In the face of such challenges, it is vital that you become very clear as to what you think the fundamental principles of organizational behavior are and how they square with your personal values, beliefs, and vision of the role you want to play in your career.

ASSUMPTIONS, BELIEFS, BEHAVIORS

Everyone in every culture accepts certain implicit basic assumptions about people, their human nature, the nature of human relationships, the nature of human activity, and the nature of the relationships between people and their environment. These assumptions are called basic assumptions because they give rise to our beliefs and values and, ultimately, the way we behave toward others.[1] The basic assumptions are learned in infancy and develop as we mature and are educated. They become so thoroughly internalized that they are taken for granted and are shared with and supported by others around us. The assumptions become an invisible part of the warp and woof of life, and they are rarely thought about enough to be considered or discussed.

These basic assumptions—invisible and so taken for granted as to be rarely thought about, much less talked about—give rise to values and beliefs that we are more readily aware of. Because we may discuss them from time to time, the values and beliefs are therefore more public than the basic assumptions from which they arise. For example, one of the marvels of the Declaration of Independence is that it publicly articulated the clear linkage between basic assumptions about the nature of humankind held by the Founding Fathers and the political beliefs that, in their view, ultimately arose from those assumptions.

Moreover, actions (that is, behaviors) flow from the values and beliefs that people embrace. In the case of the Founding Fathers the compelling logic of their assumptions about human nature, that all men are created equal, led them to the treasonable acts of declaring independence from and ultimately taking up arms against arguably the mightiest kingdom of the time. Few of us have the intellectual and moral integrity of the Founding Fathers, however, and sometimes a peculiar dissonance separates the beliefs and values that we publicly espouse and the organizational behavior that we engage in.

Examples of such hypocrisy abound in education, as they do everywhere in our culture. Much is said about the need for children to get a good early start in schooling, with a rich and diverse program to lay a strong foundation for success in later years. However, we persist in spending minimally for preschool and early childhood education and spend increasingly more money at the middle and secondary school levels, despite the signs of seemingly intractable academic difficulty that are already well established early on.[2] Yet few would explicitly acknowledge that their basic assumption is that early childhood education is relatively unimportant and the "real work" of schooling begins after elementary school. Women's rights activists, people of color, the growing impoverished underclass, and oppressed racial and ethnic minorities in our culture discomfit many by pointing to similar discrepancies between espoused beliefs and values in the schooling enterprise, on the one hand, and actual schooling practices, on the other hand. If we want to make a difference in the organization we call school it is first necessary to carefully make our basic assumptions manifest and consider how logical the connections are between those assumptions, our publicly espoused values and beliefs, and the organizational behavior in which we engage in professional practice.

As you undoubtedly know, this is a difficult, though necessary, thing to do. One reason that it is difficult is epistemological: what do we know about organizational behavior in education and how do we know it? Just as the social sciences and the humanities are now in a period of great philosophical and epistemological turmoil, so is the field of organizational behavior. Therefore, much as you need to know how we know what we know, there is no quick, simple answer: you must become at least somewhat aware of the academic turmoil that is going on and how this book is positioned in it.

MODERNIST AND STRUCTURALIST THOUGHT

Certainly, at least until the mid-twentieth century, the pervasive assumption in Western cultures was that the world we live in must be characterized by some underlying patterns of logic, system, and order. From that assumption arose the belief that these patterns could be discovered only by using systematic methods of study, generally called the scientific method, that were controlled and circumscribed by strict rules of procedure and evidence. It was thought that once the orderly, presumably recurring, patterns were made manifest and described, they would reveal the keys to controlling the course of events so as to improve the human condition. In many fields, organizational behavior included, this meant that credible ways of knowing must base their claims to knowledge only on behavior or other phenomena that could be observed directly, measured, and quantified, preferably under carefully controlled conditions. Claims to knowing based on other rules of procedure and evidence could be dismissed as intuitive, anecdotal, or otherwise unscientific and therefore not to be taken terribly seriously. Today, this rather dogmatic view of ways of knowing is often referred to as modernism.

A related assumption was that the world, being an orderly and logical place, could be described by classifying the relative parts, usually in some sort of hierarchical schema. Who can forget, for example, memorizing the classification systems that we were taught in biology for sorting out the various kinds of plants and animals and showing their logical relationships in the scheme of things?

Such classification systems are called taxonomies. Many readers of this book will recall what is generally called Bloom's *Taxonomy of Educational Objectives,*[3] which has had extraordinary impact on thinking and practice in both curriculum development and teaching methods. To create the taxonomy, according to which all educational objectives could be classified, Bloom and his colleagues created an admittedly arbitrary (though apparently logical) hierarchy of six major classes of objectives that started with knowledge and, in ascending order, went on to comprehension, application, analysis, synthesis, and evaluation. Thus, the schema sought to build a conceptual structure of educational objectives that ascended from the simple to the complex, the concrete to the abstract.[4] Teachers, curriculum developers, and textbook writers embraced this powerful idea as a new and better way to organize instruction into a more logical, orderly, and systematic pattern. Above all, the taxonomy was generally accepted as being "scientific": objective, neutral, value-free, dispassionate. The Bloom taxonomy is mentioned here as simply one of the more distinguished examples that illustrate the structuralist approach to understanding the interface between human behavior and the school as a context, one that has had enormous influence on the ways in which teachers organized and managed

instruction in their classrooms. It has also had great impact on organizational behavior thought and administrative practice in education inasmuch as organizational
theorists have, until recently, accepted the structuralist view of knowledge. Essentially, that is what past organizational theories—such as bureaucratic theory and social systems theory, to mention two of the best known—have been about.
Cherryholmes' observation on structuralism is well worth noting:

> Structuralism as a pervasive and often unacknowledged way of thinking has influ-
> enced twentieth-century thinking in important ways. It promises order, organization,
> and certainty. Structuralism is consistent with teaching for objectives, standardized ed-
> ucational assessment, quantitative empirical research, systematic instruction, ratio-
> nalized bureaucracies, and scientific management. As long as structural assumptions
> remain unacknowledged, they are immunized against criticism.[5]

POSTMODERNISM AND POSTSTRUCTURALISM

In the period of postmodernism and poststructuralism, a growing number of academic iconoclasts are engaged in processes of bringing the previously unexamined
assumptions, from which our cultural and professional beliefs and values arise, into
the open, making them explicit, questioning them, and seeking to forge a consensus around new assumptions on which to rebuild our thinking about truth, knowledge, and epistemology in organizational behavior. You will recognize that we are
now entering an area of philosophical discourse of such complexity that it cannot
be dealt with in great depth here. But it is such an important emerging issue in the
study of organizational behavior today that it must be acknowledged and at least
briefly described.

Poststructuralism was fueled by growing awareness that there is often an obvious disjunction between publicly espoused values and what we do in schools. We
say, for example, that we believe in equity and equality, but many women, people
of color, and poor people find inequality and inequity to be a dominant characteristic in their lives in schools. But it is difficult for members of minority groups to
raise questions about that issue because those who control the schools are usually
able to suppress, sidetrack, redefine, or otherwise control the colloquy. French intellectual Michel Foucault pointed out that the issue is an invisible web of power in
the culture that controls our aspirations, how we think of ourselves, and what we do
to deal with those issues in our lives.[6] Through that invisible web of power, those
who control the culture decide what may be discussed, who is credible, and who is
allowed to speak.

For example, college students who want to become teachers generally take the
prescribed courses. Because they want to become teachers, and therefore want to be
viewed as "successful" students, they manifest the beliefs and behaviors that will further those ends and that the faculty of the college espouses, rewards, and controls.
Thus, the college weaves a web of visible and invisible power that influences students
to espouse the "appropriate" values and beliefs and behave in "desirable" ways so
that they will be seen as "good" potential teachers, meanwhile perhaps submerging

and even extinguishing some of their own inner assumptions. Later, as professionals in the schools, they "adapt as a matter of everyday professional life to contractual organizational demands, to demands of professional discourse, to expectations of professional peers, and to informal as well as formal job expectations. Power helps shape subjective feelings and beliefs. . . . Often power is most effective and efficient when it operates as desire, because desire often makes the effects of power invisible."[7]

Power, more particularly the asymmetrical distribution of power in the culture, makes this part of the poststructuralist view of the world a political view. It is thus that polemic enters academic discourse that previous generations prized for its evenhandedness, "objectivity" (which postmodernists now doubt can exist), and dispassion. Thus, in academic discourse on organizational behavior and educational leadership today, one commonly hears such hot-button political terms as oppression, powerlessness, political struggle, and repression being used with greater frequency as radical iconoclasts seek to develop a vocabulary intended to bring long-held, hidden basic assumptions into the open for reconsideration and thus to confront traditional thought. In this way, postmodernism contains an element of confrontation between radical members of minority groups and more conservative inheritors of power; the former seek to legitimize preoccupation with the differences that create our particular identities (such as differences in race, ethnicity, sexual orientation, class, and gender), and the latter seek to emphasize universality and amalgamation in attempting to merge our personal identities with traditionally espoused group values.[8]

This is not some arcane philosophical discussion: it is, for example, the field on which the future direction of the school curriculum and teaching in U.S. schools is being forged. Defenders of traditional values and cultural norms such as William J. Bennett and Allan Bloom strongly advocate emphasis on traditional Western literature, music, art, languages, history, and culture in the classic tradition of Western civilization, which they think of as universal elements in good school curricula. Postmodernists—including women's rights activists, race and ethnic minorities, "new" immigrants from non-European countries, and the poor—argue for a more diverse curriculum, one that is more inclusive of the literatures and histories of the majority of humankind. Thus they argue for "Women's Studies, African-American, Asian, African, Latin American, Hispanic, and Asian-American Studies."[9]

Poststructuralists also tend to think of ways of knowing, that is, research, less in the coolly detached terms of objective science and more in the sense of people's experience, feelings, intuition, and common sense. Poststructuralists often think of research in educational organizations as practitioners and academicians mutually engaged in a collaborative search for understanding rather than as aloof scientists studying their nameless "subjects" (or, worse, "S's") in the detached impersonal way formerly associated with scientific investigations of organizational behavior in education. Evidence of this lies in the rapid increase of the use of various qualitative research methods, especially ethnography, which seek to examine life in schools primarily through the experiences, assumptions, beliefs, values, and feelings of the participants.

However, as will be described in the chapters ahead, no overarching, all-encompassing theory or metanarrative of organizational theory exists that would generally be agreed upon by "everyone" today. Except on the general conceptual level that was stated earlier, there is no coherent body of thought that may accurately be described as *the* theory of organizational behavior. There is, though, an enormous body of literature that has been building at least since the mid-1920s, when organizational behavior was "discovered." That literature contains the thought, experience, and research of generations of scholars and practitioners as they struggled to understand human behavior in the workplace and its implications for effective management and leadership. As you might expect, while that vast literature reveals great diversity, it also reveals a steadily growing consensus about what we know.

That is why, as will be discussed more fully in later chapters, most people today believe that it matters very much what kind of climate or culture prevails in a school. As teachers know well, many schools tend to evoke behavior that is conventional, conforming, submissive, and controlled—many would describe such schools as oppressive (students tend to say "jails")—by emphasizing powerful social norms and expectations that support and reward such behavior. Conversely, the norms of such schools discourage behavior that questions the established order and proposes changes that challenge the conventional ways of the past. In the United States today, many people—not only those from traditionally oppressed or ignored groups, such as women, people of color, ethnic and minority groups, and the burgeoning underclass—find such educational institutions incompatible with their own strongly held personal values such as empowerment, self-growth, personal fulfillment, and sense of self-worth. This book will help you to explore ways of understanding the extraordinarily powerful relationship between the school as an organization and the behavior of people who work in it, and what implications for praxis in educational leadership these understandings suggest.

Knowledge of organizational behavior is not only very powerful but is arguably central to the most pressing issues in educational leadership today. This is a time of great intellectual turmoil in the field of education, a time of great epistemological skepticism in which all ideas rooted in the past are suspect. Indeed, some people seek to reject all theory and insist on a pragmatic approach to understanding organizational life in schools without seeming to understand that pragmatism is, in itself, a theory and an epistemological philosophy. Although this book takes a pragmatic approach to understanding behavior in education, it is based on understanding and accepting the fact that pragmatism is both an epistemological theory and philosophy. Because of the epistemological skepticism that is rampant today, and the antitheory bias that is sweeping through all the behavioral studies, let me disclose at least the essence of the growing intellectual heritage that underlies this book.

WHAT DO WE KNOW ABOUT ORGANIZATIONAL BEHAVIOR AND HOW DO WE KNOW IT?

In 1933, a brilliant young psychologist quietly slipped away from his prestigious position as a professor of psychology on the faculty of the world-renowned University of Berlin, stole to Norway, and then, wisely, took passage to New York. Kurt Lewin had been a rising star in Berlin's then-great academic citadel, but he had also seen the soaring Nazi terror invade the sheltered halls of the academy, poison the erstwhile learned discussions of colleagues and students alike, and literally place some people, such as Jews like himself, in fear for their very lives. Though already a respected international scholar, Lewin was practical enough to know that not merely was the university threatened, but that the future of European society was on a slippery slope. His mother could not bring herself to believe such a thing of her beloved native land and would soon meet her death in a concentration camp.

Once in the United States, one would think that, even in the depths of the Great Depression, Lewin would have had little difficulty procuring a faculty position in one of the major universities that were then beginning to harbor serious aspirations to world-class status. His scholarly background was both impeccable and impressive, and he held extraordinary promise for future achievements in the then still-unfledged field of psychology. One of his laboratory assistants, Ferdinand Hoppe, had already done major landmark research in 1930–31 on the roles of self-confidence, expectations, and aspirations in the motivation of people; his research remains fundamental in our thinking about organizational behavior to this day.

Moreover, Lewin had some connections through Americans who had studied in the celebrated University of Berlin and who had been impressed by what he taught. Would not any psychology department in one of the major U.S. universities have eagerly snatched him up? The answer is no, they would not and they did not; no offers came from any psychology faculty, distinguished or otherwise, in the United States. Nothing from Stanford, Chicago, Harvard, or any of the other prestigious universities then poised in the wings for greatness on the world stage. Ultimately, Lewin did find a job in the Child Welfare Research Station at the University of Iowa, one of the unique land-grant universities in the United States, which were then best known for their research and teaching in agriculture. In this way Kurt Lewin began to rebuild his career far from the academic bastions in psychology, shunned because he had already begun to question the fundamental concepts of psychology as the academic power wielders of the time understood it. In 1945, Lewin would receive an appointment at the Massachusetts Institute of Technology, which by then was scrambling to modernize its psychology department. However, that was a scant two years before his death. He was an iconoclast of his time, and academe is not always a welcoming place for iconoclasts.

Therein lies a story that you should know more about if you want to understand what we know about organizational behavior in education today and how we know it.

THE FIRST FORCE IN PSYCHOLOGY: PSYCHOANALYSIS

By 1933, when Lewin was job hunting in the United States, two major concepts had emerged to create the foundations of the rising field of psychology. The first of these was based on the pioneering work of Sigmund Freud and his followers, notably Carl

Jung. Psychoanalysis was the key method of choice to explore the unconscious drives and internal instincts that were thought to motivate people and, thus, be the causes of behavior. In fact, it was Freud who introduced the revolutionary notion of *psychic energy:* a previously overlooked source of energy, different from physical energy, from which human thoughts, feelings, and actions arose.[10] Both Freudian and Jungian psychoanalytic approaches tended, at that time, to focus on the need to diagnose and treat what was thought to be deviant or, at least, problematic behavior and tended to concentrate on such issues as social maladjustment and behavior disorders. The reader will no doubt recall such familiar concepts as the id, ego, and superego, which were of bedrock importance in teaching and studying human behavior as it was understood by psychoanalysts. The preferred method of treatment of perceived behavioral disorders was, and still is, psychotherapy.

Psychoanalysts and psychotherapists of various stripes and colors were important actors in some academic departments of psychology in U.S. universities of 1933, but they were far from dominant in the field because their research methods had little to do with such things as the design and execution of laboratory experiments, objective measurement, and mathematical analyses—all of which had become the hallmark of the scientific method and academic respectability in the status-conscious denizens of the upwardly mobile U.S. academy of the time. Nevertheless, the psychoanalytic/psychotherapeutic concepts of psychology were—as they still are—a widely known and influential force in the development of psychology.

Today, many U.S. teachers have studied the application of psychotherapeutic concepts to schooling through the work of such practical psychoanalysts as Bruno Bettelheim,[11] whose writing has been very popular among the general public as well, especially among parents and others interested in his chosen field of dealing with emotionally disturbed children.

THE SECOND FORCE IN PSYCHOLOGY: BEHAVIORISM

The second force in the development of psychology, and the dominant one in U.S. universities when Kurt Lewin began his job search in 1933, was behaviorism. Behaviorist psychology rejected most of the assumptions and methods of psychoanalysis, including (1) the emphasis on discovering the inner drives of people as causes of behavior and (2) the psychoanalytic methods of discovering these inner drives, which depended so heavily on the anecdotes of patients.

Behaviorists sought to develop a science of human behavior in the classic modernist sense. The epitome of the research method was the controlled laboratory experiment. The rules of evidence of this, the quintessential scientific method, required psychologists to limit their data collection to behaviors that could be observed directly in an "objective," "scientific" manner under controlled conditions. Thus, observations could, and should, be reduced to quantifiable terms: How many times was the behavior observed? In what time frame? In what sequence? Because intrinsic (or inner) motivations so central to psychoanalytic thought and practice cannot be observed, much less quantified or controlled, but depend on anecdotal evidence, behaviorists discounted them altogether. Because they could not observe and measure internal motivation, behaviorists focused on extrinsic motivation: rewards and punishments intended to reinforce desired behaviors and extinguish undesired behaviors. Food and release from pain were among the quantifiable, manipulable extrinsic rewards often used in the carefully controlled laboratory experiments that constituted the method of choice of behaviorists and became their hallmark.

Thus, human beings were not only reduced to being merely objects under study by behaviorists but they were actually replaced in the laboratory by rats, pigeons, and other animals, which were both cheaper and easier to control. "Animals, from a breeding house and often newly obtained fresh from American Railway Express platforms, were starved to three quarters or two thirds of their body weight to insure adequate 'motivation.' When it is remembered that these rats were two to three months old, 'teenagers' in the human time scale, at the outset of the experimentation (to have waited longer would have increased laboratory costs), it is no wonder" that the psychology that emerged could be described as the psychology of desperate rats.[12]

Nonetheless, behaviorism had clearly emerged by 1933 as the definitional approach to understanding human behavior in academic departments of psychology in U.S. universities. B. F. Skinner is undoubtedly the practitioner best known to U.S. teachers and educators for his widely practiced proposals for applying behaviorism to schooling, especially the pedagogical methods for teaching children with maladaptive behavior.

By the 1970s, behaviorism, and particularly its Skinnerian form, had mushroomed into a large-scale movement in U.S. schooling and remained so well into the 1980s. Behaviorism still remains influential in curriculum and instruction circles. It has been embraced, knowingly or otherwise, by many advocates of school reform. Such pedagogical notions as programmed instruction, diagnostic-prescriptive teaching, and behavior modification are behaviorist ideas familiar to many U.S. teachers. Much of the use of computers in the classroom is based on behaviorist notions of pedagogy. "The technology of behaviorism that Skinner [advocated] for the schools is to decide on goals, to find the reinforcers to produce those responses, to implement a program of reinforcers that will produce the desired behaviors, and finally to measure very carefully the effects of the reinforcers and to change them accordingly."[13] Thus behaviorism, especially B. F. Skinner's brand, was far from some idle academic theory that had little relevance to the real world of schools: in fact, it has been a powerful force in defining how U.S. teachers, administrators, reformers, and others think about students, teaching praxis, and the organization and leadership of schools. For example, Schmuck and Schmuck viewed with some alarm the impact of Skinnerian behaviorism on schooling in the United States. In 1974, they observed that, in the behaviorist view, "Evidence of learning consists of prescribed responses to stimuli presented in a program, on a standardized test, or by the teacher's question. In a good [behaviorist] program, the objectives are behaviorally defined, the information is presented in a logical and sequential manner"[14] and there are systematic methods for evaluating behaviors to be used as evidence of reaching the program's objectives. Systematic methods for evaluating the outcomes of instruction should be, in the behaviorist view, "objective" and tend to emphasize standardized testing. Skinner, moreover, made it very clear that since the processes of learning are not themselves either directly visible or quantifiable, the pedagogical techniques of behaviorism "are not designed to 'develop the mind' or to further some vague 'understanding' . . . they are designed on the contrary to establish the very behaviors which are taken to be *evidence of learning.*"[15]

A THIRD FORCE EMERGES IN PSYCHOLOGY: HUMANISTIC AND SOCIAL PSYCHOLOGY

Kurt Lewin was among the first to raise serious, prickly questions about behaviorism. Why, he wondered, should it be that human behavior could be studied only in the laboratory under controlled conditions? Did chasing rats in a laboratory maze really produce insights into the human condition that were germane to significant social problems? Was there only one acceptable way of searching for truth and understanding, or were there acceptable alternative ways? Couldn't one go out into the real world, where people lived and worked, and study behavior in legitimate ways? Furthermore, didn't people's attitudes, feelings, values, and beliefs matter in the formation of behavior? Didn't they have anything significant to do with the way people behaved? Coming from Europe, where he had looked around thoughtfully, Lewin noted that being a member of a group seemed to have impact on how people behaved. He had, personally, seen and felt the furious rage of groups of his fellow citizens directed at the Jews—a group of people to whom he belonged. He had also seen, or knew of, similar murderous group enmities elsewhere in Europe (in Eastern Europe, the Balkans, and so on), often having a heritage extending back into the forgotten mists of time. Shouldn't psychologists study these important social problems so that, by understanding their causes better, we might find better ways of educating younger generations and otherwise effecting some amelioration of these age-old scourges of human civilization? A few simple questions, earnestly argued, and Lewin was suddenly typecast as an iconoclast taking on the establishment, a petty upstart to be barred from the company of the academic barons who controlled the psychology departments of universities in the United States. Surely Foucault was right: there was an invisible web of power by which the dialogue was controlled.

It was thus, in the cut-and-thrust still so typical of academic politics, that Lewin found himself without a job, at least in a psychology department and presumably sidetracked to oblivion. He would be dead in fourteen years: plenty of time to be a leader in founding and developing social psychology, pioneer new research methods and rules of evidence to be used in real-world settings, forge new linkages among psychology and sociology and anthropology, and inspire a generation of younger scholars to address practical social-psychological problems of urgent importance. As I will describe, many others with new ideas of their own, but inspired by the work of Lewin, his associates, and his students, would develop a new and very different approach to psychology.

Lewin is widely accepted as one of the founders, if not the founder, of social psychology, and moved beyond that to become a pioneer in the development of third force, or humanistic, psychology. The latter accepts, first, that behavior arises from interactions between individuals, whose temperaments and personalities are idiosyncratic and variable, and their environment—that is, B = $f(p \cdot e)$—and, second, that a primary value of organizational life is to support and facilitate continuing growth, development, and expansion of the potential of the people in the organization.

When working in schools, as in any organization, an extraordinarily powerful aspect of the environment in shaping and molding behavior of participants is the culture and the climate provided by the organization. Although educational leaders have scant influence over the temperaments or personalities of the individuals whom they would lead, they have a wide range of possibilities for influencing the characteristics of the culture and the climate of the organization. Because the organization has no independent physical reality but exists only as a socially constructed reality, and because our construction of reality is dependent on our perception of what is real, it becomes clearer how the organization emerges as a primary factor in evoking behavior of people in it. This web of interactions between people and organization, and its implications for leadership, is not simple but it is powerful in influencing and shaping the behavior of people at work in educational organizations. It is the subject of the rest of this book.

SOCIOLOGICAL AND PSYCHOLOGICAL POINTS OF VIEW

The study of psychology took root in the United States in the years preceding World War I. The pioneers in the field, such as G. Stanley Hall (who was awarded the first U.S. doctorate in psychology in 1878) and William James, took intense interest in pedagogy and schooling and had enormous impact on educational thought. By the early 1920s, normal schools and, later, university schools of education had developed strong departments of educational psychology that reflected their views; these departments soon established themselves as dominant in shaping the curriculum of teacher education, and thus the thinking of U.S. educators.

Today, psychology remains a predominant element in the core of teacher education. Departments of educational psychology in schools of education commonly exert strong influences not only on the content of courses in teaching methods and curriculum but also on the content and methods of data collection and research. That is why courses in such topics as tests and measurements and statistics loom so large in the undergraduate and graduate studies of teachers: they represent critically important skill areas for the researcher in the laboratory of behavioral psychology and are commonly assumed to be somehow useful in teaching praxis. We know from the widespread belief that teachers often voice that such courses are viewed as having little application to teaching practice. The longtime dominance of educational psychology on educational thought in schools of education also helps to explain why present-day in-service education programs for teachers tend to focus so narrowly on technical aspects of pedagogy, usually with emphasis on instructional techniques in the classroom. It is commonplace for teachers to view such programs as of dubious value to them in improving practice.

Sociology, on the other hand, developed in its early years with scant reference to schooling other than as institutions that reflected such issues as social class, the effects of desegregation, and the role of schools in society. By the late 1970s, however, a small number of sociologists grew interested in the sociology of organizations, including educational organizations. They began to pick up on some of the ideas that had been explored by the sociologists who conducted studies in industrial settings, notably in units of the Western Electric Company, and to extend that field of inquiry. As the reform movement of the 1980s unfolded, educators became disenchanted with many of the proposals coming from psychologists—for example, proposals for more testing, increased emphasis on basic skills, and refinement of pedagogical techniques—and they began to listen more carefully to the thoughts of sociologists.

In thinking about schooling, psychologists and sociologists generally agree that the goals of schooling are

- academic achievement
- effective work habits
- civic values
- social behavior
- self-esteem
- self-reliance[16]

But they disagree on what must be emphasized to achieve these outcomes better. Psychologists focus on how individual pupils learn, including the particular learning styles, motivation, and relationships with both the teacher and classmates. "Sociologists," on the other hand, "look at the entire school and how its organization affects the individuals within it."[17] Thus, to achieve the goals of schooling, educational psychologists tend to focus on such things as

- the expectations that teachers have for the achievement of students
- the relationships between students and teachers
- the motivation of students
- time spent on teaching and learning
- the relationships between individual students and their peers

To achieve the same goals, organizational and educational sociologists tend to emphasize such things as

- how schools are led and managed
- how students are grouped

✦ the involvement of parents and community

✦ the ways in which students and teachers are assigned to work together

✦ the ways in which important decisions are made in the school as a whole

One should be careful about emphasizing the apparent dichotomy of these two different points of view. It is not a new idea in psychology that behavior is heavily influenced by the characteristics of organizational environment on which organizational sociologists tend to focus. Working independently, both Kurt Lewin and Henry A. Murray,[18] each a giant in the founding of modern psychology, accepted the premise as early as the 1930s that behavior is a function of the interaction between the person and the environment. This remains today a basic concept in understanding organizational behavior.

In this book, that idea is expressed as $B = f(p \cdot e)$.[19] This is a powerful understanding that has informed and inspired much of the study of organizational culture and organizational climate in schools. The study of organizational behavior is, in fact, the study of the internal needs and personality characteristics of the individual in dynamic tension with the environment created by the educational organization.

The recent trend to emphasize restructuring of schools to achieve school reform emanates largely, but by no means exclusively, from contemporary thought of organizational sociologists, which generally has not been well represented in the curricula of schools of education. Many currently popular buzzwords in school reform reflect the renewed understanding that the interface of people with the organization is the nexus of school reform efforts. Thus, the vernacular of school reform in the 1990s resounds with calls for empowerment and power sharing, "reinventing" the school, school site management, restructuring the school, participative decision making, and humanizing the school. All of these suggest major changes in the organization of the school to improve the growth-enhancing characteristics of their environments.

The sixty-year-long development of the field of organizational behavior has been characterized by two main strands that are endlessly intertwined, sometimes in conflict yet often not even in contact. One strand is provided by those who perceive educational organizations as enduring hierarchical bureaucratic systems in which power and authority are and ought to be exercised from the top down, a structure into which people must fit on terms that the organization demands. The other strand is provided by those who perceive educational organizations as human social systems in which members are the most valuable resources in creating a working environment that continually supports their personal growth and development over time in order to encourage the most effective and appropriate organizational behavior.

Although U.S. schools have tended throughout their history to ape the values and views of industry, commerce, and the military, it is becoming increasingly clear that schools are in fact distinct, if not unique, kinds of organizations that are different in important ways from industrial, commercial, governmental, or military organizations. Because schools are unique among organizations they require ways of thinking, styles of leadership, and approaches to administrative practice that are especially suited to them.

The uniqueness of educational organizations resides in their educative mission, which demands that they be growth-enhancing organizations: fostering learning and personal growth and development of participants, encouraging never-ending processes of maturing, enhancing self-confidence and self-esteem, satisfaction, taking initiative, and seeking responsibility for one's actions. Educative organizations seek to increase the personal and interpersonal competencies of the organization's participants, to constantly develop the skills of the group in collaborating, to make hidden assumptions explicit and to examine them for what they mean in terms of individual and group behavior, to enact cooperative group behavior that is caring and supportive of others, to manage conflict productively and without fear, and to share information and ideas fully and without fear. It is the business of schools, therefore, to develop a culture that places high value on, and supports and enhances, openness, high trust, caring and sharing, that always strives for consensus but supports and values those who think differently, and that prizes human growth and development above all. Educational leaders, then, strive for a vision of the school as one that seeks to be engaged in a never-ending process of change and development, a "race without a finish line," or *kaizen,* as the Japanese speak of constant growth achieved through small incremental steps, rather than one that seeks the big dramatic breakthrough, the mythical "silver bullet," that will, supposedly, finally make everything right.

The processes of becoming[20]—of people growing and developing as individuals and as groups, and of the organization doing so as well—combine to create the essence of enduring vitality in organizational life while academic outcomes are transient, ephemeral evidence that the processes are working. The conundrum of power is a major characteristic of the environment of the educational organization: hierarchy prevails; we really have never found a substitute for it in organizational life, but there is much that we can ethically and honestly do to share power, and distribute it more equitably in efforts to minimize its deleterious effects on the behavior of people in the organization. In the process, we can make the school an ever more growth-enhancing environment.

SUGGESTED READING

Aronowitz, Stanley, and Henry A. Giroux, *Postmodern Education: Politics, Culture, and Social Criticism.* Minneapolis: University of Minnesota Press, 1991.

> A polemical discussion of the politics of class, race, and gender in the present postmodernist period of U.S. education. The writing is dense and often obscure, but knowledgeable, passionate, and important information for those who have not kept abreast of this emerging field.

Cherryholmes, Cleo H., *Power and Criticism: Poststructural Investigations in Education.* New York: Teachers College Press, 1988.

> An excellent tour of poststructuralist thought in education that provides an always challenging, often exciting, discussion of newer ways of thinking about schools and how they are being studied.

Foster, William, *Paradigms and Promises: New Approaches to Educational Administration.* Buffalo, NY: Prometheus Books, 1986.

> A book on theory in administration that explains critical theory and strongly advocates it as a basis for the study of educational administration. "Administrators of educational settings are critical humanists. They are humanists because they appreciate the usual and unusual events of our lives and engage in an effort to develop, challenge, and liberate human souls. They are critical because they are educators and are therefore not satisfied with the status quo; rather, they hope to change individuals for the better and to improve social conditions. A scientific model of administration, to the degree that this depends on a positivist model of science, comes under attack here because we feel that it inadequately considers the many social, cultural, and educational issues in our society" (pp. 17–18).

NOTES

1. I am indebted to Edgar Schein's analysis of the relationships between basic assumptions, values and beliefs, and behavior; his views are described more fully later in this book. See Edgar H. Schein, *Organizational Culture and Leadership* (San Francisco: Jossey-Bass, 1985).
2. We now have extensive documentation and literature on this. See, for example, Theodore R. Sizer, *Horace's School: Redesigning the American High School* (New York: Houghton Mifflin, 1992).
3. Benjamin S. Bloom, Edward J. Furst, Walker H. Hill, and David R. Krathwohl, *Taxonomy of Educational Objectives: Cognitive Domain* (New York: David McKay, 1956).
4. Cleo H. Cherryholmes, *Power and Criticism: Poststructural Investigations in Education* (New York: Teachers College Press, 1988), p. 29.
5. Ibid., p. 30.
6. See, for example, Michel Foucault, *Power/Knowledge* (New York: Pantheon Books, 1980). For a broader overview of Foucault's ideas, see Hubert Dreyfus and Paul Rabinow, eds., *Michel Foucault: Beyond Structuralism and Hermeneutics,* 2nd ed. (Chicago: University of Chicago Press, 1983).
7. Cherryholmes, *Power and Criticism,* p. 35.
8. Sharon Welch, "An Ethic of Solidarity and Difference," in *Postmodernism, Feminism, and Cultural Politics: Redrawing Educational Boundaries,* ed. Henry A. Giroux (Albany, NY: State University of New York Press, 1991), pp. 83–84.
9. Ibid., p. 84.
10. Martin V. Covington, *Making the Grade: A Self-Worth Perspective on Motivation and School Reform* (Cambridge: The Cambridge University Press, 1992), p. 25.
11. Perhaps his opus magnum was *Love Is Not Enough* (New York: The Free Press, 1949).
12. Richard Klee, "Humanist Perspective," in *Humanistic Psychology: A Source Book,* eds. I. David Welch, George A. Tate, and Fred Richards (Buffalo, NY: Prometheus Books, 1978), p. 4.
13. Richard A. Schmuck and Patricia A. Schmuck, *A Humanistic Psychology of Education: Making the School Everybody's House* (Palo Alto, CA: National Press Books, 1974), p. 45.
14. Ibid., p. 49.
15. B. F. Skinner, *The Technology of Teaching* (New York: Appleton-Century-Crofts, 1968), p. 26. Emphasis added.
16. The following discussion on the differences between the approaches used by psychologists and sociologists to making schools better follows Amy Stuart Wells, "Backers of School Change Turn to Sociologists," *The New York Times,* Education Supplement, Wednesday, January 4, 1989, p. 17.
17. Wells, "Backers of School Change," p. 17.
18. Henry A. Murray and others, *Explorations in Personality* (New York: Oxford University Press, 1938).
19. Lewin originally stated it as $B = f(P,E)$. See Kurt Lewin, *A Dynamic Theory of Personality* (New York: McGraw-Hill, 1935).
20. Carl R. Rogers, *On Becoming a Person* (Boston: Houghton Mifflin, 1961).

Mainstreams of Organizational Thought

ABOUT THIS CHAPTER

Over the course of the last century we have learned that there are, essentially, two ways of thinking about educational organizations. One is the traditional way: to think of organizations as hierarchical systems in which power and intelligence are concentrated at the top, hence initiative and good ideas originate there and are passed down through command and control as programs and procedures that people in the lower levels put into practice. The other, newer way—discovered in chrysalid fashion over the course of the century—is to think of organizations as co-operative, collegial, even collaborative systems in which good ideas exist everywhere in the organization and can be made manifest and put into action only when those in the hierarchy of command and control act in ways that release the capabilities and motivations of subordinates. There is a lot more to it than that, of course, and Chapter 1 gives you some background on the history of the development of these ideas. Without that background, one cannot intelligently engage in the current debate on school reform because the debate—though often openly political rather than educational—nearly always arises from the different concepts that the debaters have about such issues as how to make an organization more effective and what leadership is.

Like most readers of this book, you are very probably an experienced and highly skilled professional teacher who is preparing to qualify for a position of leadership where you work: perhaps as a chairperson, an assistant principal, or a principal. If so, you are undoubtedly not only a busy person but inclined to be tough minded and practical, not especially interested in academic discourse that is not directly related to your needs. Therefore, you may ask yourself, why should I be studying organizational behavior in education? What is important to me in this first chapter? Let me deal with this in the form of three questions.

Why Study Organizational Behavior?

The short answer is, because organizational behavior provides the indispensable foundation of knowledge that is absolutely essential if one hopes to achieve success in educational leadership. After all, leadership, and administration as well, means *working with and through other people to achieve organizational goals.* Although those who are appointed as school principals are usually selected from the ranks of teachers who are thought to be especially effective, after their appointments they engage very little in the technical aspects of teaching that earned them their reputations. Indeed, the shift from classroom teaching to a school leadership position, such as the principalship, is really a career change—so different are the skills needed to do the work, and the outcomes by which one's success is judged, that one literally leaves teaching and enters a new and very different occupation. Often, newly appointed school leaders find that knowledge of such traditional subjects in the curriculum of educational administration—such as school law, curriculum theory, or educational finance—do little to assure success in leadership.

After appointment as principal, one's work consists primarily of working with and through other adults: one confers with people, individually and in small groups; one plans and runs meetings, sometimes small and sometimes large; one has innumerable encounters with people, some planned but many impromptu and necessarily hurried. It is often assumed that intelligent adults, such as successful teachers, are smart enough to work with and through other people effectively. Yet if you are a school teacher, you may have already witnessed school principals at work who are simply not as capable as they should be in motivating teachers and parents, leading them, and developing the dynamic teamwork in the school and its community that is demanded in this era of school reform. A major cause of such failure is often the fact that the principal simply does not have a strategic plan, sometimes called a vision, as to how to deal with the all-critical human dimension of the school enterprise.

Many newly appointed principals have good intentions about improving the performance of the school by improving morale, enriching the quality of life in the school, and building teamwork. Many wish to introduce new technical changes as well: adding new curricula, perhaps, or reorganizing the structure of the school. But very often they are ill prepared by traditional course work to think through and plan their approach to school leadership and have given little thought to the relationship between their day-to-day and hour-by-hour behavior on the job and the outcomes that they so earnestly desire as leaders. Study of organizational behavior in education can help you, first, by focusing your attention on these issues and, second, by encouraging you to making some personal decisions as to how you would plan to practice being a leader on the job. Aside from a general knowledge of pedagogy and schooling, perhaps the single most useful professional too] that the teacher can bring to the role of educational leader is skill at planning for both long-range and short-range activities on the job. One of the outstanding characteristics of successful teachers is their skill at planning their work, both in the formal sense of written plans as well as in the sense of coherent mental maps of what work to do and how to do it. Astonishingly, this is the very skill that many people seem to abandon first when appointed to the principalship and, instead, go in to work every day more or less waiting to see what crises will unfold. Every principal quickly finds that there are always many, many crises and emergencies sure to arise that seem to fill every hour of the day, compete urgently for attention, and keep one "putting out fires" from early in the morning until the evening hours. Such a demanding job, with its never-ending time pressures, requires a principal who not only understands organizational behavior and its importance to school leadership, but has internalized a personal commitment to constantly keep leadership and human concerns very high on the list of priorities.

Why Study the History of Organizational Behavior?

This chapter presents a history of the development of modern organizational thought from its beginnings in 1887 to the present time. Prior to that time, little serious consideration had been given to organizational thought, other than the concept of hierarchical command that arose in the mists of time past and was perpetuated in monarchic dynasties and their military and ecclesiastical establishments. It is the patrimony of many of their intellectual heirs in present-day business, government, and military organizations. But, as we shall see, since 1887 a great deal of thought and study has been given to the search for alternative ideas for organizing and leading that are better suited to modern realities. The central theme of that search, which developed throughout the twentieth century, has been growing awareness and understanding of human behavior and its importance in determining the effectiveness of the organization. But new knowledge has not replaced the old. Traditional concepts of organization continue to compete with newer knowledge and, indeed, are still dominant in the marketplace of ideas. But, in Western cultures at least, there has been a growing trend in which the importance of the human dimension of the organization is increasingly understood and recognized.

As the twentieth century draws to a close, we know that we can deliberately choose from between two competing alternative strategies of leading and organizing: traditional top-down hierarchy or a more collegial participative approach. Today both strategies are being used in education, as well as in business, government, and the military, and each has its sometimes fierce advocates. As a school leader you may be certain of one thing, at least: you will be constantly pulled by advocates of traditional authoritarian leadership and hauled by those who see the fundamental importance of the human dimension of the school. You may be certain that, as an educational leader, you will regularly be called on to make personal decisions as to which path to follow. Only by knowing the contributions of those who came before us, those who pioneered in building the knowledge that we have for thinking about organizations and leadership, can you prepare yourself to make the strategic and tactical decisions that will undergird your leadership with steadfast purpose, consistency, and effectiveness.

Why Study Theory?

This chapter describes a number of theories about organization that were developed mostly in the last half of the twentieth century. But, the practical-minded reader may ask, why study theory? Why not just tell us what works and leave the theorizing to someone else? The answer to the question lies in the fact that there is often confusion about what theory is. This is explored more thoroughly in Chapter 2, where you will find a definition and discussion of theory. But for the moment it should be understood that one cannot even think about different ways of organizing human beings in collective effort without using theory. Simply to speak of such common organizational notions as leadership or top-down hierarchical authority is to engage in theoretical discussion. Trying to discuss educational organization without some reference to theory is a lot like trying to discuss the prevention of sickness and disease without reference to such basic sanitary practices as washing, bathing, and constructing sealed wells for drinking water, ideas that rest on the germ theory of disease. It is insufficient for us to know that one should wash one's hands regularly, bathe from time to time, and have a source of safe drinking water. It is when we know *why* these are good, healthful practices that we become personally, deeply committed to them as being very important to achieving an important goal in life. Thus, no matter how busy we are we do not fail to keep these practices high on our list of daily priorities: whereas they are theoretically important to us, they are equally as important in a practical sense.

It is theory that provides the rationale for what one does. Practice simply cannot be isolated from theory. Paul Mort said it well: "There is nothing impractical about good theory. . . . Action divorced from theory is the random scurrying of a rat in a new maze. Good theory is the power to find the way to the goal with a minimum of lost motion and electric shock."[1]

PUBLIC ADMINISTRATION AS A BEGINNING

In one sense, administration is one of the most ancient of all human endeavors. There is little question, for example, that the Egyptians organized and administered vast complex enterprises that required sophisticated planning, complex organization, skilled leadership, and detailed coordination at least two thousand years before the birth of Christ. To put it in perspective, it has been estimated that the task of constructing the Pyramids—which took one hundred thousand men twenty years to complete—was equivalent to administering an organization three times the size of the Shell Oil Company.

Similarly, the Chinese are known to have had highly systematic, large-scale administrative systems at about the same time as the Pyramids were built, which used many of the management concepts still in use today. Moses, implementing the plan given to him by his father-in-law by which the people of Israel would be ruled, is cited in modern management textbooks as establishing the pyramidal design of organization still so much in vogue today. The administrative system of the Catholic church, a far-flung organization at one time numbering nearly a half-million cardinals, archbishops, bishops, and parish priests, is still studied for its remarkably centralized administrative system and is compared with the vastly more complex administrative system of modern-day General Motors. And, of course, great military leaders from Alexander the Great to Caesar, to Napoleon, to Douglas MacArthur have long been studied for what they can teach us about planning, organizing, leading, and motivating.

Nearer to us in time, and better known to most of us, are the ideas and concepts that underlay the establishment of the reputable civil services of Europe and Great Britain in the nineteenth century. Two key notions provided the essential rationale for those Western-European civil services:

1. The idea that administration is an activity that can be studied and taught separately from the content of what is being administered. For example, a mail carrier need not administer a postal service, nor must tax attorneys administer the collection of taxes. This gave rise to the notion that administration could, in itself, have a productive work role in the organization.

2. The belief that decisions about the policies and purposes of government belong to the realm of political action but that these decisions are best implemented by civil servants whose jobs are not dependent on the whims of politics and who are free to develop good administrative procedures. This includes much more than the U.S. idea of a civil service as an alternative to corruption and the "spoils system." This belief is based on the concept that a disinterested administrative organization can become more effective than one that is involved in the policy-making process. In the twentieth century, the Secretariat of the United Nations and the Foreign Service of the United States State Department are good illustrations of efforts to apply this concept in practice.

In the United States in the nineteenth century, the term "administration" was also used in the context of government, and the ideas it represented gave rise to the growth of public administration, although "civil service" in the United States tended to connote a system designed to insure honesty and fairness rather than the expertness associated with the European and British systems. Woodrow Wilson crystallized early thinking about the professionalization of administration with the publication of his now-famous essay, "The Study of Administration," in 1887. He felt that the improvement of administrative techniques depended on scholarly study and learning in the specialized field of administration itself.

"The object of administrative study," he wrote in an often-quoted statement, "is to rescue executive methods from the confusion and costliness of empirical study and set them upon foundations laid deep in stable principle."[2] A thirty-one-year-old assistant professor when he published this article, Wilson was far ahead of his time in arguing earnestly for the inclusion of the study of administration as a subject fit for serious treatment by universities. Forty years were to pass before the first textbook on the principles in public administration for which he called was published (1927). The search for principles was essential to the development of an administrative science, as differentiated from administrative folklore or custom.

IMPACT OF THE INDUSTRIAL REVOLUTION

At about the close of the nineteenth century—the time of Woodrow Wilson's scholarly contributions—businesspeople in Western Europe and the United States were stepping up their efforts to increase profits from industry. Then, as now, it was generally believed in that burgeoning era of industry that greater profitability required lowering the unit cost of producing goods. One way to do this, of course, was to step up mass production through the use of such innovations as the assembly line. The leadership of pioneering industrial giants, such as Henry Ford, is widely recognized in connection with such technological breakthroughs. In this era of industrial expansion, the key people were the engineers and technically oriented scientists—as they are in our own day of technological revolution. These were the people who could build the machines and then combine them into assembly line units. This was the era of the engineering consultant and the drive for efficiency.

Frederick W. Taylor is a name well known to many students of administration. He had been an engineer at the Midvale and the Bethlehem steel companies at the close of the 1800s and, in the early 1900s, became one of the top engineering consultants in U.S. industry. We know that Taylor read Wilson's essay and was influenced by it. From about 1900 to 1915, as he worked to solve practical production problems in factories all over the United States, Taylor developed what later became known as his four "principles of scientific management":

1. Eliminate the guesswork of rule-of-thumb approaches to deciding how each worker is to do a job by adopting scientific measurements to break the job down into a series of small, related tasks.

2. Use more scientific, systematic methods for selecting workers and training them for specific jobs.

3. Establish the concept that there is a clear division of responsibility between management and workers, with management doing the goal setting, planning, and supervising, and workers executing the required tasks.

4. Establish the discipline whereby management sets the objectives and the workers cooperate in achieving them.

Notice, especially, the last two of Taylor's principles: they formally differentiate between the roles and responsibilities of managers, on the one hand, and workers, on the other hand. They mandate a top-down hierarchical relationship between managers and workers. This traditional concept of labor-management relationships was hardly original with Taylor, but its formalization as a basic principle of organization and management has proven to be extremely powerful in shaping the assumptions and beliefs of managers and thus their thinking about such concepts as collaboration and teamwork, which were to emerge in the years ahead. These two of Taylor's principles still provide the justification for many school administrators and school board members to resist—openly or covertly—such ideas as collegial, collaborative approaches to goal setting, planning, and problem solving and other "bottom-up" approaches to school reform in favor of more traditional authoritarian approaches. Indeed, over the course of the next seventy-five years—certainly until the present time—these two of Taylor's principles of scientific management would be the arena in which new and very different ideas about management behavior would evolve.

Frederick Taylor's principles of scientific management became enormously popular, not only in industry but also in the management of all kinds of organizations, including the family. A bestseller of the 1950s, *Cheaper by the Dozen*, vividly recounts how "efficiency" invaded every corner of the family life of Frank B. Gilbreth, one of Taylor's closest colleagues and an expert on time-and-motion study. Taylor's principles of scientific management were aimed primarily at lowering the unit cost of factory production, although he and his followers claimed that these principles could be applied universally;[3] they became almost an obsession in the press and throughout our society.[4] In practice, Taylor's ideas led to time-and-motion studies, rigid discipline on the job, concentration on the tasks to be performed with minimal interpersonal contacts between workers, and strict application of incentive pay systems.[5]

At the same time that Taylor's ideas and their application were having such enormous impact on life in the United States, a French industrialist was working out some powerful ideas of his own. Henri Fayol had a background quite different from Taylor's, which helps to account for some of the differences in perception of the two men. Whereas Taylor was essentially a technician whose first concern was the middle-management level of industry, Fayol had the background of a top-management executive. It would be useful to mention briefly some of the ideas Fayol advanced, to give us a better perspective on what he contributed to the growth of thought in administration:

1. Unlike Taylor, who tended to view workers as extensions of factory machinery, Fayol focused his attention on the manager rather than on the worker.
2. He clearly separated the processes of administration from other operations in the organization, such as production.
3. He emphasized the common elements of the process of administration in different organizations.

Fayol believed that a trained administrative group was essential to improving the operations of organizations, which were becoming increasingly complex. As early as 1916, Fayol wrote that administrative ability "can and should be acquired in the same way as technical ability, first at school, later in the workshop."[6] He added that we find good and bad administrative methods existing side by side "with a persistence only to be explained by lack of theory."[7]

In his most notable work, *General and Industrial Management*,[8] Fayol established himself as the first modern organizational theorist. It was Fayol who defined administration in terms of five functions: (1) planning, (2) organizing, (3) commanding, (4) coordinating, and (5) controlling. It should be noted that, in the sense that he used these terms, commanding and controlling mean what are now called leading and evaluating results. More than sixty years after its initial publication, many still find this insightful approach to administration practical and useful.

Fayol went further by identifying a list of fourteen "principles," among which were (1) unity of command, (2) authority, (3) initiative, and (4) morale. Avoiding a rigid and dogmatic application of his ideas to the administration of organizations, Fayol emphasized that flexibility and a sense of proportion were essential to managers who adapted principles and definitions to particular situations—quite a different interpretation from that of Taylor, who held firmly to the uniform, emphatic application of principles.

By the time of Fayol and Taylor, it was clear that the Western world was becoming an "organizational society." As giant industrial organizations grew in the early 1900s, so did government and other organizational aspects of life grow. The relatively simple social and political structures of the preindustrial era seemed inherently inadequate in an urban industrial society. Life was not always completely happy in this new social setting, and a great deal of friction—social, political, and economic—resulted. The increasing sense of conflict between people and organizations became a major factor in the struggle of learning to live successfully with this new kind of world, this industrial world in which the individual was, at every turn, a part of some organization. The years before World War I were punctuated by frequent outbursts of this conflict, such as labor unrest, revolution, and the rise of Communism. In this setting, a German sociologist, Max Weber, produced some of the most useful, durable, and brilliant work on an administrative system; it seemed promising at that time and has since proved indispensable: *bureaucracy.*

At a period when people and organizations were dominated by the whims of authoritarian industrialists and entrenched political systems, Weber saw hope in bureaucracy. Essentially, the hope was that well-run bureaucracies would become fairer, more impartial, and more predictable—in general, more rational—than organizations subject to the caprices of powerful individuals. Weber felt that well-run bureaucracies would be efficient, in fact, would be the most efficient form of organization yet invented. Such a viewpoint may not reflect modern experiences with bureaucracies, but Weber was convinced that a *well-run* bureaucracy would be very efficient for a number of reasons, one of which was that bureaucrats are highly trained technical specialists, each skilled in a specific, limited portion of an administrative task.

According to Weber, the bureaucratic apparatus would be very impersonal, minimizing irrational personal and emotional factors and leaving bureaucratic personnel free to work with a minimum of friction or confusion. This, he concluded, would result in expert, impartial, and unbiased service to the organization's clients. In the ideal bureaucracy Weber envisioned certain characteristics that are, in a sense, principles of administration:

1. A division of labor based on functional specialization.
2. A well-defined hierarchy of authority.
3. A system of rules covering the rights and duties of employees.
4. A system of procedures for dealing with work situations.
5. Impersonality of interpersonal relations.
6. Selection and promotion based only on technical competence.[9]

Part of Weber's genius lay in his sensitivity to the dangers of bureaucracy, while at the same time he recognized the merits of bureaucracy in *ideal* circumstances. He emphasized very strongly the dangers of bureaucracy, even so far as to warn that massive, uncontrollable bureaucracy could very well be the greatest threat to both Communism and free enterprise capitalism.[10] It is helpful, in trying to understand the flow of ideas that guided the development of administration, to be aware that—although he produced his work at about the same time that Taylor and Fayol did (that is, from about 1910 to 1920)—Weber was almost unknown in the English-speaking world until translations of his work began to appear in the 1940s. This helps to explain why his systematic work on bureaucracy did not receive widespread attention in educational administration until after World War II.

We have thus far considered three people of ideas who represent many others as well and a prodigious field of effort in their time. Each pointed to the need for the principles and the theories that, by 1900, were generally regarded as essential if the administration of our growing organizations was to become more rational and more effective. The American, Taylor, emphasized the principles that viewed administration as management—the coordination of many small tasks so as to accomplish the overall job as efficiently as possible. Efficiency was interpreted to mean the cheapest net-dollar cost to produce the finished article. Taylor assumed that labor was a commodity to be bought and sold, as one buys oil or electricity, and that by "scientific management" the manager could reduce to a minimum the amount of labor that must be purchased.

The Frenchman, Fayol, emphasized broader preparation of administrators so that they would perform their unique functions in the organization more effectively. He felt that the tasks that administrators perform are, presumably, different from those that engineers perform, but equally as important.

Germany's Max Weber held that bureaucracy is a theory of organization especially suited to the needs of large and complex enterprises that perform services for large numbers of clients. For Weber, the bureaucratic concept was an attempt to minimize the frustrations and irrationality of large organizations in which the relationships between management and workers were based on traditions of class privilege.

THE RISE OF CLASSICAL ORGANIZATIONAL THEORY

These three individuals—Taylor, Fayol, and Weber—were giants in the pre–World War I years and led the way in the early efforts to master the problems of managing modern organizations. There is no precise and universally agreed-upon beginning or end of this era; however, the period from 1910 to 1935 generally can be thought of as the era of scientific management. "Scientific management" had a profound and long-lasting impact upon the ways in which schools were organized and administered. Raymond E. Callahan, in *Education and the Cult of Efficiency,* vividly portrayed how school superintendents in the United States quickly adopted the values and practices of business and industrial managers of that time.[11] Emphasis was on efficiency (that is, low per-unit cost), rigid application of detailed, uniform work procedures (often calling for minute-by-minute, standard operating procedures for teachers to use each day throughout a school system), and detailed accounting procedures. Though some educational administrators harbored doubts about all of this, there was a rush among school superintendents to get aboard the bandwagon of the day by adopting the jargon and practices of those with high status in the society—business executives. Typifying this, Ellwood Cubberly—long one of the leading scholars in U.S. education—took the clear position in 1916 in a landmark textbook that schools were "factories in which the raw materials are to be shaped and fashioned into products to meet the various demands of life."[12]

This view was widely held over the span of years running roughly from before World War I until very close to the outbreak of World War II. Because the concept of scientific management called for the scientific study of jobs to be performed, professors of educational administration undertook to describe and analyze what school superintendents did on the job. Fred Ayer, at the University of Texas, for example, surveyed superintendents to find out what kind of work they did in 1926–1927. Nearly all reported "attending board meetings, making reports, and supervising teachers, 80 percent . . . reported that they went to the post office daily; and each week half of them operated the mimeograph machine, . . . 93 percent inspected toilets, and 93 percent inspected the janitor's work."[13] To prepare individuals to become school superintendents, therefore, programs of study often featured courses in budgeting, heating and ventilating, methods for performing janitorial services and sanitation tasks, writing publicity releases, and record keeping. Professors of educational administration, in turn, commonly conducted studies to determine, for example, the cheapest methods of maintaining floors—such as the most efficient techniques for mopping or sweeping, oiling and/or waxing—so that they could provide prospective school superintendents with the skills necessary to train janitorial workers.

As the study of the problems of organization, management, and administration became established more and more firmly in the universities—just as Wilson and Fayol had predicted—the principles of scientific management received increased attention and also challenge from scholars and practitioners. In particular, as the hierarchical-authoritarian notions of organizational life formalized by Taylor and his followers gained ascendancy, mounting conflict arose from the clash between the demands of the organization for submissiveness and discipline of the part of workers and the need of individuals to experience a reasonable sense of reward and satisfaction from their work. This was publicly manifested in the 1920s and 1930s by increasing labor unrest. Nevertheless, management specialists continued to focus on developing and refining top-down hierarchical ideas about the management of organizations.

Luther Gulick and Lyndall Urwick stand out among the many scholars who attempted to synthesize what is now known as the "classical" formulation of principles, which would be useful in developing good, functional organizations. Central to the work of these two men was the idea that elements of the organization could be grouped and related according to function, geographic location, or similar criteria. They emphasized the drawing up of formal charts of organizations that showed the precise ways in which various offices and divisions were related. Gulick and Urwick published a widely acclaimed book in 1937[14] and were still highly influential after World War II.[15] Many school administrators are familiar with some of the organizational concepts that were popularized by such classical writers.

Organizational Concepts of Classical Theory

Classical organizational theorists have sought to identify and describe some set of fixed "principles" (in the sense of "rules") that would establish the basis for management. The best known of these dealt with organizational structure. For example, central to the classical view of organization is the concept of hierarchy, which, in the jargon of classical theorists, is the *scalar principle*. (In practice it is usually referred to as "line and staff.") The contention is that authority and responsibility should flow in as direct and unbroken a path as possible from the top policy level down through the organization to the lowest member. This general principle is rather widely accepted by organizational theorists today, being most often attacked because of the rigid insistence with which many classical thinkers tend to apply the concept in practice, limiting lateral relationships between parts of the organization. It is, thus, no accident that organizational charts of U.S. school districts today frequently show vertical lines of authority and responsibility with little or no interconnection between operating divisions of the organization. Thus, the organizational chart of a typical school district will show the elementary schools reporting up the line through the director of elementary education to the superintendent, with no interconnections with the middle schools or the secondary schools. In fact, in such a district there ordinarily is no functional connection between the three levels or divisions of the district.

Another central classical principle of organization is *"unity of command"*: essentially, that no one in an organization should receive orders from more than one superordinate. Fayol, a strict interpreter of this point, was sharply critical of Taylor because the latter favored something called "functional foremanship," which permitted a worker to receive orders from as many as eight bosses (each being a specialist). As organizations and work became more complex over time, this principle has been greatly weakened by the need to modify it so often to meet changing conditions. The organizational charts of school districts frequently reflect this principle, although in actual operation the concept is routinely ignored.

The *"exception principle"* holds that when the need for a decision recurs frequently, the decision should be established as a routine that can be delegated to subordinates (in the form of rules, standard operating procedures, administrative manuals). This frees those in higher positions from routine detail to deal with the exceptions to the rules. This principle, too, has received wide acceptance: it underlies the delegation of authority and the concept that all decisions should be made at the lowest possible level in the organization. This has proved to be the most generally applicable principle of classical theory.

"Span of control" is the most discussed of the major ideas from classical organizational theory. The essence of the concept is to prescribe (and thereby limit)

the number of people reporting to a supervisor or administrator. Much of the thinking about this principle arose from military organizations, which—under highly stressful, unstable, emergency conditions—need a dependable system of control and coordination. The problems in applying the concept to other kinds of organizations have led to more controversy than understanding. Whereas many theorists suggest having a small number of people reporting to an administrator (usually somewhere between three and six), many firms deliberately put executives in charge of larger numbers of people so as to force them to delegate more decision making to their subordinates.

The Ideas of Mary Parker Follett

The work of Mary Parker Follett was unique in the development of management thought. Her ideas were rooted in the classical traditions of organizational theory but matured in such a way that she, in effect, spanned the gap between scientific management and the early industrial psychologists. Follett's first organizational study, done for her master's thesis at Radcliffe, was a major analysis of the speakership of the House of Representatives of the United States Congress, a significant administrative and leadership position that had received little systematic study until that time. It was successfully published as a book that was a standard in the literature for years. Then, for many years, she managed an innovative volunteer program in Boston that offered a large-scale program of educational and recreational opportunities in public school facilities during the afternoon and evening hours. The program was designed specifically to meet the needs of the large number of homeless boys, street kids, who were found in abundance in Boston and other major U.S. cities at the turn of the century and who badly needed safe places where they could study in the evening, receive supportive guidance, and engage in wholesome recreational activities. Much of the financial support for this volunteer social program came from business executives, and through working with them Follett came to learn a great deal about U.S. corporate leaders and what they thought about organizations and workers. She increasingly became concerned that corporations, through their management practices, were doing much to create the problems that her programs were attempting to ameliorate. The stock market crash of 1929, followed by the Great Depression, was a galvanizing event for her and for many others that starkly illuminated the realization that large business corporations had become social institutions whose concentration of power called into question the U.S. tradition of unrestrained corporate action.

Her ideas were instrumental in modifying the trend toward rigidly structuralist views in classical management theory, provided a rationale that was helpful in ushering in the human relations movement, and pioneered conceptualizing about what today is called contingency theory.

Follett, first, viewed management as a social process and, second, saw it inextricably enmeshed in the particular situation. She did not see authority as flowing from the top of the organization's hierarchy to be parceled out among those in lower ranks. It was better practice, in her view, that orders should not be given by one person; rather, all should seek to take orders from the situation itself. She saw that the administrator has three choices of ways to handle conflict: (1) by the exercise of power, (2) by compromise, or (3) by "integration" (that is, bringing the conflict into the open and seeking a mutually acceptable, win-win resolution).

In 1932, Follett sought to summarize her views by developing four principles of sound administration. The first two were *Coordination by direct contact of the responsible people concerned* and *Coordination in the early stages*. These clashed with the typical classical preoccupation with hierarchical communication and control: she advocated placing control in the hands of those in the lower levels of the organization, which requires opening up communication horizontally across the organization as well as down the hierarchy. The third principle was *Coordination as the reciprocal relating of all the factors in the situation* (which laid the basis of the "law of the situation"). This emphasized the importance of linking departments in ways that enabled them to self-adjust to the organization's needs at lower levels of the organization. Finally, *Coordination as a continuing process* recognized that management is an ever-changing, dynamic process in response to emerging situations—a sharp contrast to traditional, static, classical views that sought to codify universal principles of action.

Classical and Neoclassical Administrative Concepts

Though classical concepts of organization and administration—that is, the concepts associated with bureaucracy and "scientific management"—were developed early in this century and stood for a time unchallenged by competing concepts, it would be an error to view the classical approach as something that once flourished and is now gone from the scene. Nothing could be further from actuality.

Bureaucracies flourish among us today, of course: government bureaucracies, such as the Internal Revenue Service and state departments of motor vehicles, are among obvious examples encountered every day. Even in the case of nonbureaucratic organizations, however, many scholars as well as administrators essentially believe that the classical views are the best basis for administrative practice.

Many contemporary advocates of accountability programs, competency-based programs, and management by objectives operate from classical organizational concepts. These newer manifestations of the older classical concepts are often referred to as *neoclassical* or, in some cases, *neoscientific*.

Numerous federal interventions in public schooling—such as the Elementary and Secondary Education Act (ESEA), P.L. 93-380, the Emergency School Assistance Act (ESAA), P.L. 92-318, and the Comprehensive Employment and Training Act (CETA), P.L. 93-203—are organized and administered in conformity with classical concepts of bureaucracy. Planning, Programming, and Budgeting Systems (PPBS) and Zero-Based Budgeting (ZBB) are designed to implement the basic ideas of classic bureaucratic organizational strategies (as are most so-called rational planning and management systems). They are examples that are widely called *neoclassical* today.

THE HUMAN RELATIONS MOVEMENT

In time, as the principles of scientific management were applied to industry with greater care, a need to be more precise about the effect of human factors on production efficiency was felt. The Western Electric Company was one of the more enlightened industrial employers of the time and, in routine fashion, cooperated with the National Research Council in a relatively simple experiment designed to determine the optimum level of illumination in a shop for maximum production efficiency. Western Electric's Hawthorne plant near Chicago was selected for the experiment. Before the research was over, an impressive team of researchers was involved; of its members, Elton Mayo is probably the best known to educators.

The original experiment was very well designed and executed, and it revealed that there was no direct, simple relationship between the illumination level and the production output of the workers. Because one of Taylor's "principles" suggested strongly that there would be such a relationship, this study raised more questions than it answered.

After pondering the surprising results from their initial experiment, the investigators sought to answer six questions that they hoped would explain their findings:

1. Do employees actually become tired?
2. Are pauses for rest desirable?
3. Is a shorter working day desirable?
4. What is the attitude of employees toward their work and toward the company?
5. What is the effect of changing the type of working equipment?
6. Why does production decrease in the afternoon?

These were rather simple, straightforward questions, but it is obvious that the answers to a number of them would be psychological, rather than physical, in nature. These questions triggered one of the most far-reaching series of experiments in the history of administration, which became known as the Western Electric studies and which led to discoveries that are not yet fully understood. However unexpected it may have been, one major finding of these studies was the realization that human variability is an important determinant of productivity. Thus, in the 1920s the basis for the human relations movement was established.[16]

New concepts were now available to the administrator to use in practice. Among them were (1) morale, (2) group dynamics, (3) democratic supervision, (4) personnel relations, and (5) behavioral concepts of motivation. The human relations movement emphasized human and interpersonal factors in administering the affairs of organizations. Supervisors, in particular, drew heavily on human relations concepts, stressing such notions as "democratic" procedures, "involvement," motivational techniques, and the sociometry of leadership.

The human relations movement attracted social and behavioral scientists, particularly group dynamicists who had already been studying the phenomena of human behavior of individuals interacting with one another in dyads and in groups. Numerous studies carried out in group and organizational settings laid the groundwork for better understanding the nature of human groups and how they function. Illustrative of the better early work of group dynamicists is that of Jacob Moreno, who developed and refined the techniques of sociometric analysis. Moreno sensed that within groups there are informal subgroups—identifiable clusters of people that form essentially on the basis of how much they like or dislike one another.[17] Moreno developed techniques of gathering information from members of organizations as to the attraction they had for one another; the data were often gathered by interview, but other techniques (such as simple questionnaires) also were used. From such information, *sociograms* were developed that portrayed the dynamics of the *informal social structure* of human groups. A typical sociogram of a group of five people might look like Figure 1–1, for example. By asking the members of the group simple questions (such as with whom they would be most willing to work), it is possible to ascertain a great deal about the informal social structure of the group.

Another fruitful line of investigation emanating from the human relations approach was the work of Robert Bales. He developed a systematic technique for analyzing the patterns of interaction between the members of a group. Essentially, Bales's interaction analysis technique consisted of recording key facts about the discussions that occurred between individuals: how many took place between specific individuals, who initiated them, which of these were between two individuals and which were addressed to the group as a whole, and so on.[18] Bales's work not only provided a workable technique that others could use to study the interaction pat-

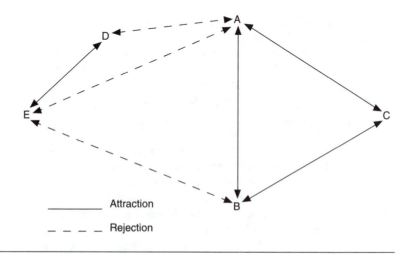

FIGURE 1–1   Simple sociogram of five-person group.

terns of groups, but also permitted him to draw some generalizations about groups that have proved to be useful.

For example, Bales was the first to document that successful groups tend to have people in them who play two key roles: it is necessary for someone (or, perhaps, several individuals in a group) to keep the group focused on *accomplishing its task,* and, at the same time, it is necessary for every successful group to have someone to see that the group pays attention to *maintaining productive human relations* within the group. These two dimensions of group behavior—task orientation and maintenance orientation—have proved to be of lasting value in understanding the dynamics of group functioning.

Leadership has long been a subject of great interest to those concerned with organizations, and social scientists were not long in realizing that—unlike the classical view—leadership is not something that "great people" or individuals with formal legal authority do to their subordinates, but rather is a process involving dynamic interaction with subordinates. Benjamin Wolman, for example, found that members of groups tend to elect to leadership positions individuals who are perceived to have the ability (or "power") to satisfy the needs of the group and who are, at the same time, perceived as ready to accept the responsibility.[19] Bales noted that groups tend to confer leadership on individuals, not so much on the basis of how well they are liked as on the basis of the ideas that the individuals contribute to the groups and the help that they give the groups in carrying out the ideas.[20] Helen Jennings found that dominant, aggressive people are not likely to be perceived by group members as leaders but, in fact, are likely to be rejected and isolated by the group.[21]

These few examples may serve in this discussion to illustrate some of the kinds of sociological, psychological, and social psychological investigations that were undertaken in large numbers during the human relations era. This was a time when, in fact, social psychology began to mature as a scientific and academic discipline. Kurt Lewin contributed richly to studies of organizational behavior during this period, especially in the area of group decision making.[22] More importantly, Lewin early developed crucial insights and theoretic views that were of great help to those who came after him. His work and that of his students, for example, inspired the laboratory method of personal growth training (that is, T-Groups or sensitivity training), which, in turn, laid the basis for the contemporary practice of organization development, discussed in Chapter 9.

Muzafer Sherif, whose studies of street gangs as human social systems became landmarks of insight and research methodology, went on to produce one of the early textbooks in social psychology.[23] George Homans (*The Human Group,* 1950), Felix Roethlisberger (*Management and Morale,* 1950), William Foote Whyte ("Human Relations in the Restaurant Industry," 1948), Fritz Redl ("Group Emotion and Leadership," 1942), Philip Selznick ("The Leader as the Agent of the Led," 1951), and Alvin W. Gouldner (*Studies in Leadership,* 1950) are only a few of the more famous contributors to the outpouring of theory and research during this period that was to establish an irreversible trend in thought and understanding about behavior in human organizations.

In U.S. education, the human relations movement had relatively little impact on school district administrators (for example, superintendents of schools), as compared with rather a substantial impact upon supervisory levels (for example, supervisors, elementary school principals). Superintendents, in general, continued to emphasize such classical concepts as hierarchical control, authority, and formal organization, whereas supervisors emphasized to a much greater extent such human relations concepts as morale, group cohesiveness, collaboration, and the dynamics of informal organization. A review of the proceedings and publications of representative organizations, such as the American Association of School Administrators (AASA) and the Association for Supervision and Curriculum Development (ASCD) readily reveals that, for the most part, those who saw their roles as educational administrators tended to emphasize attention to budgets, politics, control, and the asymmetrical exercise of power from the top downward, whereas those who were primarily concerned with instruction and curriculum placed much more emphasis on participation, communication, and de-emphasis on status-power relationships. This difference in emphasis persisted at least into the 1980s, though administrators moved somewhat to embrace human relations ideas.

THE ORGANIZATIONAL THEORY MOVEMENT

Classical and bureaucratic approaches to organizations tend not only to emphasize organizational structure and the highly rational logic of hierarchical control over people, but reify these concepts: treating the organization as tangible, concrete, virtually touchable and even living. In the early literature on organization this was called the *formal* organization. Today, it is generally known as *structuralism.* Structuralists tend to think that a properly structured organization will improve organizational performance. When we combine small school districts into larger ones, or adopt school-based management, or modify the interface between elementary schools and high schools by creating middle schools, structuralist thought is guiding our administrative practice.

But the organization, with all its formal structure and the rules and regulations to interpret and reinforce that structure, is populated by human beings with their very human and personal beliefs, attitudes, assumptions, hopes, and fears, and such inner states of these people, collectively, go a long way to make the organization what it actually is. Thus, psychological thinking enters the study of organization and administration. Those who emphasize this concept of organization are convinced that changes in the relations between human beings in the organization have enormous power to affect the performance of the organization. This is variously called the *informal* organization or, as it was indelibly labeled in 1960, the *human side* of the organization. Often today it is referred to simply as *people approaches* to organization. When we seek to involve people more fully in making decisions that affect them, attend to their motivational needs more adequately, or increase collegiality and collaboration through teamwork, we are using people approaches to organizational problems.

In the five-year span between 1937 and 1942, however, three significant books appeared that laid the groundwork for what was to develop during the post-World War II era into a new, major influence on thought and practice in administration. The first of these landmark books was Chester Barnard's *The Functions of the Executive,* which appeared in 1938. Barnard, a vice president of the New Jersey Bell Telephone Company, selected and integrated concepts from the many schools of thought that had appeared since Wilson's essay, and he introduced a number of new insights of his own. Barnard was in close communication with the scientists who conducted the Western Electric studies. One of his most important contributions, and one that is germane to this discussion, was to illuminate the crucial importance of better understanding the relationship between the *formal organization* and the *informal organization.* In this pioneer work Barnard made it clear (1) that it was illusory to focus exclusively on the formal, official, structural facets of administering organizations and (2) that the effective executive must attend to the interaction between the needs and aspirations of the workers, on the one hand, and the needs and purposes of the organization, on the other hand.

In the very next year, 1939, the second of these three significant books appeared: *Management and the Worker,* by Felix J. Roethlisberger and William J. Dickson. These two scholars presented a new view of the dynamic mutual interaction between the formal organization and the informal organization (the latter being the informal social structure that exists among workers). Based on evidence gathered from the Western Electric Company research, the authors described and documented, for example, the surprising sophistication of the informal organization and its power to exercise control over not only the behavior of workers but also (without their realizing it) over the behavior of supervisors and managers who thought that they were exercising the control. Their emphasis on "individual needs, informal groups, and social relationships was quickly endorsed by other social scientists and led to a 'philosophy of management' concerned primarily with human relationships in formal organizations."[24]

Finally, the third of this triumvirate of early books was Herbert A. Simon's *Administrative Behavior,* which was published in 1947. Even the title, with its emphasis on behavior, foreshadowed a fresh approach to understanding administrative practice. Simon—a professor with a strong background in political science, psychology, and business administration—sought to illuminate the importance of human behavior in such critical administrative processes as making decisions. This book, more than any other, established a fresh new concept of administration and set the pace for social and behavioral scientists who sensed in that post–World War II era that there was great promise in this new approach.

Although the adherents of classical and human relations approaches did not vanish in the years that followed, the most vigorous administrative research was in the areas of extending and developing the newer behavioral concepts. Scientists from a number of disciplines, or traditions, were to publish a steady stream of research and theory during the ensuing years. A listing of a few of the better-known books published in the 1950s through the 1960s, roughly classified by the academic tradition of their authors, presents a rather clear overview of the way the field developed:

PSYCHOLOGY AND SOCIAL PSYCHOLOGY

CHRIS ARGYRIS, *Personality and Organization* (1958)
BERNARD M. BASS, *Leadership, Psychology, and Organizational Behavior* (1960)
ALVIN W. GOULDNER, ED., *Studies in Leadership* (1950)
MUZAFIR SHERIF, ED., *Intergroup Relations and Leadership* (1962)
RENSIS LIKERT, *The Human Organization: Its Management and Value* (1967)

SOCIOLOGY

PETER M. BLAU AND W. RICHARD SCOTT, *Formal Organizations* (1962)
AMITAI ETZIONI, *A Comparative Analysis of Complex Organizations* (1961)
CHARLES PERROW, *Organizational Analysis: A Sociological View* (1970)

ANTHROPOLOGY

WILLIAM FOOTE WHYTE, *Men at Work* (1961)
ELIOT DISMORE CHAPPLE AND LEONARD R. SAYLES, *The Measure of Management* (1961)
HARRY F. WOLCOTT, *The Man in the Principal's Office* (1973)

POLITICAL SCIENCE

VICTOR A. THOMPSON, *Modern Organization* (1961)
ROBERT V. PRESTHUS, *The Organizational Society* (1962)
MARILYN GITTEL, *Participants and Participation: A Study of School Policy in New York City* (1967)

MANAGEMENT

DOUGLAS MCGREGOR, *The Human Side of Enterprise* (1960)
RENSIS LIKERT, *New Patterns of Management* (1961)
ALFRED J. MARROW, DAVID G. BOWERS, AND STANLEY E. SEASHORE, *Management by Participation* (1967)

Human Relations and Organizational Behavior

The term "human relations" is a broad one that refers to the interactions between people in all kinds of situations in which they seek, through mutual action, to achieve some purpose. Thus, it can properly be applied to two people seeking to develop a happy and productive life together, a social club, a business firm, a school, or, indeed, an entire government or even a whole society. The social structure that regulates the human interactions that are the subject of human relations may be formal, clear, and readily apparent (for example, a government, a firm), or it may be informal, even diffuse, and therefore difficult to describe accurately (for example, the power structure of a group of prison inmates, the social system of a school faculty, or a neighborhood).

"Organizational behavior" is a narrower, more precise term that falls under the broader, more general meaning of human relations. Organizational behavior is a discipline that seeks to describe, understand, and predict human behavior in the environment of formal organizations. A distinctive contribution and characteristic of organizational behavior as a discipline is the explicit recognition that (1) organizations create internal contextual settings, or environments, that have great influence on the behavior of people in them and (2) to some extent the internal environment of an organization is influenced by the larger context in which the organization itself exists (for example, the social, political, economic, and technological systems that support the organization). Moreover, the internal environment or context of the organization (which is so influential in eliciting and shaping human behavior) is not merely physical and tangible but also includes the social and psychological characteristics of the living human system.

Because management/administrative science has effective performance of goal-seeking formal organizations as its central focus, organizational behavior is closely linked with that science also. Management and administration necessarily must bear responsibility for establishing internal arrangements of the organization so as to achieve maximum effectiveness. In the early years of human relations it was common for managers and administrators to speak of the human relations of employees or human relations of the firm as though the organization and the wellsprings of its employees' behavior were separate though related. Contemporary administrative science, on the other hand, views goal-directed organizational behavior as essential to results-oriented, cooperative endeavor that cannot be teased out from the management policies and administrative practices of the system.

Educational administration was affected very little by the evolution of administration as a field of study until the middle of this century, largely because the teaching of educational administration was sequestered from the mainstreams of scholarly thought and research. Schools of education in even the most prestigious universities tended to have almost no contact with the business schools and the behavioral science departments on their own campuses. Traditionally, educational administration had been taught by former school superintendents whose knowledge of their subject came largely from years of hard-earned experience in the "front lines." Courses in educational administration tended to focus on practical, "how-to-do-it" problems, drawing on the past experience of practicing administrators. Emphasis was typically given to sharing the techniques of these administrators for solving problems—techniques that had been tried in school districts such as the ones with which the students were familiar.

Research in educational administration during the first half of this century consisted principally of status studies of current problems or the gathering of opinion. With rare exceptions, little research in educational administration dealt with the testing of theoretical propositions, and virtually none of it involved the insights and research methods that had been developed by behavioral scientists. As Van Miller has observed:

> A lot of the study of administration has been a matter of looking backward or sideways at what was done or what is being done. It is striking to contemplate how much administrative experience has been exchanged and how little it has been studied scientifically. The current excitement arises from the fact that within recent years educational administration has become a field of study and of development as well as a vocation.[25]

By the mid-1950s a new concept of organization was gaining wide acceptance among students of educational administration. This new concept recognized the dynamic interrelationships between (1) the structural characteristics of the organization and (2) the personal characteristics of the individual. It sought to understand the behavior of people at work in terms of the dynamic interrelationships between the organizational structure and the people who populated it.

Using this insight, students of organization began to conceptualize organizations—such as school systems and schools—as *social systems.* Although it is true that nearly any human group[26] constitutes a human social system (including such diverse groups as street gangs, hobby clubs, and church congregations), the concept that began to emerge in this post–World War II era was that *organizations* constitute a *particular kind* of social system: essentially, it is characterized by a clear and relatively strong *formal* structure. For example, unlike such informal human social systems as the office bowling team or the secretaries who eat lunch together, school systems and schools (and, indeed, all formal organizations) may be characterized as follows:[27]

1. They are specifically goal oriented.
2. The work to be done so as to achieve goals is divided into subtasks and assigned as official duties to established positions in the organization.
3. These positions are arranged hierarchically in the formal organization, and authority relationships are clearly established.
4. General and impersonal organizational rules govern, to a large extent, what people do in their official capacity and also, to a large extent, shape and delimit the interpersonal interactions of people in the organization.

Beginning in the mid-1950s, increasing attention was devoted to efforts to better understand the relationships among (1) these characteristics of organizational structure, (2) the personality (and consequent "needs") of individuals in the organization, and (3) behavior on the job. For example, numerous studies of leader behavior conducted in the 1950s and 1960s revealed remarkable agreement on the point that leadership can be best understood in terms of two specific kinds of behaviors: (1) behavior that gives structure to the work of the group (for example, how the work is to be done, when, by whom, and so forth) and (2) behavior that is per-

ceived by subordinates as showing consideration for the subordinates as human beings. These empirically derived insights were widely applied to business, industry,
the military, and many other kinds of organizations, as well as to school systems
and schools.[28]

The generalization that seemed to arise from empirical tests of this view was
that one leadership style promised to be more effective than any other: namely, a
style characterized by behavior that emphasized *both* initiating structure *and* consideration for people. In this way, of course, both the demands of the organization
and the needs of individuals to deal with the organization would be met. One study
typical of this period, using the popular social systems model, found that school
principals who displayed a style that emphasized concern for people tended to view
teachers as professionals to a greater extent than did principals who stressed the role
of initiating structure in the work group.[29]

In the years from roughly 1955 to 1970, there was a great outpouring of theorizing and research in educational administration which explored the basic concepts of social system (either explicitly or implicitly) as applied to public school
systems and schools. Neal Gross, using sociological methods of inquiry, sought to
illuminate the reasons why school board members and school superintendents in
New England made the decisions that they did.[30] Daniel Griffiths initiated landmark
work on decision making in educational administration which added considerably
to our understanding of the importance of the decision-making behavior of administrators.[31] One of many studies based on Griffiths's work, for example, suggests
that if the administrator confines himself or herself to establishing clear processes
and procedures for making decisions (rather than actually making the final decisions), the administrator's behavior will be more acceptable to subordinates.

A team of researchers, who were especially interested in understanding the
processes of curriculum change in schools, conducted a study to explore the question, "To what extent do administrators and teachers in a given school system tend
to agree or disagree in their perceptions of decision-making roles and responsibilities?" Among the many findings arising from this complex and comprehensive
study, one of the most outstanding—according to Griffiths—was that consideration
for subordinates is more valuable behavior for the superintendent to exhibit than behavior intended to initiate structure in the group.

University graduate programs of study for educational administrators soon
reflected the influence of social and behavioral science views of organizational
behavior. In many cases, courses featuring some of the newer behavioral views—
such as leadership, motivation, decision making, organizational climate, conflict
management, and organizational change—took their place alongside courses on
budgeting, financing, law, and school plant, site, and facilities. It soon became
standard practice for writers of textbooks on the school principalship, general administration, and personnel administration to attempt to establish the relevance of
organizational behavior research and concepts to the specific areas that the book
addressed. Many professors, in their research and consulting activities, used these
new ideas in their analysis of practical problems in actual schools, as well as in the
design of in-service training activities.

CONCLUSION

Much of the current debate about school reform and educational leadership—whether in academic literature, the popular press, or in discussions between practitioners—manifests different, frequently incompatible, ideas about the nature of schools as organizations and the behavior of people who work in them. This debate has its roots in the larger debate about whether organizations are best understood as hierarchical, bureaucratic systems or as collegial, collaborative systems. That debate emerged in the first half of the twentieth century with the publication of the Western Electric studies and has been continually stimulated by the growth and spread of research in group dynamics and human resources development. Though the human resources view has over time steadily grown in influence in the realms of business and the military as well as in education, many individuals in executive and leadership positions still cling to classical notions of hierarchical power relationships. It is important for the student of education to be aware of this and especially important for him or her to examine the issues and make a clear personal commitment as to where to stand on those issues as a guide to professional practice in educational leadership.

The struggle to develop understanding of human resources approaches to organizational behavior has led to the development of a number of theoretical views that can be helpful in clarifying issues confronting the educational leader. Chapter 2 examines a number of these newer views.

SUGGESTED READING

Callahan, Raymond E., *Education and the Cult of Efficiency.* Chicago: University of Chicago Press, 1962.
> Recounts the events of an early period in the twentieth century when U.S. business and industrial leaders sought to improve public schooling by forcing school boards across the country to adopt their organizational values and goals. If you think that what goes around comes around, you will find a powerful message for today in this fascinating account.

Etzioni, Amitai, *Modern Organizations.* Englewood Cliffs, NJ: Prentice-Hall, 1964.
> A remarkably lucid, easy-to-read explanation of the fundamentals of modern organizational thought. Truly a classic in the literature of organization and behavior.

Morgan, Gareth. *Images of Organization.* Beverly Hills, CA: Sage Publications, 1986.
> This well-written book describes seven different ways of thinking about organizations, using such metaphors as organizations as machines, as political systems, as cultures, and so on. The author goes on to describe the advantages and disadvantages of using each metaphor.

NOTES

1. Paul R. Mort and Donald H. Ross, *Principles of School Administration* (New York: McGraw-Hill Book Company, 1957), p. 4.
2. Woodrow Wilson, "The Study of Administration," *Political Science Quarterly,* 2, no. 2 (June 1887), 197–222.
3. Frederick Taylor, *The Principles of Scientific Management* (New York: Harper & Row, Publishers, 1911), p. 8.

4. For a vivid description of this period and the power of business and industrial leaders to force their values on school administrators, see Raymond E. Callahan, *Education and the Cult of Efficiency* (Chicago: University of Chicago Press, 1962).

5. Amitai Etzioni, *Modern Organizations* (Englewood Cliffs, NJ: Prentice-Hall, 1964), p. 21.

6. Henri Fayol, *General and Industrial Management,* trans. Constance Storrs (London: Sir Isaac Pitman & Sons, 1949), p. 14.

7. Ibid., p. 15.

8. Fayol's work was published in French in 1916 (when he was chief executive of a mining firm) and immediately received wide acclaim in Europe. His views swept into a dominant position (and remained there well into the 1940s) following their appearance in English translation, in *Papers on the Science of Administration,* eds. Luther Gulick and L. Urwick (New York: Columbia University, Institute of Public Administration, 1937).

9. Richard H. Hall, "The Concept of Bureaucracy: An Empirical Assessment," *The American Journal of Sociology,* 69, no. 1 (July 1963), 33.

10. J. P. Mayer, *Max Weber and German Politics* (London: Faber & Faber, 1943), p. 128.

11. Raymond E. Callahan, *Education and the Cult of Efficiency* (Chicago: University of Chicago Press, 1962).

12. Ellwood P. Cubberly, *Public School Administration: A Statement of the Fundamental Principles Underlying the Organization and Administration of Public Education* (Boston: Houghton Mifflin, 1916), pp. 337–38.

13. David B. Tyack and Robert Cummings, "Leadership in American Public Schools before 1954: Historical Configurations and Conjectures," in *Educational Administration: The Developing Decades,* eds. Luvern L. Cunningham, Walter G. Hack, and Raphael O. Nystrand (Berkeley, CA: McCutchan, 1977), p. 61.

14. Luther Gulick and L. Urwick, eds., *Papers on the Science of Administration* (New York: Institute of Public Administration, Columbia University, 1937).

15. Luther Gulick, *Administrative Reflection on World War II* (University, AL: University of Alabama Press, 1948).

16. These studies, often called the Western Electric studies, may be known to the reader for another reason: they also led to identification of the so-called Hawthorne Effect, which became important in improving techniques of behavioral research. These studies are summarized in Fritz J. Roethlisberger and William J. Dickson, *Management and the Worker* (Cambridge, MA: Harvard University Press, 1939).

17. Jacob L. Moreno, "Contributions of Sociometry to Research Methodology in Sociology," *American Sociological Review,* 12 (June 1947), 287–92.

18. Robert F. Bales, *Interaction-Process Analysis: A Method for the Study of Small Groups* (Reading, MA: Addison-Wesley, 1950).

19. Benjamin Wolman, "Leadership and Group Dynamics," *Journal of Social Psychology,* 43 (February 1956), 11–25.

20. Robert F. Bales, "The Equilibrium Problem in Small Groups," in *Working Papers in the Theory of Action,* eds. Talcott Parsons, Robert F. Bales, and Edward A. Shils (Glencoe, IL: The Free Press, 1953).

21. Helen H. Jennings, *Leadership and Isolation,* 2nd ed. (New York: Longman, 1950).

22. Lewin, who defined *field theory* in social psychology, is often thought of as the father of social psychology. See his "Field Theory and Experiment in Social Psychology: Concepts and Methods," *American Journal of Sociology,* 44 (1939), 868–96, and "Group Decision and Social Change," in *Readings in Social Psychology,* eds. Theodore M. Newcomb and Eugene L. Hartley (New York: Holt, Rinehart & Winston, 1947), pp. 330–44.

23. Muzafer Sherif, *An Outline of Social Psychology* (New York: Harper & Row, Publishers, 1948).

24. Dorwin Cartwright, "Influence, Leadership, Control," in *Handbook of Organizations,* ed. James G. March (Chicago: Rand McNally & Company, 1965), p. 2.

25. Van Miller, *The Public Administration of American School Systems* (New York: Macmillan, 1965), pp. 544–45.

26. As distinguished from a collection of individuals.

27. This discussion follows that of Max G. Abbott, "Intervening Variables in Organizational Behavior," *Educational Administration Quarterly,* 1, no. 1 (Winter 1966), 1–14.

28. See, for example, John K. Hemphill and Alvin E. Coons, *Leader Behavior Description* (Columbus: Ohio State University Press, 1950). For later research using their concept, see Andrew W. Halpin and B. J. Winer, *The Leadership Behavior of the Airplane Commander* (Columbus: Ohio State University Press, 1952); and Andrew W. Halpin, "The Behavior of Leaders," *Educational Leadership,* 14 (1956), 172–76.
29. Daniel Griffiths, "Administrative Theory," *Encyclopedia of Educational Research,* ed. R. L. Ebel (Toronto: Macmillan, 1969), p. 18.
30. Neal Gross, *Who Runs Our Schools?* (New York: John Wiley & Sons, 1958).
31. Daniel E. Griffiths, *Administrative Theory* (New York: Appleton-Century-Crofts, 1959).

Organizational Theory in the Modern Period

ABOUT THIS CHAPTER

From its beginnings in the mid-1920s until roughly the mid-1970s, the search for understanding of organizational behavior was dominated and controlled by scholars who believed in traditional methods of laboratory science, which were drawn from logical positivism. This is now referred to as the modern period. Through subsequent decades, therefore, the scholars who dominated the study of organizational behavior demanded the use of a single way of thinking about organizations and the behavior of people in them. They demanded the use of theory and scientific techniques for testing theory—techniques that they thought were objective, detached from the people being studied, and relied on mathematical proof as the highest goal of investigation. However, as we shall see more fully in Chapter 3, it eventually became obvious that this severely delimited approach of the logical-positivist tradition borrowed from the physical sciences was relatively barren for the school practitioner, yielding little that could be applied with confidence to the praxis of educational leadership. Indeed, some leading scholars had endeavored to point out that the fundamental fatal flaw in this narrowly "scientific" approach lay in the rigid demand by influential academicians that only hypothetico-deductive ways of thinking be used in attempting to understand organizational life. Nevertheless, a number of ways of thinking about organizations—that is, a number of useful organizational theories—were developed during the modern period that have proved over time to be useful to school leaders in thinking about and talking about leadership strategies. These theories also can be helpful to you in thinking about organizations and the behavior of people in them. This overview starts with a brief grounding as to what theory is, then proceeds to compare and contrast bureaucratic theory and human resources theory. Finally you are presented with several systems models of organization, in which various scholars have sought to describe their understanding of the interrelationships between the notion of organizational structure and the people who populate the organization.

Describing systems models of organizational life is a great deal like the chalk-talk diagrams that a TV commentator uses during a football game. They can lay out and describe the concepts that underlie the game, but they must be understood in the context of the uncertainty and unpredictability that is always present in human endeavor. Models are useful for giving you a mental road map of how organizations work, something that you can use in the practical business of sorting out organizational problems and planning to solve them. They are helpful in clarifying important issues involving organizational behavior. But they are not *literal* depictions of an organizational mechanism, as they are sometimes mistakenly taken to be. For example, some people have rhapsodized about systems theories of organizations using the metaphor of old-fashioned clockworks, in which pendulums swing with unerring predictability, gears whir, springs unwind, balance wheels, cogs, escapement, and other parts all move synchronously in near-perfect predictable relationships to produce the desired result, namely, to tell the correct time. Organizations, after all, especially educational organizations, are human endeavors, and—to the despair of those seeking simplicity, precision, system, order, and certainty in human affairs— cannot be reduced to mechanistic systems. We are dealing with *human social systems.*

ORGANIZATIONAL THEORY

Discussion of different perspectives that may be used in thinking about organizations— such as bureaucratic and nonbureaucratic—is really discussion of organizational theory. Many practicing educational administrators are skeptical of theory, often thinking of it as some ideal state or idle notion (commonly associated with the pejorative "ivory tower"), whereas they must deal with the tough practicalities of daily life. The position being taken here is that, far from being removed from daily life, theory is crucial in the shaping of our everyday perception and understanding of commonplace events.

Theory Defined and Described

Theory is systematically organized knowledge thought to explain observed phe- nomena. Just as we have theories about the causes of disease, the forces that make it possible for airplanes to fly, and the nature of the solar system, we also have the- ories about organizations and how they work. Just as there are theoretical reasons that underlie the fact that we know that we should wash our hands frequently, ex- ercise regularly, and maintain a nutritionally sound diet, there should be theoretical underpinnings to our understanding of schools as organizations and how to make them ever more effective.

Theory is useful insofar as it provides a basis for thinking systematically about complex problems, such as understanding the nature of educational organi- zations. It is useful because it enables us to *describe* what is going on, *explain* it, *predict* future events under given circumstances, and—essential to the professional practitioner—think about ways to exercise *control* over events.

TWO MAJOR PERSPECTIVES ON EDUCATIONAL ORGANIZATIONS

Since the dawn of organizational studies in the twentieth century, people have gen- erally elected to conceptualize organizations in one of two disparate ways. One, the classical, traditional view is often called "bureaucratic" though in the rhetoric of ed- ucational reform in recent years many choose to speak of it as "the factory model" of organization. Whatever name is used, bureaucratic organization is epitomized by the image of the eighteenth-century army of Frederick the Great with its characteristically mechanical regimentation, top-down authority, "going by the book." To this day, bureaucratic organization remains worldwide by far the most common ideal of organization. Indeed, to many people, this is the defining concept of what an organization is.

As time passed two things developed that have wrought seemingly irreversible challenges to bureaucratic concepts of organization and have given rise to newer ways of thinking about organization:

1. *The constant growth and accelerating tempo of change in the world.* The seemingly geometric acceleration in the development of technology, and changes in politics, economics, and society have generally left rigid bureaucracies floundering and unresponsive.

2. *The worldwide rise in expectations for increased democracy, personal freedom, individual respect and dignity, and opportunities for self-fulfillment.* Whereas prior to World War II teachers perforce submitted to the authority of the bureaucratic organization and unhesitatingly accepted its dictates with little thought of marching to their own personal drummer, that era in educational organizations is long gone, and seemingly gone forever.

Organizations, particularly educational organizations, are so ubiquitous—so commonplace—that we frequently deal with them with scant examination of the assumptions about them that we often take virtually for granted. A major concern of contemporary organizational views is to clarify and differentiate between the assumptions that underlie the two major competing views of what organizations are all about: classical (or bureaucratic) views on the one hand and the newer perspectives, often called human resources development, on the other hand. Consider, for example, two contrasting approaches to the problem of coordinating and controlling the behavior of people to achieve the goals of the organization.

Bureaucratic Views

The bureaucratic approach tends to emphasize the following five mechanisms in dealing with issues of controlling and coordinating the behavior of people in the organization:

1. *Maintain firm hierarchical control of authority and close supervision of those in the lower ranks.* The role of the administrator as inspector and evaluator is stressed in this concept.

2. *Establish and maintain adequate vertical communication.* This helps to assure that good information will be transmitted up the hierarchy to the decision makers and orders will be clearly and quickly transmitted down the line for implementation. Because the decision makers must have accurate information concerning the operating level in order to make high-quality decisions, the

processing and communicating of information up the line is particularly important but often not especially effective. The use of computers to facilitate this communication is highly attractive to adherents of this concept.

3. *Develop clear written rules and procedures to set standards and guide actions.* These include curriculum guides, policy handbooks, instructions, standard forms, duty rosters, rules and regulations, and standard operating procedures.

4. *Promulgate clear plans and schedules for participants to follow.* These include teachers' lesson plans, bell schedules, pull-out schedules, meeting schedules, budgets, lunch schedules, special teacher schedules, bus schedules, and many others.

5. *Add supervisory and administrative positions to the hierarchy of the organization as necessary to meet problems that arise from changing conditions confronted by the organization.* For example, as school districts and schools grew in size, such positions as assistant principal, chairperson, director, and coordinator appeared. As programs became more complex, positions for specialists appeared; director of special education, coordinator of substance abuse programs, school psychologist, and school social worker are a few examples.

The overwhelmingly widespread acceptance of these as the preferred mechanisms for exercising control and coordination in schools is illustrated by the reform movement that burst upon the scene in the early 1980s. The effectiveness of schools arose as a major theme in the public agenda on education in the 1980s to join the linked duo that had been inherited from the 1970s—equality and access. Although there had been a steadily growing body of research literature on effective schools and what they were like, a virtually unrelated "reform movement" suddenly erupted in 1982 that—in the popular press and electronic media, at least—seized the center stage and strongly influenced numerous efforts to improve the functioning of schools. This is of interest to us here because it illustrates the very strong conviction of many educational leaders that bureaucratic theory is highly useful in thinking about schools and how to improve them.

During the biennium of 1982–1983, led by *A Nation at Risk,* issued by the National Commission on Excellence in Education, no fewer than ten major reports were published on the state of public education in the United States. Each of these cataloged various deficiencies perceived by the reporters and proffered an array of corrective measures to deal with them. If nothing else, they stand as testimony to the widespread concern about the effectiveness of public schooling at the time and they were the source of considerable popular discussion of the shortcomings of public schooling in the press and electronic media. Indeed, for the first time in the history of the Republic—thanks in large part to the interest stimulated by these reports (and approximately twenty others that were to appear by mid-1985)—the president of the United States chose to elevate the discussion of the condition of U.S. public schools to the level of presidential discourse and politics. The Educational

Commission of the States counted no fewer than 175 state-level, active task forces on education that were issuing recommendations in 1983. By 1985, a total of some thirty reports and calls for reform had appeared in print. This extraordinary outpouring of concern for the effectiveness of public schools in the United States resulted in a dazzling array of observations and recommendations for improvement and an unprecedented, broad-scale discussion of what became known as the movement for public school "reform." One veteran observer called it "the best opportunity for school renewal we will get in this century." Considering that a mere sixteen years then remained in the century, that seemed like a hardly overoptimistic assessment.

The profusion of recommendations emanating from this body of work was preponderantly based on traditional assumptions about the nature of schools held by at least some of those who conducted the studies and certainly of many who read them. Of course, there were many variations and differences among the recommendations of the reports, some being partially in conflict with one another. Essentially, however, the gist of the major recommendations in them ran as follows.

Somehow, goals of the schools (then described by John Goodlad as being mired in a conceptual swamp) should be simplified, clarified, and limited; all students should be required to complete some sort of core curriculum (bereft of "soft, nonessential courses" as the Education Commission of the States put it); mastery of the English language should be emphasized, but greater stress should also be given to math, the sciences, and computer technology; teachers should be paid more, trained better, and provided with better working conditions; schools should be more effectively linked to outside leadership groups—principally partnerships with business and more effective relationships with the state and federal governments; the school day and school year should be extended and reorganized with a keen eye to time on task, and more homework should be assigned to students; the status of teaching and teachers should be enhanced by such means as improving compensation, creating career ladders so as to reward superior teachers for superior teaching performance, and professionalizing the working environment of teachers; and stronger educational leadership should be developed, chiefly at the level of the school principalship.

In sum, the recommendations emanating from these reports on the state of education in the United States have been described as barren in terms of large-scale influence, containing few fresh ideas and few promising initiatives, and offering essentially warmed-over ideas of modest conceptual strength.[1] In response to the stimulus of the various reports, every state and numerous local school districts sought quickly to implement some of the recommendations. Predictably, the manner of implementation has weighed heavily on the side of traditional bureaucratic mandates intended to compel schools to effect change.

For example, many states issued new rules, regulations, and mandates to "toughen-up" the curriculum in local schools. Frequently, these were aimed at such things as reducing the number of elective courses and increasing the number of required courses, as well as dictating the assignment of homework by teachers. The impact of such efforts at reform in effecting improved instructional effectiveness of schools remains problematic.

This is well illustrated by the effort to extend both the school year and the school day. At the time of its appearance in 1983, one of the popular recommendations of *A Nation at Risk* was that "school districts and state legislatures should consider the seven-hour school day and the 200 or 220 day school year" as a means of providing more time for instruction. This would appear to be a relatively simple change to effect, requiring only a clear mandate from the state. Though several states did mandate additional days to be added to the minimum pupil-teacher contact days, the net effect nationwide was simply to move some states closer to the already existing national average of 180 days of instruction per year. Arkansas, for example, decided to move from its 175-day school year to a 180-day year by 1989. Colorado went from 172 school days per year to 176 in 1984. Several other states extended the work year *for teachers,* while holding the number of instructional days *for students.* Thus Florida, Tennessee, and North Carolina each requires 180 days of student-teacher contact time while permitting the employment of teachers for additional days to cover emergency closings, in-service training programs, and other administrative purposes. The net effect has been scant change nationally. In 1985 the school year ranged from a high of 184 days in Washington, D.C., to a low of 173 days in North Dakota with 29 states clustered at the national average of 180 school days. Viewing the resistance to a longer school calendar from employers in agriculture and the travel industry as well as from the general public the Education Commission of the States concluded in 1985 that the 200 or 220 day school year was "not realistic" and that "there may be a bigger payoff in wringing more honest instruction time out of the regular day, and this may be the only acceptable solution as far as parents and the public are concerned."[2] In other words, it does not appear likely that schools will move much beyond the "time on task" concept that had been widely implemented in schools long before the appearance of the report.

Virtually all of the "reform" proposals have assumed a "top-down" strategy similar to this; that is, decisions are made in the legislature or another place high in the hierarchy, such as the state education department, and handed down to be implemented by teachers in their classrooms. For example, the California Business Roundtable—composed of large business corporations in the state—managed to get the legislature to enact (and the governor to sign) a new major education law for California that was funded for $2.7 billion over a two-year period—money that the schools desperately needed in the wake of the stringent cutbacks that had been imposed as a result of Proposition 13. The new law—150 pages long—prescribed in detail things that were to be done in the classrooms (for example, what textbooks to use, how many minutes of instruction would be given in a particular subject) and specified how the state education bureaucracy would audit and verify compliance with all these complex provisions. Similarly, the New York State Board of Regents developed an Action Plan accompanied by the "Part 100 Regulations" that enabled the Regents to reach into virtually every public school classroom in the state to direct, implement, and verify compliance with a comprehensive set of highly detailed directives for changes in school practice. These specify not only policy directions (such as the goals or intent desired), but also, by directives, such things as requiring certain remedial instruction to be carried on in rooms separate from regular classrooms, specifying the types of instruction to be used, and indicating the periods of time. In the 1980s, every state developed and implemented similar plans—more or less comprehensive, perhaps, but virtually all using bureaucratic assumptions as the basis for change strategy. The federal government continued its now long-established tradition of direct top-down mandates to the public schools of the nation. The Hatch Act, for example, in establishing open and equal access to the schools for certain religious groups, went so far as to specify the permissible actions of children, teachers, administrators, and other adults in its mandate to encourage before-school and after-school voluntary assemblies of students who were interested in religion.

Clearly, there is a strong tendency for contemporary educational reformers to have in mind a set of assumptions about the nature of schools on which the logic of their efforts pivots. Those assumptions are the same as those underlying the old-fashioned factory, in which management decided what was to be done, directed the workers to do it, then supervised them closely to be sure that the directives were followed in full. Denis Doyle and Terry Hartle observed:

> It simply doesn't work that way. The impulse to reform the schools from the top down is understandable: it is consistent with the history of management science. The explicit model for such reform was the factory; Frederick Taylor's scientific management revolution did for the schools the same thing that it did for business and industry—created an environment whose principal characteristics were pyramidal organization. . . . The teacher was the worker on the assembly line of education; the student, the product; the superintendent, the chief executive officer, the school trustees, the board of directors; and the taxpayer, the shareholder.[3]

Human Resources Development Views

Doyle and Hartle go on to present a different set of assumptions about the organizational characteristics of schools and the behavior of teachers in their classrooms—a view that places the teacher foremost in creating instructional change and, therefore, questions the wisdom of any change strategy that seeks to force change upon the teacher arbitrarily and without his or her participation in the processes of deciding what should be done. As we have seen, this is far from a new view of organization. But recent failures of bureaucratic methods to rectify severe organizational difficulties—especially in the corporate world—coupled with the emergence of such newer organizational perspectives as loose coupling and the power of organizational cultures to influence behavior has brought human resources development concepts to the fore as a major new way to think about organizational problems.

Whereas bureaucratic theory stresses primacy of the organization's officially prescribed rules, and their enforcement, as a means of influencing individual participants to perform dependably in predictable ways, human resources development emphasizes using the conscious thinking of individual persons about what they are doing as a means of involving their commitment, their abilities, and their energies in achieving the goals for which the organization stands. The central mechanism through which the organization exercises coordination and control is the socialization of participants to the values and goals of the organization, rather than through written rules and close supervision. Through this intense socialization the participant identifies personally with the values and purposes of the organization and is motivated to see the organization's goals and needs as being closely congruent with his or her own. Thus, the culture of the organization epitomizes not only what the organization stands for but also the aspirations of the individual participants themselves.

The culture of an organization makes clear what the organization stands for— its values, its beliefs, its true (as distinguished from its publicly stated) goals—and provides tangible ways by which individuals in the organization may personally identify with that culture. The culture of an organization is communicated through symbols: typically stories, myths, legends, and rituals that establish, nourish, and keep alive the enduring values and beliefs that give meaning to the organization and make clear how individuals become and continue to be part of the saga of the organization as it develops through time.

In this view, close inspection and supervision are far from the only means of assuring the predictable performance of participants. Personal identification with the values of the organization's culture can provide powerful motivation for dependable performance even under conditions of great uncertainty and stress. Consider, for example, what it is that causes an individual to join an organization, stay in it, and work toward that organization's goals. A response to this fundamental question is facilitated by Douglas McGregor's Theory *X* and Theory *Y*.[4]

THEORY *X* AND THEORY *Y*

Theory *X* rests on four assumptions that the administrator may hold:

1. The average person inherently dislikes work and will avoid it whenever possible.
2. Because people dislike work, they must be supervised closely, directed, coerced, or threatened with punishment in order for them to put forth adequate effort toward the achievement of organizational objectives.
3. The average worker will shirk responsibility and seek formal direction from those in charge.
4. Most workers value job security above other job-related factors and have little ambition.

Administrators who—tacitly or explicitly—accept the assumptions underlying this explanation of humankind will, of course, use them as a guide to action in dealing with employees in the organization. Theory *Y,* however, embraces some very different assumptions about the nature of people at work:

1. If it is satisfying to them, employees will view work as natural and as acceptable as play.
2. People at work will exercise initiative, self-direction, and self-control on the job if they are committed to the objectives of the organization.
3. The average person, under proper conditions, learns not only to accept responsibility on the job but to seek it.
4. The average employee values creativity—that is, the ability to make good decisions—and seeks opportunities to be creative at work.

Administrators who—tacitly or explicitly—favor this explanation of the nature of human beings at work could reasonably be expected to deal with subordinates in ways that are quite different from those who hold Theory *X* views.

These theories are not presented here as something for the reader to accept or reject; they are merely proffered as a simple illustration of how organizational views are actually used by practitioners of educational administration in their work—a guide to rational decisions and actions "on the firing line."

Theory *X* and Theory *Y* are obviously two different, contrasting explanations of real-world conditions. They are clearly based on differing assumptions about people. Those of us with administrative, management, or leadership responsibilities tend to believe that one or the other of these theoretic statements is more accurately representative of the nature of human beings than the other. Those of us whose behavior is congruent with our beliefs and perceptions will act in ways that are harmonious with the theoretic statement that we think is "true." Those who tend to hold a Theory *X* view of people, for example, will tend to believe that motivation is basically a matter of the carrot and the stick; they will tend to accept readily the necessity for close, detailed supervision of subordinates, and they will tend to accept the inevitability of the need to exercise down-the-line hierarchical control in the organization. Collaborative, participative decision making will tend to be viewed as perhaps a nice ideal in the abstract but really not very practical in the "real" world.

As Chris Argyris put it, Theory *X* views give rise to Behavior Pattern *A* on the part of leaders.[5] This pattern of behavior may take one of two principal forms:

1. Behavior Pattern *A, hard,* is characterized by no-nonsense, strongly directive leadership, tight controls, and close supervision.
2. Behavior Pattern *A, soft,* involves a good deal of persuading, "buying" compliance from subordinates, benevolent paternalism, or so-called good (that is, manipulative) human relations.

In either case, Behavior Pattern *A,* whether acted out in its hard or its soft form, has the clear intention of manipulating, controlling, and managing in the classical sense. It is based on Theory *X* assumptions about the nature of human beings at work.

Argyris went on to explain that Theory *Y* assumptions about people give rise to Behavior Pattern *B*. This is characterized by commitment to mutually shared objectives, high levels of trust, respect, satisfaction from work, and authentic, open relationships. Pattern *B* leadership may well be demanding, explicit, and thoroughly realistic, but it is essentially collaborative. It is a pattern of leader behavior that is intended to be more effective and productive than Pattern *A*, because it is thought to reflect a more accurate understanding of what people at work are "really" like.

In this discussion of the relationship between theory and understanding organizational behavior in schools, it should be emphasized—as Argyris cautioned— that Behavior Pattern *A*, *soft*, is often superficially mistaken for Behavior Pattern *B*. This ambiguity has caused considerable confusion among those trying to apply these theoretic ideas to schools:

> Behavior associated with Theory *Y* assumptions . . . is basically developmental. Here supervisors focus on building identification of and commitment to worthwhile objectives in the work context and upon building mutual trust and respect in the interpersonal context. Success in the work and the interpersonal contexts are assumed interdependent, with important satisfactions for individuals being achieved within the context of accomplishing important work.[6]

The important differences in the assumptions that underlie Behavior Pattern *A*, *soft*, and Behavior Pattern *B* are compared and contrasted in Figure 2–1.

But the Behavior Pattern *A*, *soft*, approach often used by supervisors to manipulate teachers into compliance with what is basically highly directive management—in the guise of "good human relations"—has done much in U.S. education to discredit the plausibility of Theory *Y* as applicable to the "real" world of schools and school systems. "By treating teachers in a kindly way," Sergiovanni observes, "it is assumed that they will become sufficiently satisfied and sufficiently passive so that supervisors and administrators can run the school with little resistance."[7]

The utility of theorizing in this way is illustrated by the work of Rensis Likert. In more than thirty years of research in schools as well as in industrial organizations, Likert has identified a range of management styles, called Systems 1, 2, 3, and 4. Further, his studies support the hypothesis that the crucial variable that differentiates more effective from less effective organizations is human behavior in the organization:

> The main causal factors [of organizational effectiveness or ineffectiveness] are the organizational climate and the leadership behavior which significantly affect how subordinates deal with each other individually and in work groups in order to produce the end results. These variables can be used to define consistent patterns of management. . . . The range of management styles begins with System 1 which is a punitive authoritarian model and extends to System 4, a participative or group interaction model. In between is System 2, a paternalistic authoritarian style that emphasizes [person-to-person] supervision in a competitive (or isolative) environment, and System 3, which is a [person-to-person] consultative pattern of operation.[8]

ASSUMPTIONS UNDERLYING BEHAVIOR PATTERN A, SOFT (Theory X, soft)	ASSUMPTIONS UNDERLYING BEHAVIOR PATTERN B (Theory Y)
With Regard to People	
1. People in our culture, teachers among them, share a common set of needs—to belong, to be liked, to be respected.	1. In addition to sharing common needs for belonging and respect, most people in our culture, teachers among them, desire to contribute effectively and creatively to the accomplishment of worthwhile objectives.
2. Although teachers desire individual recognition, they, more importantly, want to *feel* useful to the school.	2. The majority of teachers are capable of exercising far more initiative, responsibility, and creativity than their present job or work circumstances require or allow.
3. They tend to cooperate willingly and to comply with school, department, and unit goals if these important needs are fulfilled.	3. These capabilities represent untapped resources that are currently being wasted.
With Regard to Participation	
1. The administrator's basic task is to make each teacher *believe* that he or she is a useful and an important part of the team.	1. The administrator's basic task is to create an environment in which teachers can contribute their full range of talents to the accomplishment of school goals. The administrator works to uncover the creative resources of the teachers.
2. The administrator is willing to explain *his* or *her* decisions and to discuss teachers' objections to his or her plans. On routine matters, teachers are encouraged in planning and in decision making.	2. The administrator allows and encourages teachers to participate in important as well as routine decisions. In fact, the more important a decision is to the school, the greater are the administrator's efforts to tap faculty resources.
3. Within *narrow* limits, the faculty unit or individual teachers who comprise the faculty unit should be allowed to exercise self-direction and self-control.	3. Administrators work continually to expand the areas over which teachers exercise self-direction and self-control as they develop and demonstrate greater insight and ability.
With Regard to Expectations	
1. Sharing information with teachers and involving them in school decision making will help satisfy their basic needs for *belonging* and for individual recognition.	1. The overall quality of decision making and performance will improve as administrators and teachers make use of the full range of experience, insight, and creative ability that exists in their schools.
2. Satisfying these needs will improve teacher morale and will *reduce* resistance to formal authority.	2. Teachers will exercise responsible self-direction and self-control in the accomplishment of worthwhile objectives that they understand and have helped establish.

FIGURE 2–1 Comparison of assumptions underlying Argyris's Behavior Pattern *A, soft,* and Behavior Pattern *B.* Adapted from Thomas J. Sergiovanni, "Beyond Human Relations," in *Professional Supervision for Professional Teachers,* ed. Thomas J. Sergiovanni (Washington, DC: Association for Supervision and Curriculum Development, 1975), pp. 12–13.

Essentially, these four categories of "management systems" are descriptions of conditions that may be found in schools and school systems. By the 1970s, Likert and others were conducting a number of studies in school settings to ascertain whether these same factors of organizational behavior are applicable to the unique characteristics of effective school systems. Those studies support the view that "the more effective schools are those with a participative environment more toward System 4, while the less effective are much more authoritarian, toward a System 1 pattern of operation."[9]

Figure 2–2 shows that there is a remarkable compatibility between Douglas McGregor's work and that of Likert. Both were basically concerned, not with being nice to people or making work pleasant, but with understanding how to make work organizations more effective, which is as pressing a need in business and industry as it is in education. This general point of view is widely and strongly supported by

THEORY X   *System 1*   *Management is seen as having no trust in subordinates.*
   a. Decision imposed—made at the top.
   b. Subordinates motivated by fear, threats, punishment.
   c. Control centered on top management.
   d. Little superior-subordinate interaction.
   e. People informally opposed to goal by management.

System 2   *Management has condescending confidence and trust in subordinates.*
   a. Subordinate seldom involved in decision making.
   b. Rewards and punishment used to motivate.
   c. Interaction used with condescension.
   d. Fear and caution displayed by subordinates.
   e. Control centered on top management but some delegation.

System 3   *Management seen as having substantial but not complete trust in subordinates.*
   a. Subordinates make specific decisions at lower level.
   b. Communication flows up and down hierarchy.
   c. Rewards, occasional punishment, and some involvement are used to motivate.
   d. Moderate interaction and fair trust exist.
   e. Control is delegated downward.

THEORY Y   *System 4*   *Management is seen as having complete trust and confidence in subordinates.*
   a. Decision making is widely dispersed.
   b. Communication flows up and down and laterally.
   c. Motivation is by participation and rewards.
   d. Extensive, friendly, superior-subordinate interaction exists.
   e. High degree of confidence and trust exists.
   f. Widespread responsibility for the control process exists.

FIGURE 2–2   Likert's Management Systems Theory related to McGregor's Theory *X* and Theory *Y.*

a vast amount of organizational research. Robert R. Blake's and Jane Srygley Mouton's organizational research,[10] Gordon Lippitt's studies of organizational renewal,[11] and Paul Berman's and Milbrey McLaughlin's extensive studies of change in U.S. schools[12]—are only a few of the many studies that support the general theoretic position that pioneers such as McGregor and Likert held.

Traditional classical organizational views would indicate the opposite point of view: tighten up, exercise stronger discipline and tougher management, and demand more work from subordinates. In the parlance of neoclassical theory, the focus is: teacher accountability, specified performance objectives, and cost-benefit analysis. Yet much of the best research in organizational behavior strongly suggests that this latter approach would be, at best, self-defeating.

A word of caution is in order here. Bureaucratic and human resources perspectives have been compared and contrasted as ideal cases for the purpose of clarifying and delineating the very real, basic differences between them. In the "real world" of educational administration, of course, one rarely encounters ideal cases, which is not to suggest that organizations cannot properly be classified as being bureaucratic or nonbureaucratic. Indeed, they can be and often are. However, it does not mean, either, that to be described as nonbureaucratic an organization must be totally devoid of policies, regulations, standard operating procedures, or hierarchical organization, or that to be described as bureaucratic an organization must be totally devoid of sensitivity to or respect for people. This is particularly true of schools, which are bureaucratic in some ways and nonbureaucratic in some very important ways. What it does suggest is that organizations may be properly described as *relatively* bureaucratic or nonbureaucratic. It also suggests that schools are undoubtedly far more organizationally complex than has been traditionally understood prior to the mid-1980s.

ORGANIZATIONAL STRUCTURE AND PEOPLE

A major theme, perhaps the dominant one, in organizational theory for at least a half-century has been the interaction between organizational structure and people. It can be argued, for example, that the structure of an organization is the prime determinant of the behavior of people in the organization. Charles Perrow pointed out that

> one of the persistent complaints in the field of penology, or juvenile correctional institutions, or mental hospitals, or any of the "people-changing" institutions is the need for better workers. Their problems, we hear, stem from the lack of high-quality personnel. More specifically, the types of individuals they can recruit as guards, or cottage parents, or orderlies typically have too little education, hold over-simplified views about people, tend to be punitive, and believe that order and discipline can solve all problems.[13]

He went on to describe a study in which applicants for positions in a juvenile correction institution were, when tested, found to be quite enlightened and permissive, whereas after they had worked in the institution for a while they had become less permissive and took a punitive, unenlightened view regarding the causes of delinquency and the care and handling of delinquents. Perrow offered this as an illustration of the power of organizations to shape the views and attitudes—and, thus, behavior—of participants.

On the other hand, much of the literature of organizational theory is devoted to the view that the people in the organization tend to shape the structure of the organization. Much attention is given to the impact of the behavior of people—in the processes of making decisions, leading, and dealing with conflict—on the structure, values, and customs of organizations. Increasingly, attention has been devoted to the possibilities of improving organizations by means, not of changing their structures as a way of inducing more effective organizational behavior, but of training participants in more effective group processes as a way of bringing about desirable changes in organizational structure.

GENERAL SYSTEMS THEORY

Attempts to describe, explain, and predict organizational behavior generally depend—as does much of modern scientific thought—on systems theory. A biologist, Ludwig von Bertalanffy, is generally credited with having first outlined, in 1950, the notion of what is now known as general systems theory.[14] The nature of his work and its significance to the science of biology is suggested by the following statement:

> An organism is an integrated system of interdependent structures and functions. An organism is constituted of cells and a cell consists of molecules which must work in harmony. Each molecule must know what the others are doing. Each one must be capable of receiving messages and must be sufficiently disciplined to obey. You are familiar with the laws that control regulation. You know how our ideas have developed and how the most harmonious and sound of them have been fused into a conceptual whole which is the very foundation of biology and confers on it its unity.[15]

This statement captures the basic ideas of a way of considering and analyzing complex situations that have come to be preeminent in both the physical and the social sciences.

If we substitute *organization* for organism, *group* for cell, and *person* for molecule in the above statement about biology, it has relevance for thinking about organizations:

> An *organization* is an integrated system of interdependent structures and functions. An *organization* is constituted of *groups* and a *group* consists of *persons* who must work in harmony. Each *person* must know what the others are doing. Each one must be capable of receiving messages and must be sufficiently disciplined to obey. . . .[16]

Two Basic Concepts of System

The system approach to understanding and describing phenomena is well established in both the physical sciences and the social sciences. Social scientists tend to draw their illustrations and analogues from the biological sciences.

A young child, for example, might think of a nearby pond as a wonderful playground, away from the ever-watchful eyes of grownups. A fisherman might see it as a great place in which to fill his creel. A farmer might think of it as a good source of water for irrigating his crops. A biologist, however, would tend to view the pond as a system of living things, all of which are interdependent in many ways and all of which are dependent in some ways on the larger environment in which the pond exists (for example, the air and sunlight). In terms of understanding the pond and being able to describe it, it is obvious that we are dealing with different levels of insight. However, in terms of being able to predict more accurately the consequences of things that might be done to the pond—such as pumping a large volume of water from it or removing large numbers of its fish—the biologist clearly has the advantage.

It is this advantage in dealing with cause and effect that has made systems theory so attractive to those concerned with organizational behavior. There is a strong tendency in our culture to ascribe single causes to events; in fact, the causes of even relatively simple organizational events are often very complex. We may be unwilling to accept this fact and, as a way of rejecting it, choose to apply simplistic cause-and-effect logic to our problems.

This was illustrated by congressional interest in reducing automobile accidents in this country, which started out by concentrating on the automobile as a primary "cause" of accidents. From this flowed a logical line of thought: if we require automobile manufacturers to improve the design of their cars and install certain mechanical safety features, the result would be a reduction in the appalling carnage on our highways.

In fact, however, more careful study seemed to show that automobile accidents are "caused" by an enormously complex, interrelated set of variables. Automobile design is clearly one, but others include road conditions and such relatively intangible factors as social mores and the psychological state of the driver. As we dig behind each of these conditions (for example, Why was the road built that way? Why was the driver drunk? Why didn't the driver yield the right of way?) we find that each is part of a complex set of interrelated factors of its own. Clearly, significant reduction in automobile accidents must eventually require analysis of the interrelated factors of these complex subsystems of causative factors.

Systems theory, then, puts us on guard against the strong tendency to ascribe phenomena to a single causative factor. Similarly, if our car is not running well, we often take what is, in effect, a systems approach to the problem: we get a tune-up from someone who understands the functions and interrelatedness of the subsystems (for example, the ignition system, the fuel system, the exhaust system) that comprise the engine.

These two concepts—the concept of subsystems and the concept of multiple causation—are central to systems theory.

SOCIAL SYSTEMS THEORY

Systems can be divided into two main classes: "open" systems, which interact with their environments, and "closed" systems, which do not interact with their environments. Social systems theory generally deals with so-called open systems, because it is virtually impossible to envisage a social system, such as a school, that is not interactive with its environment. When observers describe certain schools or school systems as "closed systems," they generally mean that those organizations tend to try to limit the influence of the community and tend to proceed as though unrelated to the larger real world in which they exist. Thus, in the late 1960s and into the 1970s, it was popular to describe unresponsive school systems that resisted constructive change as "closed systems." Though the calumny has a certain ring of scientific credibility, it is in fact technically impossible. The input-output relationship of the school to its larger environment is an endless cyclical interaction between the school and its larger environment.

In Figure 2–3 we show schooling as a process involving (1) *inputs* from the larger societal environment (for example, knowledge that exists in that society, values that are held, goals that are desired, and money), (2) *process* that occurs within the social system we call a school (involving subsystems of organizational structure,

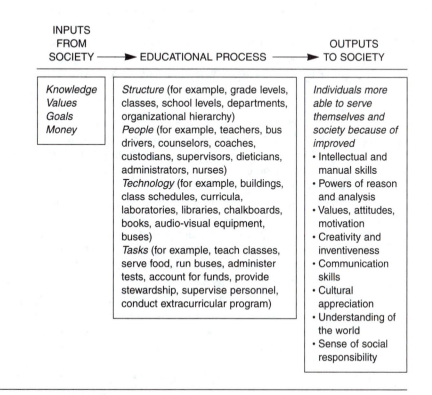

FIGURE 2–3   Schooling as an input-process-output system.

people, technology, and work tasks), and—resulting from that process—(3) *outputs* to society (in the form of changed individuals). In this sense it is impossible for a school to be, in fact, a closed system. Indeed, in recent years professional educators have become increasingly aware of the extent and importance of the interaction between the school and its environment—which is, conceptually, the basis for much of what goes on under the rubrics of accountability and community relations.

A Contextual Approach

The input-output concept is often called a "linear model"; it is, in effect, a theory that attempts to explain how things can be described in the "real world." It is a seductive concept—seemingly logical, rational, and orderly. It lends itself well to concepts of efficiency, such as cost effectiveness; one can relate the value of inputs to the value of outputs and arrive at relative cost efficiency. It has been extremely popular in analyzing the apparent relative effectiveness of competing programs and technologies. By the late 1970s, however, it was becoming increasingly apparent that this theoretical model contributed little to our understanding of the ways in which educative organizations function. For example, it presupposes that when students and teachers go to school each day, their dominant concerns are to achieve the formal, official goals of the school. Even a casual observer soon learns, however, that actually these people bring to school with them a host of their own beliefs, goals, hopes, and concerns that are more significant and more powerful to them. Clearly, the many subtle ways in which teachers, administrators, and students accommodate to the rules, regulations, and discipline of the school have more to do with the need to "survive" in a frustrating, crowded environment than with commitment to the achievement of some remote and often ambiguous educational goals.

A more useful approach to understanding educative organizations and the behavior of people in them is to focus our attention on what actually goes on in them. Thus, our attention is centered on examining the inner workings of that system we call an organization. This requires us to see the organization as a whole system that creates the setting, the context in which the whole pattern of human behavior that characterizes the organization occurs. With this approach we seek to study organizations as systems that create and maintain environments in which complex sets of human interactions (both group and individual) occur with some regularity and predictability. In this view, our understanding of educative organizations requires us to examine the relationships between human behavior and the context (environment, ecology) that are characteristic of the organization. Thus, as I shall discuss in detail in Chapter 5, the organizational culture (climate, ecology, ethos) of the system we call an organization becomes critical to our understanding.

The realm of organizational behavior tends to focus primarily on the school district or on the school as a system. Some scientists, in studying organizational behavior, have unwittingly encouraged the illusion that a school can, in fact, be a closed social system. Andrew Halpin and Don Croft, for example, in their highly influential study of the organizational climate of schools "concentrated on internal organizational characteristics as though they function independently from external influences"[17] and, further, used the terms "open" and "closed" to describe the profiles of schools that represented selected characteristics of what they chose to call organizational climate.[18] This was, to some extent, a convenience for the researchers: it is, indeed, difficult to study and discuss the behavior of people in a system without assuming (implicitly or otherwise) that the organization is separate from its environment. Many studies of organizational behavior in schools have, in fact, focused on the internal functioning of schools—that is, have treated the schools as "closed systems"—as though they function independently of influences from their larger, outside environments.[19]

In the physical realm, a burning candle has become a classic illustration of an open system: it affects its environment and is affected by it, yet it is self-regulating and retains its own identity. If a door is opened, the candle may flicker in the draft, but it will adjust to it and return to normal at the first opportunity—provided, of course, that the environmental change (the draft) was not so overwhelming as to destroy the system (that is, to extinguish the flame).

It is not so simple to describe *social* systems on even this superficial level. Daniel Griffiths spoke of the organization (the system) as existing in an environment (the suprasystem) and having within it a subsystem (the administrative apparatus of the organization). His diagram is presented in Figure 2–4. The boundaries of the various systems and subsystems are suggested in the figure by the tangential circles; however, we must bear in mind that these boundaries are permeable, permitting interaction between the systems and their environments. One application of this viewpoint can be illustrated by labeling the figure, as in Figure 2–5. It then becomes obvious that factors that interfere with the interactive and adaptive relationships among the components of the interrelated parts of the system could pose a threat to the functioning of the whole. One form of interference would be a loss of permeability of one or more of the boundaries, thus tending to make the system "closed" and less sensitive to environmental change.

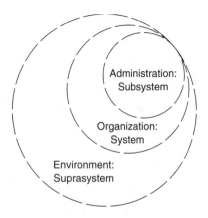

FIGURE 2–4

An organization viewed as an open social system. From Daniel E. Griffiths, "Administrative Theory and Change in Organizations," In *Innovation in Education,* ed. Matthew B. Miles (New York: Teachers College Press, 1964), p. 430. © 1964 by Teachers College, Columbia University. Reproduced by permission of the publisher.

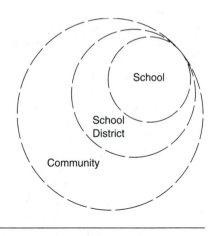

FIGURE 2–5
A social systems view of the school.

Where does the individual fit into all of this? This becomes clearer if we modify the original model, as in Figure 2–6. Here, again, relabeling the diagram can specify—a little more clearly at least—one way in which the view would apply to people working in schools. The individual is functioning in the organization not only as an individual but also as one who occupies a certain *role* within the social system in the organization. In the hypothetical case illustrated in Figure 2–7, the person occupies the role of "teacher" in the chemistry department of John F. Kennedy Senior High School, a situation possessing a number of useful implications for anyone interested in analyzing, predicting, and perhaps controlling organizational behavior.

When we consider the individual person carrying out a unique role in an organization, we become concerned with the complex web of human involvement and its attendant behavior in organizational life. As the individual, with all the needs,

FIGURE 2–6
Levels of interaction of the individual and the organization. From Richard C. Lonsdale, "Maintaining the Organization in Dynamic Equilibrium," in *Behavioral Science and Educational Administration,* ed. Daniel E. Griffiths. The Sixty-Third Yearbook of the National Society for the Study of Education, Part II (Chicago: National Society for the Study of Education, 1964), p. 143.

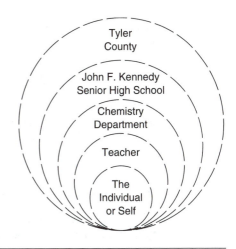

FIGURE 2–7
A social systems view of the individual in a hypothetical
school organization.

drives, and talents that human beings have, assumes an official role, he or she shapes that role to some extent and is also shaped by it. The dynamic interaction of people with varying psychological makeups in the organizational setting is the domain of role theory.

ROLE THEORY

In attempting to analyze face-to-face, interpersonal behavior of people in organizations, Erving Goffman, in *The Preservation of Self in Everyday Life,*[20] drew a useful analogy between "real-life" situations and the unfolding of a play on the stage. People in organizations have definite roles to perform, and many interactive factors help to determine precisely what kind of "performance" each role will receive. Each "actor" must interpret his or her role, and this interpretation depends to some extent on what the individual brings to the role. But behavior in a role as part of an organization—no less than for an actor on the stage—is influenced to some extent by dynamic interplay with other people: other actors and the audience. Role performances are also shaped by the expectations of the director and others attempting to control the situation. Presumably, each actor attempts, to some degree, to behave in conformity with these expectations—and the expectations of colleagues and other referent groups as well. Goffman described the actors in an organization as being on stage when they are formally carrying out their roles, but he points out that backstage there is a different behavioral standard. Those of us connected with schools, for example, know that a certain kind of behavior is exhibited by teachers in the presence of students and their parents, which differs from their behavior in the teachers' cafeteria.

Role theory has been used extensively by observers and researchers in many kinds of organizations to better understand and predict organizational behavior. A vocabulary of generally understood terms is fairly well established in the literature. Some of the more commonly used terms are described below.

Role.   Role[21] is a psychological concept dealing with behavior enactment arising from interaction with other human beings. The various offices or positions in an organization carry with them certain expectations of behavior held by both onlookers and by the person occupying the role. These expectations generally define role, with some additional expectation that the individual will exhibit some idiosyncratic personality in role behavior.

Role description.   This refers to the actual behavior of an individual performing a role or, more accurately, one's perception of that behavior.

Role prescription.   This is the relatively abstract idea of what the general norm in the culture is for the role. What kind of role behavior is expected of a teacher in this country, for example?

Role expectation.   This refers to the expectation that one person has of the role behavior of another. Teachers, for example, expect certain behaviors from a principal, and the principal has expectations of behaviors for teachers. Thus, as teacher and principal interact in their roles in the school, they have complementary role expectations.

Role perception.   This is used to describe the perception that one has of the role expectation that another person holds for him or her. In dealing with the PTA president, for example, the principal knows that the president has some role expectation of the principal. The principal's estimate of that expectation is role perception.

Manifest and latent roles.   Naturally, a person plays more than one role in life; indeed, an individual may well play more than one in an organization. In the case of multiple roles, the term *manifest role* refers to the obvious role that one is performing, but one also occupies *latent roles*. For example, in the classroom, a teacher's manifest role is "teacher"; but the teacher may also be the building chairperson for the teachers' union, and that role—while he or she is teaching—is a latent role. A history teacher may also be an activist in a consumers' rights organization and thus holds a latent, as well as a manifest, role.

Role conflict.   This is commonly thought to be a source of less-than-satisfactory performance in organizations. There are many sources of role conflict, all of which inhibit optimum performance by the role incumbent. An obvious role conflict is a situation in which two persons are unable to establish a satisfactory complementary, or reciprocal, role relationship, which can result from a wide variety of causes and—not infrequently—may involve a complex set of conflict behaviors. Confusion over role expectation and role perception is commonly observed.

Moreover, role conflict frequently exists within a single individual. The role expectation may well clash with the individual personality needs of the role incumbent. A case in point is that of a school principal who was employed by a school district largely because of his innovative skill and strong leadership qualities; when a taxpayers' revolt in the school district suddenly caused a sharp reversal of school board policy, the superintendent was dismissed, and the school board put strong emphasis on economy of operation and conformity to mediocre educational standards. The school principal was plunged into a role conflict situation in which he could not perform to his, or anyone else's, satisfaction and ended up seeking another job with a more manageable amount of conflict.

A common source of tension from role conflict is the expectation that the incumbent, perhaps an administrator, will be empathetic and understanding in dealing with his or her subordinates and will still enforce the rules of the organization and strongly support the school board in dealing with teachers as members of a collective bargaining unit. Many administrators feel this sort of conflict when they zealously attempt to build trust, confidence, and high morale in the teaching staff and then are required to conduct a formal evaluation or to participate in a grievance procedure that seems to be in conflict with those goals.

Role ambiguity.   This arises when the role prescription contains contradictory elements or is vague. Role ambiguity is rather commonly observed in the attempt to preserve the distinction between administration and supervision: the first is generally seen as a "line" authority, whereas the other is thought to be a "staff" responsibility. Yet supervisors are often perceived as being in hierarchical authority over teachers; not infrequently, supervisors feel that they are being maneuvered, against the spirit of their role, into the exercise of authority over teachers, which threatens their more appropriate, collegial relationship with them.

Role conflicts such as those described produce tensions and uncertainties that are commonly associated with inconsistent organizational behavior. In turn, this inconsistent behavior, being unpredictable and unanticipated, often evokes further tension and interpersonal conflict between holders of complementary roles. Frequently, those who must perform their roles under the conditions of ambiguity and tension outlined here develop dysfunctional ways of coping with the situation.

Thus, although we may find such socially acceptable avoidance behavior as joking about the conflict or ambiguity, in organizations in which this kind of avoidance is not acceptable rather elaborate and mutually understood avoidance patterns may exist. These can include a studied avoidance of any discussion of the problem or substituting any kind of "small talk" instead. A common avoidance technique is found in ritualistic behavior that permits parties to get through their role performances with a minimum of actual conflict. Vagueness, pomposity, complex structure, clichés, and overly obscure vocabulary in communication are popular avoidance techniques.[22]

Role set.   The notion of *role set* is helpful in clarifying some of the concepts of role theory as they are found to be operational in organizations. If we were to observe a work group, we would, of course, find it possible to sort out the participants into subgroups in a variety of ways. One way would be in terms of role. In the case of the role set that will be used here as an illustration, the pivotal role player may be thought of as an administrator.[23] Naturally, he or she has superordinates in the hierarchy of the organization, people to whom he or she reports (see Figure 2–8).

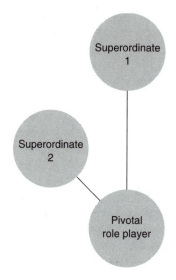

FIGURE 2–8
Relationship of role player to superordinates in the work group.
Adapted from Warren G. Bennis, *Changing Organizations* (New
York: McGraw-Hill Book Company, 1966), p. 193.

These are key people in the individual's referent group, and they convey their role
expectations in many ways. But the administrator not only has superordinates; he
or she also has subordinates, or people who report to him or her. As shown in Figure 2–9, subordinates also are significant persons in the administrator's group, and
they, too, communicate role expectations to the administrator. Thus, the role
player's position becomes pivotal, and it is obvious that the role expectations being
communicated are likely to be somewhat in conflict.

The role set is incomplete, however, until a third group of referents is added:
the role player's colleagues. With their addition to the role set, as in Figure 2–10,
we see the administrator in a pivotal position in relationship to subordinates and superordinates. When we realize that, in this example, twelve persons—two superordinates, four subordinates, and six colleagues—are acting as *role senders* (that is,
they are communicating role expectations to the administrator), it is evident that the
interpersonal dynamics of the role set are complex.

Undoubtedly some role conflict will be present in such a situation, as well as
some role ambiguity. Robert Kahn and his colleagues have used this operational
concept of role theory to describe and measure role conflict and role ambiguity and
to correlate their presence with attitudes that members of the set have toward their
work situation and to the behavioral functioning of these people in the work
group.[24] Thus, the role set is an important concept in a consideration of the ecology of the social setting in which the individual makes his or her contribution to the
organization. It is a useful way of conceptualizing the connection between the person and the organization.

To possess knowledge of role theory and some of its concepts is, in itself, of
little use. However, the construct can be useful in analyzing some of the interpersonal behavior that we encounter in the work groups of organizations. For example,

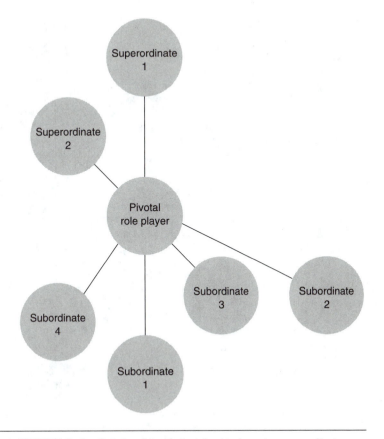

FIGURE 2–9   Relationship of pivotal role player to superordinates and subordinates in the work group. Adapted from Warren G. Bennis, *Changing Organizations* (New York: McGraw-Hill Book Company, 1966), p. 193.

leaders are concerned with facilitating the acceptance, development, and allocation of roles that are necessary for the group to function well.

Functional Roles in the Group

Kenneth Benne and Paul Sheats have pointed out that a group must fill three types of roles:[25]

1. *Group task roles.* These roles help the group to select the problems to be worked on, to define these problems, and to seek solutions to these problems.
2. *Group building and maintenance roles.* These roles facilitate the development of the group and its maintenance over time.
3. *Individual roles.* These roles enable group members to satisfy their own idiosyncratic needs as individuals.

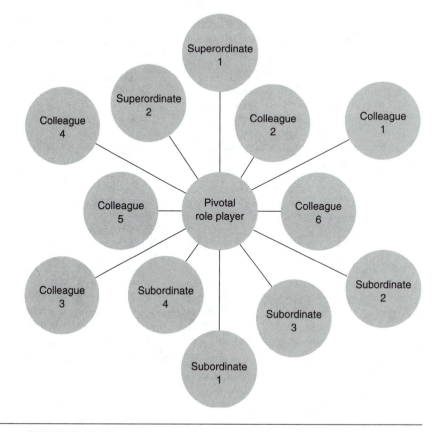

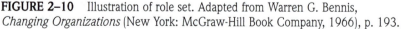

FIGURE 2–10   Illustration of role set. Adapted from Warren G. Bennis, *Changing Organizations* (New York: McGraw-Hill Book Company, 1966), p. 193.

Although we must be wary of too much labeling, let us consider Benne and Sheats's further description of possible specific roles that are available to group members in meeting two critical needs of a group:

Group task roles: These are roles that help the group to achieve its tasks. They include the roles of (a) initiating action and contributing ideas, (b) seeking information, (c) seeking opinions from the group, (d) giving information, (e) giving one's opinion, (f) coordinating the work of group members, (g) helping to keep the group focused on goals, (h) the evaluator-critic, (i) the energizer who prods the group to action, (j) the procedural technician who attends to routine "house-keeping" tasks of the group, and (k) the recorder.[26]

Benne and Sheats stressed that each of these roles must be played by someone in the group; the leader must either assume these essential roles or see that they are allocated to other members of the group. Part of the leader's responsibility is to provide for the creation of an environment in the group in which these roles can be developed and carried out. Other specific roles are suggested under the second major category:

> *Group building and maintenance:* These roles help the group develop a climate and processes that enable the members to work harmoniously and with a minimum of lost time, such as (a) encouraging members to keep at the task, (b) harmonizing differences between ideas and between individuals, (c) facilitating communication (for example, by helping silent individuals to speak up and encouraging equal use of "air time"), (d) setting high standards of performance for the group, (e) providing the group with feedback as to its own processes and actions.[27]

These roles are obviously quite different in nature and function from the group task roles. Of course, it is possible that an individual group member will take on more than one role or that two or more members will share a given role.

ROLE RELATED TO SOCIAL SYSTEMS THEORY

The foregoing discussion enables us to return to social systems with somewhat more insight. The basic notion is that the organization may be understood as a *social system.* Jacob Getzels and Egon Guba described this view as follows:

> We conceive of the social system as involving two major classes of phenomena, which are at once conceptually independent and phenomenally interactive. There are, first, the *institutions* with certain *roles* and *expectations* that will fulfill the goals of the system. Second, inhabiting the system are the *individuals* with certain *personalities* and *need-dispositions,* whose interactions comprise what we generally call "social behavior." . . .
>
> . . . [T]o understand the behavior of specific role incumbents in an institution, we must know both the role expectations and the need-dispositions. Indeed, needs and expectations may both be thought of as motives for behavior, the one deriving from personal propensities, the other from institutional requirements. What we call social behavior may be conceived as ultimately deriving from the interaction between the two sets of motives.
>
> The general model we have been describing may be represented pictorially as indicated [in Figure 2–11]. The nomothetic [organizational] axis is shown at the top of the diagram and consists of the institution, role, and role expectations, each term being the analytic unit for the term next preceding it. . . . Similarly, the idiographic [individual] axis, shown at the lower portion of the diagram, consists of individual, personality, and need-dispositions, each term again serving as the analytic unit for the term next preceding it. A given act is conceived as deriving simultaneously from both the nomothetic and the idiographic dimensions. That is to say, social behavior results as the individual attempts to cope with the environment composed of patterns of expectations for his behavior in ways consistent with his own independent pattern of needs.[28]

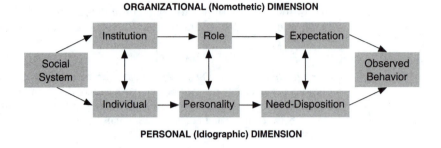

ORGANIZATIONAL (Nomothetic) DIMENSION

PERSONAL (Idiographic) DIMENSION

FIGURE 2–11   Model of the organization as a social system (the so-called Getzels-Guba model). Adapted from Jacob W. Getzels and Egon G. Guba, "Social Behavior and the Administrative Process," *The School Review,* 65 (Winter 1957), 423–41.

Viewed in this way, each behavioral act is seen as stemming simultaneously from the nomothetic and the idiographic dimensions. But how do these dimensions interact? What proportion of each dimension is present in organizational behavior? That depends, of course, on the individual and on the institutional role and is best expressed as a function of the interplay between the two dimensions. Getzels gave us this general equation to express it:

$$B = f(R \times P),$$

where B = observed behavior,
      R = institutional role, and
      P = personality of the role incumbent.[29]

Thus the school, as an organization, creates certain offices and positions that are occupied by individuals. The offices and positions represent the nomothetic dimension of the organization and role expectations held by the organization for incumbents are specified in a number of ways. These may range from elaborate written job descriptions to the more subtle (and usually more powerful) group norms established by custom and tradition. By this means, the organization establishes not merely some formal, minimal level of job performance that would be acceptable but also communicates rather elaborate specifications of behavior in role that may well extend to the kinds of clothes worn on the job, the manner of speech used, and so on.

But the individuals who are incumbent in the offices and positions have their own personality structures and needs, which represent the idiographic dimensions of the organization. To some extent, even in highly formal organizations, the role incumbents mold and shape the offices in some ways in order to better fulfill some of their own expectations of their role.

The mechanism by which the needs of the institution and the needs of the individual are modified so as to come together is the work group. There is a dynamic interrelationship in the work group, then, not only of an interpersonal nature but also between institutional requirements and the idiosyncratic needs of individual participants. The shaping of the institutional role, the development of a climate within the social system, and the very personality of the participants all dynamically interact with one another. Organizational behavior can be viewed as the product of this interaction.

How much organizational behavior can be ascribed to role expectation and role prescription, and how much is traceable to the personality needs of the role incumbent? In other words, if $B = f(R \times P)$, what values can be assigned to R and P, respectively? A useful way of picturing the problem is shown in Figure 2–12. We can see that, for some people, a role can have far greater influence in prescribing behavior than for others.

For example, there has been considerable study of individuals who exhibit an authoritarian personality syndrome and of their impact on others.[30] Such an individual possesses a combination of personality characteristics that are stable, describable, and go far in shaping his or her view of the world. Typically the authoritarian individual tends to think in terms of relatively simple dichotomies: things are seen in black-or-white terms (with few shades of gray), concrete ideas are typical (with little patience for abstract thinking or ambiguity), and he or she identifies strongly with the "in" group (and particularly with authority figures). Authoritarian individuals, being insecure in ambiguous circumstances, place little trust in others and seek to control as much of the environment as possible (including the people around them). Such a person tends to seek a role in which he or she is seen as strong and in which control can be exercised. Behavior in that role tends to be relatively consistent: dogmatic, seeking absolute solutions to complex problems, and exercising power for personal gratification.

Mary Crow and Merl Bonney describe the impact of such people when they take on the leadership roles of a school district:

> Picture a moderate-sized urban school system in Middle America. The clean-cut, conservatively dressed superintendent has made it clear who is on his side and who isn't. Among his supporters are the building principals, men who are much more like the

FIGURE 2–12
The interplay of role personality in organizational behavior. Behavior is a function of organizational role and personality, or $B = f(R \times P)$. Adapted from Jacob W. Getzels, "Administration as a Social Process," in *Administrative Theory in Education,* ed. Andrew W. Halpin (Chicago: Midwest Administration Center, University of Chicago, 1958), p. 158.

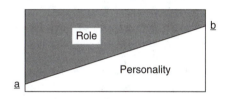

superintendent: wanting to be tough disciplinarians, yet subservient to the boss. Of these principals, teachers will tell you that more competent candidates were often passed over for principalships in favor of these supporters who would be no threat to the superintendent's job. . . . At the first faculty meeting of the year, the superintendent comes across forcefully. He stresses how important it is that his teachers be honest, upstanding citizens, maintain good discipline in their classes, and work hard if they wish to be successful in his system. . . . Students are afraid of teachers; teachers are afraid of principals; principals are afraid of the superintendent; and the superintendent is afraid of the board.[31]

Though this is admittedly a stereotype of one kind of personality frequently found in leadership roles in U.S. school districts, everyone shapes his or her own role to *some* extent; hence, as shown in Figure 2–12, point *a* would not ordinarily be at zero; on the other hand, in any organization everyone plays some sort of institutional role, and, therefore, point *b* is somewhat below the 100 percent mark. The line *ab,* however, suggests the possible range of variation of the function of role and personality that organizations normally encounter.

Different kinds of roles in different kinds of organizations do suggest that some role players will be closer to point *a* (that is, will permit very little infusion of personality into the role). Conversely, we know that some kinds of roles demand greater personality involvement, as illustrated in Figure 2–13. One generally supposes that the role of an army private is very largely prescribed and clearly limits the extent to which the private can meet his or her individual personality needs. Closer to the other extreme would be an artist who exhibits highly creative behavior, with a minimum of organizational constraint, and who expresses personal idiosyncratic needs to a great degree.

Equilibrium

People participate in organizations in order to satisfy certain needs. Presumably, the organization has needs of its own, which are fulfilled by the participants who function in its various roles. This is illustrated by the Getzels-Guba social systems

FIGURE 2–13

Personality and role factors in organizational behavior of army private and artist (proportions are approximate). Adapted from Jacob W. Getzels, "Administration as a Social Process," in *Administrative Theory in Education,* ed. Andrew W. Halpin (Chicago: Midwest Administration Center, University of Chicago, 1958), p. 158.

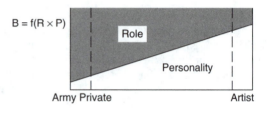

model, with its stress on the interplay between the nomothetic (organizational) needs and the idiographic (personal) needs of the "actors" who fill the various roles. There is obviously a *quid pro quo* relationship between the role player and the organization, the maintenance of which can be thought of as a state of *equilibrium* between the needs of the organization and those of the individual. As long as this state of equilibrium exists, the relationship presumably will be satisfactory, enduring, and relatively productive.

On a very rudimentary level, the notion of equilibrium between the needs of the organization and its participants is illustrated by the well-known case of Schmidt at Bethlehem Steel. Schmidt, as he was called in Frederick W. Taylor's description,[32] was a pig-iron handler who picked up, carried, and loaded pig iron— 12.5 tons in a ten-hour day for $1.15 per day. Obviously, the company needed men to do the pig-iron handling, and this need was satisfied by the men whose role was that of "handler." Presumably, as long as the needs and satisfactions exchange was in a state of balance or equilibrium, the organization functioned adequately. In his account Taylor described how he applied his "scientific principles" to the task of rigorously training Schmidt to increase Schmidt's daily workload to 47.5 tons. The needs-inducements balance was maintained by boosting the pay by 60 percent, to $1.85 per day. Schmidt and the company apparently found the needs-inducements arrangements mutually satisfactory, because Schmidt was described as staying on the job for "some years."

Chester Barnard discussed equilibrium as "the balancing of burdens by satisfactions which results in continuance"[33] of participation of both the individual and the organization in a mutual relationship. In his lexicon, the term "effectiveness" was the "accomplishment of the recognized objectives of cooperative action."[34] "Efficiency" referred to the ability of the organization to sustain the continued participation of individuals by offering adequate satisfactions to them.

Barnard described the organization as inducing cooperation by distributing its "*productive* results" to individuals. "These productive results," he wrote, "are either material or social, or both. As to some individuals, material is required for satisfaction; as to others, social benefits are required. As to most individuals, both material and social benefits are required in different proportions."[35] Barnard pointed out—and this is familiar to us all—that the definition of what constitutes "adequate satisfactions" to individuals in the organization varies, depending in great measure on the makeup and circumstances of the individual involved. Some people certainly find great satisfaction in material reward, especially money, and in order to get it will accept an organizational role that may be insecure, unpleasant, or strenuous. Regardless of the many possible negative aspects of such a role, as long as there is enough material reward such people may well find the inducement satisfying. Others, for whatever reasons, might find a higher income not worth the price that must be paid.

In the recent history of educational administration this can be seen in connection with the role of the superintendent of schools and, to a lesser degree, with that of the high school principal. Although the salaries being offered to superintendents are reaching very high levels, many qualified people are not attracted to these roles, and many incumbents have shifted to university teaching or to other fields altogether. Long working hours, arduous demands, and enormous pressures are some of the drawbacks of the superintendency; in many cases there is little reward in terms of achievement or self-fulfillment. In order to attract and hold capable people as superintendents, school districts must proffer a combination of material and psychological rewards that incumbents will find attractive.

Similarly, not many years ago an important problem in the United States was attracting good teachers to rural areas and keeping them there in spite of the low pay, inadequate school facilities, and limited cultural opportunities, which made teaching in such areas relatively unrewarding to many. Today, of course, the situation is reversed; other careers and schools in nonurban areas offer considerable reward to many teachers, whereas the bleak, hostile, frustrating environment of the teacher in the poor urban school is barely adequate—both in terms of money and a sense of fulfillment—for many capable teachers.

In discussing organizational equilibrium from the systems-theory point of view, we must remember that there is not only a needs-inducements relationship between the individual participant and the organization; the organization itself is part of a larger system. Further, if the system is "open"—as in the case of schools and school systems—the organization will interact actively with the external systems that comprise its environment. An expanded version of the Getzels-Guba social system model, shown in Figure 2–14, depicts this interaction of school with its larger environment. Presumably, changes in the environment will stimulate a reaction by the organization, either *static* or *dynamic*. If the reaction is static, the system responds so as to keep relationships in their original state, that is, the *status quo* is maintained. Dynamic equilibrium, however, is characterized by a rearrangement of the internal subsystems of the organization or by a change in its goals in order to adjust to changing circumstances in its external environment. Dynamic equilibrium, in other words, helps to keep the system in a steady state by being adaptable.

Homeostasis

This biological term has been applied to organizations and refers to the tendency of an open system to regulate itself so as to stay constantly in balance. The biological organism tends to retain its own characteristics, to maintain itself and to preserve its identity, but, at the same time, it has compensatory mechanisms that enable it to adapt to and survive environmental changes within certain limits. Homeostatic processes in human beings include the body's tendency to maintain a constant temperature and to maintain blood pressure by repairing a break in the circulatory system through coagulation. Homeostatic mechanisms in school systems and schools, such as well-developed communication systems and decision-making processes, enable them to adapt to and deal effectively with changes in their environment.

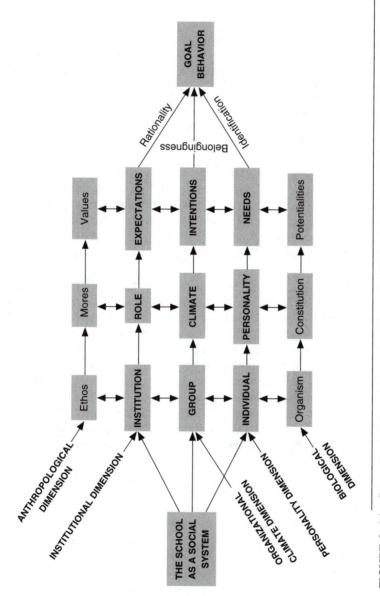

FIGURE 2–14 Dimensions of the school as a social system. Adapted from Jacob W. Getzels and Herbert A. Thelen, "The Classroom Group as a Unique Social System," in *The Dynamics of Instructional Groups: Sociopsychological Aspects of Teaching and Learning*, ed. Nelson B. Henry. N.S.S.E. Yearbook LIX, Part II (Chicago: National Society for the Study of Education, 1960), p. 80.

Feedback

Feedback is described by John Pfiffner and Frank Sherwood:

> In its simplest form, feedback is the kind of communication an actor receives from a live audience. If the crowd is enthusiastic, the performer reacts with similar enthusiasm. There is in a way a closed circuit between performer and audience with continuing interchange of information. . . . Essential to feedback is the notion that the flow of information is actually having a reciprocating effect on behavior. This is why the term loop is frequently associated with feedback. This circular pattern involves a flow of information to the point of action, a flow back to the point of decision with information on the action, and then a return to the point of action with new information and perhaps instructions. A primary element in this process is the sensory organ, the instrument through which information is obtained.[36]

Systems that do not have sensitive antennae picking up accurate feedback information, or—perhaps worse—that do not provide for the accurate transmission of feedback information to decision makers, find it difficult to react appropriately to environmental changes. Such systems tend to be in a static, rather than in a dynamic, equilibrium with their environments. They tend to lack the self-correcting, homeostatic processes essential to maintaining themselves in environments characterized by change.

We have, then, in the social systems view, an organization that is, by definition, an open system. This means, in part, not only that the organization has internal subsystems but also that it is part of a suprasystem. Moreover, the organization is in an interactive relationship with this suprasystem: it exchanges inputs and outputs with it. To some extent, the organization affects its environment (the suprasystem) and is also affected by changes that occur in the suprasystem.

It can resist and deny changes in the suprasystem or environment by ignoring or fighting them or by attempting to insulate itself from them (that is, by becoming more "closed"). It can attempt to accommodate to environmental change by homeostatic adaptation (that is, by adopting a policy of "business as usual"). Or, finally, the organization can adapt to environmental changes by developing a new balance, a new equilibrium. In a world such as ours, dominated by rapid and extensive change, it would appear that the organization with poor feedback mechanisms or weak homeostatic characteristics would show declining performance and increasing evidence of disorganization.

It is important to remember that essential to systems theory is the concept that *systems are composed of subsystems that are highly interactive and mutually interdependent.* It would seem clear from the Getzels-Guba model of the school as an open social system, which has already been described, that at least two subsystems can be identified and their interaction at least suggested: (1) the organizational or institutional system and (2) the human system. However, useful as this model was in early attempts to understand the dynamics of organizational behavior, it is incomplete. By the mid-1980s it was clear that organizations possess more than these two subsystems and that analysis of organizational behavior requires us to use more complex concepts. One of the more currently useful approaches is to conceptualize organizations—for example, the school system and the school—as *sociotechnical systems.*

SOCIOTECHNICAL SYSTEMS THEORY

By definition, an organization exists for the purpose of achieving something: reaching some goal or set of goals. It seeks to do this by accomplishing certain tasks.[37] Rationally, of course, the organization is structured, equipped, and staffed appropriately to accomplish its mission. The main goal of a school district, for example, requires it to operate schools, a transportation system, and food services. The district must employ people, provide legally mandated services, and perhaps engage in collective bargaining. There are numerous tasks that the school district must organize internally in order to achieve its goals.

In order to achieve an assigned task—which may include a large number of subtasks and operationally necessary tasks—we build an organization: that is, we give it *structure.* It is the structure that gives an organization order, system, and many of its distinctive characteristics. The structure establishes a pattern of authority and collegiality, thus defining role: there are top-management executives and middle-management supervisors, bosses and workers, each of whom attempts to know the extent of his or her own legitimate authority as well as that of others. Structure dictates, in large measure, the patterns of communication networks that are basic to information flow and, therefore, to decision making. Structure also determines the system of work flow that is, presumably, focused on achieving the organization's tasks.

The organization must have *technological resources* or, in other words, the "tools of its trade." Technology, used in this sense, does not only include such typical hardware items as computers, milling machines, textbooks and chalk, and electron microscopes. Technology may also include program inventions: systematic procedures, the sequencing of activities, or other procedural inventions designed to solve problems that stand in the way of organizational task achievement. Thus the teacher's daily lesson plan, the high school class schedule, and the district's curriculum guides are illustrative of technology in educational organizations.

Finally, of course, the organization must have *people.* Their contribution to the task achievement of the organization is ultimately visible in their acts—that is, their organizational behavior. It is this behavior that selects, directs, communicates, and decides.

These four internal organization factors—*task, structure, technology,* and *people*[38] (Figure 2–15)—are variables that differ from time to time and from one organization to the next. Within a given organization these four factors are highly interactive, each tending to shape and mold the others. As in any system, the interdependence of the variable factors means that a significant change in one will result in some adaptation on the part of the other factors. Important in determining the nature and interrelationship of these internal organizational arrangements in a

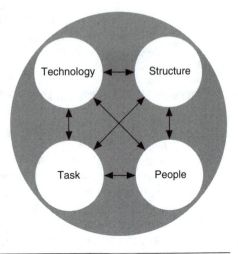

FIGURE 2–15
Interacting subsystems in complex organization.
Adapted from Harold J. Leavitt, "Applied Organizational
Change in Industry: Structural, Technological and
Humanistic Approaches," in *Handbook of
Organizations,* ed. James G. March. © 1965 by Rand
McNally & Company, Chicago, Figure 1, p. 1145.

school district or school is the response of the organization to changes occurring in
the larger system in which it exists.

Suppose, for example, that an academically oriented high school admits limited numbers of talented students by competitive examination for the express purpose of preparing them for college. If the board of education rules that the school
be converted into a comprehensive high school to meet the needs of the total youth
population (which, of course, would be a change in the organization's goal), it is
apparent that a number of internal adjustments would be necessary for the school
to achieve its new goal reasonably well. Many of these changes would be compensatory in nature. For example, in order to accommodate those students interested in
a business career it would be necessary to teach courses in business (task). To do
this, business education equipment would have to be installed (technology), business education teachers would have to be employed (people), and a department of
business education might be created (structure). However, some of the changes
flowing from the board's directive might be retaliatory rather than compensatory.
For example, if some people in the school sought to resist these changes, then their
former cooperative and productive behavior would be replaced by alienation and
conflict. This, in turn, could disrupt the normal communications patterns in the
school, thereby producing a structural change.

A technological change, such as the introduction of a comprehensive, computer-
related instructional system in a high school, could bring about important side effects: it could change the goals of the school by making it possible to achieve new
things and, simultaneously, by rendering certain traditional tasks obsolete. A change
in people would include the employment of new personnel with technical skills,
affecting the work activities of others in the school by making some activities unnecessary and requiring certain new activities to be introduced. Finally, the intro-

duction of new departments and changes in those involved in the decision-making processes would be structural changes flowing out of the technical change originally initiated.

Thus, in coordinating the internal processes of the school district or school, it is necessary to attend to the dynamic interaction of the four subsystems: people, structure, technology, and task. However, if it is proposed to introduce a significant change through primarily one of the target variables, it is clear that the other variables soon will be affected. Change efforts that are basically technological in nature result in some compensatory or retaliatory behavior on the part of people and in some structural adjustments within the organization. Those who seek to bring about significant structural rearrangements in the school, such as differentiated staffing plans, must reckon with the people involved and the way they will react to the change.

Although it is easy to speak of different administrative strategies and to categorize various tactics and procedures as "belonging" to one strategy or another, we must recognize the symbiotic interrelationship that exists among the internal organizational subsystems with which we are concerned: task, technological, structural, and behavioral.

The schematic diagram in Figure 2–16 illustrates the key internal and external relationships of a school system or school. In the figure I have provided only a few illustrative examples of the many things that are normally included in the task, technology, and structure subsystems. In conceptualizing the human subsystem, the reader is cautioned to note that it is insufficient to name or label the occupational roles of participants (such as teachers, nurses, and custodians). In terms of the dynamics of internal organizational functioning, the values, beliefs, and knowledge possessed by individuals in the human system are fully as important as the facts that the individuals are present and that the organization has formalized ways of dealing with them (such as rules, grievance procedures, and personnel policies). It should be obvious that the human subsystem is the only one that has nonrational (that is, affective, not irrational) capability.

CONTINGENCY THEORY

Theorizing, thinking, research, and experience with organizations have been accompanied by an observable tendency for individuals (whether theorists or practitioners) to adopt advocacy positions. Those who favor classical approaches to organization, for example, have consistently supported the notion that a hierarchy of authority based upon rank in the organization is essential to the very concept of organization. Human relations adherents may differ on many points but are almost unanimous in espousing supportive, collaborative, people-centered leadership and highly participative management styles as superior to other approaches. Behavioral adherents have, with a fair degree of consistency, sought to find the best, most productive way to integrate the key elements of the classical and human relations

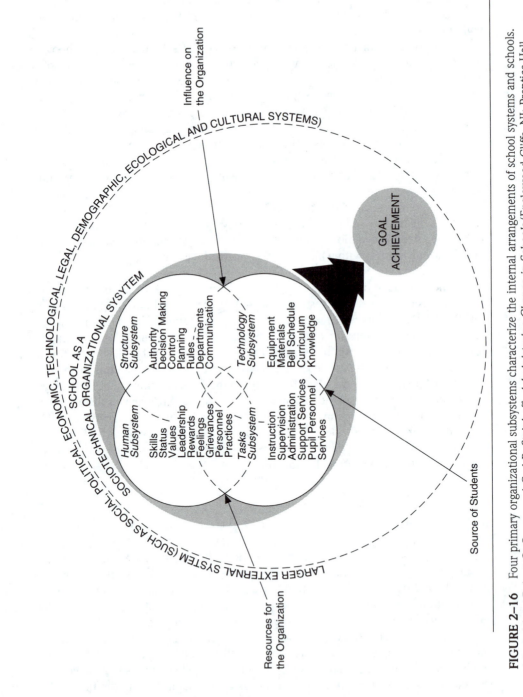

FIGURE 2–16 Four primary organizational subsystems characterize the internal arrangements of school systems and schools. Adapted from Robert G. Owens and Carl R. Steinhoff, *Administering Change in Schools* (Englewood Cliffs, NJ: Prentice-Hall, 1976), p. 143.

approaches. The result, for many years. was the development of competing advocacy positions, which showed very mixed results when attempts were made to apply any one of the positions to organizations: none of the three approaches is demonstrably superior in *all* situations.

Traditional (classical or neoclassical) approaches to the administration of school systems and schools have tended not only to use a hierarchical model of organization (drawn from the tradition of the military and large corporations) but also to emphasize the importance of rational, logical, and potentially powerful control systems, whereby decisions are made at the top of the hierarchy and implemented at the bottom. As a conceptually ideal state, at least, the whole is characterized by hierarchically maintained order, system, and discipline. Remember, as in the discussion of Douglas McGregor's Theory *X* presented earlier in the chapter, classical concepts may be used in either hard (coercive) or soft (manipulative) form.

Rational Planning Models

These models, such as Planning, Programming, and Budgeting Systems (PPBS), Program Evaluation and Review Technique (PERT), Management by Objectives (MBO), and Zero-Based Budgeting (ZBB) are adapted from massive, military-industrial enterprises that were created for such purposes as building and maintaining huge fleets of enormous, technologically complex systems of weapons (such as intercontinental ballistics missiles, atomic-powered submarines, and giant aircraft) and, lest we forget, carrying out vast space exploration programs.

The approach, characterized by use of modern rational systems concepts and technology (as differentiated from *social* systems concepts), is traditional, classical in viewpoint, and *mechanical* in operation. Organizations are said to be mechanical when the primary basis for managing the system features the following:

1. Highly differentiated and specialized tasks with precise specification of rights, responsibilities, and methods.

2. Coordination and control through hierarchical supervision.

3. Communication with the external environment controlled by the top offices of the hierarchy.

4. Strong, downward-oriented line of command.

5. One-to-one leadership style emphasizing authority-obedience relationships.

6. Decision-making authority reserved for top levels of the hierarchy.

The concepts of *mechanical* and *organic* systems are widely discussed in the literature of organizational theory.[39] These concepts help us to discuss and analyze specific organizational situations without resorting to such potentially pejorative dichotomies as the bureaucratic-humanistic or democratic-authoritarian ones, which, in our culture, are obviously value-laden. Organic organizational systems are recognizable by the fact that they emphasize a different approach to managing the system:

1. Continuous reassessment of tasks and responsibilities through interaction of those involved, with functional change being easy to arrange at the working level.

2. Coordination and control through interaction of those involved, requiring considerable shared responsibility and interdependence.

3. Communication with external environment relatively extensive and open at all levels of the organization.

4. Emphasis on mutual confidence, consultation, and information sharing—up and down, laterally, and diagonally across the organization—as the basis of organizational authority.

5. Team leadership style, featuring high levels of trust and group problem solving.

6. Wide sharing of responsibility for decision making at all levels in the organization.

These two views of organization in public education have long represented what John Goodlad described as two irreconcilable modes of thought that have struggled for dominance.

> They have been with us for a long time. William James characterized them as "the hard and the tough" and the "soft and the tender." . . . So far as the rhetoric of schooling is concerned, these two themes rise and fall like tides, one usually flooding as the other ebbs. Each during its high [tide] deposits its share of debris on the beach and occasionally changes the shoreline a little. But the vast interior of schooling is disturbed scarcely at all.
>
> During the 1960s, both modes of thought struggled for attention. But the avant garde was represented by the soft and tender. Teachers were exhorted to open up their classrooms; open-space schools were the work of an enlightened school district. But all of this [was] replaced [in the late 1970s] with the rhetoric of "back to the basics." . . . The cry is picked up in the daily press, on radio and television, and at P.T.A. meetings. There is a flurry of activity—more of it outside the schools than within. Hundreds of conventions carry the theme; legislative bills are enacted—for accountability by objectives, competency-based teacher education and, of course, proficiency tests for high school students. This activity builds up for two or three years, is intense for from three to five years, but then . . . falls from its own weight. . . . What bothers me most is that educators contribute so significantly to these excesses. Indeed, they pick them up and, for a brief while, make dubious reputations out of them. Usually, too, they are just a little late so that they are swinging exuberantly to one drumbeat at about the time an alternate drumbeat is coming on strong.[40]

The ebb and flow of the tides of rhetoric and viewpoint, alternately bringing a mechanical-bureaucratic-hierarchical emphasis to the fore, then a soft human relations–humanistic sweep followed, perhaps by a more manipulative, "soft" mechanical emphasis, historically has been painfully evident in the administration of U.S. public schooling. Many school superintendents, principals, and others, having witnessed this reality, have decided to eschew any theoretical or analytical approach, but have elected what is generally described by practitioners as an eclectic or pragmatic approach: to go out into the "real world" of school districts and to do whatever seems to "work." After all, the argument goes, "theory doesn't make any difference." This is not only a gross misreading of what organizational studies have to teach us, but it also offers no hope whatever of setting educational administration on a solid foundation of knowledge from which systematic administrative practice may be developed.

A contingency approach to organization takes a different view: although there is no one best way to organize and manage people in all circumstances, there are certain designs of organizational structure and describable management methods that can be identified as being most effective under specific situational contingencies. The key to understanding and dealing effectively with organizational behavior, from a contingency point of view, lies in being able to *analyze* the critical variables in a given situation. Effective administrator behavior (that is, behavior likely to increase achievement of the organization in attaining its goals, to improve the culture for working and learning, and to deal as productively as possible with conflict) is not seen as characterized by a universal fixed style (for example, "nomothetic" or "idiographic") but reveals a repertoire of behavioral styles tailored to the contingencies of the situation. In sum, three basic propositions underlie the contingency approach to organizational behavior in schools:

1. There is no one best universal way to organize and administer school districts and/or schools.

2. Not all ways of organizing and administering are equally effective in a given situation: effectiveness is contingent upon appropriateness of the design or style to the situation.

3. The selection of organizational design and administrative style should be based upon careful analysis of significant contingencies in the situation.

Open System Related to Contingency Theory

As I have described, contingency theory represents "a middle ground between (a) the view that there are universal principles of organization and management and (b) the view that each organization is unique and that each situation must be analyzed separately."[41] Contingency approaches represent a rather sensible theoretical development that seems to have value in dealing with the theory-practice gap.[42] The basic contribution of contingency thinking lies not in providing ready-made, pat answers to complex problems or easy recipes for "how-to-do-it"; it lies, rather, in providing us with new ways of analyzing the interrelationships within and among the interacting parts of the organizational system.[43] One critical set of relationships arises from the interaction of the organization (which, remember, is an open system) with its environment.

One of the early influential attempts along this line was the work of Paul Lawrence and Jay Lorsch,[44] who viewed organizations as open systems that are capable of differentiating their internal subsystems in response to a variety of environmental contingencies. Organizations that deal successfully with uncertain environments (that is, environments that are apt to call for relatively sudden change in the organization) tend to differentiate internally more than less successful organizations do; yet they are able to maintain high levels of integration between the various subunits. Such organizations are characterized by joint decision making, clear interdepartmental linkages, and well-developed means of dealing with conflict between units of the organization. Organizations that function in environments characterized by change and instability must, to be effective, organize differently to meet the need for planning, decision making, and conflict management than do those organizations that deal with relatively stable environments.

As environmental conditions change, the organization needs to adapt by responding with an appropriate structure and administrative system. Stable technologies and stable environmental conditions call for mechanistic organizations, characterized by rigidity and by explicitly defined tasks, methods, and job descriptions. In contrast, organizations facing unstable or changing technologies and environments require relatively flexible structures, with emphasis on lateral rather than on vertical communications, expert power (rather than hierarchical power) as the predominant base of influence, loosely defined responsibilities, and emphasis on exchanges of information rather than on giving direction.[45]

Response to Technological Change

Critics who fault U.S. schools for failing to make full use of modern technology often have "hardware" technologies in mind (such as computers, television and videotape, and other machines) and have a limited grasp of the extensive "software" technology that is widely used in U.S. education. The term "technology" properly includes such "software" as procedures for sequencing instruction; scheduling the interface of time, people, and material resources; specialized programs and curriculum guides; and techniques for generating and managing information. Thus the term—when applied to school organizations—must include such diverse forms as curriculum guides, the high school schedule, biology laboratories and band rooms, the testing program, and methods for classifying, grouping, and promoting students. The array of technology utilized in schooling has considerable power to affect behavior in the entire sociotechnical system, as was suggested earlier.

But, again, technology is usually developed outside of the school system or school; its impact is a result of the interaction of the open sociotechnical system with its environment. New technological developments of every description tend to alter the contingencies that affect the internal arrangements of the school. They are, in effect, one aspect of the large environment in which school systems or schools as organizations exist.

Interaction with External Environment

The school system or school, as a sociotechnical system, is in constant dynamic interaction with the larger external environment in which it exists. As used here, environment refers to the suprasystem in which the school district or school exists: the social, political, and economic systems of our culture. Thus, demographic shifts resulting in changing enrollments and increasing percentages of older people in the population, changing attitudes toward individual freedom, emphasis on women's rights to equality, shifting patterns of social mobility, dissatisfaction with the performance of schools, massive changes in legal-judicial philosophy, increased taxpayer resistance, organization of teachers into labor unions, and even mounting distrust of authority and institutions in our society in general are among the many environmental contingencies to which public school organizations have had to adapt in recent years.

Internal arrangements of the organization are largely contingent upon circumstances in that environment. Changes in the environment cause the organizational system to respond with changes in its internal arrangements. Those internal arrangements are best understood as containing four dynamically interactive subsystems: *tasks* to be performed, *structure* of the organization, *technology* utilized to perform the tasks, and the *human* social system.

One way that the social, political, and cultural environment of the school district or school has an impact is in setting goals to be achieved. Although educators play a part in establishing the goals of schooling, the process is ultimately in the political realm: state legislatures representing the body politic, for example, are normally instrumental in formalizing important aspects of the goals of schooling. Legislation of minimum competency standards for graduation and/or promotion can have a powerful impact on what schools seek to achieve. Federal initiatives have had a widespread, direct effect on school goals—not only for youngsters with special educational needs but also on virtually all other students as well.

Other political processes, such as approving budgets and levying taxes or electing school board members, also serve as means for influencing the goals of schools. Frequently, a display of potential political power is sufficient to effect reassessment and revision of organizational goals. Not infrequently, of course, judicial intervention is a means of implementing goal changes in schooling. This is readily observable in situations in which federal district courts not only have ordered the desegregation of school districts but also have specified the means by which this is to be achieved (for example, intradistrict transportation and interdistrict transportation). Courts also have not infrequently required changes in curricula, testing procedures, and methods of selecting and assigning staff. All of these represent some of the ways that the environment of the school organization affects the internal functioning of the organization; the organization will either adapt smoothly and easily, or it may resist.

Thus, a groundswell of popular support for "back to basics" might appear in a local school district that motivates the board of education and the administrative staff to initiate a goal-setting and educational planning project with community involvement. As a result, the schools would likely revise their curricula, shift their teaching style, perhaps reorganize their grade structure, and adopt new textbooks—that is, make internal rearrangements in response to changes in the organization's environment.

Not infrequently, however, schools will resist external changes and maintain the *status quo,* almost regardless of the degree or power of the new environmental contingencies. Our history with regard to desegregation, equal rights, and nondiscriminatory practices—even in the face of concentrated, massive, statutory, judicial, and political action—makes it clear that there are many occasions when schools attempt to close off the organizational system in order to deflect the impact of changes in the larger environment, rather than seek ways of making appropriate internal rearrangements so as to adapt to them. From a contingency point of view, this tends to put the school or school system out of touch with the real-world contingencies in which these organizations exist. In terms of organizational behavior, a negative result in such a case is likely to be the leadership and administrative styles that—in the long run—are not the most effective and may even be counterproductive.

Contingency Theory and Organizational Behavior in Schools

Operationally, using the contingency approach in the practice of school administration does not necessarily have to be terribly exotic or to require highly sophisticated methods. It does, however, require the administrator to use some analysis of relevant contingencies in the situation at hand as a basis for selecting a way of dealing with them. Since *administration is working with and through individuals and groups to achieve organizational goals,* a fundamental contingency to consider is, "What will likely yield the most productive behavior (in terms of achieving organizational goals) from my subordinates in this situation?" An important assumption underlying this kind of question is, of course, that different administrative styles are likely to evoke predictably different responses from people.

For example, an issue that often confronts the administrator concerns leadership style. Is a good leader one who sets goals, directs subordinates as to what to do, and checks closely to see that they do things as directed? Or is a good leader one who involves subordinates in setting goals, collaborates with them in deciding what to do and how to do it, and provides coordination of the group in evaluating progress and results? In the parlance of public school administrators, which is better: directive leadership or "democratic" leadership?

A contingency approach to this issue starts with clarifying what is meant by "good." Because the administrator's intent is to maximize the achievement of organizational goals, "good" is probably best redefined as "effective." The question then becomes: which leadership style is most effective—that is, which will likely contribute most to the goal performance of the school system or school?

As I shall discuss more fully in Chapter 6, contemporary understanding of the dynamics of leader behavior makes it clear that there is apparently no one most effective style: effectiveness of leadership style clearly depends upon its appropriateness in terms of the critical contingencies in a given situation. The power of the leader, the quality of relationships with subordinates, the clarity of the structure of the task to be done, the degree of cooperation required to implement decisions, and the levels of skill and motivation of subordinates are a few of the many contingencies that can be assessed by the administrator and related to predictable outcomes of various, specific, alternative ways to lead. In the contingency view, the effective leader is able to match leadership style to the contingencies of the situation in order to achieve the behavior on the part of subordinates that will contribute most to achieving the goals of the school district or school.

Similarly, a contingency orientation is helpful in dealing with issues of motivation, decision making, organizational change, organizational culture, and conflict management. The remaining chapters of this book explore these aspects of organizational behavior in schools.

CONCLUSION

Open systems theory is the basis for contemporary analysis of organizational behavior. Social systems theory, such as the Getzels-Guba model, has provided a useful way of conceptualizing organizational behavior as a function of the interaction between the demands of organizational requirements and the needs-dispositions of individuals in the organization. Although the Getzels-Guba model often has been used to stress this internal dynamic relationship of the organization, the expanded version of the model clearly illustrates the dynamic relationship between the organizational system itself and its external larger environment, the suprasystem.

Role theory not only helps us to understand the idiographic-nomothetic relationship in greater detail but also illuminates many of the broader interpersonal relationships that exist in schools and school systems. Although role theory lacks the power to explain the organization in its entirety, it is useful as a framework for examining relationships between person and organization, as well as interpersonal behavior.

Sociotechnical concepts help us to understand the dynamic interrelationship among the structure, tasks, technology, and human aspects of educational organizations as a force in evoking and molding the behavior of people. In the typical high school, for example, people's daily lives are deeply affected by "the schedule" that governs all and often defines the possible. Architects design buildings that evoke psychological responses and shape behavior. The choice to equip a classroom with movable desks or "screwed-down" desks has an impact on behavior. A curriculum that mandates individually prescribed instruction also mandates behavior. The need to transport students to and from school on buses has an impressive impact on the school as an organization and on the behavior of people in it.

But the fact that educational organizations are *open* systems has additional behavioral consequences. A school, for example, is subject to two major external forces that define the very nature of its internal arrangements. One of these forces is the fact that the school *is* a school: it is probably more like other schools from coast to coast than different from them. Professional standards and expectations expressed through teacher training institutions, accrediting associations, the entrance requirements of colleges, the wares of the educational-industrial complex, and the speakers at annual conventions—all of these are but a representative few of the many "professional" influences that reach in from the outside and define what a school *is* in behavioral terms.

The *second* cluster of these forces represents the broader social-cultural influences that reach in from the outside and establish "norms" for behavior in the school. These include such diverse sources as community standards, tradition, judicial decisions, statutory law, and—not least, by any means—the broad generalizations embodied in such concepts as "Western culture." More specifically, perhaps, is the impact of the "youth subculture" that has become so influential in Western nations. Because the school is an open system, this facet of the school's environment has a powerful impact on its internal functioning. The fact that children watch television, are exposed to a drug culture, and are developing new concepts of sex, marriage, and the family does shape the nature of life in schools. All of these, together, combine to create an *organizational* culture that is powerful in determining how people perceive things, value them, and react to them.

Thus, the concept of the educative organization as an open sociotechnical system enables one to see the internal arrangements of a particular organization as at once unique and part of an interaction with its larger suprasystem. This is the view of schools that people like Goodlad have when they speak of the "culture" of the school, and it is discussed again in Chapter 5, on organizational culture.

In contemporary organizational theory, this concept is coupled with contingency theory: the view that there is no one universal "best" way of dealing with organizational issues. Contingency approaches to organizational behavior require developing a systematic understanding of the dynamics of organizational behavior in order to be able to diagnose or analyze the specific situation that exists.

Organizational theory provides a systematic body of knowledge upon which we base assumptions about the nature of organizations and the behavior of people in them. Far from being the impractical plaything of scholars, theory is used constantly by administrators—albeit often in an intuitive and unexamined way—as a basis for the professional work they do every day.

Bureaucratic theory has long been, by an overwhelming margin, the most widely used perspective in developing assumptions about educational organizations. Human resources theory has, however, been steadily developing and gaining greater acceptance as research following the tradition of the Western Electric studies has been pushed forward and as bureaucratic responses to the problems of schools have failed to work as well as had been expected. Since the 1960s human resources development theory has been considerably strengthened by the emergence of such newer perspectives as concepts of loose coupling.

It is recognized today that, as a broad generalization, schools characteristically tend to use human resources approaches in the management of the instructional behavior of teachers and to use bureaucratic approaches in the management of other, more routine aspects of the enterprise. Each of these two theoretic approaches gives rise to different assumptions about the nature of people and, therefore, of effective ways of managing them—Theory *X* and Theory *Y.*

A word of caution to the reader is in order here. Bureaucratic and human resources perspectives have been compared and contrasted as ideal cases for the purpose of clarifying and delineating the very real, basic differences between them. In the "real world" of educational administration, of course, one rarely encounters ideal cases, which is not to suggest that organizations cannot properly be classified as being bureaucratic or nonbureaucratic. Indeed, they can be and often are. However, it does not mean, either, that to be described as nonbureaucratic an organization must be totally devoid of policies, regulations, standard operating procedures, or hierarchical organization; or that to be described as bureaucratic an organization must be totally devoid of sensitivity to or respect for people. This is particularly true of schools, which have been described here as being dual organizations: bureaucratic in some ways and nonbureaucratic in some very important ways. What it does suggest is that organizations may be properly described as *relatively* bureaucratic or nonbureaucratic. It also suggests that schools are undoubtedly far more organizationally complex than has been traditionally understood.

SUGGESTED READING

Firestone, William A., and Bruce L. Wilson, "Using Bureaucratic and Cultural Linkages to Improve Instruction: The Principal's Contribution." *Educational Administration Quarterly,* 21 (Spring 1985), 7–30.
> Discusses the two kinds of "linkages" available for principals to use in influencing the instructional behavior of teachers: bureaucratic and cultural. An excellent source of references to the literature for those who wish to probe this topic more fully.

Meyer, John W., and Brian Rowan, "The Structure of Educational Organizations." In John W. Meyer and W. Richard Scott, eds., *Organizational Environments: Ritual and Rationality.* Beverly Hills, CA: Sage Publications, 1983.
> A provocative analysis of schools from a sociological perspective that challenges the conventional tradition of bureaucratic logic and order. The entire book, of which this chapter is part, will be of great interest to the serious student.

Meyer, Marshall W., *Theory of Organizational Structure.* Indianapolis: Bobbs-Merrill Educational Publishing, 1977.
> In this seventy-eight-page book, sociologist Meyer first discusses the various functions of organizational theory. He then goes on to describe a theory of organizational structure that departs from traditional bureaucratic concepts. Much in this book is directly related to the emerging new perspectives on the structure of educational organizations.

Weick, Karl E., "Educational Organizations as Loosely Coupled Systems." *Educational Administration Quarterly,* 21 (1976), 1–19.
> While Weick did not invent the concept of loosely coupled systems, in this article he did lay the foundation for a major shift in the theory of schools as organizations. This is a classic that should be read in the original.

NOTES

1. Luvern L. Cunningham, "Leaders and Leadership: 1985 and Beyond," *Phi Delta Kappan,* 67 (September 1985), 20.
2. Education Commission of the States, "Tracking the Reforms," *Education Week* (September 18, 1985), 18.

3. Denis P. Doyle and Terry W. Hartle, "Leadership in Education: Governors, Legislators, and Teachers," *Phi Delta Kappan,* 67 (September 1985), 24.

4. Douglas M. McGregor, *The Human Side of Enterprise* (New York: McGraw-Hill Book Company, 1960), pp. 37–57.

5. Chris Argyris, *Management and Organizational Development* (New York: McGraw-Hill Book Company, 1971), pp. 1–26.

6. Thomas J. Sergiovanni, "Beyond Human Relations," in *Professional Supervision for Professional Teachers,* ed. Thomas J. Sergiovanni (Washington, DC: Association for Supervision and Curriculum Development, 1975), p. 11.

7. Ibid.

8. Albert F. Siepert and Rensis Likert, "The Likert School Profile Measurements of the Human Organization" (paper presented at the American Educational Research Association National Convention, February 27, 1973), p. 3.

9. Ibid., p. 4.

10. Robert R. Blake and Jane Srygley Mouton, *Building a Dynamic Corporation through Grid Organization Development* (Reading, MA: Addison-Wesley, 1969).

11. Gordon L. Lippitt, *Organizational Renewal: Achieving Viability in a Changing World* (New York: Appleton-Century-Crofts, 1969).

12. Paul Berman and Milbrey Wallen McLaughlin, *Federal Programs Supporting Educational Change, Volume VIII: Implementing and Sustaining Innovations* (Santa Monica, CA: Rand Corporation, 1978).

13. Charles B. Perrow, *Organizational Analysis: A Sociological View* (Monterey, CA: Brooks/Cole Publishing Co., 1970), pp. 3–4.

14. Ludwig von Bertalanffy, "An Outline of General Systems Theory," *British Journal of Philosophical Science,* 1 (1950), 134–65. A more complete work, by the same author, is *General Systems Theory* (New York: George Braziller, 1968).

15. Andre Lwoff, "Interaction among Virus, Cell and Organization," *Science,* 152 (1966), 1216.

16. F. Kenneth Berrien, "A General Systems Approach to Organizations," in *Handbook of Industrial and Organizational Psychology,* ed. Marvin D. Dunnette (Chicago: Rand McNally & Company, 1976), p. 43.

17. Ronald G. Corwin, "Models of Educational Organizations," in *Review of Research in Education,* ed. Fred N. Kerlinger and J. B. Carroll (Itasca, IL: F. E. Peacock, Publishers, 1974), p. 263.

18. Andrew W. Halpin and Don B. Croft, *The Organizational Climate of Schools* (Washington, DC: Cooperative Research Report, U.S. Office of Education, 1962).

19. Some examples are James G. Anderson, *Bureaucracy in Education* (Baltimore: The Johns Hopkins University Press, 1968); Neal Gross and Robert E. Herriott, *Staff Leadership in Public Schools: A Sociological Inquiry* (New York: John Wiley & Sons, 1965). These may be compared with later studies, such as the Rand investigations of educational change conducted by Berman and McLaughlin. See, for example, Paul Berman and Milbrey Wallin McLaughlin, *Federal Programs Supporting Educational Change, Volume VII: Factors Affecting Implementation and Continuation* (Santa Monica, CA: Rand Corporation, 1977), especially pp. 16–20.

20. Erving Goffman, *The Presentation of Self in Everyday Life* (New York: Doubleday & Co., Anchor Books, 1959): A later study in a similar vein by the same author is *Encounters* (Indianapolis: The Bobbs-Merrill Co., 1961).

21. The term, "role," is a highly useful metaphor that is widely used in human relations research and practice. Because there is such extensive literature on role theory in psychiatry, psychology, sociology, and education, not surprisingly there is some imprecision attached to the use of this metaphor. It should be clear, however, that what is under discussion here is a psychological concept and not merely job titles or job descriptions. For discussion of the problem of definition, see Theodore R. Sarbin and Vernon L. Allen, "Role Theory," in *The Handbook of Social Psychology,* vol. 1, 2nd ed., eds. Gardner Lindzey and Elliot Aronson (Reading, MA: Addison-Wesley, 1968).

22. Robert Boguslaw, *The New Utopians: A Study of System Design and Social Change* (Englewood Cliffs, NJ: Prentice-Hall, 1965), pp. 170–77.

23. The material presented here on role set is based on Warren G. Bennis, *Changing Organizations* (New York: McGraw-Hill Book Company, 1966), pp. 193–96.

24. Robert L Kahn, Donald M. Wolfe, Robert R. Quinn, and J. Diedrick Snoek, *Organizational Stress: Studies in Role Conflict and Ambiguity* (New York: John Wiley & Sons, 1964).
25. The following discussion of role allocation is based on Kenneth D. Benne and Paul Sheats, "Functional Roles of Group Members," *Journal of Social Issues,* 4, no. 2 (Spring 1948), 41–49.
26. Ibid., pp. 43–44.
27. Ibid., pp. 44–45.
28. Jacob W. Getzels and Egon G. Guba, "Social Behavior and the Administrative Process," *The School Review,* 65 (Winter 1957), 423–41. This version of the organization as a sociopsychological system is based upon the earlier work of Talcott Parsons and was first suggested by Getzels in 1952 in his "A Psycho-Sociological Framework for the Study of Educational Administration," *Harvard Educational Review,* 22, no. 4 (1952), 235–46. Later, in collaboration with Egon Guba, the model was developed to include *psychological* concepts (such as personality), *sociological* notions (for example, role expectation), *anthropological* concepts of culture, and *social-psychological* concepts (for example, group norms and organizational climate). This more elaborate model—the so-called Getzels-Guba model—is discussed later in this chapter (see Figure 2–14).
29. Jacob W. Getzels, "Administration as a Social Process," in *Administrative Theory in Education,* ed. Andrew W. Halpin (Chicago: Midwest Administration Center, University of Chicago, 1958), p. 157.
30. There is extensive literature on the authoritarian personality. Classic works are Theodore W. Adorno, Else Frenkel-Brunswik, Daniel J. Levinson, and R. N. Sanford, *The Authoritarian Personality* (New York: Harper & Row, Publishers, 1950); and Milton Rokeach, *The Open and Closed Mind* (New York: Basic Books, Publishers, 1960).
31. Mary Lynn Crow and Merl E. Bonney, "Recognizing the Authoritarian Personality Syndrome in Educators," *Phi Delta Kappan,* 57, no. 1 (September 1975), 40.
32. Frederick W. Taylor, *The Principles of Scientific Management* (New York: Harper & Row, Publishers, 1911). pp. 42–43.
33. Chester I. Barnard, *The Functions of the Executive* (Cambridge, MA: Harvard University Press, 1938), p. 57.
34. Ibid., p. 55.
35. Ibid., p. 57.
36. John M. Pfiffner and Frank P. Sherwood, *Administrative Organization* (Englewood Cliffs, NJ: Prentice-Hall, 1960), p. 299.
37. The following discussion is adapted from Robert G. Owens and Carl R. Steinhoff, *Administering Change in Schools* (Englewood Cliffs, NJ: Prentice-Hall, 1976), pp. 60–63 and 143 and is based on the concepts developed by Harold J. Leavitt cited below.
38. This view is based on the concepts developed by Harold J. Leavitt, *Managerial Psychology,* 2nd ed. (Chicago: University of Chicago Press, 1964). See also by the same author, "Applied Organizational Change in Industry: Structural, Technological, and Humanistic Approaches," in *Handbook of Organizations,* ed. James G. March (Chicago: Rand McNally & Company, 1965), pp. 1144–70.
39. See, for example, Wendell L. French and Cecil H. Bell, Jr., *Organizational Development* (Englewood Cliffs, NJ: Prentice-Hall, 1973), pp. 183–85, whose description is reflected in this discussion.
40. John I. Goodlad, "Educational Leadership: Toward the Third Era," *Educational Leadership,* 35, no. 4 (January 1978), 330.
41. Fremont E. Kast and James E. Rosenzweig, *Contingency Views of Organization and Management* (Chicago: Science Research Associates, 1973), p. ix.
42. Dennis Moberg and James L. Koch, "A Critical Appraisal of Integrated Treatments of Contingency Findings," *Academy of Management Journal,* 18, no. 1 (March-June 1975), 109–24.
43. Donald Hellriegel and John W. Slocum, Jr., *Organizational Behavior: Contingency Views* (St. Paul: West Publishing Co., 1976), p. 6.
44. Paul R. Lawrence and Jay W. Lorsch, *Organization and Environment* (Homewood, IL: Richard D. Irwin, 1967).
45. Stephen P. Robbins, *The Administrative Process: Integrating Theory and Practice* (Englewood Cliffs, NJ: Prentice-Hall, 1976), pp. 272–73.

Building Human Capital

ABOUT THIS CHAPTER

The previous chapter introduced some systematic ways of thinking about organizations and the people who work in them, which is the field of systems theory of organization. Many of these ways of thinking, or theories, such as the Getzels-Guba model, have proven almost indispensable to students in educational administration. However, in this chapter we shall see that these ways of thinking have some distinct limitations. Perhaps the most serious is that, although they depict relationships between the organizational structure and the people who populate the organization in graphic ways, they tend to subscribe to a theory of action that emphasizes bureaucratic control over the human realities in organizations.

This chapter describes some aspects of the very important shift in organizational theory from traditional modernism, with its emphasis on perfecting and refining bureaucratic management strategies and techniques, to a postmodern approach, which emphasizes the potential for improving organizational performance from within, from the bottom up, by fostering the growth and development of the people who inhabit the organization. The overarching concept of this approach is that of building human capital: that organizations are made more effective as the people in them grow and develop personally and professionally over time so that they become increasingly effective not only in their individual work but as participants in a work group that also is becoming increasingly more adept and effective in cooperative endeavor.

RECONCEPTUALIZING THE NATURE OF ORGANIZATIONS

This book addresses the problem of understanding the behavior of people at work in educational organizations. This is the central problem confronting educational administrators because administration is defined as "working with and through other people, individually and in groups, to achieve organizational goals." In terms of administrative practice, then, we need to address an essential question: which are the best and most effective ways of working with and through other people?

This is no arcane academic question. How you answer it goes to the heart of how you go about the work of school administration, whether as a department chairperson, a school principal, a superintendent of schools, or any position in between. Nor is it a simple question. Teachers know, from working with children and their parents, that people are complex, idiosyncratic, full of contradictions, and that their behavior often seems baffling and difficult to grasp.

Moreover, we understand now much better than we did twenty years ago that schools, as organizations, are complex and confusing places that are—at their best—filled with contradiction, ambivalence, ambiguity, and uncertainty. These understandings help us realize that many of the most important problems confronting school administrators are neither clear-cut nor amenable to technical solutions.

This is not a problem peculiar to school administration nor is it limited to schools as organizations. It is a problem that is generally shared by all professions and all organizations. Consider how Donald Schön describes what he calls a "crisis of confidence in professional knowledge":

> In the varied topography of professional practice, there is a high, hard ground overlooking a swamp. On the high ground, manageable problems lend themselves to solutions through the application of research-based theory and technique. In the swampy lowland, messy, confusing problems defy technical solution. The irony of this situation is that the problems of the high ground tend to be relatively unimportant to individuals or society at large, however great their technical interest may be, while in the swamp lie the problems of greatest human concern. The practitioner must choose. Shall he remain on the high ground where he can solve relatively unimportant problems according to prevailing standards of rigor, or shall he descend to the swamp of important problems . . . ?[1]

For many years now, educational administrators have been urged to concentrate on technical solutions to the problems of education. Educational administrators have long been exhorted to apply new technologies as a means of solving both the manageable problems in the high ground as well as the more urgent yet messy and confusing problems of great human concern. This includes not only the use of electronic technology, such as computers and the Internet, but also structural technology, such as the creation of magnet schools, charter schools, and other forms of school choice, as well as instructional technology, such as the invention of new curriculum patterns and formalized pedagogical techniques in the classroom. The perspective of schools and school reform that has been adopted by many people who advocate these various technologies has been tightly bound to the image of schools as production organizations in which teaching is viewed as routinized labor which, if properly systematized and subjected to bureaucratic controls, will lead logically to the desired outcomes. Adherents of these views of schools have tended to believe that teachers can only learn through formal training that normally consists of lectures, directed workshops, and formal conferences, all of which are controlled and directed by external experts who know what the problems are and what the teachers need to deal effectively with them. Thus we have witnessed the rise of a virtual obsession to develop "programs" to meet every conceivable problem confronting the schools as well as a proliferation of "expert" consultants ready to fly in to dispense their wisdom and quickly depart with their high fees safely in their pockets.

But important educational problems, those that are in the swampland that Donald Schön described, are typically messy: ill defined, ill understood, and complicated. Messy problems tend to be understood, or framed, in terms of the things about them that we are apt to notice. What you may notice, though, comes mainly from your own background, values, and perspectives. As Schön observed,

> A nutritionist, for example, may convert a vague worry about malnourishment among children in developing countries into the problem of selecting an optimal diet. But agronomists may frame the problem in terms of food production; epidemiologists may frame it in terms of diseases that increase the demand for nutrients or prevent their absorption; demographers tend to see it in terms of a rate of population growth that has outstripped agricultural activity; engineers, in terms of inadequate food storage and distribution; economists, in terms of insufficient purchasing power or the inequitable distribution of land or wealth.[2]

Similarly, as administrators seek to deal with the problems of education, their approach depends primarily on how they conceptualize their options, how they frame the problems. As in the case of malnutrition of children, there are many ways of framing a response. But people are limited in their ability to make sense of problems, to frame them, by the number and variety of frames that they are familiar with and that they can draw on to give them insight and perspective on the messy, ill-defined problems that every professional encounters in the swampy lowlands.

As I have described, for much of the last century one single perspective has dominated thinking about educational organizations: the structural perspective. This is the familiar notion of hierarchical control, bureaucratic offices, the familiar organization chart, and rules and regulations such as "standard operating procedures."

After 1975, organizational thought took a major turn away from such formal theorizing, which emphasized the machinelike characteristics that many scholars believed underlay the ways in which they worked, toward a markedly increased emphasis on the human dimensions of organization. This shift was caused by a combination of several forces that came together simultaneously. One of these forces was intellectual: the development of a new analysis of the fundamental concept of what an organization actually is.

COLLAPSE OF TRADITIONAL ORGANIZATIONAL THEORY

As I have described, the period from the early 1950s into the mid-1970s produced a great outpouring of theory and research in educational administration, so much so that in retrospect the period—the modern period—is often called the era of The Theory Movement in educational administration. However, by the 1970s concern was being increasingly expressed that the theories and the research that had been spawned did not fully describe schools as they were experienced by people in them. Research, and indeed the academic establishment in leading universities at that time, was dominated by those who accepted logical-positivist assumptions about schools as organizations and about ways of understanding them. In other words, they assumed that there was some rational, logical, systematic order underlying the organizational realities of schools that must be discovered. Further, they thought that the means of discovery must be the approach to inquiry that emphasizes measurement, sampling, quasi-experimental methods, and quantification. Moreover, it was believed that these assumptions and these methods of discovery were the only way to improve the training of educational practitioners. Wayne Hoy and Cecil Miskel claimed, for example, that "The road to generalized knowledge can lie only in tough-minded scientific research, not in introspection and subjective experience."[3]

However, by 1974, T. Barr Greenfield articulated serious concerns about then-existing organizational theory that had been developing among both practitioners and a growing number of scholars. The crux of the concerns was that academicians, in their search to understand educational organizations and the behavior of people in them—to make sense of the "swamp" that Donald Schön spoke of—had become transfixed with the wish to be objective, to emphasize mathematical descriptions, and, worst of all, they had come to think of organizations as tangible, concrete entities that exist independently and that are governed by systematic laws and principles. "In common parlance," Greenfield said, "we speak of organizations as if they were real."[4] But they are not real, he went on to explain: "they are invented social realities"[5] that actually exist only in the minds of people, rather than as tangible, independent realities. Thus, the argument runs, we anthropomorphize when we speak of organizations as imposing themselves on people or of organizational systems "behaving" in certain ways. The essence of organization is human beings who populate the organization; it is they who choose, act, and behave, even if in their own minds they reify the organization as they do so.

Nevertheless, we are continually confronted by evidence that academic assumptions often contrast remarkably with the experiences of individuals engaged in the work of school administration. This pervasive discrepancy between the academic view of the world and that of the practitioner may well explain the lack of enthusiasm that practitioners chronically express toward the preparation that they have received at the university.[6] For example, striking differences exist between academic literature on the principalship and the principals' written reflections on their own practice:[7]

+ Principals describe concrete everyday experiences, whereas academics emphasize theory and abstract relationships.

+ Principals communicate through metaphors, examples, and stories, whereas academics use models and the language of science.

+ Principals are aware of limits on rationality, whereas academics stress rationality and defining problems in formal terms.

✦ Principals describe schools in human and emotional terms wherein school personnel agonize over and celebrate their daily ups and downs, whereas academics describe them in terms of detached abstraction.

✦ Principals see schools as ambiguous and even chaotic places, whereas academics describe an image of rationality and orderliness.

RISE IN QUALITATIVE RESEARCH METHODS

As early as 1964, James Bryant Conant—Nobel laureate, former president of Harvard University, and chairman of the National Defense Research Committee during World War II—had reported that when he undertook studies of U.S. schools in the 1950s it became necessary for him to eschew the hypothetico-deductive way of thinking that he had used for so many years in chemistry; instead, he had to learn to use inductive reasoning because the nature of educational problems was so different from that of scientific problems. In a readable little book called *Two Modes of Thought: My Encounters With Science and Education,* he discussed the differences between kinds of thinking appropriate to the sciences and education. In it he observed, "What goes on in schools, colleges and universities may be classified as applied social science, or a practical art in which the social sciences were now impinging."[8]

In 1963, Carl Rogers discussed "three ways of knowing" about human behavior and the contexts in which it occurs:

1. Subjective knowing, which "is fundamental to everyday living."
2. Objective knowing, which Rogers thought was not really objective but actually more of a consensus between and among trusted colleagues who were thought to be qualified to make judgments about the "truth" of observed events.
3. Interpersonal, or phenomenological, knowing, in which one can know about the internal frame of mind of an individual by checking hypotheses with the individual or, alternatively, by validating hypotheses by checking independently with several other observers. Rogers gave a simple example in describing the situation in which you may feel that a colleague is sad or depressed. How can you confirm that hypothesis? One way would be to simply ask the person in an empathetic way. Another would be to wait and see if others comment to you on their own independent observations and feelings about the colleague's state of mind. Rogers believed that in a mature behavioral science all three ways of knowing would be acknowledged and used in combination, rather than using one way and ignoring the others.[9]

Twenty-five years later, in 1988, Arthur Blumberg enriched this line of thinking about educational organizations when he suggested that it is useful to think of school administration as a craft rather than as a science, and so to think about knowledge and understanding as craft workers do. A craft, he contended, is unlike science in important ways. A craft (he used pottery as one example) is learned in day-to-day practice with tools and materials in which the practitioner develops "a nose for things," an intimate feel for the nature of the materials being worked with, a sense of what constitutes acceptable results, an almost intuitive sense of process, an understanding of what to do and when to do it, and a feel for the need for action. Blumberg argued convincingly that by shifting from the concept of science to the concept of craft one discovers new and useful ways of knowing about organizational behavior in education.[10] However, like many people who advocate the use of pragmatic approaches such as this in our search for understanding of behavior in schools, Blumberg failed to recognize that the use of the craft metaphor is but another theoretical approach to understanding as had been the work of Rogers, Conant, and so many others who sought to break out of the straitjacket of logical positivism.

By the 1980s many students of education, who were well aware of these discrepancies, began to eschew traditional formal theorizing and the limitations of traditional quasi-experimental research methods and to find better ways of studying human behavior in schools. They began to go into the schools, instead of sending questionnaires and compiling statistics, to see what was going on and to talk to school individuals in order to understand how they were experiencing their lives. The results of such inquiries produced lively, rich narrative descriptions of life in present-day schools that illuminated the confusions, inconsistencies, ambiguities, and general messiness so characteristic of schools' organizational life.

Indeed, studies using these research methods, called *qualitative* or *ethnographic methods,* became the intellectual backbone of the educational reform movement of the 1980s. Gone were the spare statistical studies, so often elegant in style but yielding "no significant difference"; they were replaced by lively, richly documented accounts of human beings at work that yielded insight and understanding of what was happening to people and how they were responding to their experiences.

This was a major shift in ways of thinking about and studying organizational behavior, and it directly arose from abandoning the old certainties of logical positivism in favor of significant new directions in understanding organizational behavior in schools. To get some flavor of the newer thinking, we turn now to a brief explanation of some of the ideas about organization that began to emerge as traditional organizational theory collapsed.

Educational Organizations as Loosely Coupled Systems

Commonly, we are apt to think of and describe a school system or a school in classical structural terms: for example, as a hierarchically linked pyramid of units subject to strong central control and command (as bureaucracies and military organizations are usually described). Students of organization have recognized for quite some time, however, that school systems and schools are in fact characterized by structural looseness: schools in a district have considerable autonomy and latitude, and teachers in their classrooms are under only very general control and direction of the principal. As Charles Bidwell has pointed out,[11] this is a functionally necessary arrangement, given the nature of the school's task, clients, and technology. Karl Weick captured this reality with vivid imagery, which he credited to James G. March:

> Imagine that you're either the referee, coach, player or spectator in an unconventional soccer match: the field for the game is round; there are several goals scattered haphazardly around the circular field; people can enter or leave the game whenever they want to; they can throw balls in whenever they want; they can say "that's my goal" whenever they want to, as many times as they want to, and for as many goals as they want to; the entire game takes place on a sloped field; and the game is played as if it makes sense. And if you now substitute in that example principals for referees, teachers for coaches, students for players, parents for spectators, and schooling for soccer, you have an equally unconventional depiction of school organizations. The beauty of this depiction is that it captures a different set of realities within educational organizations than are caught when these same organizations are viewed through the tenets of bureaucratic theory.[12]

We can contrast this image of reality with the conventional explanation of how schools go about doing things: namely by planning, goal setting, and applying such rational processes as cost-benefit analyses, division of labor, job descriptions, authority vested in official office, and consistent evaluation and reward systems. The only problem with this latter, conventional view is that it is rare to find schools that actually work that way; more often than not, people in educational organizations find that rational concepts such as these simply do not explain the way the system functions.

Because so much of educational organization defies explanation by existing rational concepts, the suggestion is that we give serious thought to newer, more unconventional ideas that may lead us to more accurate understanding, such as the notion of "loose coupling." In general, the term, loose coupling, means that although subsystems of the organization (and the activities that they carry out) are related to one another, each preserves its own identity and individuality. In a high school, for example, the guidance office is usually shown on an organization chart as reporting to the principal's office; yet the linkage is usually loose, with relatively infrequent interaction and typically slow responses of one to the other; the linkage is, in short, relatively weak and unimportant. The coupling—the very glue that holds the organization together—may be described as, at best, "loose."

Educational Organizations as Dual Systems

The concept of loose coupling as a distinctive characteristic of schools and other educational organizations has been powerful in explaining aspects of their organization that were previously ill understood. It does not, however, explain them fully: an observer can easily find much in schools that smacks of bureaucratic or classical organization as well as much that is loosely coupled.

By the mid-1980s there was general agreement among students of organizations that educational organizations are loosely coupled in some significant ways and are highly bureaucratic in other ways, and that this is important in understanding them and the behavior of people in them. For example, in reporting the results of a study of one hundred eighty-eight elementary schools in thirty-four school districts in the San Francisco area, John Meyer and Brian Rowan showed that

> the inspection of instructional activity is delegated to the local school and takes place infrequently. For example, only one of the thirty-four superintendents interviewed reported that the district office evaluates teachers directly. Nor does it appear that principals and peers have the opportunity to inspect and discuss teachers' work: Of the principals surveyed, 85 percent reported that they and their teachers do not work together on a daily basis. Further, there is little evidence of interaction among teachers: A majority of the principals report that there are no day-to-day working relations among teachers within the same grade level, and 83 percent report no daily work relations among teachers of different grades. Teachers reaffirm this view of segmented teaching. Two-thirds report that their teaching is observed by other teachers infrequently (once a month or less), and half report a similar infrequency of observation by their principals.[13]

Considerable other research evidence corroborates the observation that supervision by school administrators is rather infrequent.[14]

Of course, control may be exerted by means other than direct inspection (which public school people usually call supervision). For example, evaluating student learning, maintaining close and detailed specification of the curriculum, and ensuring that students have mastered the work of a previous grade before being promoted to the next are among the many ways that schools may exercise strong control over teaching. However, the San Francisco area research and other studies reported by Meyer and Rowan provide evidence that these techniques are little used in meaningful ways.

Thus the central core activity of the school—instruction—is viewed as being loosely coupled to the extent that it is not directly controlled under the authority of administrators. Although administrators bear general responsibility for the instructional programs of schools, their authority to control the instructional behavior of teachers is rather limited and, since the advent of collective bargaining, appears to be declining. For example, Meyer and Rowan reported that only 12 percent of the principals they studied indicated that they have real decision power over the methods that teachers use, and a mere 4 percent said that they are extremely influential in determining the instructional methods used by teachers.[15]

Administrators, however, do have access to bureaucratic means by which to structure the work of teachers and, thereby, have indirect means of influencing the instructional behavior in the school. *The control of time* is one means: time schedules, the frequency with which students are pulled out for special classes and other activities, the frequency of interruptions of classroom instruction, and the burden of paperwork required of teachers all mold the teaching behavior of teachers and all are influenced by the administrator as a key actor. *The assignment of students to classes* (how many and what kind) is also considerably influenced by administrators and constrains the teachers' work behavior. *Grouping* is another way by which administrators can influence instruction—for example, students may be grouped heterogeneously or homogeneously; teachers may work alone in self-contained classrooms, on teaching teams, or in departments. Principals also influence instructional behavior of teachers through their *control of resources:* teaching space, the availability of equipment, access to the copying machine, and even the availability of such mundane basic supplies as paper and pencils. Yet, although these bureaucratic means are powerful in some ways in influencing the instructional behavior of teachers, they are relatively indirect. Further, as teachers have come to realize the power of these mechanisms, they have increasingly sought to gain some share in controlling them through collective bargaining. Thus, principals are increasingly constrained in their ability to dictate teaching schedules and class sizes, and even in their ability to impose paperwork on teachers.

Whereas the core technical activity of the school is, thus, loosely coupled (as contrasted with what one would expect from a classic bureaucratic organization), noninstructional activities are often tightly coupled. The issuing of paychecks in timely fashion, the deployment of buses, the management of money, and pupil accounting (attendance, for example) are among the numerous noninstructional activities that are closely controlled by administrators and therefore may be described as tightly coupled. In contrast to the nebulous authority that administrators reported over the instructional activities of teachers in their research, Meyer and Rowan reported that 82 percent of the principals surveyed claim to make decisions about scheduling, 75 percent about the assignment of pupils to classes, and 88 percent (either alone or in consultation with other school administrators in the district) about hiring new personnel. These activities may be said to be tightly coupled inasmuch as they are carefully controlled by direct administrative oversight.

One may conclude that looseness in controlling the instructional behavior of teachers is somehow "wrong" and insist—in the tradition of classic bureaucratic thought—that it be tightened up. Indeed, many contemporary observers take such a view, and this explains many political initiatives undertaken in recent years by governors, legislatures, and a few state departments of education to "toughen up" standards and educational requirements by imposing new requirements and limitations on schools. These often include adding required instruction to the curriculum, increased testing of both students and teachers, and more detailed specification of teaching methods. However, the issue being raised here is not whether schools "ought" to be loosely coupled or tightly coupled. Our interest is in better understanding the organizational characteristics of educational organizations *as they exist* (rather than as someone may wish they are) so that we may better understand the management of people in them.

Indeed, recent studies strongly suggest that there are powerful mechanisms through which the organization exerts considerable control over the instructional activities of teachers that have heretofore been largely unseen and unrecognized. These mechanisms are in contrast with the hierarchical line of authority embodied in classical bureaucratic thought. Whereas we traditionally think of organizations exercising control exclusively through such formal mechanisms as supervision down the line of authority, a useful newer perspective is that, in educational organizations at least, powerful control is exercised through the use of far more subtle and indirect means: the development of organizational culture. Understanding this can be a powerful insight in understanding schools and universities and how to lead them effectively.

BUILDING HUMAN CAPITAL

Capital is ordinarily thought of in terms of tangible assets such as cash, raw materials, real estate, machinery and equipment, and intellectual property such as ideas, inventions, and creations. But economists have, for a long time, understood the concept of *human* capital: that is, that the knowledge that people have, their skills, attitudes, and social skills, are also assets to any human enterprise. The human resources available to an organization are, therefore, a form of human capital. In fact, it turns out that they are potentially highly valuable assets that can increase in value over time—which, by definition, assets should do—or decrease in value, depending largely on how they are managed.

Applied to societies, nations, or regions this concept helps to explain why some societies, though rich in tangible assets such as minerals or water power, may be less productive in others. Those societies and nations in which people have high levels of education, well-developed work skills, are favorably disposed toward the discipline of the workplace, and have a social tradition that places high value on hard work and productivity tend to become wealthier than those that do not.[16] This concept was demonstrated spectacularly in Western Europe shortly after World War II with the Marshall Plan.

Most of Europe lay in ruins after World War II: many factories were gone, equipment ruined or worn out, currency systems in shambles, distribution and transportation systems nearly wrecked, and not a few cities and towns reduced to rubble. As a result, unemployment was rampant, poverty commonplace, and despair was everywhere. George C. Marshall and Harry S. Truman persuaded a reluctant Congress to fund a large-scale plan, the Marshall Plan, to rebuild the currency and banking systems, the cities, the factories, the transportation and communications systems, and, generally, to get people back to work and productive once again. A key to the plan was that the human capital needed to bring recovery about was already in place in Western European nations: Western Europeans were a well-educated populace, possessing high levels of work skills and managerial skills; they were not only able but wanting to work; and they had a long tradition of pride in high-quality work and achievement. Because these human resources were in place, the infusing of a substantial amount of start-up money enabled Western Europe to quickly rebuild, and citizens rapidly achieved levels of productivity that were higher than had existed prior to the war.

The concept of building human capital underlies much of the historic effort to improve the lot of societies through the spread of education and the development of social infrastructures as well as the physical and economic infrastructures of third-world nations through international aid. Today, many developing nations that are emerging as prosperous societies with rising standards of living, especially countries in the Pacific Rim area such as South Korea, Taiwan, Hong Kong, Thailand, Singapore, and China, manifest the power of the concept of human capital. Not a few business leaders in the United States view the need to reform U.S. schooling through the lens of human capital, often referring to the reform of education as an investment in human capital. The concept is apt for application to thinking about organizations as well and lies at the heart of the notion of human resources management.

Administrators are customarily held accountable for the financial and physical assets of the school district, such as buildings, equipment, and money. The processes of preparing and approving the annual budget, then the administration of the budget over the course of the fiscal year, and finally a formal accounting of stewardship are familiar and important activities in every school district. Permitting tax-levy funds to be used unwisely or allowing assets to deteriorate through misuse or neglect are, justifiably, considered to be evidence of mismanagement. Only in the 1970s, however, did accountants as well as organizational theorists begin to realize the extent to which mismanagement of an organization's human resources can be detrimental to the organization's effectiveness.

One form of mismanagement is, obviously, to spend too much on human resources; this has led to downsizing, outsourcing, contracting for services, using temporary and part-time employees, and other efforts to reduce payroll costs. Another form of mismanaging human resources, perhaps more important because it is less obvious and often unseen immediately, is failing to place adequate value on the skills, abilities, motivations, and commitment of the people in the organization. Consider, for example, the prophetic observation that was made about IBM in 1976:

> [T]here are currently 148 million shares of International Business Machines (IBM) stock outstanding. At a recent market price of $200 a share, the marketplace values the corporation at approximately $30 billion. Now, part of that value includes the knowledge, skills, abilities, and commitment of the more than 250,000 employees of IBM; but the company's financial statements do not reflect the value of these quarter-million employees. Actually, if every one of these employees—or even a large proportion—were to quit, the value of IBM stock would undoubtedly tumble, because investors know that even though financial statements do not include the value of the human factor, the organization, which is made up of people, will succeed or fail based upon the skills, abilities, motivations, and commitment of these people.[17]

Within ten years that is precisely what happened. IBM did, indeed, undertake a cost-cutting program of retrenchment that sharply reduced its number of employees through layoffs, buyouts, and attrition. The result: during 1996 IBM was being actively traded on the New York Stock Exchange within a range of $83.12 to $166 per share and the once-unchallenged world champion in the computer industry was reduced to scrambling for market share in head-to-head competition with a number of rivals that had previously been considered bush leaguers.

In a typical U.S. school district, over 80 percent of the annual operating budget is allocated to personnel services and related costs. Obviously the human resources of the school enterprise require a substantial outlay of tax-levy funds. Not only are the administrators responsible for maintaining the quality and effectiveness of these resources, but they also must manage them—as one would manage any assets—so that their value to the school district increases over time. People, therefore, should be managed so that their skills, motivations, attitudes, and knowledge develop, improve, and increase over time rather than level off at a steady state or, worse yet, decline. This way of managing, so as to develop and increase the value of the organization's human resources, is the process of building human capital.

Human Resources as Assets

In building human capital, it is insufficient to assume that if employees do not actually quit, the state of the organization's human resources is acceptable. Research has shown, for example, that the processes of building and administering the budget are often handled in ways that create considerable pressure on individuals and groups, which leads to strife, apathy, tension, strain, aggression, and pervasive feelings of failure. These responses tend, of course, to give rise to counterproductive behaviors that are directly related, not to the fact that budget decisions had to be made, but to the leadership processes that leaders and administrators choose to employ in dealing with the budget.[18]

As Rensis Likert observed, "if bickering, distrust, and irreconcilable conflict become greater, the human enterprise is worth less; if the capacity to use differences constructively and engage in cooperative teamwork improves, the human organization is a more valuable asset.[19] Many problems stem from a negative climate in the organization—such as low morale, inadequate effort, lack of cooperation, complaints, and employee turnover.[20] Thus there is impressive evidence that the internal characteristics of the organization that tend to evoke destructive organizational behavior arise largely from the choices that administrators make in deciding how to carry out their work. Indeed, it is often largely the behavior of administrators that needlessly causes the dysfunctional feelings and behaviors commonly observed in struggling or failing organizations.

A continuing difficulty in dealing with this issue has been to find ways to make administrators aware of the dense relationship between their behaviors, policies, and practices and their impact on the human side of the enterprise. In dealing with tangible assets, such as money or real estate, it is often possible for accountants to demonstrate with numbers the bottom-line results of choices that managers make affecting the value of tangible assets entrusted to their care. One can show that deferring maintenance on buildings is an expensive practice, that purchasing wisely can save money, or that turning down thermostats reduces fuel costs. It is much more difficult to make such cause-and-effect linkages between administrative practices and their impact on the value of human resources. A local taxpayer association may cheer on a heavy-handed administrator who ruthlessly cuts teaching positions to slash the budget, but what is the cost if student achievement nosedives and dropout rates soar? Antiunion residents may be elated to see the superintendent of schools get tough at contract bargaining time, but what is the cost if resentment undermines the motivation of teachers and teamwork between administrators and classroom teachers falters? The American Accounting Association has supported a great deal of work to develop ways of dealing with such human resources issues in industrial and commercial organizations. This is called human resources accounting. The central continuing problem with human resources accounting lies in the difficulty of measuring and quantifying the impact of management behavior on human attitudes, motivation, and work behavior. However, this work has given rise to a set of concepts that are helpful in understanding organizational behavior.

Human resources are valuable. In fact, in the case of educational organizations, they are often the most valuable resources available to create and maintain a high-performing organization. If thought of and treated as assets, the people in the organization—the human resources from which human capital is formed—are expected to have greater value in the future than at the present time. This is the essential nature of assets. Therefore, one can properly think of the costs of recruiting and hiring new people, training and supporting them, encouraging their professional growth and development, and managing them sensitively and skillfully as investment in people and—one would hope—their eventual higher productivity as return on that investment.

Instead of increasing in value over time, however, it is commonplace to assume that the human resources in schools decline in value over the years. For example, many observers of schooling complain that school faculties contain a lot of "deadwood," particularly older teachers, who are often described as "burned out." This is often thought to be a consequence of tenure, which allegedly causes teachers to become not only complacent but uncaring. As a proposed remedy, legislation is frequently called for that would make it easier to fire teachers for little substantial cause. If this is true, it is not only costly but—worse—hinders the school's effective performance. But if it is true, one must ask, what is the cause? Is it that teachers tend to be a basically selfish and uncaring lot who, once they have some job security, shed any sense of professional responsibility? Is it that teaching is somehow a young person's game and at some point teachers should be dismissed because of age? Perhaps, but there is little that we know about organizational behavior that supports either of these propositions. Rather, research in organizational behavior suggests that it is more likely that in a supportive organizational environment, one that facilitates continuous personal growth and professional fulfillment, teachers turn out to be increasingly more effective over the course of time. This fortuitous state of affairs is ordinarily found to exist in schools that are described as highly effective. Creating such a growth-enhancing organizational environment is the responsibility of those in charge of the schools, namely school administrators. It is the process through which one builds human capital in schools.

Organizational Culture as a Bearer of Authority

Like all workplaces, an educational organization—each school and each university—is characterized by a distinctive organizational culture. In this sense "organizational culture" refers to the *norms* that inform people about what is acceptable and what is not, the dominant *values* that the organization cherishes above others, the *basic assumptions and beliefs* that are shared by members of the organization, the *"rules"* of the game that must be observed if one is to get along and be accepted as a member, the *philosophy* that guides the organization in dealing with its employees and its clients. These elements of organizational culture are developed over a period of time by the people in the organization, working together. They evolve during the history of the organization and are shared and subscribed to by those who are a part of that history.

The culture of the educational organization shapes and molds assumptions and perceptions that are basic to understanding what it means to be a teacher. The culture informs the teachers as to what it means to teach, what teaching methods are available and approved for use, what the pupils or students are like—what is possible, and what is not. The culture also plays a large role in defining for teachers their commitment to the task: it evokes the energy of the teachers to perform the task, loyalty and commitment to the organization and what it stands for, emotional bonds of attachment to the organization and its ideals. These give rise to teachers' willingness not only to follow the rules and norms governing their behavior in the organization but, more than that, to accept the ideals of the organization as their own personal values and, therefore, to work energetically to achieve the espoused goals of the organization.[21]

Do certain, specific kinds of organizational cultures promote greater effectiveness in educational organizations? The evidence is fragmentary at present. However, considerable evidence for the idea that certain kinds of organizational cultures create improved organizational performance is emerging from studies on business corporations. For example, Terrence E. Deal and his associates have contended that it is strong organizational culture that distinguishes high-performing companies from less successful companies in competitive markets.[22] In a highly popular and best-selling book, Thomas J. Peters and Robert H. Waterman, Jr., argued that successful U.S. corporations are characterized by the presence of specific, describable cultures that clearly differentiate them from others that would seek to compete with them.[23] Similarly, Rosabeth Moss Kanter has argued persuasively that companies that have what she calls an "open culture" are more innovative and more successful than those that do not.[24] Edgar Schein has described the relationship between organizational culture and the ability of administrators to exercise leadership.[25] A growing body of literature concerning the role of organizational culture in educational organizations (discussed in later chapters of this book) strongly suggests that organizational culture is as powerful in creating effective educational organizations as it is in creating profit-making corporations.

NONTHEORETICAL INFLUENCES ON ORGANIZATIONAL THOUGHT

Academic theorizing is hardly the only force that develops our understanding of educational organizations and behavior in them. Two powerful and highly pragmatic emerging influences have largely ignored traditional organizational theory yet have substantially buttressed the kinds of thinking just described. One of these is the *effective schools research;* the other is the much larger, broader *school reform movement* that gathered momentum in the 1980s.

Effective Schools Research

The now-substantial body of research literature on effective schools had its origins in despair. In the 1970s, big-city high schools were generally perceived as performing so badly that some were beginning to wonder, "Can big-city high schools be made to work for their poor, ethnic minority students? Do any big-city high schools exist in which student achievement levels are satisfactory? And, if they do, what can we learn from them that will help us to improve other schools?" An analysis of the reading-achievement test scores of big-city high schools quickly revealed that, at least on the basis of those scores, some—albeit, at the time, a few—inner-city high schools were clearly performing better than others.

Researchers began visiting these apparently effective schools to see what they were like, to observe what went on in them, and to write case studies describing them. Over the years, this body of qualitative research has grown not merely in volume but also in scope and sophistication. It has powerfully influenced our understanding of the organizational characteristics and the work behaviors of people in effective schools and how they differ from those in their less-effective counterparts.

Findings of the Effective Schools Research

First, a word of caution. Ever since the first research on effective schools began to appear in the literature in the 1970s, there have been repeated efforts to synthesize the findings and extract the essence of what the research tells us. The differences between early efforts to synthesize the work and those that were done later, when the research literature was more substantial and more sophisticated, are striking. Perhaps premature, the earlier efforts now appear to be relatively simplistic and somewhat misleading. By the late 1980s, considerable agreement had emerged among students of effective schools research as to what the key findings were.

Five Basic Assumptions of Effective Schools

First, let us look at five basic assumptions that underlie the concept of effective schools:[26]

1. Whatever else a school can and should do, its central purpose is to teach: success is measured by students' progress in knowledge, skills, and attitudes.

2. The school is responsible for providing the overall environment in which teaching and learning occur.

3. Schools must be treated holistically: partial efforts to make improvements that deal with the needs of only some of the students and break up the unity of the instructional program are likely to fail.

4. The most crucial characteristics of a school are the attitudes and behaviors of the teachers and other staff, not material things such as the size of its library or the age of the physical plant.[27]

5. Perhaps most important, the school accepts responsibility for the success or failure of the academic performance of the students. Students are firmly regarded as capable of learning regardless of their ethnicity, sex, home or cultural background, or family income. "Pupils from poor families do not need a different curriculum, nor does their poverty excuse failure to learn basic skills," Stewart Purkey and Marshall Smith assert, adding, "Differences among schools do have an impact on student achievement, and those differences are controllable by the school staff."[28]

Thus, the effective schools concept turns 180 degrees from traditional educational thought that tends to blame the victim, namely the student, for low academic achievement. Though one of the outstanding characteristics of effective schools is that they take responsibility for meeting the educational needs of students to a greater degree than their less-successful counterparts, this is still a concept that many educational practitioners find difficult to accept. Especially in those schools seemingly overwhelmed, as many inner-city and not a few suburban schools are, by poor children, children from diverse cultural backgrounds, and children from nontraditional families, it is not easy to focus the responsibility for the motivation and achievement of students on the school rather than on the students or forces outside the school. Nevertheless, this is the essential lesson from the effective schools research.

The question remains: what is it, specifically, that the schools do in order to fulfill this responsibility? Listen to Purkey and Smith, who developed a penetrating analysis of the effective schools research literature in the mid-1980s:

> The most persuasive research suggests that student academic performance is strongly affected by school culture. This culture is composed of values, norms, and roles existing within institutionally distinct structures of governance, communication, educational practices and policies and so on. Successful schools are found to have cultures that produce a climate or "ethos" conducive to teaching and learning . . . efforts to change schools have been most productive and most enduring when directed toward influencing the entire school culture via a strategy involving collaborative planning, shared decision making, and collegial work in an atmosphere friendly to experimentation and evaluation.[29]

Thus the effective schools research suggests "increased involvement of teachers and other staff members in decision making, expanded opportunities for collaborative planning, and flexible change strategies that can reflect the unique 'personality' of each school. The goal is to change the school culture; the means requires staff members to assume responsibility for school improvement, which in turn is predicated on their having the authority and support necessary"[30] to create instructional programs that meet the educational needs of their students.

Seeking an Effective Schools Formula

The early effective schools research was quickly seized upon as the basis for developing programs for improving the performance of schools. Regrettably, some of the early popularizers of the effective schools research emphasized interpretations that consisted of a rather simple five- or six-factor formula. Effective schools, ran that early message, share the following characteristics:

+ Strong leadership by the principal.

+ High expectations for student achievement on the part of teachers and other staff members.

+ An emphasis on basic skills.

+ An orderly environment.

+ Frequent and systematic evaluation of students.

+ Increased time on teaching and learning tasks.[31]

Many major-city school systems—including Chicago, New York, Minneapolis, Milwaukee, St. Louis, San Diego, and Washington, D.C.—and also several states established school-improvement projects based on a list of variables such as the one above. The secretary of education embraced the concept in 1987, and a bill was introduced into the U.S. Congress, although it did not pass, for the federal funding of school-improvement projects based on this notion.

Recent examination of the effective schools research continues to support the belief that we can identify and describe the essential organizational characteristics of effective schools and the behavior of people in them. However, installing in schools these five or six "correlates," as they soon came to be called, is not in itself sufficient to improve the effectiveness of schools.

Emerging Approach to Effective Schools

Purkey and Smith have identified thirteen characteristics of effective schools from the reported research.[32] They fall into two groups. The first group contains nine characteristics that can be implemented quickly at minimal cost by administrative action:

1. School-site management and democratic decision making, in which individual schools are encouraged to take greater responsibility for, and are given greater latitude for, educational problem solving.

2. Support from the district for increasing the capacity of schools to identify and solve significant educational problems; this includes reducing the inspection and management roles of central office people while increasing support and encouragement of school-level leadership and collaborative problem solving.

3. Strong leadership, which may be provided by administrators but also may be provided by integrated teams of administrators, teachers, and perhaps others.

4. Staff stability, to facilitate the development of a strong cohesive school culture.

5. A planned, coordinated curriculum that treats the students' educational needs holistically and increases time spent on academic learning.

6. Schoolwide staff development that links the school's organizational and instructional needs with the needs that teachers themselves perceive should be addressed.

7. Parental involvement particularly in support of homework, attendance, and discipline.

8. Schoolwide recognition of academic success, both in terms of improving academic performance and achieving standards of excellence.

9. Emphasize time on teaching and learning; for example, reduce interruptions and disruptions, stress the primacy of focused efforts to learn, and restructure teaching activities.

These are not the only characteristics of effective schools and certainly they are not the most crucial. However, they are relatively easy and inexpensive to implement quickly and they set the stage for the development of a second group of four characteristics that have great power to renew and increase the school's capacity to continue to solve problems and increase effectiveness over time:

10. Collaborative planning and collegial relationships that promote feelings of unity, encourage sharing of knowledge and ideas, and foster consensus among those in the school.

11. Sense of community, in which alienation—of both teachers and students—is reduced and a sense of mutual sharing is strengthened.

12. Shared clear goals and high achievable expectations, which arise from collaboration, collegiality, and a sense of community and which serve to unify those in the organization through their common purposes.

13. Order and discipline that bespeak the seriousness and purposefulness of the school as a community of people, students, teachers and staff, and other adults, that is cohered by mutual agreement on shared goals, collaboration, and consensus.

Clearly, the critical school characteristics listed in the second group are more complex than those in the first group, more difficult to achieve and sustain over time, yet they combine to produce great power to establish the improvement of educational effectiveness as a central focus of life within the school. The power, of course, lies in developing within the school a culture—norms, values, beliefs—that unites those in the school in their unending quest of seeking increased educational effectiveness. Many if not most school-improvement plans can be faulted precisely for seeking to "install" the relatively simpler first-order characteristics and falling short of seriously engaging in the culture-rebuilding suggested by the more complex second-order characteristics cited here.

THE SCHOOL REFORM MOVEMENT

The school reform movement, which got under way in the early 1980s with the publication of *A Nation at Risk: The Imperative for Educational Reform,*[33] had at the outset little connection with either the new developments in organizational thought or the effective schools research. It has, however, spawned a large number of studies of schools. Many of these studies were qualitative and describe the need to change schools drastically in ways that are highly compatible with the findings of the effective schools research literature.

The First Wave of School Reform

Many observers describe the school reform movement of the 1980s as unfolding in two "waves." The so-called first wave of reform—the initial reaction to the outpouring of critiques of schooling that began with the publication of *A Nation at Risk* in 1983—was composed largely of an astonishing increase in regulatory mandates imposed on the schools by the states. Such regulations facilitated the reach of governmental bureaucracies directly into the classroom—a reach that was mimicked at the local level by many school district central office organizations—by specifying, for example, what textbooks must be used, how many minutes of time should be devoted to instruction, what teaching techniques were to be used, and by establishing elaborate systems of examinations and reporting through which compliance could be audited by governmental agencies.

By the 1990s, however, many thoughtful observers were expressing alarm that such regulatory approaches with their requisite detailed top-down bureaucratic administration of regulations were, in fact, counterproductive in two major ways:

> *First,* regulatory approaches were driving schools to new heights of mindless rigidity that often failed to take into account the specific individual educational needs of students and the specific circumstances of the schools that they attended. Heightening the bureaucratic control of schools, it was argued, hampered teachers in making the professional judgments about the curriculum and teaching that a particular child needed—decisions that are best made not by the fiat of some faceless distant bureaucratic office but by today's highly qualified teachers who in face-to-face interaction with the student can bring their professional insights to bear on the problem.
>
> *Second,* a growing body of research made clear that teachers—highly qualified and motivated to do the best for their "clients," namely the students—were increasingly frustrated by their growing inability to exercise their professional judgments in a school environment that was becoming steadily bureaucratized. This was reflected not only in the then-growing teacher shortage, as people left the profession and others declined to enter it, but also in growing evidence of alienation and declining morale of the teachers who remained on the job.

The Second Wave of School Reform

These concerns ushered in what became known as the second wave of school reform, which recognized that the increased regulatory practices of the first wave of reform were, as Alvin Toffler had put it, "a classic response to a need for fundamental change—the initial tendency is to work the old system harder." Through the promulgation of ever-more regulations, more courses were required and fewer electives were permitted, more hours of classes required, more services made available, more pay offered to teachers, more equipment provided; but these only made the old system work harder and improved schooling only marginally, at best. Why? Because they failed to deal with the fundamental need for change itself: the need for more productive human relationships in schools, the need by students to assume greater responsibility for their own learning, and the need for greater professional autonomy for teachers in diagnosing and solving instructional problems that confront them both in the school and in the classroom.

The old system, which the first wave of reform had taken for granted, saw teachers as low-level functionaries of public hierarchical bureaucracies who were accountable to officials in the higher echelons "above" them in those bureaucracies, who, in turn, are accountable to the public through the political mechanisms of school boards, legislatures, and state boards of education. Indeed, this structure of U.S. public schools is so generally taken for granted that we are not aware of how powerfully it influences the relationships of the players and in turn influences how people behave when they are at work in the schools. The omnipresence of this view has caused us to see public schooling as a function delegated to a government agency, and any other model is literally inconceivable. Thus, education became understood in the bureaucratic mind as the "delivery of educational services," rather than as the mutual striving of teachers and students working together to achieve shared goals of success.

The second wave of school reform took a remarkably different view: that the "front line" of schooling lies in the individual school rather than in some distant bureaucratic government agency and that it is there—in the individual school and in its classrooms—that educational problems can best be identified, puzzled over, and solved. The second wave of school reform recognizes the professional role of teachers, as contrasted with the bureaucratic role. This requires giving teachers sufficient professional autonomy and leeway to exercise their abilities to understand and solve educational problems at the school level, where they are closest to those problems and where they see the complex factors that may be involved in them, and to hold teachers responsible for the results of their decisions and actions.

This new approach to school reform calls for a restructuring of roles and relationships between people at work in the schools. Rather than teachers who passively await mandates to be handed down from above for them to implement, it calls for teachers who are actively involved in studying professional problems, making decisions as to what to do about them, and being committed to achieving results in implementing those decisions. The vision is of a collaborative school environment with teachers more fully engaged than in the past, more highly motivated because of their increased "ownership" of the action.

WOMEN'S ISSUES IN ORGANIZATIONAL BEHAVIOR

As we have seen, organizational behavior in education as we understand it today is the result of a century-long process of continuous inquiry and study. Knowledge of organizational behavior is slow to emerge for at least two reasons:

1. The behavior of people in educational workplaces is neither simple nor self-evident.

2. Our basic assumptions about human nature, and the values about human beings that arise from these assumptions, are continually changing and developing.

These give rise to ambiguity, complexity, and the general messiness that is inherent in the study of organizational life. Thus, developing a body of knowledge in organizational behavior requires, as does the effort to understand any aspect of complex human experience, a process of repeated iterations of developing theory, research to test the theory, and criticism of resulting outcomes in a continuous effort to build and expand the body of knowledge. All of this is, of course, essential to the development of any body of scientific knowledge and scholarship.

By the 1980s it had become obvious to women scholars that educational administration has traditionally been a male bastion that has generally resisted women who seek admission. The preponderance of scholars who studied administration and organizational behavior in education have traditionally been men as well. Moreover, despite the doubt that has been cast on the tradition of authoritarianism in school administration by emerging knowledge in organizational behavior and despite the enlightened views of schools advocated by many students of school reform who deplore the widespread alienation commonly found in them, many Americans still harbor the belief that the solution to seemingly intractable problems in schooling lies in the greater exercise of coercion from the top down. Because of this, given the gender stereotypes that are so prominent in our culture, doubt still lingers as to whether women are as able as men to be effective in school administration. For example, some doubt that women possess the toughness traditionally thought to be necessary to maintain discipline in high schools. Yet, as we shall see, the feminist critique posits that women possess abilities that suit them well to exercise leadership in schools that are much in need of change from the past. Women, runs the critique, not only can succeed in administrative work but they can excel at it. Moreover, schools would perhaps be better than they are if their organizational cultures more fully reflected the thinking, the values, and the perspectives of women than they traditionally have.

In the context of the general movement in recent years toward gender equity, these facts and ideas cried out for study and explanation. The result has been a recent critique of scholarship in organizational behavior, centered on gender issues.

This critique challenges the ways in which we typically think about organizations, organizational behavior, organizational theory, and administration that has traditionally been done by men from the perspective of men. The literature in these areas of theory and research is described as having been androcentric, that is, male centered. Because it is, the theories and the results of research based on those theories may well be biased and, therefore, flawed.

Androcentrism

All scientific inquiry, including inquiry into organizational behavior, reflects some basic assumptions and fundamental beliefs that the inquirer implicitly holds. These include assumptions about human nature, the nature of human relationships, the nature of reality, and the nature of human activity.[34] A hazard for any scholar lies in the fact that many of these basic assumptions are so taken for granted by the scholar, so implicitly held, and so thoroughly internalized as to be virtually invisible to the individual who holds them. Each of us holds some assumptions that seem to be so obviously true, so commonplace, that "everyone" shares them. They are shared among colleagues, friends, and others in one's group or in one's culture. Because such assumptions are commonplace, they become invisible, and are not discussed because no one even thinks to raise the subject. When that happens, members of the group believe that any other premise is inconceivable. This is precisely the basis of the gender issues that have been raised about scholarship in organizational behavior.

The systematic development of knowledge in educational administration and in organizational behavior may be viewed as effectively describing the world as men have understood it, a description of the world as viewed through a "male prism"[35] or a "male lens."[36] Critics describe organizational behavior research as having been largely done by men who studied populations comprised mostly of men and who used the unexamined worldview of men in theorizing and carrying out the investigations. Women were virtually uninvolved in much of the research, either in conceptualizing it or as the subjects of the investigations. "The underlying assumption is that the experiences of males and females are the same, and thus research on males is appropriate for generalizing to the female experience. In developing theories of administration, researchers didn't took at the context in general and, therefore, were unable to document how the world was different for women. When female experience was different, it was ignored or diminished,"[37] according to one observer.

This dominance of the male worldview in research and knowledge, this "male-defined scholarship," has been called *androcentrism*.[38] Androcentrism in organizational behavior research is thought to introduce a bias into the study of organizational behavior in schools especially because schools are predominantly female workplaces while efforts to understand those workplaces are essentially derived from male-based scholarship.[39]

Androcentrism in scholarship and research methods should not be confused with prejudice or a particular bias against women as a class of people, which would be sexism.[40] Rather, androcentrism in organizational studies refers to the virtual overlooking of women, their absence from the scholarship itself, the unexamined assumption held by those who conducted the studies that men and women experience organizational life in essentially the same ways. Recent critiques, largely from women scholars, raise serious questions about this assumption.

The history of the development of the study of organizational behavior during this century as a linchpin of educational administration has largely coincided with the post–World War II entry of men into teaching and educational administration. Almost a century after Catharine Beecher popularized the notion of teaching as "woman's true profession,"[41] men returning from military service in World War II began to take women's places in teaching in large numbers with the help of education under the GI Bill. Early in the century, the majority of elementary school principals were women although high school principalships and superintendencies were largely held by men. Beginning in the 1930s, however, there was a trend toward selecting men for elementary school principalships as well. By the early 1950s, the dominance of women in administrative positions in the elementary schools had clearly given way to men. This ushered in the modern era in which administration has been largely a man's preserve whereas teaching has been largely a woman's preserve.

The decades of the 1950s and 1960s were also marked by the profound development of research and theory in such aspects of organizational behavior as motivation, leadership, organizational climate, conflict management, and decision making. This body of organizational behavior knowledge quickly became, and still largely is, the foundation on which modern concepts of educational administration stand. Virtually all research and teaching of educational administration in universities in the Western world draw on organizational behavior as fundamental to understanding educational administration. However, the charge of androcentrism became a major challenge to traditional theorizing and study of organizational behavior from a feminocentric[42] perspective.

The Feminocentric Critique

The feminocentric critique posits that for a variety of reasons men and women understand and experience the world in significantly different ways. Women "see" things differently from men, hold different values, seek different goals, and have different priorities. For example, one reason given for this is the belief that men, from boyhood into adulthood, receive more direct feedback on their behavior, in the form of both criticism and praise, than do women. Some speculate that men are thus better able to learn appropriate work behaviors and deal effectively with the give-and-take that ordinarily occurs between supervisor and teacher.[43] Other reasons often given in the literature of the feminocentric critique include that women are more concerned about relationships and caring for others than are men, who are depicted as concerned about territoriality and justice.

Thus the educational workplace is described as having two cultures—a male culture and a female culture—and these two overlap only partially; they are not coterminous. These differences have been little recognized until now and, in the feminocentric view, that leads to errors in the body of literature that describes, interprets, and predicts organizational behavior. What differences are we talking about?

In summarizing the findings of the feminocentric literature, Charol Shake-shaft discussed five characteristics of the female world in educational organizations and how they contrast with what she perceives to be the misogynous[44] male world that exists in schools:

1. "Women spend more time with people, communicate more, care more about individual differences, are concerned more with teachers and marginal students, and motivate more," Shakeshaft says. Consequently, she claims, "staffs of women administrators rate women higher, are more productive, and have higher morale. Students of schools with women principals also have higher morale and are more involved in student affairs. Further, parents are more favorable toward schools and districts run by women."[45]

2. Women administrators exhibit greater knowledge of teaching methods and techniques, are more likely to help new teachers and supervise all teachers directly, and create a climate more conducive to learning that is orderly, safer, and quieter. "Not surprisingly," Shakeshaft adds, "academic achievement is higher in schools and districts in which women are administrators."[46]

3. "Shakeshaft also notes that women exhibit a more democratic, participatory style . . . involve themselves more with staff and students, ask for and get higher participation, and maintain more closely knit organizations. Staffs of women principals have higher job satisfaction and are more engaged in their work than those of male administrators."[47]

4. The woman administrator is always on display and always vulnerable to attack in the misogynous male world of educational administration. Whether or not "the assault actually occurs is less important than the knowledge that it is always possible. Women perceive their token status."[48]

5. Women are more likely than men to behave the same way in public as they do in private and this often results "in behavior that men often label inappropriate."[49]

Patricia Schmuck has reported that androcentrism, which takes men's experience as representative of all human experience and simply excludes women as a particular group to be studied, is merely the first of five stages of thinking about women in educational organizations.[50] The second stage is called "compensatory thinking," in which the underrepresentation of women in the ranks of school administration is recognized and efforts are undertaken to recruit women to ameliorate that deficiency. The third stage is called a "psychological deficiency model," in which the low number of women is explained away and interpreted in psychological terms. The fourth stage of thinking generally conceptualizes women as being oppressed by organizational arrangements. The fifth and last stage of thinking about these issues is what Schmuck calls the "New Scholarship," in which gender becomes central in disciplined inquiry that seeks to describe, understand, and explain the deficiencies of traditional androcentric organizational research, Thus, in the fifth stage, "Research is modified to include women as well as men as the objects and subjects of study. This scholarship is corrective: it provides alternative points of view and transforms existing knowledge." This neat five-level model is problematic even from the feminine perspective,[51] but it does illustrate the current struggle by feminocentric scholars to conceptualize serious reservations about which all students of organizational behavior in education, both men and women, are concerned and wish to eliminate.

Women scholars have generally used two different ways to modify administrative research so as to include women. As I shall explain next, one way has been to reexamine existing research and theory to show that it is androcentric and therefore seriously flawed methodologically. Another way has been to engage in new research using research methods that are thought to be more appropriate to understanding the organizational behavior of both women and men in educational administration.

Feminocentric Critique of Existing Research

In perhaps the most prominent feminocentric critique of existing research, Charol Shakeshaft and Irene Nowell selected the following five distinguished examples of scholarly work for careful examination:[52]

1. The social systems model of organization created by Jacob Getzels in 1952[53] and elaborated with the assistance of Egon Guba in 1957.

2. The Leader Behavior Description Questionnaire (LBDQ) created by John Hemphill and Alvin Coons in 1950.

3. The Organizational Climate Description Questionnaire (OCDQ) created by Andrew W. Halpin and Don B. Croft in 1962.

4. The contingency theory of leadership developed by Fred E. Fiedler in the early 1960s.

5. The theory of human motivation created by Abraham H. Maslow in 1943.

The concepts and theories embodied in each of the works listed are truly seminal. Each has spawned a substantial literature of research based on their concepts and theories, and each is described in virtually every textbook on administrative theory. The present textbook describes each of them. Indeed, few individuals who have taken even an introductory course in school administration have failed to be exposed to them. They can be taken, therefore, as representative of the concepts and theories that have guided thinking about important aspects of organizational behavior in education.

Shakeshaft's critique makes a strong case that these theorists largely ignored women in their thinking and seem to assume that their theories and research illuminate the organizational behavior of men and women equally. She has pointed out that, in describing their social systems model, Getzels and Guba simply ignored women and did not investigate their actual experience of role conflict as teachers, for example.

Although the Leader Behavior Description Questionnaire (LBDQ) was originated in the research of Helen Jennings, in which she studied the leader behavior of girls in a New York State residential institution, much of the development work of the LBDQ instrument was done in military and corporate settings, which were then predominantly male.

In conducting extensive research to test his contingency theory of leadership, Fred Fiedler not only ignored the gender of the leader (though he had women in his research samples) but also engaged in some speculation about aspects of women's organizational behavior that Shakeshaft derided as "masculist" and "uninformed."

Finally, Maslow's approach to motivation has been described by Shakeshaft as reflecting patronizing views toward women of one who believes that the work of women does not require intelligence, talent, or genius.[54]

In their pioneering study of organizational climate in schools, in which they developed and used the now-classic Organizational Climate Description Questionnaire (OCDQ), Halpin and Croft described perceptions of principals by teachers as a major factor in organizational climate. Despite the high likelihood that virtually all principals in their research sample of elementary schools were men whereas undoubtedly virtually all teachers were women, Halpin and Croft completely ignored the possibility that gender may play some part, perhaps a very significant part, in molding these critical perceptions.

One might be tempted to dismiss the feminocentric critique as being merely another of a long series of criticisms, from various perspectives, that this body of venerable scholarly work has inevitably and properly endured during the many years that it has been in the central core of the marketplace of ideas about organizational behavior. However, the critique was given added significance by a study of the articles reporting administrative research that were published in a leading scholarly journal, *Educational Administration Quarterly,* over a span of ten years.[55] The study found that the majority of articles published in that distinguished journal could properly be described as exhibiting androcentric bias inasmuch as

1. Reviews of research literature rarely examined how gender issues had been accounted-for in previous work.

2. The instruments and survey strategies used were often biased.

3. In articles describing the research samples used, 90 percent were samples of men only.

4. The research results were described as generalizable to the population as a whole with no discussion of possible limitations in terms of gender.

Remember that before articles are accepted for publication in such a journal each manuscript must be reviewed by a panel of reputable scholars who scrutinize it in terms of its intellectual and methodological rigor and significance. Because the scholarly standards are rigorous, most work submitted is rejected. However, the findings of this study clearly imply that the androcentric qualities of this ten-year body of work had gone unnoticed not only by a substantial group of scholars who served as reviewers but also by readers of the journal. It would seem apparent that the charge of androcentrism in this field of scholarship is strongly supported.

Feminocentric Scholarship

Over the years, many female scholars have written on educational administration and organizational behavior. Generally, their work is indistinguishable in the body of literature from the work authored by men. For example, Paula Silver's book, *Educational Administration: Theoretical Perspectives on Practice and Research,*[56] does not differ in terms of its treatment of theory, concepts, or topics covered from the many textbooks prepared by males that compete with it in the marketplace. "Taken as a whole," Daniel Griffiths has stated that "there appear to be no theoretical or methodological differences [in the work written by women] from the literature written by men."[57] However, in addition to the feminocentric critique that has been discussed, a new body of research literature that specifically addresses the concerns of women is emerging. This is what Patricia Schmuck alluded to as "the new scholarship." It is, at this point, a small but growing body of literature. Its central characteristic is that it addresses questions and issues of deep and personal concern to women.

Characteristics of "The New Scholarship"

A central characteristic of the new scholarship is, of course, an avowed interest in gaining a better understanding of the experience of women in the organizational life of education. This interest has tended to focus the research on three main areas:

1. Studies of such things as the ways in which women fit into organizations, what motivates them, the ways in which they get satisfaction from their work, and how they move from teaching into administration.

2. Studies of attitudes toward women such as negative attitudes toward them that they encounter as they seek to become administrators and the general bias in favor of men that they encounter in their administrative careers.

3. Descriptions of women school administrators at work, their effectiveness in administrative positions, and comparisons of the behavior of administrative women with that of their male counterparts.

A second characteristic of this body of research is methodological. Increasingly, inquiries into women's issues in organizational life make use of a broader array of techniques for gathering data than had heretofore been customary. For example, many women investigators find it useful to collect data by going into educational organizations to observe the behavior of people in them and to conduct open-ended unstructured interviews. Such research methods are called *qualitative* (or *ethnographic*) and contrast markedly with the more impersonal questionnaires that were traditionally the principal means for gathering data in the survey research typical in administrative studies prior to the emergence of the feminocentric critique.

TWO STUDIES OF WOMEN'S ISSUES

Although the history of research on women administrators in educational organizations is relatively new, it has produced a growing and very diverse body of published literature. This, of course, indicates the intense and rising interest that the field of study has attracted. From that large body of research literature, I will describe two recent studies that are of particular interest to those concerned with organizational behavior in schools.

Women Who Aspire to School Administration

Ever since the 1960s, the number of women enrolling in university courses in educational administration has risen dramatically. By the 1980s, women comprised over 50 percent of the students in such courses.[58] This, of course, indicates rising aspirations of women for administrative careers. However, although the number of females being appointed to administrative positions in the schools has increased over time, the rate of increase was disappointing to many women. Studies have sought to understand the barriers to women seeking to develop administrative careers in education. Gladys Johnston and her colleagues examined the patterns of the employment of women administrators in public education[59] and found that the perception that women do not fare well in the job market is well founded. Another study examined prejudice against female school administrators by the public and explored the possibilities of changing what is considered to be an unfavorable situation.[60] Others have explored possible strategies and tactics for facilitating the appointment of women to administrative positions and their advancement through the ranks.[61] Flora Ortiz examined the problems and opportunities confronting a female administrator who sought to scale the hierarchy of a school system.[62] Numerous other studies relevant to women in administration cover topics as varied as women dealing with stress in administration,[63] networking for administrative women,[64] and ways of handling the combination of career and home responsibilities.[65]

Although these early studies, and many others, suggest that men are part of the problem by being hostile or indifferent not only to the aspirations but also to the abilities of women, more recent research suggests that that traditional male view may be waning. Sakre Edson, for example, used qualitative research methods (principally interviews) to conduct a nationwide study in which she followed, for a period of five years, the careers of 142 women who wanted to get into educational administration.[66] One conclusion from that research was that the attitudes of male administrators toward women who wish to become administrators is becoming more supportive and helpful. Many of the women in the study credited men administrators with initiating their interest in administration, encouraging them, and being helpful colleagues and mentors. As Edson reported,

> Some men find it difficult to alter their long-held beliefs about female administrators; however, women appreciate the efforts of those men who earnestly try to change their perceptions about women's management abilities. . . . [M]any aspirants sense a new

openness towards women seeking school management positions. Although hiring statistics fail to document their optimism, many feel it is only a matter of time before genuine change will occur. Throughout the country, female aspirants admit that they might never have considered aspiring to administration except for the encouragement of those male colleagues who are changing their attitudes about women.[67]

Edson attributes the more favorable climate toward women administrators to "the women's movement" and to recent equity legislation.

School Boards and Women Superintendents

Although, as Edson's study shows, some women have high aspirations for administrative work and while enrollments of women in preparatory courses soar and those of men decline, the number of women being appointed to administrative positions has not risen appreciably. Indeed, the American Association of School Administrators reported that although in 1981–1982 some 25 percent of school administrators in the United States were female, by 1984–1985 the figure had risen to only 26 percent. Moreover, the higher the administrative position, the lower the proportion of women being appointed. Although about 21 percent of the school principals in the United States were women in 1984–1985, only 16 percent were deputy, assistant, or associate superintendents, and fewer than 3 percent of school superintendents were female.[68] Colleen Bell and Susan Chase reported that a 1987 survey of U.S. state departments of education found that 2.8 percent of superintendents in K–12 school districts were women.[69] This state of affairs has caused thoughtful investigators to seek to understand more fully how women experience the superintendency.

Bell and Chase examined the experiences of three women superintendents, including the procedures used to evaluate and select candidates when they were considered for appointment, as well as their experiences on the job.[70] Because a key aspect of the superintendency lies in the unique relationship between the members of the school board, collectively and individually, and the superintendent, this relationship became a focus of the study. The investigators used qualitative methods to conduct the study: they went to the school districts to

- ✦ observe the behavior of people on the scene,
- ✦ conduct lengthy unstructured interviews with the superintendents and also with members of the boards of education, and
- ✦ study documents ranging from newspaper stories to such official documents as minutes of school board meetings and copies of the school district budgets.

The women who were ultimately selected by the largely male school boards to be superintendents were described as being highly qualified: they were experienced administrators and, in most cases, had doctorates. Furthermore, the boards had considered not only women but also some male candidates. But many board members had acknowledged their discomfort and doubt about the ability of women to perform the tasks of the superintendency. In each case the school board had initially been inclined to favor male candidates even though school board members acknowledged that the credentials of the women were superior. As the selection process went forward, however imperfect as it was, each woman finally emerged as successful and got the job. But, Bell and Chase wondered, why would a school board be inclined to select a less-qualified man when these well-qualified women were in the running?

The answer, the researchers think, has to do with social conformity: this is the notion preferred by Rosabeth Moss Kanter[71] that organizations have many characteristics that create pressure for members to conform to accepted standards. School boards, for example, face a great deal of uncertainty, ambiguity, and not a little conflict in fulfilling their mandate to govern the schools. Naturally, in looking for a superintendent, board members want to reduce that uncertainty, yet they realize that the superintendent must exercise wide-ranging discretionary authority on their behalf. Therefore, board members want a superintendent on whom they feel they can rely, one whom they can trust, whose behavior they feel they can predict. In this situation they tend to look for someone whose values, experience, and language they share; someone like themselves and like other superintendents with whom they have worked. This is social homogeneity and it increases confidence, predictability, ease of communication, and trust that, as Kanter has pointed out, is essential in all effective organizations. When people who are "different" are brought into the inner circle of organizations it becomes difficult to preserve the culture of trust that homogeneity fosters. "Thus," Bell and Chase have argued, "what the preferred candidates [men] had going for them and what operated against the women who applied [for the job] was a social homogeneity factor; that is, male board members find it easier to communicate and interact with, and hence to trust, male candidates for the superintendency."[72]

SOME FINDINGS OF FEMINOCENTRIC RESEARCH

Men, and women as well, are often uncomfortable in thinking about and discussing gender issues. The sources of this discomfort run deep in the traditions of our cultural heritage and will not be readily assuaged, let alone eradicated. The need to deal with the issues, and the discomfort, also runs deep and is hardly new. George Bernard Shaw built a considerable reputation (and not inconsiderable fortune) by bringing wit and satire to bear on the battle of the sexes in such plays as *Man and Superman* and *Pygmalion,* which continue to draw audiences to this day. Noël Coward gained a sort of immortality by bringing his genius for song and sophisticated comedy to the discussion. And many people still remember Professor Higgins's puzzlement, in the Broadway musical, *My Fair Lady,* as to why a woman cannot be more like a man. If nothing else, the feminocentric critique of traditional administrative research and the contributions of what Patricia Schmuck has called "the new scholarship" have made it clear that, in organizational life of education at any rate, Professor Higgins's question is not the one posed today.

Increased Awareness of Androcentrism in Administrative Thought

A major contribution of feminocentric criticism and research has been to increase the awareness of men and women alike to a serious shortcoming in our understanding of organizational behavior in education. The message, sometimes delivered in the measured dispassionate tones of traditional scholarly discourse and sometimes in rhetoric that is on the cusp of hostility, has been received and accepted at least by leading theoreticians and scholars. For example, the *Administrative Science Quarterly* not only printed the critique documenting its own contribution to androcentrism but has responded by including women more often and more centrally in its own decision-making processes. Moreover, its pages, as well as the pages of other scholarly journals, have since carried a number of articles further illuminating aspects of gender issues in organizational life. Indeed, it would be difficult today to have a manuscript accepted for publication in a major scholarly journal that ignored women's issues.

Another example is in the *Handbook of Research on Educational Administration,*[73] which appeared in 1988. This landmark scholarly tome included a number of women on its editorial advisory board and it features a chapter on women in educational administration and another on equity. Some other chapters also reveal awareness of, sensitivity to, and knowledge about the new scholarship in women's issues in organizational behavior. Regrettably, a number of other chapters—such as the one on motivation, work satisfaction, and organizational climate—ignore the topic altogether.

The American Educational Research Association, as a matter of policy, has for some years encouraged the participation of women, and their research has been well represented among the presentations of papers and at seminars of its annual meetings. Progress in areas such as these seem to suggest that, at least at the level of awareness among scholars, a good deal of progress has been made. Because this progress is formalized and institutionalized it strongly suggests that the new direction will be enduring and increase in vigor and leverage as time goes on.

Better Understanding of the Differences Between the Ways That Men and Women Do Administrative Work

Consider the description by Anne Wilson Schaef that the "world" of white males and the "world" of females and minority people are very different, in effect creating at least two different cultures.[74] Because the white male culture is dominant, everyone who would deal effectively with that world must learn its culture and how to deal with it. Women, however, and minority people as well, also live in a culture that excludes white males and about which white males know very little. However, recent studies of the world of women have done a great deal to help both women and men to better understand how they see and respond to things in different ways. More than that, these studies explain the ways in which the resulting differences in behavior of men and women administrators may well make women more effective in at least some kinds of administrative work.[75]

For example, the new scholarship raises the distinct possibility that women may, in fact, be better suited for the elementary school principalship than men.[76] But, then, this has been well known for many years but little discussed. A large-scale landmark study of elementary school principals that was published in 1962 drew the following conclusions after analyzing massive amounts of data that had been collected nationwide:

> In considering the question, "Should men be appointed as elementary school principals in preference to women?" it would appear that the answer is probably no.
>
> The study does not present evidence that a woman principal should always be preferred over the man who may also be a candidate. It does indicate, however, that as a class men are not overwhelmingly superior to women as elementary school principals. The evidence appears to favor women if the job of the principal is conceived in a way that values working with teachers and outsiders; being concerned with objectives of teaching, pupil participation, and the evaluation of learning; having knowledge of teaching methods and techniques; and gaining positive reactions from teachers and superiors.[77]

This is a startling finding from some of the most distinguished students of U.S. public schooling who very properly went where the data took them. But it is a finding that was, in effect, buried in obfuscation. As Shakeshaft has drily pointed out, a question more consistent with the data provided by the researchers would be, "Should women be appointed as elementary school principals in preference to men? That answer, based upon their findings, would be *probably yes.*"[78]

Feminocentric research has produced a much larger body of research literature than can be reviewed here. Broad and diverse in scope, it documents significant characteristics of women and their world and how these affect women's performance in the male world of administration. Moreover, it suggests that replacing much of the present dominant male culture of administration with female culture may well improve administrative practices and the effectiveness of schools as well.

As an aspect of the older and larger women's movement, the feminocentric critique of administrative research and the rapid development of the new feminocentric scholarship has already caused reconsideration of many traditional male assumptions. Students of organizational behavior in education now readily concede that the behaviors of men and women school administrators differ in some crucial ways that we are now only beginning to understand. This body of knowledge and thought is in its early stages and it appears likely to endure, to continue to expand, and to develop growing impact over time. How much it will contribute to the breakdown of long-entrenched biases in educational organizations and in the public and also increase opportunities for women to move into positions of leadership in education remains to be seen.

CONCLUSION

The essay "The Study of Administration," which Princeton's Assistant Professor Woodrow Wilson published in *Political Science Quarterly* in the summer of 1887, marked the beginning of serious study of administration. During the century that was to follow, students of organization struggled to do what had never before been done: to increase through systematic inquiry our understanding of organizations and the behavior of people who work in them. Two very clear long-term trends developed that, together, set the stage for where we are now and where we are going.

The Effort to Create an Administrative Science

The search for deep and stable principles believed to be the foundations of administrative thought and practice led first to the quest for a science of administration. The effort was fueled by the conviction that some fundamental rational logic, system, and order must underlie organization. These were to be discovered through objective, value-free scientific research using measurement and expressing descriptions in mathematical terms.

Once these factors were discovered, it was thought, systematic principles for engaging in the practice of administration could be scientifically derived from them. By the middle of the twentieth century, though, many observers were having doubts, not merely about the assumptions of system and rationality in organizations that guided the processes of scientific discovery but doubts that the assumed order and logical system even existed at all. These doubts arose from two main observations. First, that practicing administrators saw little relationship between the reality of organizational life as they experienced it and the theories of organizational life that academicians espoused. Second, scant convincing evidence was generated to support the "scientific" assumptions as being more valid than other insightful, thoughtful views.

Formal challenges to this logical-positivist paradigm began to be published in 1974, the so-called theory movement collapsed, and today students of educational administration, at least, have coalesced around a new paradigm that is in the process of being developed at this time. The new paradigm rejects anthropomorphism, which can lead us to reify organizations and think of them as existing in some sort of free-standing way independent of human beings, when organizations actually are social inventions that exist only in the minds of people. We now think not so much of analyzing organizations in mathematical terms but of making sense of them in human terms. We accept that organizations do not "act" or "think"; people do.

Thus, at the dawn of the second century of organizational study, few seriously believe that the time is yet ripe to develop a science of administration if, indeed, such a science ever will be developed. This does not mean, however, that we have failed either to discover some basic principles of organizational behavior or to develop increased understanding of organizational life. Far from it. The patient theorizing and research carried out over the course of a century has produced a rich legacy of knowledge that administrators can use in practice. But it is not marked by the logical precision and mathematical certitude that the pioneer scholars had expected it to have.

Centrality of the Human Dimension of Organization

Perhaps the most powerful learning to have arisen during the first century of organizational studies concerns what is now obvious: that the key to understanding organization lies in understanding the human and social dimensions. Early scholars emphasized organizational structure, chiefly as a hierarchy of power, and the discipline of inducing those of the lower ranks to submit to the power and authority, perceived as legitimate, of those in the higher ranks of the hierarchy. Toward the middle of the twentieth century, triggered by the Western Electric researches, students of organization began to grasp what Douglas McGregor was later to describe as "the human side of enterprise." This was the realization that human motivation, aspiration, beliefs, and values have wondrous power in determining the effectiveness of efforts to lead and develop organizations.

At first, still obeisant to the then widely held conviction of the legitimacy of hierarchical authority, this was interpreted as "human relations," meaning taking steps to ameliorate and reduce the resistance of workers to their powerlessness. "Human relations," as it was interpreted by administrators, typically became ameliorative inducements for people to submit to organizational authority. The inducements ranged from health insurance plans to simple civility in daily encounters; from providing pleasant working environments to legitimizing the feelings of employees about their work. But through the human relations era, administrators clung to the notion that—while they might act civilly, even kindly, to subordinates—power in the organization is hierarchical and, of a right, ought to be exercised asymmetrically from top down.

But the "battle of the century," both in organizational studies and in the larger world, has been the struggle between centralized authority and individual freedom, between entrenched power elites and ordinary people. Organizations of all kinds, often once revered, are now suspect, viewed with hostility, and often described as oppressive. The ability to establish and maintain organizational discipline through traditional top-down hierarchical exercise of power has been rapidly eroding in all kinds of organizations from nation-states to school districts. The larger canvas, the backdrop, is of course revealed in the collapse of traditional political hegemonies that began to unfold in the late 1980s in Eastern Europe, the former Soviet Union, and South Africa as people around the world demanded greater power and freedom from centralized organizational constraints, greater control over their own lives and destinies.

In the world of U.S. education this theme is insistently echoed, if in muted tones, in oft-repeated themes that call for efforts to improve the performance of schools by restructuring them so as to increase the power of teachers to make critical educational decisions, facilitate collaborative decision making, and create collegial growth-enhancing school cultures. This is, of course, a marked departure from traditional thinking and is based on the conviction that overemphasis on bureaucratic structures, top-down exercise of power, and centralized control have demonstrably failed to produce the organizational results that advocates of traditional organizational theory had claimed it would.

Where We Are and Where We Are Going

At the present time, traditional bureaucratic approaches to organization and the newer approaches that emphasize the human dimensions of organization exist side by side and often compete for the attention and loyalty of educational administrators. Bureaucracy is far from dead in educational organizations, and many people are confident that imposing change from the top down is the most effective way to reform them. On the other hand, nonbureaucratic approaches to organizing and administering have been rapidly gaining support in recent years. These two approaches will continue to compete in the marketplace of ideas for years to come, with the concept of building human capital continuing to gain ground because it so well meets contemporary conditions.

SUGGESTED READING

Edson, Sakre Kennington, *Pushing the Limits: The Female Administrative Aspirant.* Albany: State University of New York Press, 1988.

> A penetrating study that illumines the world of the contemporary woman student of educational administration who aspires to that first administrative appointment. Rich in the actual language of those whose story it tells, this research transports the reader to the world of these women as they see it and understand it.

Meyer, Marshall W., and Associates. *Environments and Organizations.* San Francisco: Jossey-Bass, 1978.

> Structuralism, in the classical bureaucratic tradition, has long dominated thinking about organizations in sociology. This important book marks a sharp departure from that tradition and introduces the newer organizational theorizing that is emerging in that discipline. Excellent chapter on "The Structure of Educational Organizations." Highly recommended.

Mintzberg, Henry, *The Structuring of Organizations.* Englewood Cliffs, NJ: Prentice-Hall, 1979.

> A well-organized, comprehensive, and lucid discussion of contemporary problems of designing and building organizations. Describes the characteristics of five specific kinds of organizations and their implication for administration.

Peters, Thomas J., and Robert H. Waterman, Jr., *In Search of Excellence: Lessons from America's Best-Run Companies.* New York: Harper & Row, 1982.

> Long on the best-seller lists, this is a "must" for those who want to find out how modern organizational theory is being used in the competitive corporate world. Though it focuses on business and industry, it contains a great deal of food for thought for educators.

Schmuck, Patricia A., and W. W. Charters, Jr., eds., *Educational Policy and Management: Sex Differentials.* New York: Academic Press, 1981.

> A scholarly sourcebook on significant policy issues in sex equity in U.S. public schooling.

Shakeshaft, Charol, *Women in Educational Administration.* Newbury Park, CA: Sage Publications, 1987.

> A briskly written, well-researched survey of the "state of the art" that has received a respectful and responsive hearing from the community of scholars in educational administration.

NOTES

1. Donald A. Schön, *Educating the Reflective Practitioner* (San Francisco: Jossey-Bass, 1987), p. 3.
2. Ibid., pp. 4–5.
3. Wayne K. Hoy and Cecil G. Miskel, *Educational Administration,* 2nd ed. (New York: Random House, 1982), p. 82.
4. T. Barr Greenfield, "Theory About Organization: A New Perspective and Its Implication for Schools," in *Administering Education: International Challenge,* ed. M. G. Hughes (London: Athlone, 1975), p. 71.
5. Ibid., p. 81.
6. Robert W. Heller, James A. Conway, and S. L. Jacobson, "Here's Your Blunt Critique of Administrative Preparation," *The Executive Educator* (September 1988), 18–30.
7. Roland S. Barth and Terrence E. Deal, *The Effective Principal: A Research Summary* (Reston, VA: Association of Secondary School Principals, 1982).
8. James Bryant Conant, *Two Modes of Thought: My Encounters With Science and Education* (New York: A Trident Press Book, 1964).
9. Carl R. Rogers, "Toward a Science of the Person," *Journal of Humanistic Psychology* (Fall 1963).
10. Arthur Blumberg, *School Administration as a Craft: Foundations of Practice* (Boston: Allyn and Bacon, 1988).
11. Charles E. Bidwell, "The School as a Formal Organization," in *Handbook of Organizations,* ed. James G. March (Chicago: Rand McNally & Company, 1965).
12. Karl E. Weick, "Educational Organizations as Loosely Coupled Systems," *Administrative Science Quarterly,* 21 (March 1976), 1.
13. John W. Meyer and Brian Rowan, "The Structure of Educational Organizations," in *Organizational Environments: Ritual and Rationality,* eds. John W. Meyer and W. Richard Scott (Beverly Hills, CA: Sage Publications, 1983), p. 74.
14. For examples see Van Cleve Morris, Robert L. Crowson, Emanuel Hurwitz, Jr., and Cynthia Porter-Gehrie, *The Urban Principal: Discretionary Decision Making in a Large Educational Organization* (Chicago: College of Education, University of Illinois at Chicago Circle, 1981); and N. A. Newberg and A. G. Glatthom, *Instructional Leadership: Four Ethnographic Studies of Junior High School Principals* (final report of grant number NIE G–81–0088, 1983).
15. Meyer and Rowan, "The Structure of Educational Organizations," p. 75.
16. Economists have long recognized the value of human resources. See, for example, Gary S. Becker, "Investment in Human Capital: A Theoretical Analysis, *The Journal of Political Economy* (Supplement), 70 (October 1962); and Theodore W. Schultz, "Capital Formation by Education," *The Journal of Political Economy,* 68 (December 1960).
17. Stephen P. Robbins, *The Administrative Process: Integrating Theory and Practice* (Englewood Cliffs, NJ: Prentice-Hall, 1975), pp. 425–26.
18. Chris Argyris, "Human Problems with Budgets," *Harvard Business Review,* 31 (January-February 1953), 97–110.
19. Rensis Likert, *The Human Organization: Its Management and Value* (New York: McGraw-Hill Book Company, 1967), p. 148.
20. Ray A. Killian, *Human Resource Management* (New York: AMACOM, 1976), p. 140.
21. William A. Firestone and Bruce L. Wilson, *Using Bureaucratic and Cultural Linkages to Improve Instruction: The High School Principal's Contribution* (Eugene: Center for Educational Policy and Management, College of Education, University of Oregon, 1983), pp. 14–15.
22. Terrence E. Deal and A. Kennedy, *Corporate Cultures: The Rites and Rituals of Corporate Life* (Reading, MA: Addison-Wesley, 1982); and Lee G. Bolman and Terrence E. Deal, *Modern Approaches to Understanding and Managing Organizations* (San Francisco: Jossey-Bass, 1984).
23. Thomas J. Peters and Robert H. Waterman, Jr., *In Search of Excellence: Lessons from America's Best-Run Companies* (New York: Harper & Row, Publishers, 1982).
24. Rosabeth Moss Kanter, *The Change Masters: Innovation and Entrepreneurship in the American Corporation* (New York: Simon & Schuster, 1983).
25. Edgar H. Schein, *Organizational Culture and Leadership,* (San Francisco: Jossey-Bass, 1985).

26. S. C. Purkey and M. S. Smith, "School Reform: The District Policy Implications of the Effective Schools Literature," *The Elementary School Journal,* 85 (December 1985), 353–89.

27. Ibid., p. 355.

28. Ibid., p. 355.

29. Ibid., p. 357.

30. Ibid., p. 357.

31. L. C. Stedman, "It's Time We Changed the Effective Schools Formula," *Phi Delta Kappan* (November 1987), 215–24.

32. This discussion follows the analysis of Purkey and Smith, "School Reform," pp. 358–59.

33. National Commission on Excellence in Education (Washington, DC: Government Printing Office, 1983).

34. Edgar H. Schein, *Organizational Culture and Leadership* (San Francisco: Jossey-Bass, 1985), p. 14.

35. J. Bernard, "Afterword," in J. A. Sherman and E. T. Beck, eds., *The Prism of Sex* (Madison: University of Wisconsin Press, 1979), pp. 267–75.

36. Charol Shakeshaft, *Women in Educational Administration* (Newbury Park, CA: Sage Publications, 1987), p. 150.

37. Ibid., p. 148.

38. Ibid., p. 150.

39. Ibid., p. 149.

40. Dorothy E. Smith, "A Peculiar Eclipsing: Women's Exclusion from Man's Culture," *Women's Studies International Quarterly,* 1, no. 4, 281–95.

41. Nancy Hoffman, *Woman's "True" Profession: Voices from the History of Teaching* (Old Westbury, NY: Feminist Press, 1981), 2–17, 35–56.

42. If androcentrism is "the practice of viewing the world and shaping reality from a male lens" then, conversely, we can take feminocentrism to be the practice of viewing the world and shaping reality from a female lens. See Shakeshaft, *Women in Educational Administration,* p. 150, and Carol A. B. Warren, *Gender Issues in Field Research* (Newbury Park, CA: Sage Publications, 1988), p. 8.

43. Charol Shakeshaft, "The Gender Gap in Research in Educational Administration," *Educational Administration Quarterly,* 25 (1989), 324–37.

44. Misogyny means the hatred of women.

45. Shakeshaft, *Women in Educational Administration,* p. 197.

46. Ibid.

47. Ibid.

48. Ibid., p. 198.

49. Ibid.

50. Patricia A. Schmuck, ed., *Women Educators: Employees of Schools in Western Countries* (Albany: State University of New York Press, 1987).

51. Gabrielle Lakomski, review of Patricia Schmuck, *Women Educators,* in *The Journal of Educational Administration,* 26, no. 1. (March 1988), 117–20.

52. Charol Shakeshaft and Irene Nowell, "Research on Theories, Concepts and Models of Behavior: The Influence of Gender," *Issues in Education,* 2 (Winter 1984), 186–206.

53. J. W. Getzels, "A Psycho-Sociological Framework for the Study of Educational Administration," *Harvard Educational Review,* 22 (1952), 225–46.

54. Shakeshaft, *Women in Educational Administration,* p. 158.

55. Charol Shakeshaft and M. Hanson, "Androcentric Bias in the Educational Administration Quarterly," *Educational Administration Quarterly,* 22 (1986), 68–92.

56. New York: Harper & Row, Publishers, 1983.

57. Daniel E. Griffiths, "Administrative Theory," in Norman J. Boyan, ed., *Handbook of Research on Educational Administration* (New York: Longman, 1988), p. 47.

58. Jill Y. Miller, "Lonely at the Top," *School & Community,* 72 (Summer 1986), 9–11; M. M. McCarthy, G. Kuh, and J. Beckman, "Characteristics and Attitudes of Doctoral Students in Educational Administration," *Phi Delta Kappan,* 61 (1979), 200–203; and Sakre Oller, "Female Doctoral Students in Educational Administration: Who Are They?" *Sex Equity in Educational Leadership Report 7* (Eugene, OR: Center for Educational Policy and Management, 1978).

59. G. S. Johnston, C. C. Yeakey, and S. E. Moore, "An Analysis of the Employment of Women in Professional Administrative Positions in Public Education," *Planning and Changing,* 11 (1980), 115–32.

60. J. Stockard, "Public Prejudice Against Women School Administrators: The Possibility of Change," *Educational Administration Quarterly,* 15 (1979), 83–96.

61. K. D. Lyman and J. J. Speizer, "Advancing in School Administration: A Pilot Project for Women," *Harvard Education Review,* 50 (1980), 25–35.

62. F. I. Ortiz, "Scaling the Hierarchical System in School Administration: A Case Analysis," *Urban Review,* 11 (1979), 111–25.

63. A. T. Elshof and E. Tomlinson, "Eliminating Stress for Women Administrators," *Journal of the National Association for Women Deans, Administrators, and Counselors,* 44 (1981), 37–41.

64. A. Stent, "Academe's New Girl Network," *Change,* 10 (1978), 18–21.

65. A. W. Villadsen, and M. W. Tack, "Combining Home and Career Responsibilities: The Methods Used by Women Executives in Higher Education." *Journal of the National Association of Women Deans, Administrators, and Counselors,* 45 (1981), 20–25.

66. Edson, *Pushing the Limits.*

67. Ibid., p. 146.

68. E. Jones and X. Montenegro, *Women and Minorities in School Administration* (Arlington, VA: American Association of School Administrators, 1982), 5–15.

69. Colleen S. Bell and Susan E. Chase, "Women Superintendents and School Boards: Their Experiences and Perceptions of Gender Issues." Paper presented at the annual meeting of the American Educational Research Association, 1988. A revised version of this paper, entitled "Organizational Influences on Women's Experience in the Superintendency," *Peabody Journal,* is in press.

70. Ibid.

71. Rosabeth Moss Kanter, *Men and Women of the Corporation* (New York: Basic Books, Publishers, 1977).

72. Bell and Chase, "Women Superintendents," p. 10.

73. Norman J. Boyan, ed., *Handbook of Research on Educational Administration* (New York: Longman, 1988).

74. Anne Wilson Schaef, *Women's Reality: An Emerging Female System in the White Male Society* (Minneapolis: Winston Press, 1981).

75. J. M. Frasher and R. S. Frasher, "Educational Administration: A Feminine Profession," *Educational Administration Quarterly,* 15 (1979), 1–15.

76. A. Fishel and J. Pottker, "Performance of Women Principals: A Review of Behavioral and Attitudinal Studies," in J. Pottker and A. Fishel, eds., *Sex Bias in the Schools* (Cranbury, NJ: Associated University Presses, 1977).

77. John K. Hemphill, Daniel E. Griffiths, and Norman Frederiksen, *Administrative Performance and Personality* (New York: Teachers College Press, 1962).

78. Shakeshaft, *Women in Educational Administration,* p. 168.

Motivation

CHAPTER 4

ABOUT THIS CHAPTER

Having described organizational behavior as arising from interactions between the person in the organization and characteristics of the organizational environment, or $B = f(p \cdot e)$, this chapter focuses on the person—individual—in that equation. The remaining chapters of the book focus on characteristics of the organizational environment in the equation.

THE MEANING AND PATTERNS OF MOTIVATION

Motivation deals with explanations of why people do the things they do. Why, for example, do some teachers regularly come to work and do as little as necessary, whereas others are full of energy and ideas and throw themselves zealously into the job? Why do some principals seem to focus only on the day-to-day operations in the school with no apparent vision of where the school should be headed, whereas others seem to embrace a clear, coherent vision of the school as it ought to be and pursue it consistently over the course of years? Why are some professors boring, monotonous lecturers whose classes students avoid, whereas other professors are so enthusiastic, vibrant, and creative that their classes are interesting, always fresh, and are so popular with students that they are closed out early during registration?

For millennia, the mysteries of why people behave as they do have fascinated dramatists, artists, writers, composers, philosophers, theologians, and other observers of the human condition, as the libraries and museums of the world attest. For a century now, scholars have added their efforts to probing the enigma of human motivation and have produced a body of literature that is staggering in scope and size and illuminating as well. From all this we have learned a great deal about the links between motivation and human behavior, and we still have more to learn. This chapter discusses some of what we know and the pragmatic implications of that knowledge for the practice of leadership in educational organizations.

Although many theories of motivation exist, with new ones appearing every year, and much disagreement about them among scholars, there is also substantial agreement on what we are talking about when discussing motivation. Scholars generally agree, for example, that when we observe the variation in human behavior in organizations, at least three motivational patterns are evident.

First Pattern: Direction in Making Choices

One of the first indicators of motivation is the apparent pattern of choices that individuals make when confronted with an array of possible alternatives. When a person attends to one thing rather than others, the observer may make some motivational inference from the behavior of choosing but, of course, cannot know what actually caused the choice to be made. For example, one teacher might habitually arrive at school early in the morning, pick up the mail promptly, and proceed briskly to the classroom to prepare for the day's work so as to be ready and relaxed before the students arrive. Another teacher might wander in much later, chat and socialize in the office until the last moment, then dash to the classroom to begin work by fumbling with papers as the students sit at their desks waiting. A similar example is the professor who, seeing the academic job as demanding only three days a week on campus, regularly spends two days on the golf course or at the tennis club, whereas a colleague spends every spare moment studying and preparing articles for publication in academic journals that not only do not pay for them but reject three times more manuscripts than they publish.

Second Pattern: Persistence

A second critical indicator of motivation is the persistence with which one pursues the chosen course of action. One dimension of persistence is the amount of time a person devotes to the chosen activity. Whether it is refinishing antiques or creating plans for a new teaching project, some people will work intensely for long hours seeking to produce meticulous, high-quality results, whereas others may give the task a "lick and a promise," consider the result good enough to get by, and let it go at that. Indeed, an individual may show great persistence in pursuing one activity meticulously and show remarkably little persistence in pursuing another. Another dimension of persistence is observed when an individual returns to a task time and again to achieve the desired results. Some teachers, for example, never seem to have the job done and frequently take work home to spend more hours on it, whereas others usually close up shop as soon as the buses have left and won't think about their work again until tomorrow. Some professors pull old yellowed lecture notes from the file year after year, whereas others spend many hours every year not merely editing, revising, and polishing their lectures but creating new methods of instruction in the hope of making classes not only more informative but more interesting as well.

Third Pattern: Intensity

The intensity with which a person attends to doing something is a third behavioral indicator that seems to be linked to motivation. One person can work with apparent high energy, seemingly concentrating intensely, engrossed in the work, whereas another might be observed to be much less intensely involved when attending to a task. Observations of intensity have to be interpreted more carefully than either direction or persistence, because factors beyond the control of the individual may be involved, such as the environment and the skill of the individual. For example, observing work behavior in environments where there are many uncontrolled interruptions, as is common in some schools, makes it difficult to determine whether the level of intensity is a matter of individual choice or the result of environmental disturbance. Similarly, an individual may be observed as being little involved as a participant in meetings, apparently merely waiting quietly for the time to pass that will bring the meeting to a close. The problem here could easily be environmental, such as a social climate in the meeting not being conducive to participation; or it may be that the individual has never developed the behavioral attitudes and skills that one needs to participate confidently in the give-and-take of effective meetings; or it may simply be that the topic under consideration is neither interesting nor relevant to the individual.

THE EXTRINSIC-INTRINSIC DEBATE

Two major approaches have dominated thinking about motivation in organizational behavior during this century. One has been described as *The Great Jackass Fallacy*.[1] That is the age-old metaphor of the carrot and the stick, which prescribes that a combination of proferring some mix of rewards and punishments is a way to motivate people in organizational life. It is associated with behaviorist psychology in which external control of the individual is emphasized.

The other approach, associated with both cognitive psychology and humanist psychology, emphasizes the psychic energy of internal thoughts and feelings as the primary source of motivation.

Extrinsic, or Behaviorist, Views

Managers have traditionally sought to motivate people with a carrot and a stick. They long ago found that people who are hurt tend to move in order to avoid pain and people who are rewarded tend to repeat the behavior that brought the reward. This is a behaviorist concept of motivation, and it has long been highly influential in management thought. Managers using such techniques would say, "We're motivating the employees!"

The behaviorist view of motivation, that people can be motivated through manipulation of positive reinforcers (the carrot) and negative reinforcers (the stick), has been widely embraced and used in educational organizations. Merit pay plans, demands for accountability, emphasis on formal supervision, annual performance reviews tied to reappointment to position, and "teacher recognition days" are but a few of the many ways that this motivational concept is routinely used in public school praxis. In the same vein, universities often practice an "up-or-out" policy to motivate newly appointed junior faculty members. They are commonly given a stipulated number of years to demonstrate growing research production through publication of their works; at the end of the time period, they know that they may be either rewarded for their behavior by being promoted and granted tenure or punished by dismissal.

Intrinsic Views of Motivation

Some contend that the behaviorist approach has nothing to do with motivation. As Frederick Herzberg said of the carrot-and-the-stick approach, "Hell, you're not motivating them. You're moving them."[2] Herzberg's observation points to a major criticism of the behaviorist approach to motivation: it in fact does not deal with motivation at all.

The view is that although people can be *controlled* by external forces such as rewards and punishments, a crucial factor in the *motivation* of people lies within the individuals themselves. The cognitive and humanistic views of motivation spring from an understanding of people as unfolding and developing both physiologically and psychologically from biological givens. The internal capacities of individuals, primarily emotional and cognitive, give rise to feelings, aspirations, perceptions, attitudes, and thoughts, and it is these that can be motivating or demotivating. In this view, motivation is thought of as creating conditions in the organization that facilitate and enhance the likelihood that the internal capacities of members will mature both intellectually and emotionally, thus increasing their inner motivation. In sum, the behaviorist tends to view motivation as something that one does *to* people, whereas the cognitive or humanist tends to view motivation as tapping the inner drives of people by creating growth-enhancing environments.

INDIVIDUAL AND GROUP MOTIVATION

Let's now focus on the motivation of people in organizations, as distinguished from the more general, broader concept of motivation of individuals qua individuals. A crucial point to remember in understanding *organizational* behavior is that, as a member of an organization, the person does not act alone and independently: the organization member always acts as a member of a group, and that concept is probably central to understanding organizational behavior. Groups are dynamic social systems that establish interdependent relationships between and among people.

Thus, if you find yourself hurrying along a crowded city street you would hardly think of the throng as a group of which you are a member. On the other hand, if you step to the curb and take your place in a queue to wait for a bus, you have joined a group, albeit a primitive one. The members of that group, the bus queue, share certain purposes, values, and expectations for behavior that bond them in common purpose and modify not only your own behavior but your attitudes and beliefs as well. Thus, if someone had the temerity to cut in line near the head of the queue, you would probably become concerned and join with fellow group members in remonstrating with the individual in an effort to get him to abide by the behavioral norms tacitly shared by the group.

The character and quality of the group's internal dynamics are often described in terms of group cohesion and morale. These dynamics of the group give rise, in turn, to basic assumptions and values that are shared between and among the members of the group as "truth" and "reality." The latter point, which is the essence of group climate and culture, is discussed in greater depth in the next chapter.

The power of group norms in motivating people at work, having been first clearly identified in the Western Electric studies more than sixty years ago, is well established in the literature of organizational behavior and is widely understood and accepted. Let's take a moment to consider once again and more exactly what was learned in those studies.

THE WESTERN ELECTRIC STUDIES REVISITED

Most students of education have heard something about the Hawthorne studies or the Western Electric studies, if in no other way than to have learned about the so-called Hawthorne effect, about which I shall say more in a moment. This classic research has had such profound impact on the understanding of motivation at work, and has been so widely misunderstood in educational circles, that we should take a moment to review it here. This discussion draws on only two of the many studies that composed this very sizable research project.

The Illumination Studies

The Hawthorne Works of the Western Electric Company, located in Cicero near Chicago, was chosen as the site for an experimental study that was started in 1924 and ended ten years later. This particular site was selected for the experiment largely because the management of Western Electric was considered enlightened and likely to be cooperative with the investigators. The purpose of the study was to find out how much illumination was required to achieve the maximum output from workers.

> Two groups of employees doing similar work under similar conditions were chosen, and records of output were kept for each group. The intensity of the light under which one group worked was varied, while that under which the other group worked was

held constant. By this method, the investigators hoped to isolate from the effect of other variables, the effect of changes in the intensity of illumination on the rate of output.[3]

But in the early stages of the research the investigators were disappointed; it soon became obvious that no simple relationship existed between the intensity of illumination and the workers' rate of output. "The employees [reacted] to changes in light intensity in the way they assumed they were expected to react," George Homans reported, "That is, when light intensity was increased, they were expected to produce more; when it was decreased, they were expected to produce less. A further experiment was designed to demonstrate this point."[4] The lightbulbs were changed so that the workers were allowed to assume that there would be more light when, in fact, other bulbs of the same power had been installed. Of course, as we now know, each change of bulbs resulted in some increase in output by the workers regardless of the level of illumination that they provided. Clearly, the workers in the experimental group were responding to *their perceptions* of the expectations of the experimenters and not to the changes in the physical environment. Thus, the workers were responding to *psychological* factors that motivated their behavior at work and, at the time of the experiments, the nature of these psychological factors was unknown to the investigators.

The significance of this study was not lost on the researchers. Whereas traditional management theory would have posited that changes in the physical environment would have an impact on worker productivity, this experiment showed a direct relationship between productivity and *psychological* phenomena, such as the expectations of others and being the focus of attention. This is sometimes called the "Hawthorne effect," which has often been misinterpreted by many educators as suggesting that merely paying attention to people, changing some things in their environment, and expecting higher achievement from them will increase their motivation. As we shall see, there is much more to it than that.

The Relay Inspection Group Studies

After the study on the relationship between illumination and productivity was concluded, leaving more questions than answers, a new experimental study was organized in the Hawthorne Works involving workers who assembled telephone relays. The researchers used a control group, which worked in the regular shop, and an experimental group, which was given a separate work area. To initiate the experiment,

> the operators who had been chosen to take part were called in for an interview in the office of the Superintendent of the Inspection Branch [remember, this was in 1927, and the workers all were women]. . . . The nature of the test was carefully explained to these girls and they readily consented to take part in it. . . . They were assured that the object of the test was to determine the effect of certain changes in working conditions, such as rest periods, midmorning lunches, and shorter working hours. They were especially cautioned to work at a comfortable pace, and under no circumstances to try to make a race of the test. This conference was only the first of many that were

to be held during the course of the experiment. Whenever any experimental change was planned, the girls were called in, the purpose of the change was explained to them, and their comments were requested. Certain suggested changes which did not meet with their approval were abandoned.[5]

Working methodically for over a year, the researchers kept careful production records while trying different experimental interventions: rest pauses, special lunch periods, a shorter working day, and a shorter working week. Throughout the period of the experimental work, the output rose slowly and steadily. In each period of the experiment, output was higher than in the preceding period. Finally, the work conditions of the group were, with the consent of the workers, returned to the same as they had been prior to the start of the research (no rest periods, no special lunch periods, a regular-length workday and workweek). The result: productivity *continued to rise*. In fact, "the output of the group continued to rise until it established itself on a high plateau from which there was no descent until the time of discouragement and deepening economic depression which preceded the end of the test" in 1933.[6] In sum, the group had (1) become more productive and (2) had maintained that high productivity even after the experimental interventions were taken away. If rest periods and shorter working hours, plus the "special attention" of being in an experimental group, could not account for the change, what could?

Central Findings of the Studies

It took a number of people some years to analyze all the data and gradually put together a picture of what had happened. The salient facts are these:

1. The workers liked the experimental situation and considered it fun.

2. The new form of supervision (encouraging them to work at a normal pace and not to try to hurry) "made it possible for them to work freely and without anxiety."[7]

3. The workers knew that what they did was important and that results were expected.

4. The workers were consulted about planned changes, often by the superintendent himself, and during that process were encouraged to express their views and were, in fact, permitted to veto some ideas before they were ever implemented.

5. As a result, the group itself had changed and developed during the course of the experiment. Though the last step of the experiment was an attempt to return the group to the original conditions of work by taking away the experimental rest periods, new hours, and the like, it was in fact impossible to return the group to its original state because the group itself had been transformed. It had become more cohesive, it had developed a distinctive esprit, and it was functioning at a significantly more mature level than it had been in the beginning.

In sum,

> the women were made to feel that they were an important part of the company. . . .
> They had become participating members of a congenial, cohesive work group . . . that
> elicited feelings of affiliation, competence, and achievement. These needs, which had
> long gone unsatisfied at work, were now being fulfilled. The women worked harder
> and more effectively than they had previously.[8]

Or, in the vernacular of today's educational reform, the women had been empow-
ered, had participated in making decisions that were important to them and their
work, had been treated in ways that fostered personal feelings of dignity and respect, and had gained "ownership" of their work and how it was performed. However it is expressed, clearly this experience had transformed the group into a much
more effective team than it had been before, as the sustained increase in productivity over time showed.

Impact of the Studies

One very interesting aspect of this research is that at the time, when it was not unknown for companies routinely to send goons to beat up dissident workers, it was
so unusual for a company to relate to workers in these ways that many years passed
before it dawned on anyone (except a very few advanced scholars) what had happened in the Hawthorne plant during those experiments. For decades, many students
of organization and management chose to believe that the Hawthorne studies
showed that if you pay a little attention to people by changing some of their working conditions, their motivation will take an upward tick and productivity will increase. This misreading of the research is often called the Hawthorne effect.

However, it is now clear that the Western Electric studies set the stage for the
evolution of widespread research seeking to better understand the nature and needs
of human beings at work and to apply this knowledge to the development of more
effective organizations. Drawing on that large and still growing body of research,
plus extensive practical experience in applying the emerging new knowledge to a
variety of organizations, we now understand that the higher productivity achieved
during the Western Electric research resulted from the fact that under participative
leadership the groups of workers themselves developed greater cohesiveness, higher
morale, and values that were highly motivating. Once collaborative group processes
had been established, the individual participants were no longer merely working
side-by-side, but became interrelated in ways that were unique to that specific
group. Today, of course, that is commonly called teamwork and it is at the heart of
motivational concepts in work groups. Moreover, as the Western Electric studies
showed, once established, teamwork can become not only a powerful motivator but
one that tends to endure. Though school boards, school administrators, and managers who like to view themselves as being tough, failed for decades to understand
the power and significance of this simple, crucial discovery even as it was being re-
confirmed in study after study over the years, it eventually emerged in the 1980s as

the central idea in the transformation of organizational life and leadership in U.S. business and industry and, eventually, education.

Contemporary Views of the Western Electric Studies

The Western Electric studies are arguably the most seminal research of this century on organizational behavior in the workplace. They illumined a whole new approach to understanding the subject and paved the way for such modern notions as participative management, democracy in the workplace, empowerment, and more. As one would expect with any major research study, however, sixty years of close study has revealed some weaknesses and oversights.

An Androcentric Bias

Recent critiques of the Western Electric studies have pointed out that the research is marred by androcentric bias, which was inevitable given the period in history in which the research was done. For example, I have pointed out that in one major phase of the research the workers were women and the managers were men. When the studies were done, in the 1920s and early 1930s, the power relationships between managers and workers were far more unequal than they are today. This was heightened, of course, by the inequality of power that was socially sanctioned between men and women at that time. There is little question that this fact, unknowable at the time, may have been more influential in interpreting the results than has been heretofore imagined.

The fundamental importance of the Western Electric studies, however, should not be obscured by this valid criticism: they drew attention to the psychological aspects of organizational behavior with such power and authority as to have literally changed the course of management and administration history.

INDIVIDUAL DIFFERENCES

Thus far, the discussion has dwelt on some notable *environmental* factors in the basic organizational behavior equation, $B = f(p \cdot e)$, and we turn now to a discussion of useful ways of thinking about the differences in the intrinsic characteristics of the *person* in that dynamic concept. One question about motivation that commonly arises is what gets people "turned on" or "turned off." Why is it, for example, that one person will select a particular thing to do, stick with it, and work intensively on it whereas another person might show no interest whatever? Psychologists call this "turning on" to something, this energizing of human behavior, *arousal*: it is clearly an internal aspect of self, seemingly involving emotional processes as well as cognitive processes, a characteristic that lies close to the personality of the individual. Clearly, then, the individual brings unique inner personal characteristics to the dynamic social interaction processes of the group. The characteristics of these internal capacities literally determine how one perceives the environment and makes judgments about it.

In Praise of Diversity

In today's world, when all people of good will seek to avoid the bigotry of stereotyping and labeling of others, any effort to type or categorize people tends to be met with suspicion. Yet the fact is "that people are different from each other, and no amount of getting after them is going to change them. Nor is there any reason to change them, because the differences are probably good, not bad. People are different in fundamental ways. They *want* different things; they have different motives, purposes, aims, values, needs, drives, impulses, urges. Nothing is more fundamental than that. They *believe* differently: they think, cognize, conceptualize, perceive, understand, comprehend, and cogitate differently."[9] Because such inner attributes—cognitions, urges, values, perceptions, and so on—are crucial in prompting us to say what we say and do what we do, the individual differences between and among us can and do evoke a vast range of behaviors. From those behaviors we can deduce a great deal about the motivations of individuals, and create useful descriptive categories. But one must be extremely cautious not to slip into the error of labeling one behavioral style as good and another bad.

Because what is being discussed here is the inner characteristics of the person, their temperament or personality, we are unsure of the extent to which they are either learned or innate. We are therefore unsure of the extent to which they can be intentionally modified. Some take a fairly absolutist view of this, comparing psychological type to other fixed characteristics. For example, as short persons cannot make themselves tall and one cannot change the pattern of fingerprints or the color of the eyes, one cannot change the inner drives and attributes. Others believe that some modification of inner characteristics may be possible but always at the risk of distorting, destroying, or scarring the original instead of transforming it into something new.

However, a problem in all this is the all-too-common tendency to confuse various ways of perceiving, thinking, feeling, and behaving as shortcomings or flaws that need to be corrected. Keirsey and Bates reminded us of the Pygmalion story from Greek mythology and cautioned that efforts to sculpt others so that they conform to our own standard of perfection are doomed to failure at the outset.[10] Educators deal with this all the time: for example, we may understand, and perhaps accept, the idea of multiple intelligences, yet in our schools there is powerful social and cultural pressure to put a premium on certain kinds of intelligences, especially the linguistic and logical-mathematical, and value the others less in varying degrees. Thus, the logic of American cultural traditions prods schools to emphasize and extol in the official curriculum languages, math, and sciences for all students and tends to marginalize music, the arts, and bodily kinesthetic opportunities for development. In the minds of many Americans, for example, a "good" kindergarten curriculum stresses formal instruction in reading, language, and arithmetic and "wastes" little time on activities in which children move about, engage others in play, and participate in physical activities.

So we proceed from the assumption that people are fundamentally different in many ways, that we can understand important patterns of those differences, and that we can learn to make that understanding work productively for us. The converse assumption would be that people are, or should be, fundamentally all alike and our goal is to get them to behave alike. That, however, appears to be a twentieth century confusion that arises from the growth of democracy in the Western world: the idea that if we are equals, then we must be alike.[11] As the twenty-first century approaches, we celebrate a different idea: as we are equals, then we may be different from one another.

Understanding and accepting diversity between and among people in a non-judgmental way is important to understanding and working with organizational behavior in education. In praxis, this means that educational administration and leadership emphasizes creating environments in organizations that simultaneously

+ foster and enhance the growth and development of participants in terms of their own perceptions, needs, aspirations, and self-fulfillment and

+ accept the fact that not only do individuals differ from one another but that this diversity can be a source of great strength to the organization.

Archetypes

We commonly make the great diversity between and among people manageable by thinking of individuals as archetypes: "Oh," we say, "He's that kind of guy!" or "Did you hear what she asked? That's vintage Harriet Smith!" Psychologists do the same thing.

+ Howard Gardner described the differences between and among people in terms of seven kinds of intelligence.

+ Based on the work of Carl Jung, many psychologists describe individuals in terms of their temperaments, or personality types.

+ Not a few psychologists, such as Carol Gilligan, have used gender as a lens to examine and understand individual differences in organizational life.

HUMAN INTELLIGENCE

One of the ways in which many readers of this book know that people differ is in their intelligences. In his landmark work on the nature of human intelligence—or, more correctly, human intelligences—Howard Gardner drew attention to the shift during the twentieth century of philosophers and psychologists from focusing on the external objects of the physical world in explaining human behavior to focusing on preoccupation with the mind, and especially cognitive thought, that depends so heavily on symbols such as language, mathematics, the visual arts, body language, and other human symbols.[12] Gardner's great contribution to explaining human thought and behavior has been to give us a new way to think about intelligence: not as a single characteristic, nor even as a group of characteristics that can be summed up with a single measure called Intelligence Quotient. Gardner explained that there are several kinds of intelligence that are independent of one another, yet each of which enables one to engage in intellectual activity in different ways.

Gardner's Seven Dimensions of Intelligence

Howard Gardner described seven dimensions of intelligence:[13]

+ *Linguistic:* the ability to understand words and how they are combined to produce useful language. Important, of course, for writers, poets, journalists.

+ *Logical-mathematical:* the ability to see patterns, order, and relationships in seemingly unrelated events in the world around us and to engage in logical chains of reasoning. One thinks of scientists and mathematicians.

+ *Musical:* the ability to discern pitch, melody, tone, rhythm, and other qualities of musical symbolism and integrate them into intellectual activity such as reasoning. Musicians, composers, and rap artists come to mind.

+ *Spatial:* the ability to accurately perceive and think in terms of the visual qualities of the world and its dimensions and to manipulate and transform them in creative ways. Important for architects, artists, sculptors, and navigators.

+ *Bodily-kinesthetic intelligence:* the ability to control one's bodily motions and the capacity to handle objects skillfully[14] and to combine these into a language with which one may express one's self "with wit, style, and an aesthetic flair"[15] as Norman Mailer said with boxers in mind. Gardner's example of mimes, particularly Marcel Marceau, makes vivid the concept of bodily-kinesthetic intelligence, but one thinks also of dancers, figure skaters, and many athletes.

+ *Intrapersonal intelligence:* the ability to access and understand one's inner personal self: feelings, reactions, aspirations. This is the self-aware individual who understands and is comfortable with his or her own idiosyncratic personal emotions and is able to differentiate between and among feelings and use them in thinking about the world. One thinks of novelists and playwrights such as Alice Walker, Eugene O'Neill, Marcel Proust, and James Baldwin who used autobiographical themes to explore the world; cinema *auteurs* ranging from Marcel Pagnol to Woody Allen; and gurus whose wisdom transcends their own provincialism.

+ *Interpersonal intelligence:* "the ability to notice and make distinctions among other individuals and, in particular, among their moods, temperaments, motivations, and intentions."[16] This ability "permits a skilled adult to read the intentions and desires—even when these have been hidden—of many other individuals and, potentially, to act upon this knowledge—for example, by influencing a group of disparate individuals to behave along desired lines."[17] Outstanding examples would be Martin Luther King, Jr., Eleanor Roosevelt, and Mohandas Gandhi. Individuals who possess high levels of interpersonal intelligence might find it useful in exercising educational leadership, but it appears to be a form of intelligence rarely sought by university programs of preparation in educational administration.

Gardner's description of intelligences illuminates some important ways in which people bring different inner resources to the behavioral equation in organizations. It is important to remember that these different kinds of intelligences are present in each of us, but that the mix in each of us is so idiosyncratic that in any group one will find some range of individual differences. This suggests that an approach to motivation that fails to take these differences into account is flawed at the outset.

It is, moreover, important to remember that these intelligences are human characteristics, not options that individuals choose. As Gardner showed, though one's intelligences develop over time as one matures physiologically, their development also depends to a great extent on learning from the environment. Thus, one does not learn to read, write, and calculate simply because one has matured but because along the way one has seen others read, write, and calculate.[18] This underscores the importance of interaction between the person and the culture in the individual's environment in shaping human behavior.

In describing the historical underpinnings of his theory of multiple intelligences, Gardner recounted the noted meeting between William James, the first world-renowned psychology scholar from the United States, and Sigmund Freud, which took place in Worcester in 1909. The occasion was Freud's only trip to the United States, which was at the invitation of G. Stanley Hall, the psychologist who was then president of Clark University. The meeting between Freud, who had already reached celebrity in Europe, and the aging James is acclaimed in the history of the development of psychology because it set the stage for the eventual emergence of modern psychology that was to transcend the radical behaviorism that was so dominant in the United States at that time.

"What united Freud and James," Gardner explains, "and what set them apart from the mainstream of psychology both on the Continent and in the United States, was a belief in the importance, the centrality, of the individual self—a conviction that psychology must be built around the concept of the person, his personality, his growth, his fate. Moreover, both scholars deemed the capacity for self-growth to be an important one, upon which depended the possibility of coping with one's surroundings."[19] Curiously, Gardner did not mention the presence of another person on that historic occasion who was to play a pivotal role in explaining human personality and its capacity for self-growth and adaptation to the environment. Carl Jung, then 34 and a close collaborator of Freud's, would soon thereafter break away from his older colleague and create new ways of understanding the differences between and among individuals that have proven to be invaluable in understanding organizational behavior.

TEMPERAMENT AND ORGANIZATIONAL BEHAVIOR

Early psychology was dominated by the notion that people are motivated from within by a single instinct. The scholar's challenge was to identify that instinct. To Freud it was Eros, which manifested itself in different guises at different times. Adler thought that the motivating instinct was to acquire power. Others thought that the desire for social belonging was the central motivational instinct. To the existentialists it was the search for Self that informed and drove our behavior. "Each appealed to instinct as purpose, and each made one instinct primary for everybody."[20]

Carl Jung's masterwork on motivation revealed that this was not so, that individuals are motivated by different inner forces and there is wide variation in these motivational forces from person to person. But, Jung identified a pattern in these individual differences. Understanding the pattern of individual differences enables one to better understand the behavior of others and to predict their likely behaviors under different circumstances. This was the basis for understanding the concept of personality types.

Like Freud, his senior and sometime mentor, Carl Jung was a clinical psychologist. Having observed many people in his clinical practice, he began to think that the personalities of various individuals could be sorted into categories according to types. He compared his observations with studies of literature, mythology, and religions and found that the idea was often used by writers and other observers of human behavior. He published a treatise on the subject in 1920, and a student of his translated it into English in 1923;[21] both publications were largely ignored. Why? Because "in 1923, other approaches to psychology were dominant in Europe and North America. Freudian psychology was in vogue in Europe and on both American coasts, while grass-roots America was under the overwhelming influence of behaviorism. Scientific circles of the time regarded Jung as mystical and his approach antithetical to their own penchant for logic and facts."[22]

The Four Psychological Types

Cutting through the confusion that abounds in trying to understand the essential personality differences between and among people, Jung's observations led him to a simple analysis: there are three basic dimensions of human personality, and the "mix" of these dimensions varies from person to person although they cluster into patterns that are called psychological types. In the 1950s, as I shall describe, Isabel Myers and her mother, Katheryn Briggs, added a fourth dimension to the analysis, laying the basis for identifying four psychological types—or four temperaments—of people, an analysis that is widely accepted today.

When we speak of four psychological types, we are speaking of the ways in which people perceive the world around them, how they interpret what they perceive, and how they form judgments about their perceptions—that is, the extent to which people are (1) introverted or extraverted,* (2) sensing or intuitive, (3) thinking or feeling, and (4) perceiving or judging. From the perspective of psychological types, therefore, there is no objective independent reality that we call the environment: the "real" environment depends largely on how one perceives and interprets it. This is an important point in understanding organizational behavior and a central tenet of postmodern thought: the reality of organizational life lies largely in the eye of the beholder. An understanding of one's own temperament not only puts one in a better position to understand how one "sees" and deals with the organizational world, but gives one greater ability to understand the behavior of others in the organization.

Four Basic Dimensions of Human Personality

The Myers-Briggs Type Indicator (MBTI) is a paper-and-pencil instrument that seeks to identify sixteen different patterns of action that people are likely to follow in responding to certain situations. The sixteen patterns of action are combinations of four dimensions that describe the preferences that one might have in dealing with the situations. Three of the dimensions were described by Jung in the 1920s:

+ introversion—extraversion
+ sensation—intuition
+ thinking—feeling

Myers and Briggs used these three dimensions as scales to create the MBTI. As one would in creating such a personality inventory, they devised questions to represent these scales to which people taking the test would respond. During their work, Myers and Briggs created a fourth dimension that they believed was needed:

perceiving—judging

The MBTI became popular in U.S. corporate organizations as a self-assessment instrument for those who wanted to learn more about themselves as managers as well as about their colleagues. It has also been used in corporate training programs to help work groups gain a better understanding of ways to become more effective in dealing with various types of colleagues in the organization. Aside from its uses as a self-assessment instrument, the dimensions on which the MBTI is built provide an interesting way to analyze and understand organizational behavior.

*The atypical spelling of the word, extraversion, became the accepted spelling in the subject index of *Psychological Abstracts* in 1974 and has been the accepted spelling in the literature on individual differences since that time.

Introversion-Extraversion

Jung "used the term *attitude* to refer to the ways that individuals direct their psychic energy. He described two attitudes: the extraverted and the introverted."[23] Some people characteristically receive great psychic energy from external sources: people, events, and things in the environment. Typically these are very sociable individuals who like to talk to people and play and work with them; they find that meeting and interacting with others is not only fun, but that it invigorates them and recharges their psychic batteries. They are the extraverts, and whether at work, at play, or on vacation they gravitate to other people and want to be involved where the action is. Working alone in quiet places is wearisome to the extravert, who tends to find such activities as research in the library or puzzling alone over a complex problem tiring and draining.

Introverts, on the other hand, though they usually like people and often enjoy being around them, tend to find socializing taxing, tiring, draining of their energies rather than energizing. The introvert prefers quiet, even being alone at times, and in this environment is recharged and invigorated.

These dimensions—introversion and extraversion—are useful in thinking about motivation because they reveal deep-seated orientations as to how one literally perceives the world, where one gets information about the world, and how one makes judgments about what is real in the world. Two individuals, one an extravert and the other an introvert, tend to experience identical events differently, understand them differently, and respond to them differently. So saying, it is important to remind ourselves that one is not *either* an introvert *or* an extravert. This is a dimension that describes the intensity of a personality characteristic; although each of us may tend to emphasize either extravert attitudes or introvert attitudes, most of us find that both attitudes coexist in each of us.

Sensation-Intuition and Thinking-Feeling

In describing the ways in which different types of people related to their environments, Jung saw that there were two rational functions, thinking and feeling, and two nonrational functions, sensing and intuition. These allude to how one experiences, judges, and reacts to events in the environment. Normally one, or perhaps two, tend to dominate in an individual. These four functions are summarized as follows:

> The rational functions, thinking and feeling, evaluate and judge information. *Thinking* uses principled reasoning, logic, and impersonal analysis to evaluate information and situations. To make a judgment, criteria are sufficiency of data, validity, and reasonableness. *Feeling*, by contrast, uses empathy or personal values to make a judgment. Of prime importance in feeling is the impact a judgment will have upon another person. The feeling person calculates subjectively whether a judgment is important or unimportant, valuable or useless.
>
> The [nonrational] functions, sensing and intuition, simply receive and process information without evaluating or judging it. *Sensation* is sense perception, or perception mediated by the bodily senses. Its focus is on concrete, tangible realities in the

present. Sensing types of people distrust ideas that cannot be supported by the facts. *Intuition* is perception through the unconscious. The intuitive individual can arrive at a perception without being aware of the concrete basis for that perception. Intuitive types of people can make leaps from the past or the present to future possibilities, and they can perceive complex connections among various phenomena.[24]

Perceiving-Judging

As Myers and Briggs developed an instrument for identifying personality types (about which more will be said in a moment), they added a fourth dimension of behavior that people use in dealing with the world around them: perceiving and judging. A *perceiving* person is one who tends to use either sensing or intuition in making sense of the environment. On the other hand, one who tends to use either thinking or feeling in interactions with the environment is described as a *judging* type of individual.

THE MYERS-BRIGGS TYPE INDICATOR (MBTI)

After World War II, when the field of psychology underwent extraordinary ferment in which many alternatives to traditional academic behaviorism emerged, Jung's idea that these "psychological types" existed and could be identified was revisited. Myers and Briggs, triggered widespread interest in the possibilities and uses of this idea when they created a simple questionnaire that was said to be reliable and valid in determining the psychological type of individuals. The Myers-Briggs Type Indicator (MBTI)[25] makes it easy to use the four behavioral dimensions that have just been described to sort people out according to the preferences that they tend to use in dealing with the world around them. The MBTI and its offshoots have also been widely advocated in popular literature for individuals to use as a way of assessing one's own personality type.[26] To anyone who would be an educational leader, having a clear understanding of how one functions in the world—how one "reads" the environment, the kinds of information one attends to, how one interprets what is perceived—is, of course, a great advantage in dealing effectively with many kinds of people.

The idea of different personality types as a set of lenses through which one may view and understand the behavior of men and women in the organization is an interesting—and, many find, useful—alternative to the lenses demanded by, for example, radical feminist psychology, which generally describes men and women as perceiving and functioning differently and explains the differences in terms of the cultural norms associated with gender. There is little doubt that, as Carol Gilligan made clear, "psychology has persistently and systematically misunderstood women," including their motives, and when men view the world differently than women do, "the conclusion is that something may be wrong with women."[27] There is also little doubt that psychology has little understood the whole concept of personality types.

Introversion-Extraversion

For example, about 75 percent of the people in the population are thought to have extraverted attitudes and about 25 percent are thought to be introverted.[28] But as Gilligan pointed out in discussing sex differences in psychological attitudes, "it is difficult to say 'different' without saying 'better' or 'worse' since there is a tendency to construct a single scale of measurement [in one's mind]," so it is, too, in dealing with introversion-extraversion. Just as some people tend to think there is something wrong with women who do not conform to male-dominated norms of motivation,[29] so in Western cultures it is common to think that there is something wrong with those individuals who prefer a little peace and quiet, perhaps some solitude, and a little territorial breathing room. "Indeed," noted Keirsey and Bates, "Western culture seems to sanction the outgoing, sociable and gregarious temperament. The notion of anyone wanting or needing much solitude is viewed rather often as reflecting an unfriendly attitude."[30] When one considers that the attitudes of people in non-Western cultures often tend to be more supportive and approving of those who prefer to direct their psychological energy inward than those whose energy is primarily directed outward, it becomes clearer that Jung was at least close to being right in believing that introversion-extraversion reveals some combination of innate, inherited attitudes, skills that reflect learning to conform to cultural norms. For example, the introverted individual may very well learn the social skills and attitudes to deal effectively with the expectation that one occasionally attends large, noisy cocktail parties as part of professional life. The extravert, on the other hand, may learn to "work the room" expertly. The difference is that the introvert will find the experience demanding, perhaps tiring, while the extravert will find it exhilarating and just plain fun.

A Dimension, Rather Than Either-Or

In thinking about introversion-extraversion attitudes, however, it must be underscored that we are dealing with a *dimension* with two poles: introversion at one end and extraversion at the other. One's attitude will lean toward one pole or the other, but it would be rare indeed to find a "pure" type. Thus, an introvert is not totally without the ability to enjoy other people, to socialize, or to share with them, nor is an extravert unable to enjoy concentrating on lonely tasks or a break away from the "pressure cooker" of the organization. It is the balance, chiefly between sociability and territory, that identifies types in this dimension.

Intuition-Sensation

Intuition and sensation are ways of thinking about the world around us. Although differences in introversion-extraversion are important differences between and among people, intuition-sensation differences may be, more than any of the other factors in personality typing, "the sources of the most miscommunication, misunderstanding, vilification, defamation, and denigration. *This difference places the widest gulf between people.*"[31] This is probably due in large part to the fact that these two ways of receiving information about our environment are opposites, polarities—not a continuum. One who relies on sense perception to get information probably cannot also use intuition simultaneously. These two lenses on the world are opposites, and when one individual operates on the basis of sensation and the other on the basis of intuition, the groundwork is laid for misunderstanding.

Sensation is sense perception, that is, perception as it received and processed by the body, such as sight, sound, touch, taste, and feel. Sensation is real, seemingly tangible, in the immediate here and now. The person who prefers to be informed by sensation tends to be one who relies on facts and observation, who trusts the lessons drawn from practical experience, emphasizes the demonstrable, and tends to ask, "How do you know?"

The polar opposite of sensation, intuition, is a very different way of gathering information with which to make sense of the world around us. Rather than sense perception received and mediated through the body, intuition is perception through the unconscious.[32] Individuals who depend on intuition for information about the environment often develop an insight without knowing exactly the bases for it. They are often quick to spot patterns and connections between and among elements of complex situations, though they are not sure how they saw them. Intuitive people tend to be able to project ahead from the present to future possibilities. They like ingenuity and often express themselves through metaphor, fantasy, and fiction. Many times, of course, they are impatient with the attention to detail of sensation-oriented colleagues and view them as plodding and unimaginitive. For their part, sensation-oriented people—who emphasize being sensible, practical, and no-nonsense—of course often find intuitive colleagues impractical and unaware of realities.

The intuition-oriented person can be impatient with insistence on facts and hard evidence, tends to use metaphor and imagery, often fails to notice details in observation that the sensation-oriented person notes at once. The intuitive individual, not infrequently to the despair of the sensation-oriented individual, often speaks about future possibilities for making things better; tends to bounce from one vision to another, often leaving a project before it is completed to take up another; and talks a lot about the future, about what may be possible, creative, and imaginative. As we have seen, using the examples of intelligences, personality types, and gender, many psychologists focus on the role that various personal characteristics play in motivation. These personal characteristics are thought to be basic to motivation: in large measure they literally construct the environment of the individual by defining and describing what is perceived and understood; they cause a person to attend to one thing rather than another; they explain why the individual is persistent in some tasks and desultory in others. Sensemaking, viewed through the lenses of individual differences, is informed by the way one thinks, feels, and experiences as one interacts with the organizational environment.

To what extent are these personal characteristics innate or learned? In pragmatic terms, we don't know: for scholars, the debate continues. However, many theories of motivation have been constructed on the assumption that humans universally respond to certain innate needs, and new theories of this sort appear every year.

INTRINSIC MOTIVATION

Other than behaviorist theories of motivation, which emphasize motivational factors external to the individual (e.g., the carrot and the stick), two main streams of motivational thought exist: the cognitive perspective and the humanistic perspective. Both view motivation as intrinsic, or arising from within the individual.

COGNITIVE VIEWS OF MOTIVATION

One cognitive perspective on motivation is based on the belief that human beings have an innate inner drive to understand the world, to make sense of it, to gain control over their lives, and to become increasingly self-directed. This is thought to give rise to certain innate characteristics that arouse and energize individuals to work toward these ends. Following Piaget, the cognitive perspective assumes that people are motivated by a need for order, predictability, sensibleness, and logic in dealing with the world. This is equilibrium, an idea central to Piaget's theory.[33] Piaget used the term "equilibration" to describe the processes of seeking equilibrium. In applying the notion of equilibrium to organizational life, one would tend to emphasize organizational routines to develop regularity, predictability, and dependability as desirable motivating processes.

Achievement Motivation

John Atkinson thought that every individual was driven by two learned characteristics: the desire to achieve success (n Achievement or n Ach) and/or the desire to avoid failure.[34] Some people are high in their n Ach and low in the need to avoid failure (low avoidance), whereas others are low in their n Ach and high in avoidance of failure (high avoidance). The behaviors of people with these two different motivational traits obviously tend to be different. Atkinson's work, which was carried on and extended by his close colleague and longtime collaborator, David McClelland, has had enormous impact on thinking about the behavior of managers in corporate America and in conceptualizing entrepreneurship in free market capitalism. Woven into achievement motivation theory is a very strong element of competition.

It would appear that high n Ach people thrive on competition and find it zestful and energizing, whereas high avoidance people tend to shun competition and find it stressful. But it should be made clear that the approach-avoidance concept is about *potential in human characteristics*: one may exhibit high avoidance behavior in some situations, yet in other circumstances one's n Ach motives may be aroused and the individual may engage in highly competitive behavior. A shy, self-effacing young woman, for example, may shun public appearances and large glittering celebrity parties, yet step onstage before a world-class orchestra and an audience of thousands and deliver a brilliant violin solo knowing that the critics as well as her older colleagues listen knowingly, looking for the slightest flaw.

In the literature on achievement, success-oriented people (high approach to success—low in avoidance of failure) are extolled as achieving beyond and above the standards, beating the competition, being winners. High approach people are epitomized in the stereotype of the American entrepreneur as mythologized during the Reagan/Bush presidencies: hard-driving, risk taking, tough, relentless, narrowly focused on achieving a limited goal, driven by the clock, often with little consideration for others. Failure avoiders (low approach-high avoidance), on the other hand, act more defensively, are more careful to avoid losses, and indeed often restructure the situation so that failure may be redefined as success.

Although people high in n Ach anticipate and savor success and victory in competition, their counterparts seek to avoid humiliation and failure. As the achievers work hard and relentlessly to assure success, failure-avoiders *may* tend toward inaction or *may* lower their aspirations to more closely match their perception of the likelihood of success. One has to be very careful, however, not to overgeneralize too glibly. Failure-avoiders can, and often do, strive very hard, and are often highly successful in the process. Covington described it as "a frontal assault on failure— avoiding failure by succeeding! . . . These fear-driven successes can be extraordinary," he explained, "Many failure-threatened students are merit scholar finalists, class valedictorians, and National Science Fair winners. Despite such outward signs of success, however, being driven to succeed out of fear may be the ultimate academic ordeal. The individual's sense of worth comes to depend to an increasingly perilous degree on always succeeding, relentlessly, and against lengthening odds."[35] Yet the central point should not be missed: those who seek to avoid failure can be, and often are, highly motivated people.

Ferdinand Hoppe did landmark research on the roles of self-confidence, expectations, and aspirations in the motivation of people when he was Kurt Lewin's laboratory assistant in 1930–1931. Martin Covington described Hoppe's experimental work, which both Atkinson and McClelland surely knew well, in this way:

> Professor Lewin's laboratory [in Berlin] was crowded with the research paraphernalia of his time, including an odd conveyor-belt contraption that allowed a series of pegs to move on circular rollers at a uniform rate of speed, much like a row of ducks in a shooting gallery. This unlikely apparatus would provide the key to the question of how, psychologically, humans define success and failure. There are few consistent yardsticks when it comes to judging whether or not a particular achievement is successful—certainly not in the same sense that we can objectively measure height, weight, or temperature. Success and failure mean different things to different people. The same accomplishment can elicit pride in one person and self-rebuke in another, giving rise to the truism that 'one [person's] success is another [person's] failure.' However, for all the subjectivity involved, these judgments do proceed in lawful ways, as Hoppe was to discover.
>
> Hoppe invited an assortment of local tradespeople and university students to practice tossing rings on the moving pegs at various distances from the target. He found that some subjects felt satisfied after placing, say, 8 rings, whereas others expressed extreme frustration at only 12 correct tosses. Additionally, Hoppe found that the performance level needed to arouse feelings of success changed over time for each

individual. A score that was initially judged a success might well be considered unacceptable on a later practice trial.

Hoppe's revelation prompted a cascade of crucial insights. For instance it was now possible to give meaning to the concept of *self-confidence,* another psychological state of mind like success and failure. There is no accounting for self-confidence in objective terms. Some individuals may discern a gleam of hope in a situation that seems hopeless to everyone but themselves. At the same time, others may express a vote of no confidence despite the fact that they have everything going for them. Basically, self-confidence reflects the extent to which the individual believes himself or herself able to win the prize, to turn back the foe, or in Hoppe's experiment to toss enough rings correctly.[36]

McClelland and the "Spirit of Capitalism"

Having identified the need to achieve and the avoidance of failure as personality traits that are relatively stable and had some value in predicting behavior in various circumstances, McClelland proceeded to extend his thinking to the larger society and to the economic growth of nations around the world. His hypothesis was that, *first,* highly motivated people can change society itself, and therefore, *second,* a society experiences economic growth when it promotes the advancement and use of achievement motivation by its people. This could be done, McClelland believed—and many still believe strongly—by placing high value on the orientation to achievement and teaching this value in the home and in the schools as well as teaching the attitudes, skills, and habits that might develop high n Ach.

Thus McClelland elevated discourse on motivation to the realms of social, political, and economic policy. For example, in order to transform a society into a highly motivated society with a "spirit of capitalism," which he called *The Achieving Society,*[37] McClelland advocated child-rearing practices and schooling as primary points of intervention.

The belief that there is a link between high achievement motivation as a sociocultural norm and the economic productivity of a people is remarkably similar to Max Weber's observations during the Belle Epoch that led to his work on *The Protestant Ethic and the Spirit of Capitalism.*[38] Weber lived at a time when both Roman Catholicism and Protestantism were vigorous social forces omnipresent in the daily lives of people in European nations, having powerful impact on their ethical beliefs as well as child-rearing practices and schooling. Thus it was significant when Weber observed that the productivity and economic development of European Protestant countries and European Roman Catholic countries differed from one another. Weber believed that the "Protestant ethic"—with its emphasis on individual faith and independence, rejection of personal pleasure, and the belief that hard work is in itself inherently good—accounted for much of the observed difference. As one can imagine, this view aroused a good deal of controversy over the years; however, it also has had powerful impact on Western thought about the inner versus outer issues in motivation. Moreover, the extensive research carried out by McClelland and his followers lends strong support to the notion that the society that emphasizes the need for personal achievement, hard work, and personal responsibility may be inculcating the inner characteristics that will ultimately lead to the society's high productivity and economic development. Indeed, in our time, with the humiliating demise of communism, we have witnessed an unfolding of this line of thought as the Eastern European countries of the old Soviet empire struggle to transform their societies and their economies by trying to cast off the demotivating hand of Soviet-style bureaucracy and adopt the outlook, values, and work behavior of free market capitalist cultures.

In studying the need for achievement as a motivational force, McClelland discovered that individuals varied in their need for achievement, or to be successful, with some having a high need to achieve and some having less of such a need. He also discovered that other people actually have a fear of success. Matina Horner raised the possibility that fear of success is a gender-related issue.

Fear of Success

How do we find out the strength of a person's need for achievement and the strength of a person's need to avoid failure? A basic research technique that McClelland used was to have the person take the Thematic Apperception Test (TAT). The person taking the TAT is shown a picture or given a brief story line and is asked to write a story, or complete an already started story, which, in effect, tells their version of what the picture or story line portrays. This is what psychologists call a projective technique, somewhat akin in concept to the familiar Rorschach "ink-blot" test. The idea is, of course, that different people "see" different things in the events depicted and therefore tell different stories, just as Jung would have predicted.

Fear of Success as a Gender Issue

Because the TAT has been administered by many psychologists over the years, an extensive database of results was generated, which was analyzed for trends. One trend that emerged was that "sex role turns out to be one of the most important determinants of human behavior; psychologists have found sex differences in their studies from the moment they started doing empirical research."[39] One difference that caught the attention of Matina Horner was that women tend to experience more anxiety than men when confronted with situations of competitive achievement. As you have seen, McClelland's studies of men had identified two general characteristics that influenced their perception of what they saw in the TAT pictures and story lines: one was the hope or expectation of success and the other was fear of failure. Do women perceive the same options or do they perceive something different?

In research for her Ph.D. at the University of Michigan in 1968, Horner demonstrated that women tend to see something different and she identified it as a third motivation: fear of success.[40] Why would a woman fear success in a competitive situation? One answer is the woman's perception of a dilemma that men do not experience: that success will bring a loss of culturally defined femininity.

One of the test items that Horner used began, "After first term finals, Anne finds herself at the top of her medical school class." In analyzing the stories that women wrote to complete this introduction, Horner commented, "when success is likely or possible, threatened by the negative consequences they expect to follow success, young women become anxious and their positive achievement strivings become thwarted."[41] She concluded that this fear of success "exists because for most women, the anticipation of success in competitive achievement activity, especially against men, produces anticipation of certain negative consequences, for example, the threat of social rejection and loss of femininity."[42]

A Women's Issue?

Since Horner's work, there has been much discussion of fear of success in direct competition as a significant factor in the motivation of women. In the first place, however, it is not limited to women. In the second place, it is but a part of the complex human dynamics involved in dealing with issues of competition.

For example, it is commonplace for bright students to conceal their academic prowess, often using elaborate performances to avoid being thought a "brain" by their peers, one who is highly successful in the supposedly competitive environment of the school. Dissembling is a common strategy for these students. They may conceal the fact that they have actually studied, and may consistently perform below par to avoid being singled out by their peers as a winner. Indeed, it appears that one way students avoid appearing too bright in the eyes of others, yet preserve their own inner sense of being bright, is to exert little effort. If one is to fail, it is a better excuse that one didn't try than that one was not able.[43]

THE HUMANISTIC PERSPECTIVE

Although the cognitive perspective on motivation is that we are motivated from within to make sense of the world as we perceive it, to exercise control of our lives, and to be inner-directed, the humanistic perspective is that personal needs to constantly grow and develop, to cultivate personal self-esteem, and to have satisfying human relationships are highly motivating drives. This perspective is a "searching to understand what goes on inside us—our needs, wants, desires, feelings, values, and unique ways of perceiving and understanding what causes us to behave the way we do . . . it is what teachers practice as they help students to see the personal relevancy of what they are learning."[44]

Accordingly, motivation is internal—not something that is done *to* us—and emphasizes nurturing an inherent ongoing human proclivity to continue growing, developing and maturing, and being enriched by new experiences. Hence, one is always in the process of becoming. In this view there is no such thing as an unmotivated person. As Arthur Combs put it, "People are always motivated; in fact, they are never unmotivated. They may not be motivated to do what we would prefer they do, but it can never be truly said that they are unmotivated."[45] The experienced teacher who shows little enthusiasm for the latest twist in curriculum and instruction being advocated by the superintendent, the kind of teacher who is commonly described by such clichés as "deadwood" and "burned out," and who is often targeted for "weeding out," is not unmotivated: that teacher may not be motivated to do what the superintendent would prefer, but probably sees little connection between what is being demanded and her or his own internal sense of fulfillment.

Abraham Maslow: Motivation as a Hierarchy of Needs

One of the most powerful and enduring ways of understanding human motivation was developed by Abraham Maslow who, unlike the experimental psychologists of his day, decided to study the motivation patterns shown by people as they lived. He believed that people are driven from within to realize their full growth potential. This ultimate goal is sometimes called self-fulfillment, sometimes self-realization, but Maslow called it self-actualization. Some people—such as Eleanor Roosevelt, Thomas Jefferson, and Albert Einstein, all of whose lives Maslow studied—achieve self-actualization in the course of their lives, and many people do not, but all strive in that direction.

The genius of Maslow's work lies in the hierarchy of needs: that human needs start with survival, then unfold in an orderly, sequential hierarchical pattern that takes us toward continued growth and development.[46] The hierarchy is shown in Figure 4–1. *Prepotency* is the term that Maslow used to describe the fact that one cannot be motivated by a higher need until the lower needs are first met. For example, we all start out with the need to survive, and the basics for that are food, water, clothing, and shelter. The next higher need is safety: to be without fear of physical or psychological harm. The need for survival is prepotent, however: one cannot attend to the need for safety unless the needs for survival are first met. As this book is being written, this pattern is being played out every day in places like Sarajevo, where snipers routinely zero in on water wagons and bread lines to pick off people who must risk their own safety to get the food and water that they absolutely need to survive.

As the need for safety is met, one seeks affiliation: belonging, acceptance by others, love. Once one's prepotent needs for affiliation are adequately met, one is motivated by the next higher need in the hierarchy, the need for self-esteem: this comes from recognition and respect from others.

Deficiency Needs and Growth Needs

The lower four needs in Maslow's hierarchy are called deficiency needs because (1) their deficiency motivates people to meet them and (2) until the deficiencies are met, people find it difficult to respond to a higher-order need. Thus, the teacher who feels unsafe at school is unlikely to be highly motivated to seek acceptance by other members of the faculty or by the need for recognition or approval. In such a case in Maslow's view, trying to create a more supportive, accepting climate in the school or to use participative methods of decision making are likely to be more problematic than if the prepotent need—the need for safety—had first been met.

The higher-order needs are called growth needs, and they are different. The growth needs are never fully met: for example, as one learns more and develops aes-

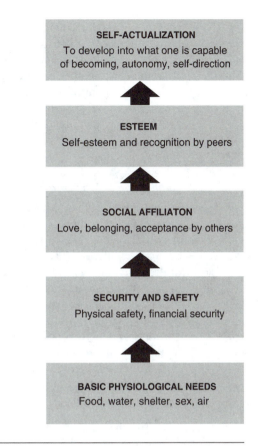

FIGURE 4–1
Hierarchy of needs as used in Maslow's theory of motivation.

thetic appreciation, the need for growth is not met; rather, it expands. The music aficionado never wearies of fine music but studies more, collects recordings, and continues attending concerts, always striving to achieve greater depth and scope of understanding and new levels of appreciation. The Civil War buff may not satisfy their curiosity by reading a book and visiting a battlefield or two: they may soon be involved to the extent of using their weekends and vacation time to attend seminars, travel to historic sites, and otherwise pursue their quest for knowing and understanding with increasing energy.

As the need for growth and self-development expands, we can understand why many people motivated by growth needs seem insatiable in their search for knowledge and understanding. Many develop an enormous scope of interests, and others probe ever more deeply into their understanding of fewer interests. Thus, responding to growth needs leads to increased growth; the cycle of personal growth is seemingly endless.

This is a very different perspective on motivation than behaviorist views, which primarily emphasize carefully regulated rewards and punishments: the prospect of modest annual increases in compensation and ultimately an unpretentious retirement income as the reward for being a "good" teacher; the threat of being demoted or sacked for being a "poor" teacher. The hierarchy-of-needs view of motivation envisions the realistic possibility of generating enormous psychic energy within and among teachers and principals, and seeing that energy expand and increase over time: first, by meeting their deficiency needs and, second, by encouraging their growth and development needs. This is the essence of *creating growth-enhancing environments* in schools as an organizational approach to motivating participants.

Application to Work Motivation

Lyman Porter adapted Maslow's concept of hierarchy of needs to creating growth-enhancing environments in work organizations.[47] An interpretation of his work is shown in Figure 4–2. In Porter's view, Maslow's hierarchy fits the organizational environment better by adding a new level in the hierarchy: *autonomy*.[48] This refers to the individual's need to participate in making decisions that affect him or her, to exert influence in controlling the work situation, to have a voice in setting job-related goals, and to have authority to make decisions and latitude to work independently. Using Porter's concept of the needs hierarchy, it is relatively easy to see the ways in which work organizations, such as school districts, schools, and institutions of higher education, can be sources for fulfilling these motivating needs.

Porter went on to conduct research that is interesting because it is representative of a whole line of inquiry that followed. Among the characteristics he attempted to measure concerning the managers he studied were the following:

1. To what extent the need characteristic (of any level of the hierarchy) *was being met* by the manager's job.
2. To what extent the manager thought the job *should* meet the need characteristic.

The differences between the first question (to what extent need was being met) and the second question (to what extent the job should meet the need) provide a measure of either (1) the amount of *need satisfaction* the person is experiencing or (2) the perceived *need deficiency* that the person is experiencing. Research such as this has been conducted widely in an effort to understand the relationship between need satisfaction and/or need deficiency and the performance of people on the job.[49]

Because such studies "contend that human behavior is goal-directed toward fulfilling unsatisfied needs, an individual's need satisfaction should be related to his job performance. And, as Maslow's theory would predict, higher-order needs should be more closely linked to job performance than lower-order needs that can be readily satisfied."[50] One generalization that seems to arise from the substantial body of research of this kind is that it is situation-bound. That is, when or where times are good and jobs plentiful (such as public education in the United States in the 1950s), such research tends to pick up little concern for the lower-order needs (for example, security and physiological needs) because they are not a significant

> **SELF-ACTUALIZATION**
> Working at full potential
> Feeling successful at work
> Achieving goals viewed as significant

> **AUTONOMY**
> Control of work situation, influence in
> the organization, participation in
> important decisions, authority to
> utilize organizational resources

> **SELF-ESTEEM**
> Titles, feeling self-respect, evidence of
> respect by others, status symbols,
> recognition, promotions, awards, being
> part of "insiders" group

> **AFFILIATION**
> Belonging to formal and informal work
> groups, friendships, professional
> associations and unions, acceptance by
> peers beyond the immediate organization

> **SECURITY**
> Pay, union, seniority, retirement plan,
> tenure, such legal concepts as "due process"
> and "fairness," statutory and policy
> protections establishing orderly evaluation
> and "RIF" procedures, the negotiated contract,
> insurance plans

FIGURE 4–2
A hierarchy of work motivation based on Porter's
model.

part of reality. But when or where there is employment instability, there appears to be a closer connection between the lower-order needs and job satisfaction. This admittedly general observation may be disconcerting to those who seek a broad, generally applicable explanation of human motivation.

It is probably unrealistic to assume that teachers are, as a group, motivated by any particular needs inducement that is applicable only to that group; the variables among teachers are too great to expect that. There are personal variables, such as life and career goals, and differing family and financial obligations. There also are differing situational contingencies; teachers who work in schools where they may have their coats stolen, or be robbed, or be in danger of being raped may very well reveal needs dispositions that are different from those of teachers in a more secure environment. Again, the point being emphasized here is the critical importance of the function of situational contingencies in attempting to describe, explain, and predict the needs inducements that lie behind the behavior of people in educational organizations.

With this caveat in mind, we should consider the studies reported by Thomas Sergiovanni and his associates, which sought to find out "at what level teachers are with respect to the hierarchy [of prepotent needs]. We need to know their level of prepotency"[51] for the simple reason that we cannot (according to the hierarchy-of-needs theory) motivate insecure teachers by offering them greater autonomy or, on the other hand, motivate teachers seeking autonomy by offering them security. Perhaps worse is the likelihood that "freshly trained school executives who overestimate the operating need level of teachers and scare them off with ultraparticipatory self-actualizing administration are as ineffective as others who deny teachers meaningful satisfaction by underestimating operating need levels."[52] To shed light on what he calls the "operating need levels" of teachers, Sergiovanni and his colleagues conducted two studies: one of the teachers and administrators of an upstate New York suburban school district and the other of the teachers in thirty-six Illinois high schools.

These studies are of interest on two levels: (1) the data-gathering instruments and techniques for analyzing the data that were used demonstrate one way to study systematically important situational contingencies in the motivation of people in educative organizations, and (2) the results drawn from the populations they studied provide some useful insights.[53] In general, "esteem seems to be the level of need operation showing greatest need deficiency for these professionals. Large deficiencies are also reported for autonomy and self-actualization, and these gaps will continue to rise as teachers make gains in the esteem area."[54] In other words, these studies suggest that (in the populations studied and at the time of the study) the teachers—overall, as a group—(1) had satisfied the lower-order needs and (2) were generally ready to respond to higher-order needs. They felt reasonably secure and reasonably affiliated with their colleagues, and, therefore, more of these kinds of inducements were unlikely to be very motivating. But, were these teachers to be given opportunities to feel better about themselves and opportunities to have greater influence in the processes of making decisions, these would likely be highly motivating opportunities. But the groups of people studied were not monolithic: the researchers report (not surprisingly, to be sure) some differences related to age (in this case, age probably was an indicator of where individuals were in the development of their careers). They found, for example, that the younger teachers (that is, ages twenty to twenty-four) seemed to be the most concerned with esteem. Slightly older teachers (ages twenty-five to thirty-four), on the other hand, showed the most unmet motivational needs, across the board. One could speculate that this is the period in a teacher's career when he or she hits a dead end: for most, there will be little opportunity for professional growth, advancement, and significant achievement in the years ahead. Perhaps even more disturbing, however, are some insights concerning older teachers (forty-five years or over). At first glance, the data seemed to indicate that older teachers had the smallest need deficiencies of all; this tends to suggest that, in the later years of their careers, teachers were finding their work rather highly motivating at all levels. When the researchers examined this phenomenon, however, there appeared to be quite a different explanation: older teachers "are not getting more in terms of need fulfillment as the years go by but, rather, are expecting less. Levels of aspiration seem to drop considerably with age. Teachers become more 're-alistic' or resigned to things as they are."[55]

The significance of findings such as these looms very large, indeed, to those who are concerned with improving the effectiveness of public schools. There is strong support for believing that job security, salaries, and benefits—though far from being irrelevant to teachers—have little likelihood of motivating them. A greater motivational need, it seems clear, is for teachers to achieve feelings of professional self-worth, competence, and respect; to be seen increasingly as people of achievement, professionals who are influential in their workplaces, growing persons with opportunities ahead to develop even greater competence and a sense of accomplishment. But in an era in which public schools (and, increasingly, institutions of higher education) have been pervaded by a powerful sense of adversarial relationships between teachers and management, there appears to be little support from the organizational hierarchy of many schools to meet these needs. Indeed, the negotiating posture of most school districts has been highly defensive on this point, viewing every gain by teachers in opportunities to develop their autonomy and participation and to increase their scope of influence as a loss of jealously guarded management authority and prerogatives.

Similarly, the widespread loss of confidence in the effectiveness of schools has led to a rash of actions that have had a direct impact on the motivating environment of educative organizations. Reductions in force (RIF), slashed budgets, mandated competency programs, legislated school reforms, and massive federal interventions at the local school level all—of course—have laudable intent in terms of overall social policy. But in terms of Maslow's needs-hierarchy theory of motivation, as applied to the organizational behavior of people at work in schools, they tend to produce disastrous results in combination.

Herzberg's Two-Factor Theory of Motivation

The two-factor theory of motivation posits that motivation is not a single dimension describable as a hierarchy of needs but that it is composed of two separate, independent factors:

1. *Motivational factors,* which can lead to job satisfaction.
2. *Maintenance factors,* which must be sufficiently present in order for motivational factors to come into play and when not sufficiently present can block motivation and can lead to job dissatisfaction.

The work of Frederick Herzberg began to appear some twelve years after Maslow's and has become widely influential in management thought around the world, particularly in profit-making organizations. He started with systematic studies of people at work, thereby producing an empirically grounded theory, rather than using an "armchair" approach. In his research Herzberg asked people to recall the circumstances in which (1) they had, at specific times in the past, felt satisfaction with their jobs, and in which (2) they similarly had been dissatisfied with their jobs.[56] Analysis of the responses indicates that there is one specific, describable cluster or group of factors that is associated with motivation and satisfaction at work and another, equally specific, group of factors that is associated with dissatisfaction and apathy. Perhaps no other theory of motivation at work has been more extensively researched and argued about than this, and in all likelihood none has been as widely applied to complex organizations.

Traditionally, it had been believed that the opposite of job satisfaction is job dissatisfaction; thus, by eliminating the sources of dissatisfaction from work, the job would become motivating *and* satisfying. But Herzberg suggested that this is not so, that the opposite of satisfaction is no satisfaction (see Figure 4–3). Thus, by eliminating sources of dissatisfaction, one may placate, pacify, or reduce the dissatisfaction of a worker, but *this does not mean that such reduction either motivates the worker or leads to job satisfaction.* For example, salary, fringe benefits, type of supervision, working conditions, climate of the work group, and attitudes and policies of the administration can be sources of dissatisfaction. However, if one improves the salary-benefit "package" and working conditions and develops a more humane, concerned administration, one can expect to reduce dissatisfaction, but one cannot expect to motivate the workers by such means. Such conditions as these, taken together, originally were called "hygiene" factors. That term was chosen because—to Herzberg, at least—they have a preventive quality. They are being called, increasingly, *"maintenance"* factors, however, and that is the appellation that is used in this book.

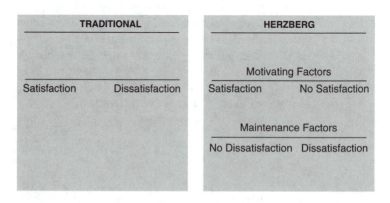

TRADITIONAL		HERZBERG	
		Motivating Factors	
Satisfaction	Dissatisfaction	Satisfaction	No Satisfaction
		Maintenance Factors	
		No Dissatisfaction	Dissatisfaction

FIGURE 4–3   Traditional concept of job satisfaction-dissatisfaction contrasted with Herzberg's concept.

Motivation appears to arise from a separate cluster of conditions, different from and distinct from those related to the sources of dissatisfaction. For example, achievement, recognition, the challenge of the work itself, responsibility, advancement and promotion, and personal or professional growth appear to motivate people and are, therefore, associated with job satisfaction. They are called motivating factors or *motivators.*

The theory, which is shown schematically in Figure 4–4, suggests that it is not possible to motivate people at work through maintenance factors. Reducing class size, developing a more amiable atmosphere, and improving the fringe benefits may well do two things: (1) reduce or eliminate the dissatisfaction of teachers and (2) create conditions wherein they may be motivated. But these kinds of efforts, in themselves, are not motivating. It does not follow, however, that the maintenance factors are unimportant: minimum levels must be maintained if we are to avoid so much dissatisfaction that motivators will not have their expected effect. For example, failure to keep the salary schedule at a level that teachers think is reasonable or threats to job security can generate such dissatisfaction that teachers cannot respond to opportunities for professional growth, achievement, or recognition. Thus, although maintenance factors are not—in themselves—motivating (or do not lead to job satisfaction), they are prerequisite to motivation.

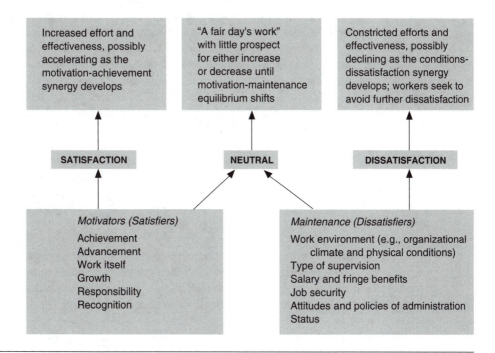

FIGURE 4–4   Model of Herzberg's motivator-maintenance theory.

An important concept in the two-factor theory is that people tend to see job satisfaction as being related to such intrinsic factors as success, the challenge of the work, achievement, and recognition, whereas they tend to see dissatisfaction as being related to such extrinsic factors as salary, supervision, and working conditions. In other words, they attribute motivational characteristics to themselves and attribute dissatisfaction to characteristics of the organization. In this context, Herzberg has suggested three main ideas for those who would practice his theory:

1. *Enrich the job,* which involves redesigning the work that people do in ways that will tap the motivation potential in each individual. This would include making the job more interesting, more challenging, and more rewarding.

2. *Increase autonomy* on the job. The reader is specifically cautioned to note here that it was not suggested that complete autonomy be somehow granted to workers but that autonomy be increased. This suggests more participation in making decisions as to how the work should be done.

3. *Expand personnel administration* beyond its traditional emphasis on maintenance factors. The focus of personnel administration should be on increasing the motivational factors present in the work. In this view, school districts in which personnel administration focuses almost exclusively on such things as contract administration, the routines of selection-assignment-evaluation-dismissal, and the details of teacher certification and pension plans are attending to important things but not to motivating things. Because 80 percent or more of the current operating budget of many school districts is allocated directly to salaries, wages, and related items, it would seem that the personnel function should be deeply involved in creating or redesigning jobs that motivate the incumbents and thus increase the effectiveness or productivity of the district's employees. This is the view that, for many, underlies the concept of "human resources administration" in contrast to more traditional views of personnel administration.

Herzberg's motivation-maintenance theory has been widely accepted and applied to the management of organizations, especially to U.S. business and industrial corporations. It has, at the same time, provided the basis for considerable academic debate. The four principal criticisms that crop up in that debate are often expressed as follows:

1. Herzberg's basic research methods tended to foreshadow the responses he got. When things went well and people felt satisfied, they tended to take the credit for it; but when things went badly on the job and the respondents were not satisfied, they tended to project the fault onto other people or onto management.

2. The reliability of his research methods is also open to question. The research design required a number of trained individuals to score and interpret the responses from the respondents. Obviously, there may be some differences in

the way individuals do the rating, with one rater scoring a response in one way and another rater scoring a similar response in another way (so-called inter-rater reliability).

3. No provision in the research covers the likely possibility that a person may get satisfaction from part of his or her job and not from another part.

4. The theory assumes that there is a direct relationship between effectiveness and job satisfaction; yet the research studies only satisfaction and dissatisfaction and does not relate either of them to the effectiveness (or productivity) of the respondents.

The first three of these criticisms are easily dealt with as merely representing typical problems of designing research that requires us to infer *causes* of behavior from observations of the behavior itself. They make the basis for nice arguments, but in fact, Herzberg's research—after exhaustive review in the literature over a period of two decades—must be accepted as representing the state of the art. The fourth criticism, however, is not so simple.

There is a chicken-or-the-egg aspect to the research literature on job satisfaction and its presumed link to effectiveness on the job. Roughly, investigators with a human relations orientation tend to think that satisfied workers are likely to be productive. Herzberg, however, is among those scholars who tend to think that satisfaction at work arises from the work itself or, more precisely, that job satisfaction comes from achievement. There is a massive body of research literature in this area; because of methodological problems as well as ideological conflicts, the overall results are inconclusive. Conversely, scant support exists for the notion that dissatisfied workers are likely to be more effective than those who report a higher level of satisfaction; the question, then, revolves around the *sources* of satisfaction (that is, maintenance factors or motivating factors). The Herzberg theory has been tested numerous times in school situations and—in this organizational setting, at least—appears to be well supported.

Ralph Savage, using interviews to obtain data from Georgia teachers, reported that Herzberg's theory was generally supported,[57] as did Rodney Wickstrom in reporting a study of teachers in the Province of Saskatchewan, Canada.[58] Gene Schmidt studied 132 high school principals in districts in the Chicago suburbs and found that, again, the two-factor theory appeared to be strongly supported by these school administrators, indicating that "recognition, achievement, and advancement are major forces in motivating them to lift their performance to approach their maximum potential."[59] In operational terms, this investigator concluded that "encouragement and support for administrators who desire to be creative, to experiment with new educational programs, and to delve into different educational endeavors are needed to allow more opportunities for achievement."[60]

Thomas Sergiovanni, in the late 1960s, after replicating Herzberg's work among teachers, reported that the theory appeared to be supported.[61] His findings were that achievement and recognition were very important motivators for teachers, along with the work itself, responsibility, and the possibility of growth. Among the dissatisfiers reported were (not surprisingly) routine housekeeping, taking attendance, paperwork, lunch duty, insensitive or inappropriate supervision, irritating administrative policies, and poor relationships with colleagues and/or parents. Sergiovanni made the point that *advancement,* frequently an important motivator in studies conducted in private-sector corporations, was missing in the study of teachers. On this significant point, he observed that "advancement was simply not mentioned by teachers because teaching as an occupation offers so little opportunity for advancement. If one wishes to advance in teaching, he must leave teaching for a related education profession such as administration, supervision, and counseling."[62]

Comments on Herzberg's Two-Factor Theory

The Herzberg two-factor theory of motivation was developed through research in which people were asked to describe critical incidents in their work lives that involved motivation and job satisfaction. Subsequently, it has been strongly supported by additional research carried out by a number of investigators using similar techniques. Together, these provide strong support for the concept. However, some investigators find it troubling that studies that use other research techniques generally fail to support the theory.

Herzberg's theory has been widely influential, however, and commonly appears in the literature of business and industry as well as that in education. Although some advocate abandoning it in favor of the newer and more complex expectancy theory, the two-factor theory remains a powerful explanation of motivation in the workplace.

INTEGRATING HERZBERG'S AND MASLOW'S THEORIES

Some of the essential differences between Maslow's hierarchy-of-needs theory and Herzberg's motivation-maintenance theory have already been pointed out. The central difference is that Maslow thought of every need as a potential motivator, with the range of human needs in a prepotent hierarchical order, whereas Herzberg argued that only the higher-order needs are truly motivating (the lower-order needs being conceptualized as maintenance factors). Another difference—not quickly apparent, perhaps—is that Maslow's was a *general* theory of human motivation, concerned, as Stephen Robbins puts it, "with the person's needs 24 hours a day,"[63] whereas Herzberg tried specifically to illuminate motivational issues *in the workplace.*

Nevertheless, a comparison of the two theories, as shown in Figure 4–5, reveals that they are basically highly compatible and, in fact, support one another. I feel (as Figure 4–5 shows) that the Porter version of the hierarchy-of-needs model lends itself to such a comparison, for the simple reason that such basic physiological drives as the need for food, water, and air have little relevance for motivating behavior at work in U.S. educational organizations. Even so, I agree with Robbins:

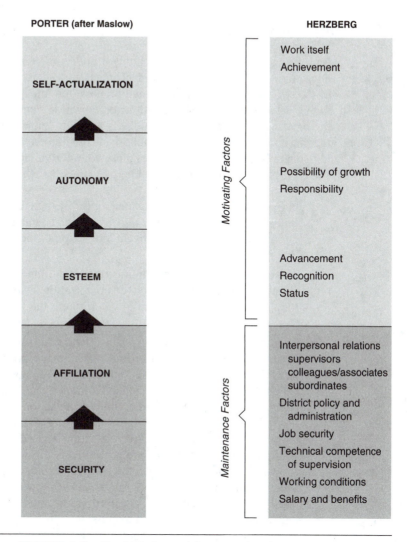

PORTER (after Maslow)

HERZBERG

SELF-ACTUALIZATION

AUTONOMY

ESTEEM

AFFILIATION

SECURITY

Work itself
Achievement

Possibility of growth
Responsibility

Advancement
Recognition
Status

Interpersonal relations
  supervisors
  colleagues/associates
  subordinates
District policy and
  administration
Job security
Technical competence
  of supervision
Working conditions
Salary and benefits

Motivating Factors

Maintenance Factors

FIGURE 4–5   Need-priority model compared with motivation-maintenance model.

The lower-order needs on Maslow's hierarchy tend to closely approximate the maintenance factors as outlined by Herzberg. Salary, working conditions, job security, [school district] policy and administration, and supervision are generally physiological and safety-oriented needs. In contrast, the intrinsic motivational factors of recognition, advancement, responsibility, growth, achievement, and the work itself tend to be closely related to the desire for esteem and self-actualization. The integrated model would also suggest that organizations have traditionally emphasized lower-order needs. If workers are to become motivated on their jobs, it will be necessary for administrators to make the alterations necessary to stimulate the motivational factors in the [jobs themselves].[64]

CONCLUSION: GENERAL PRINCIPLES

Motivating people who work in schools is not a simple matter and it cannot be reduced to a simple, certainly not a mechanical, procedure or set of procedures. Each of the two factors in the motivational process, the idiosyncratic personality of the individual and the idiosyncracies of the organization's environment, is complex and the precise nature of their interactions is not fully known. The school practitioner therefore must proceed, not with aphorisms or simple reductionism but with an intelligent holistic approach that takes these complex variables into account. Here are some pragmatic principles that will help to support such an approach.

1. Individuals are neither motivated *only* by their own internal perceptions, needs, and characteristics nor *only* by external demands, expectations, and environmental conditions, but by an interaction of the two: the generalization is $B = f(p \cdot e)$.

2. The educational leader or administrator is an important part of the organizational environment with which the organization's members interact and therefore, by definition, important in determining the nature and quality of their motivation.

3. Short-term behavioral changes can often be achieved by highly controlling strategies such as threats of serious punishments, promises of meaningful rewards, and forced competition, but these should not be confused with motivation. Such direct, coercive attempts to motivate may be useful in bringing about changes in behavior when immediate action is required in crisis situations, for example, when the performance of a teacher is so unacceptable that the school cannot wait for corrective action. Indeed, in a case such as this the controlling strategy might have a beneficial effect by permitting the teacher to achieve enough success at work so as to become responsive to motivational needs of a higher order than survival. However, even if well intended, when highly controlling strategies are used consistently enough to lead people to feel coerced, intimidated, and manipulated, then members tend to lose interest and, indeed, to develop motivational goals and strategies of their own that resist those of the organization.[65]

4. To induce and sustain long-term evolution of motivation of organizational members requires a facilitative approach, one that encourages and supports members in their efforts to grow and develop their ways of perceiving the environment they work in, their personal goals, feelings, and beliefs. A facilitative approach might, for example, seek to encourage members of the organization always to be moving up Maslow's hierarchy of needs over time, always in the direction of self-actualization with the goal of encouraging all members to become all that they can be.

5. One strategy for developing a facilitative approach to motivation in educational organizations is to change the environment factor in $B = f(p \cdot e)$, that is, to create growth-enhancing environments. This involves working with or-

ganizational culture and organizational climate. It is in this realm that the educational leader emerges as a key actor in the environment of the organization. We turn now, in Chapter 5, to a discussion of creating growth-enhancing environments.

SUGGESTED READING

Benfari, Robert with Jean Knox, *Understanding Your Management Style: Beyond the Myers-Briggs Type Indicators.* Lexington, MA: D.C. Heath and Company, 1991.

    This book applies four theoretical orientations to the understanding of one's own personality structure: (1) the Myers-Briggs Type Indicators, which are drawn directly from Jung's theory of personality; (2) the needs that motivate you; (3) the conflict management style that you use; and (4) the kinds of power that you use. It stresses the importance of assessing your own personality characteristics so that you can work from your own strengths. It's a do-it-yourself book, in a way, complete with a self-assessment test that you can take. It is also scholarly, sound, and readable.

Covington, Martin V., *Making the Grade: A Self-Worth Perspective on Motivation and School Reform.* New York: Cambridge University Press, 1992.

    While this book is focused on the motivation of students in the classroom, rather than on the motivation of adults who work in the educational organization, it is an informative and provocative discussion that has much to say to those who are interested in organizational behavior in education. Drawing heavily on the work of Atkinson and McClelland, Covington starts with the thesis that "every achievement situation implies the promise of success as well as the threat of failure. This means that all achievement situations involve approach-avoidance conflict to one degree or another" (p. 32). Entwined with this approach-avoidance, in which many students wind up struggling to avoid failure in school, is the personal sense of self-worth of the individual. A scholarly yet highly practical resource for educational leaders.

Gilligan, Carol, *In a Different Voice: Psychological Theory and Women's Development.* Cambridge, MA: Harvard University Press, 1982.

    In describing this book on the dust jacket, Lawrence Kohlberg said, "Carol Gilligan believes that psychology has persistently and systematically misunderstood women—their motives, their moral commitments, the course of their psychological growth." Gilligan describes her research into these areas and what her findings mean. This has become one of the most-cited works in the field of women's psychology.

Keirsey, David and Marilyn Bates, *Please Understand Me: Character and Temperament Types.* Del Mar, CA: Prometheus Nemesis Book Company, 1984.

    This book explains the psychological types of Carl Jung and provides a useful vocabulary and phraseology for applying the Jung-Myers concepts of different types to one's work in organizations. As the title suggests, it focuses on the communication distortions and blockages that commonly arise between and among different kinds of people who perceive and respond to the world in different ways. Readers can get feedback on their own psychological type by taking *The Keirsey Temperament Sorter* found on pp. 5–13.

NOTES

1. Harry Levinson, *The Great Jackass Fallacy* (Boston: Harvard University, 1973).
2. Quoted in William Dowling, ed., *Effective Management and the Behavioral Sciences* (New York: AMACOM, 1978), p. 44.
3. George C. Homans, "The Western Electric Researches," in *Human Factors in Management,* ed. Schuyler Dean Hoslett (New York: Harper and Brothers, Publishers, 1951), p. 211.
4. Ibid., p. 211.

5. Ibid., pp. 214–15.

6. Ibid., p. 217.

7. Ibid., p. 217.

8. Paul Hersey and Kenneth H. Blanchard, *Management of Organizational Behavior: Utilizing Human Resources,* 3rd ed. (Englewood Cliffs, NJ: Prentice-Hall, 1977), p. 46.

9. David Keirsey and Marilyn Bates, *Please Understand Me: Character and Temperament Types* (Del Mar, CA: Prometheus Nemesis Book Company, 1984), p. 2.

10. Ibid., p. 2.

11. Ibid., p. 2.

12. Howard Gardner, *Frames of Mind: The Theory of Multiple Intelligences* (New York: Basic Books, 1983), p. 25.

13. Howard Gardner and Thomas Hatch, "Multiple Intelligences Go to School," *Educational Researcher,* 18, 8 (1989), 4–10.

14. Gardner, *Frames of Mind,* p. 206.

15. Norman Mailer quoted in Benjamin Lowe, *The Beauty of Sport: A Cross-Disciplinary Inquiry* (Englewood Cliffs, NJ: Prentice-Hall, 1977), p. 255.

16. Gardner, *Frames of Mind,* p. 239.

17. Ibid.

18. Ibid., pp. 324–25.

19. Ibid., p. 238. Obviously, as late as 1983, neither Gardner nor his publisher took seriously the notion of gender-free writing that prevails today.

20. Keirsey and Bates, *Please Understand Me,* pp. 2–3.

21. Carl Jung, *Psychological Types* (Princeton: Bollingen Series, 1971).

22. Robert Benfari with Jean Knox, *Understanding Your Management Style: Beyond the Myers-Briggs Type Indicators* (Lexington, MA: Lexington Books, D.C. Heath and Company, 1991), pp. 4–5.

23. Ibid., p. 6.

24. Ibid., p. 8. Italics in the original.

25. Published by the Center for Applications of Psychological Type, P.O. Box 13807, Gainesville, FL 32604.

26. Two such books have already been mentioned: Benfari, *Understanding Your Management Style,* and Keirsey and Bates, *Please Understand Me.*

27. Lawrence Kohlberg, on the dust jacket of Carol Gilligan, *In a Different Voice: Psychological Theory and Women's Development* (Cambridge, MA: Harvard University Press, 1982).

28. Keirsey and Bates, *Please Understand Me,* p. 16.

29. Gilligan, *In a Different Voice,* p. 14.

30. Keirsey and Bates, *Please Understand Me,* p. 16.

31. Ibid., p. 17.

32. Benfari, *Understanding Your Management Style,* p. 8.

33. Jean Piaget, "Problems in Equilibration," in *Topics in Cognitive Development: Vol. 1. Equilibration: Theory, Research and Application,* eds. Marilyn H. Appel and Lois S. Goldberg (New York: Plenum Press, 1977), pp. 3–13.

34. John W. Atkinson and George H. Litwin, "Achievement Motivation and Test Anxiety Conceived as Motive to Approach Success and Motive to Avoid Failure," *Journal of Abnormal and Social Psychology,* 60 (1960), 52–63.

35. Martin V. Covington, *Making the Grade: A Self-Worth Perspective on Motivation and School Reform* (Cambridge: Cambridge University Press, 1992), p. 89.

36. Ibid., p. 26.

37. David C. McClelland, *The Achieving Society* (New York: The Free Press, 1961).

38. Max Weber, *The Protestant Ethic and the Spirit of Capitalism,* trans. Talcott Parsons (New York: Scribner, 1930). The original was published in German in 1904.

39. David C. McClelland, *Power: The Inner Experience* (New York: Irvington, 1975).

40. Matina S. Horner, "Sex Differences in Achievement Motivation and Performance in Competitive and Noncompetitive Situations." (Ph.D. Dissertation., University of Michigan, 1968). University Microfilms #6912135.

41. Ibid., p. 171.

42. Ibid., p. 125.

43. Jonathan Brown and Bernard Weiner, "Affective Consequences of Ability Versus Effort Ascriptions: Controversies, Resolutions, Quandries," *Journal of Educational Psychology,* 76, 1984, 146–158.

44. Don E. Hamachek, "Humanistic Psychology: Theory, Postulates and Implications for Educational Processes," in *Historical Foundations of Educational Psychology,* eds. John A. Glover and Royce R. Ronning (New York: Plenum Press, 1987).

45. Arthur Combs, "Motivation and the Growth of Self," in *Perceiving, Behaving, and Becoming: Association for Supervision and Curriculum Development Yearbook* (Washington, DC: National Education Association, 1962), pp. 83–98.

46. Abraham Maslow, *Motivation and Personality,* 2nd. ed. (New York: Harper & Row, 1970).

47. Lyman W. Porter, "A Study of Perceived Need Satisfaction in Bottom and Middle-Management Jobs," *Journal of Applied Psychology,* 45 (1961), 1–10.

48. Ibid.

49. For example, Edward E. Lawler III and Lyman W. Porter, "The Effect of Job Performance and Job Satisfaction," *Industrial Relations* 6 (1967), 20–28; and David G. Kuhn, John W. Slocum, and Richard B. Chase, "Does Job Performance Affect Employee Satisfaction?" *Personnel Journal,* 50 (1971), 455–60.

50. Don Hellriegel and John W. Slocum, Jr., *Management: A Contingency Approach* (Reading, MA: Addison-Wesley, 1974), p. 308.

51. Thomas J. Sergiovanni and Fred D. Carver, *The New School Executive: A Theory of Administration* (New York: Dodd, Mead & Company, 1973), pp. 58–59.

52. Ibid., p. 59.

53. This research is summarized and documented in Ibid., pp. 56–63.

54. Ibid.

55. Ibid., p. 61

56. Frederick Herzberg, *Work and the Nature of Man* (Cleveland: World Publishing Company, 1966), p. 56.

57. Ralph M. Savage, "A Study of Teacher Statisfaction and Attitudes: Causes and Effects," (unpublished doctoral dissertation, Auburn University, 1967).

58. Rodney A. Wickstrom, "An Investigation into Job Satisfaction among Teachers" (unpublished doctoral dissertation, University of Oregon, 1971).

59. Gene L. Schmidt, "Job Satisfaction among Secondary School Administrators," *Educational Administration Quarterly,* 12 (1976), 81.

60. Ibid, p. 81.

61. Sergiovanni and Carver, pp. 75–78

62. Ibid, p. 77.

63. Stephen P. Robbins, *The Administrative Process: Integrating Theory and Practice* (Englewood Cliffs, NJ: Prentice-Hall, 1976), p. 312.

64. Ibid., p. 312.

65. Richard M. Ryan and Jerome Stiller, "The Social Contexts of Internatization: Parent and Teacher Influences on Autonomy, Motivation, and Learning," in *Advances in Motivation and Achievement, Vol. 7: Goals and Self-Regulatory Processes,* eds., Martin L. Maehr and Paul R. R. Pintrich (Greenwich, CT: JAI Press, 1991), pp. 115–149.

Growth-Enhancing Environments in Educational Organizations

ABOUT THIS CHAPTER

Because the behavior of people in organizational life arises from the interaction between their inner motivational needs and characteristics (temperaments, intelligences, beliefs, perceptions) and characteristics of the environment, or because $B = f(p \cdot e)$, then it follows that the organizational environment is a key to influencing organizational behavior. Moreover, although educational leaders have little ability to alter the inner drives and motivational forces of individuals in the organization, they have considerable latitude to alter the organizational environment.

But remember, the organization, and therefore its environment, is a socially constructed reality: it is not tangible. Of course, the building is tangible enough, as are the furniture, equipment, files, and other artifacts that make up the physical entity that we often call "school." But these are not the organization. The organization exists largely in the eye and the mind of the beholder: it is, in reality, pretty much what people think it is.

Coordinating and influencing the behavior of people so as to achieve the goals of the organization is perhaps the central concern of administrators and leaders. Previous chapters in this book have pointed out that there are two different, contrasting ways of thinking about and acting on this problem. That is, there are two different theoretic approaches to it: one is the traditional bureaucratic approach, the other uses the concept of building human capital through human resources development. These two theoretic approaches were compared and contrasted in some detail in Chapter 2. You may find it helpful to review the section, "Two Major Perspectives on Educational Organizations," as a foundation for what is to follow in this chapter.

If educational administrators have little ability to directly alter or influence the inner state of organizational participants—in other words, their motivation—they have considerable ability to do so through indirect means. By fostering the creation of organizational environments that enhance the personal growth of organization members—environments that are supportive of creativity, team building, and participation in solving problems—school leaders can tap into the powerful energy of inner motivational forces that traditional organizational environments routinely repress and discourage. What is being discussed here is, of course, largely the social-psychological environment of the organization, rather than only the physical environment. It is the realm of organizational climate and organizational culture.

HUMAN RESOURCES DEVELOPMENT

As we have seen, the inner state of organizational participants is an important key to understanding their behavior. Thus, although immediate antecedent conditions may well evoke behavioral responses, so, too, do the perceptions, values, beliefs, and motivations of the participants. In other words, participants commonly respond to organizational events very much in terms of learnings that have developed through their experience over time and not merely to antecedent events immediately preceding or following their behavior. Therefore, the educational leader is much concerned with the forces and processes through which organizational participants are socialized into the organization: how they develop perceptions, values, and beliefs concerning the organization and what influence these inner states have on behavior. In contemporary organizational behavior literature, this is the realm of organizational climate and organizational culture.

Neither organizational climate nor organizational culture is a new concept. They have a long tradition in the literature of organization studies, going back at least as far as the Western Electric research of the 1930s, which noted—as described earlier— that some management styles elicited feelings of affiliation, competence, and achievement from workers, leading to more productive work than had been done previously as well as eliciting greater satisfaction from workers than under different styles of management. Beginning in the 1940s, Kurt Lewin and his colleagues and students conducted numerous studies to explore the proposition that organizations could be made more effective by using planned interventions designed to shift the social norms of managers and workers alike. Perhaps the most notable of these early efforts occurred in the Weldon Manufacturing Company, which made men's pajamas, after its merger with the Harwood Manufacturing Corporation.[1]

Many different names have been used over the years to allude to the subtle, elusive, intangible, largely unconscious forces that comprise the symbolic side of organizations and shape human thought and behavior in them.[2] In the late 1930s, Chester Barnard described culture as a social fiction created by people to give meaning to work and life.[3] In the 1940s, Philip Selznick used the term "institution" to describe what it is that creates solidarity, meaning, commitment, and productivity in organizations,[4] Marshall Meyer and his associates used the term somewhat similarly in the 1970s.[5] In the 1960s, the term "organizational climate" became very popular with students of organization, in no small measure due to the research on elementary schools by Andrew Halpin and Don Croft.[6] In his studies of universities in the 1970s, Bernard Clark used the term "organizational saga."[7] Michael Rutter and his colleagues noted the importance of "ethos" in determining the effectiveness of the high schools that they studied.[8] These studies are illustrative of a substantial body of research literature that seeks to describe and explain the learned pattern of thinking, reflected and reinforced in behavior, that is so seldom seen yet is so powerful in shaping people's experiences. This pattern of thinking and the behavior associated with it provide stability, foster certainty, solidify order and predictability, and create meaning.[9]

Defining and Describing Organizational Climate and Culture

An observer who moves from school to school ineluctably develops an intuitive sense that each school is distinctive, unique in some almost indefinable yet powerful way. This sense, seemingly palpable when we are in a school, more than describes that school: it *is* that school. As I have described, many different terms have been used to identify that sense of the unique characteristics that organizations have. People sometimes use such terms as "atmosphere," "personality," "tone," or "ethos" when speaking of this unique characteristic of a school. But the term *organizational climate* has come into rather general use as a metaphor for this distinctive characteristic of organizations. But just what is organizational climate? And how is it created?

Climate is generally defined, as *the characteristics of the total environment* in a school building.[10] But we need to understand what those characteristics are, and to lay the groundwork for that we turn to the work of Tagiuri.

Renato Tagiuri described the total environment in an organization, that is, the organizational climate, as composed of four dimensions:

1. *Ecology* refers to physical and material factors in the organization: for example, the size, age, design, facilities, and condition of the building or buildings. It also refers to the technology used by people in the organization: desks and chairs, chalkboards, elevators, everything used to carry out organizational activities.

2. *Milieu* is the social dimension in the organization. This includes virtually everything relating to the people in the organization. For example, how many there are and what they are like. This would include race and ethnicity, salary level of teachers, socioeconomic level of students, education levels attained by the teachers, the morale and motivation of adults and students who inhabit the school, level of job satisfaction, and a host of other characteristics of the people in the organization.

3. *Social system* refers to the organizational and administrative structure of the organization. It includes how the school is organized, the ways in which decisions are made and who is involved in making them, the communication patterns among people (who talks to whom about what), what work groups there are, and so on.

4. *Culture* refers to the values, belief systems, norms, and ways of thinking that are characteristic of the people in the organization. It is "the way we do things around here." This aspect of the organization's total environment is described more fully a little later in this chapter.

As Figure 5–1 shows, these four dimensions are dynamically interrelated and together give rise to organizational climate. In creating Figure 5–1, I have substituted the term *organization* for Tagiuri's original term *social system* because it seems to me to be more descriptive of what that dimension actually encompasses. Much of the organization dimension of climate arises from factors that administrators control directly or strongly influence. It is important, I think, that administrators understand the close connections between the choices they make about the way they organize and the climate manifested in the organization. To some, *social system* conveys a sense of a somewhat uncontrollable natural order of things whereas *or-*

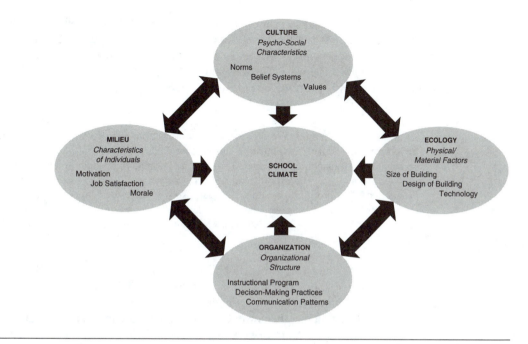

FIGURE 5–1   Interactive model showing relationships between and among key environmental factors that shape and mold school climate. Figure 2 in Carolyn S. Anderson, "The Search for School Climate: A Review of the Research," *Review of Educational Research,* 52 (Fall 1982). © 1982 by the American Educational Research Association. Adapted by Robert G. Owens with permission of the publisher.

ganization makes the influence of the administrator's responsibility for establishing that order a little clearer.

However, contemporary thought does not view each of the four dimensions as being equally potent in producing the character and quality of the climate in a given organization. Recent research has concentrated attention on the primacy of the culture of the organization in defining the character and quality of the climate of an organization.

Research on Organizational Culture

Research on organizational culture, which had stood for some time in the wings of organization studies, shifted to center stage in the two-year span of 1981–1982. It was a dramatic shift and was due to the publication of two books. The first of these, William Ouchi's *Theory Z,* appeared in 1981 and became the first book by a researcher of organizational behavior to enjoy a lengthy stay on the nonfiction bestseller lists.[11] Published at a moment when U.S. corporate managers were groping for some solution to their difficulties in meeting Japanese competition, Ouchi—a Japanese American—compared and contrasted the management styles used in the two nations. He found that Japanese management practices tended to be quite different from those applied in the United States and that some of them (not all, due to societal differences) could profitably be adopted by U.S. corporations. Taking his cue from McGregor's Theory *X*-Theory *Y*, he named his approach Theory *Z* to suggest a new alternative. Theory *Z* accepts the main assumptions of human resource development (HRD):

> Of all its values, commitment of a *Z* culture to its people—its workers—is the most important. . . . Theory *Z* assumes that any worker's life is a whole, not a Jekyll-Hyde personality, half machine from nine to five and half human in the hours preceding and following. Theory *Z* suggests that humanized working conditions not only increase productivity and profits to the company but also the self-esteem for employees. . . . Up to now American managers have assumed that technology makes for increased productivity. What Theory *Z* calls for instead is a redirection of attention to *human* relations in the corporate world.[12]

In 1982, another research report appeared on the best-seller lists. Called *In Search of Excellence,* it described eight management characteristics that sixty-two successful U.S. corporations had in common.[13] Cutting across the eight characteristics was a consistent theme: the power of values and culture in these corporations, rather than procedures and control systems, provides the glue that holds them together, stimulates commitment to a common mission, and galvanizes the creativity and energy of their participants. These values are not usually transmitted formally or in writing. Instead, they permeate the organization in the form of stories, myths, legends, and metaphors—and these companies have people in them who attend to this awareness of organizational culture: "The excellent companies are unashamed collectors and tellers of stories, of legends and myths in support of their basic beliefs. Frito-Lay tells service stories. Johnson & Johnson tells quality stories. 3M tells innovation stories."[14]

Why did organizational culture stay in the wings in the United States so long? And why is it today a central concern in U.S. management? One answer to the first question is that the human underpinning of organization has long been considered to be *soft.* Technology is *hard.* Money is hard. Organizational structure, rules and regulations, policy decisions—these are hard, in the lexicon of many administrators and managers. The things that one can measure, quantify, and control are hard. In this view, the human side of organization is soft. Values, beliefs, culture, behavioral norms have therefore widely been believed to be less potent, less powerful in getting things done. But Ouchi showed that in Japan, the current nemesis of U.S. business, managers have long taken organizational culture far more seriously than Americans have—and it is important in giving them a competitive edge. And Peters and Waterman, authors of *In Search of Excellence,* demonstrated that high-flying American corporations show similar sophistication and concern for the development of organizational culture.

Further, these books—together with Terrence Deal and Allan Kennedy's *Corporate Cultures: The Rites and Rituals of Corporate Life,* which also appeared in

1982[15]—helped to clarify what culture is: a system of shared values and beliefs that interact with an organization's people, organizational structures, and control systems to produce behavioral norms. They helped make clear that, in practical terms, *shared values* means "what is important"; *beliefs* means "what we think is true"; and *behavioral norms* means "how we do things around here." With the obvious success of companies using these ideas, and with the ideas themselves clarified, the concept of organizational culture suddenly became of practical importance to managers and administrators. As Peters and Waterman put it, "Now, culture is the 'softest' stuff around. Who trusts its leading analysts—anthropologists and sociologists—after all? Businessmen surely don't. Yet culture is the hardest stuff around, as well."[16]

It became clear to U.S. businesspeople—confronted by recession, deregulation, technological upheavals, foreign competition, and transforming economic and social change—that an organizational culture that stifles innovation and hard work may be the biggest stumbling block to adapting to uncertain times. The lesson was not lost on educational administrators: confronted by shrinking finances, faltering public support, divided constituencies with conflicting interests, and rampant charges of organizational ineffectiveness, they became riveted by the implications of organizational culture for educational organizations.

Organizational Culture and Organizational Climate Compared and Contrasted

The terms *culture* and *climate* are both abstractions that deal with the fact that the behavior of persons in organizations is not elicited by interaction with proximate events alone but is also influenced by interaction with intangible forces in the organization's environment. As I shall explain more fully, culture refers to the behavioral norms, assumptions, and beliefs of an organization, whereas climate refers to perceptions of persons in the organization that reflect those norms, assumptions, and beliefs.

Organizational Culture

Though many definitions of organizational culture are found in the literature, the high degree of agreement between and among them makes it relatively easy to understand what culture is and how it relates to and differs from organizational climate. Organizational culture is the body of solutions to external and internal problems that has worked consistently for a group and that is therefore taught to new members as the correct way to perceive, think about, and feel in relation to those problems.[17]

Culture develops over a period of time and, in the process of developing, acquires significantly deeper meaning. Thus, "such solutions eventually come to be assumptions about the nature of reality, truth, time, space, human nature, human activity, and human relationships—then they come to be taken for granted and, finally, drop out of awareness."[18] Therefore, "culture can be defined as the shared philosophies, ideologies, values, assumptions, beliefs, expectations, attitudes, and norms that knit a community together."[19] In this case, the community is an organization—a school, for example—and all of these interrelated qualities reveal agreement, implicit or explicit, among teachers, administrators, and other participants on how to approach decisions and problems: "the way things are done around here."[20]

As Terrence Deal pointed out, "At the heart of most . . . definitions of culture is the concept of a learned pattern of unconscious (or semiconscious) thought, reflected and reinforced by behavior, that silently and powerfully shapes the experience of a people."[21] This pattern of thought, which is organizational culture, "provides stability, fosters certainty, solidifies order and predictability, and creates meaning."[22] It also gives rise to simpler, though highly compatible, commonsense definitions, such as "[Organizational culture] is the rules of the game; the unseen meaning between the lines in the rulebook that insures unity"[23] or "Culture consists of the conclusions a group of people draws from its experience. An organization's culture consists largely of what people believe about what works and what does not."[24]

Although anthropologists and sociologists understand that culture—whether of a larger society or of an organization—can be inferred by observing the behavior of people, it is not really a study of that behavior. Through the observation of behavior one can develop an understanding of the systems of knowledge, beliefs, customs, and habits of people—whether it be in a larger society or an organization. In studying organizational culture, therefore, one looks at the artifacts and technology that people use, and one listens to what they say and observes what they do in an effort to discover the patterns of thoughts, beliefs, and values that they use in making sense of the everyday events that they experience. Thus, organizational culture is the study of the wellsprings from which the values and characteristics of an organization arise.

Two major themes in a definition of organizational culture

Two themes consistently pervade the literature describing and defining organizational culture: one theme is *norms* and the other theme is *assumptions*. Norms and assumptions are widely regarded as key components of organizational culture.

Norms. An important way in which organizational culture influences behavior is through the norms or standards that the social system institutionalizes and enforces. These are encountered by the individual as group norms, which are ideas "that can be put into the form of a statement specifying what members . . . should do."[25] They are, in other words, "rules of behavior which have been accepted as legitimate by members of a group."[26] They are, of course, unwritten rules, that nonetheless express the shared beliefs of most group members about what behavior is appropriate in order to be a member in good standing.[27]

Assumptions. Underneath these behavioral norms lie the assumptions that comprise the bedrock on which norms and all other aspects of culture are built. These assumptions deal with what the people in the organization accept as true in the world and what is false, what is sensible and what is absurd, what is possible and what is impossible. I agree with Edgar Schein: these are not values, which can be debated and discussed. Assumptions are tacit instead, unconsciously taken for granted, rarely considered or talked about, and accepted as true and nonnegotiable.[28] The cultural norms in the organization—informal, unwritten, but highly explicit and powerful in influencing behavior—arise directly from the underlying assumptions.

Specifying what organizational culture is

Edgar Schein described organizational culture as being comprised of three different but closely linked concepts. Thus, organizational culture may be defined as follows:

1. A body of solutions to external and internal problems that has worked consistently for a group and that is therefore taught to new members as the correct way to perceive, think about, and feel in relation to those problems.

2. These eventually come to be assumptions about the nature of reality, truth, time, space, human nature, human activity, and human relationships.

3. Over time, these assumptions come to be taken for granted and finally drop out of awareness. Indeed, the power of culture lies in the fact that it operates as a set of unconscious, unexamined assumptions that are taken for granted.[29]

Thus, culture develops over a period of time and, in the process of developing, acquires significantly deep meaning. Therefore, culture can be defined as the shared philosophies, ideologies, values, assumptions, beliefs, expectations, attitudes, and norms that knit a community together.[30] The school is viewed as having all of these interrelated qualities that reveal agreement, implicit or explicit, among teachers, administrators, and other participants on how to approach decisions and problems: "the way things are done around here."[31] As with most definitions of organizational culture, this pivots on the concept of a learned pattern of unconscious thought, reflected and reinforced by behavior, that silently and powerfully shapes the experience of a people.[32]

In Schein's model (Figure 5–2), the most obvious manifestations of organizational culture are visible and audible: these are artifacts such as tools, buildings, art, and technology, as well as patterns of human behavior, including speech. Because these are visible, they have been frequently studied usually using naturalistic field methods such as observation, interviews, and document analysis. Though these manifestations are readily visible, they are merely symbolic of the culture itself, which is not visible and which is not even in the awareness of the people we observe. Therefore, to make sense of the artifacts and the behaviors that we observe requires us to decipher their meaning, and this is difficult to do.

Below this publicly visible level of the manifestations of culture lie the values of the organization, sometimes encoded in written language such as in a "mission statement," a "statement of philosophy," or a "credo." Documents such as these move us closer to understanding the basic assumptions of the organization but they, too, merely reflect the basic assumptions that are the essence of the culture.

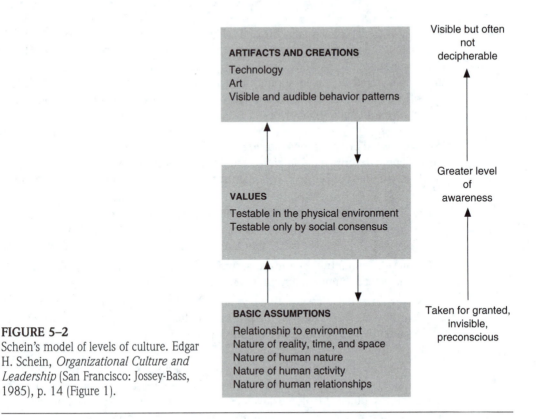

FIGURE 5–2
Schein's model of levels of culture. Edgar
H. Schein, *Organizational Culture and
Leadership* (San Francisco: Jossey-Bass,
1985), p. 14 (Figure 1).

Finally, at the third and lowest level, we find the essence of the culture: those
assumptions that are taken for granted, invisible, and out of consciousness. These
have to do with the relationships of individuals to the environment; the nature of reality, time, and space; the nature of human nature; the nature of human activity; and
the nature of human relationships. These unseen assumptions, of which the organization's members are unaware, form patterns but they remain implicit, unconscious,
and taken for granted unless they are called to the surface by some process of
inquiry.

Symbolism and culture
Though organizational culture is usually studied through inferences derived from
the observation of organizational behavior, the focus is not limited to the impact of
the environment on the behavior of individual persons. It extends to understanding
what the elements of such environments are, how they develop, and how these elements relate to one another so as to form (in effect) the lexicon, grammar, and syn-
tax of organization. Thus, for example, the study of symbolism is central to the
study of organizational culture: the rituals, myths, traditions, rites, and language
through which human meanings and values are transmitted literally from one generation of the organization to another.

A school climate may be characterized by certain perceptions held by participants as to the nature of the organization ("What things are really like here"), but how are those perceptions developed, communicated, and transmitted? A school may be viewed by members as holding certain values, extolling particular virtues, standing for describable standards and practices that have a deep effect on the behaviors of the members. But how are these made explicit and communicated to the members? What are the mechanisms used by the organization to influence and control behavior in predictable, desired ways? In schools, as well as in societies, the answer is through institutionalized rituals and symbols. Understanding these is essential to understanding culture.

In many societies, for example, marriage rites constitute powerful symbols that evoke a great deal of behavior considered "right" and "proper," if not inevitable. This might include deciding where the married couple live, how the members of the family take on new roles (such as mother-in-law), and division of labor between the sexes. Thus the institution of marriage, symbolized by ceremonies and rituals handed down through the generations, communicates values to people that the society holds to be important. Much more than that, the communication results in behaviors that may seem ordinary and even mundane to the participants but which are powerful in developing their perceptions as to what is right or wrong, or even possible.

Similarly, to join the faculty of a typical U.S. high school brings with it many obligations and expectations. Some of these are inexorably demanded by the daily schedule of classes (the bell schedule), which signals powerfully to participants who should be where—and doing what—virtually every minute of the day. To many educators the schedule is such an inherent part of the culture of the school as to be taken for granted, accepted without question, an overriding symbol of what defines the school itself. That is a powerful cultural feature of the high school, and it has great impact on what participants do, see as possible, and value as important in the life of the school. The bell schedule is one of many powerful cultural symbols that help to create the organizational climate found in a high school in the United States.

Organizational Climate

Organizational climate is the study of *perceptions* that individuals have of various aspects of the environment in the organization. For example, in their pioneer study of organizational climate in schools, Andrew Halpin and Don Croft examined "the attributes of leadership and group behavior" found to exist in elementary schools.[33] To do this, they asked teachers to describe their perceptions of certain human interactions in a sample of elementary schools that seemed to result from such causes as the principal's behavior in his or her official role in the hierarchy, the personality characteristics of individual teachers, the social needs of individual teachers as members of a work group, and such group characteristics of the teachers in the school as morale. A major outcome of the Halpin and Croft research was the demonstration that, by using the set of perceptions that the Halpin and Croft questionnaire probed, the organizational climate of elementary schools may be systematically assessed.

The notion of satisfaction is usually closely associated with the concept of organizational climate. That is, to what extent are the perceptions that participants have of the environment of the organization satisfying to them? This association of satisfaction with the perceptions of participants is implicit in some techniques for studying climate, whereas many studies have inquired directly into possible discrepancies between the participants' perceptions of the existing state of affairs in contrast to whatever desired state the respondents think ought to prevail.

Studies of organizational climate depend heavily on eliciting the perceptions of participants. This has led to the use of questionnaires in which respondents are asked directly about their perceptions. Although interviews could also be an effective means of gathering such information, this has not been done very often whereas the development of questionnaires has proliferated.

Earlier studies of organizational climate in schools tended to gather data from adults, almost always teachers, with occasional inquiries of principals. In more recent years, the trend in school climate studies has been in the direction of examining the perceptions of pupils and students, rather than adults in the school.

The Affective Aspects of Culture and Climate

The culture of an organization exerts powerful influence on the development of climate. Inasmuch as culture of the organization, even though it is intangible, influences the way that participants perceive events and make sense of those events, it is clear that culture has influence on the attitudes and feelings of participants. Rosabeth Moss Kanter captured much of the impact of organizational culture and climate in reporting her studies comparing highly successful and less successful U.S. corporations.

She speaks of high-performing companies as having a culture of pride and a climate of success. By a culture of pride she means "there is emotional and value commitment between person and organization; people feel that they 'belong' to a meaningful entity and can realize cherished values by their contributions."[34] With this feeling of pride in belonging to a worthwhile organization with a record of achievement, of being a member rather than merely an employee, the confidence of the individual is bolstered: confidence that the organization will be supportive of creative new practices and will continue to perform well and confidence also that the individual will be effective and successful in his or her own realm of work in the organization.

Kanter's research led her to believe that the culture of pride is widely found in organizations that are integrative, which means organizations that emphasize the wholeness of the enterprise, that actively consider the wider implications of things that they do, and that thrive on diversity and stimulate challenges to traditional practices. These organizations tend to a large extent to be successful because their cultures foster a climate of success.

In contrast, Kanter described less successful organizations as being segmented. In segmented organizations members find it difficult even to discover what is going on beyond their own little sphere of operations much less to deal with problems that affect the whole organization. People are kept isolated, stratified away from the larger decisions in the organization, focused on the narrow piece of action in which they are directly involved. In these organizations people find it difficult to take pride in the organization because they really know little about it and what it is doing. Thus, such organizations are characterized by climates of something other than success.

Multiple Cultures

Although a given organization will have an overall organizational culture, many organizations also have other additional workplace cultures. In other words, in describing organizational culture we must be aware that subunits of the organization have cultures of their own which possess distinctive attributes. As an example, consider the school district that has central administrative offices, a senior high school, a junior high school, and several elementary schools.

Whereas the school board and top-level administrators in such a district may understand that the district as an organization has a shared set of understandings, assumptions, and beliefs reflected in and reinforced by the behaviors of people—in short, an organizational culture—they should also understand that each individual school will be characterized by its own culture. The culture of a given school is likely to reflect certain of the principal characteristics of the school district's organizational culture and, yet, be different in some ways. Moreover, the cultures of the various schools are likely to differ. Further, it is more than likely that the central office will exhibit an organizational culture of its own that is distinctive from that of any of the schools.

To carry the illustration further, consider the organizational culture of the senior high school in that district. The school itself will have an organizational culture as I have described and it will also have workplace cultures within it. For example, the counselors in the guidance and counselling department of the school may interpret their role—and that of the department—as being supportive and helping in their relationship to students, encouraging students to grow and mature in the ability to make informed decisions regarding their lives, and to increasingly take charge of their lives. In their work, such counselors would tend to value developing high trust relationships with students in order to engender openness in dealing with problems. Across the hall, however, one might find the unit responsible for managing attendance and discipline. Quite possibly the faculty in this unit could adopt—for whatever reasons—a shared understanding that toughness counts along with fairness, that it is the responsibility of the school to be sure that students toe the mark and to mete out punishment when they fail to do so, and to leave no mistake as to who is in charge. One could go on, demonstrating that other departments in the school are likely to exhibit cultures of their own—in some ways distinctive and in other ways mirroring the culture of the school as a whole.

The fact that multiple cultures are likely to be found in school districts and schools is not surprising inasmuch as the subunits of the organization do many of the same culture-building things as the larger organization itself does. It is the subunits—such as schools and departments—that regularly bring together people who share some constellation of interests, purposes, and values; they are the settings in which people seek social affiliation in face-to-face groups; they facilitate the sharing and cooperative effort required to get the work done. These functions of the subunits provide the impetus for developing multiple cultures in the organization, rather than a single organizational culture from top to bottom.

Indeed, it appears likely that Theory *X* administrators tend to think of organizational culture as being conceptualized at top levels in the organization and managed in such a way as to be implemented down the line of authority. This approach to the development of organizational culture, which is in harmony with classical concepts of organization, is problematic inasmuch as it is difficult to change the assumptions of people and compel their sharing of assumptions with others by issuing directives. On the other hand, Theory *Y* administrators are likely to more readily accept the concept of multiple cultures existing within the organization. The development of multiple cultures within the organization is facilitated by the use of participative methods associated with HRD.

No concept in the realm of organizational behavior relies more heavily on social systems concepts than does organizational culture. Clearly, however, the culture of an organization is readily seen as important to eliciting and shaping the behavior of participants, which gives rise to the notion of *person-environment interaction*.

Group Norms

An important way in which organizational culture influences behavior is through the norms or standards that the social system institutionalizes and enforces. These are encountered by the individual as group norms, which are "an idea that can be put in the form of a statement specifying what members . . . should do."[35] They are, in other words, "rules of behavior which have been accepted as legitimate by members of a group."[36] Groups typically exert pressures on an individual to conform to group norms that are more pervasive than the individual is likely to comprehend. These pressures are often felt as an obligation to behave in certain ways; this is often manifested in positive forms, such as support from the group for opinions and behavior that the group approves and wishes to reinforce.

Especially if the individual highly values the esteem and acceptance of members of the group and, more especially, if the group is highly cohesive, the pressure to conform to group standards and expectations can even influence one's perceptions of reality. He or she tends to "see" things in terms of the expectations that the group has. Thus, the interaction of the individual with groups reaches far deeper than merely observable behavior: it strongly influences the development of perceptions, values, and attitudes.

Person-Environment Interaction

Any discussion of organizational culture has its roots in the work of Kurt Lewin, who demonstrated that understanding human behavior requires us to consider the whole situation in which behavior occurs.[37] The term "whole situation" is defined as meaning both the person and the environment. Essentially, then, behavior is a function of the interaction of person and environment. Thus, as we know, $B = f(p \cdot e)$. Consequently, in conceptualizing organizational culture, it is necessary to think of the person and the organizational environment as complementary parts of one situation. They are inseparable.

The group is an important part of the environment that the individual encounters as a member of an organization. "The postulate that behavior is a function of the interaction of organism and environment is widely accepted," Garlie Forehand and B. Von Haller Gilmer have pointed out, but "the concept of environment has been a difficult one for psychologists to deal with empirically."[38] This is, in part, because formal models of the organization (such as organizational charts) provide tidy, rational diagrams, but people often do not behave in the ways that the model depicts.[39] On the other hand, the behavior of individuals in organizational settings does not arise *only* from the personal characteristics of the individuals, but is also influenced by the total situation in which they find themselves.[40]

The perspective of organizational culture helps us to understand that the environment with which people interact is constituted of more than the immediate circumstances in which they find themselves. A crucial aspect of understanding the culture of an organization is to understand the organization's history and its traditions because individuals in an organization are socialized to accept them. Thus, unseen but present in every human encounter with the organization, is the understanding and acceptance by participants of values and expectations that are inherent in the tradition of the organization. Organizations normally expend considerable effort, both formally and informally, to transmit and reinforce these values and expectations through socialization processes.

In many a U.S. high school, to return to an earlier example, it is difficult for teachers and administrators alike to conceptualize organizing their work in any other way than by using a bell schedule built upon Carnegie Units of Instruction. Indeed, the tradition of using "units" as the building blocks of the U.S. high school's daily class schedule is so time honored and so taken for granted that few teachers today even know what a Carnegie Unit of Instruction is, even though it is one of the most dominant influences on their professional practice.

Carnegie Units were invented in 1905 by the Carnegie Foundation for the Advancement of Teaching as a way of standardizing high school instruction so that colleges would have an easier time comparing the transcripts of applicants. It was, and is, a measure of time: 120 hours of classroom instruction. Thus, one unit of a subject requires the student to be present in the classroom for 120 hours. The implications for scheduling are apparent: for example, if one decides to build a schedule around class periods that are 48 minutes long, so as to allow passing time between classes, then a one-unit class should meet 150 times during the year. This lays the basis for the traditional block-schedule that not only wields such power over the behavior of teachers and students, but shapes their perceptions of what school is and ought to be, defines what is possible and not possible, and dictates what is right and what is wrong.

This is a strong tradition in secondary education in the United States, often associated with quality and sound professional practice, that has continually been reinforced by the teachers' own experience as students in high schools, by their university training, and by their experience as professionals. It is an illustration of the forces that are always present in organizational culture as part of the unseen, intangible environment which shapes and molds the behavior of participants. The Carnegie Unit illustrates the stubborn persistence that cultural artifacts typically display, surviving to influence thinking and behavior in the organization long after they have outlived their intended purpose. For many years, educators have doubted that time spent in class is the most useful indicator that we have to gauge what kind and quality of learning a student was achieving. Yet, reinforced in law and regulation, a venerable hallmark that many people associate with the "quality" of school's instructional program, the Carnegie Unit remained unchallenged for 88 years as one of the key national quality standards in secondary schooling. In 1993 the Pennsylvania State Board of Education, the first state to do so, voted to abolish the use of the Carnegie Unit by the end of the century and to establish a set of required academic goals for students to achieve instead. The move, however—even though applauded by the Carnegie Foundation itself as desirable—has met fiercely entrenched opposition from conservatives, including Christian organizations, and the impact of the change beyond the borders of Pennsylvania may remain in doubt for some time.

The term "tradition" used in this sense does not necessarily mean repeating old solutions to newly emerging problems. Some organizations try to create what might be called new cultural traditions in an effort to break the habits of the past and emphasize the value of originality and creativity in finding fresh solutions to problems encountered in the life of the organization. Contemporary examples are readily found in the relatively young entrepreneurial computer firms in the Silicon Valley and other locations that place high value on bold thinking and inventiveness. Apple Computer is frequently cited as an illustration of an organization that was built on this concept. At this writing, with that company having developed into a large corporation whose culture was taking on values and assumptions that the original founders no longer found congenial, there was doubt whether or not the "old" corporate culture could be maintained into the future or whether it had outlived its usefulness and needed to be replaced by different cultural traditions.

Concept of Behavior Settings

Roger Barker theorized that environments have great influence in evoking and shaping the patterns of behavior of the people in them.[41] Indeed, according to his view of what is now known as "ecological psychology," the influence of environment is so great that it tends to overcome many individual differences among people who populate organizations. The result is that, in specific organizations, people tend to exhibit patterns of behavior that are so regular and distinct that we tend to view their behavior as "belonging to" those particular organizations. Barker posited, therefore, that organizational behavior is best understood in terms of *behavior settings,* referring to the whole complex physical and psychological environment with which people are in constant interaction.

In a remarkable pioneer study of the relationship between the size of high schools and the behavior of students in them, Roger Barker and Paul Gump discovered, for example, that the extent to which students participate in extraclass and extracurricular activities is directly related to the size of the school.[42] In similar research, Leonard Baird showed that the achievement of students, as well as the degree of their participation in extraclass activities, is related not only to the size of the school but also to the type of community in which the school is located (for example, small city, suburb, or large city).[43] In another study, Baird found that success at college was related not so much to the size of the high school from which students came as it was to the size of the college itself.[44]

The round of "school reform" and "school improvement" of the 1970s was notable for its emphasis on bigness: led by the studies of James B. Conant under the auspices of the Ford Foundation, the United States undertook to build bigger schools and create bigger school districts. Bigger was thought to be better because the financial economies of scale that were envisioned would permit schools to be more diverse, richer in resources, supportive of greater opportunities for students. By the mid-1990s, however, there was increasing awareness that high schools with 2,000 to 5,000 students or more were being seen "as Dickensian workhouses breeding violence, dropouts, academic failure and alienation" whereas "schools limited to about 400 usually have fewer behavioral problems, better attendance and graduation rates, and sometimes higher grades and test scores."[45] To create more growth-enhancing behavior settings in their schools, cities across the country—including New York, Philadelphia, Denver, Chicago, and San Francisco—are busily trying various ideas ranging from simply creating smaller schools in separate buildings to trying schools-within-a-school plans. Some are experimenting with the "charter school" idea in which schools that undertake to reinvent themselves are encouraged and supported by being excused from some of the legal and bureaucratic constraints that burden the public school enterprise.

Barker's work has had considerable influence on Seymour Sarason, whose book, *The Culture of the School and the Problem of Change,* speaks so lucidly and persuasively of the necessity of finding ways of altering the patterns of activities, group norms, and the temporal qualities that are characteristic of U.S. public schools before we can hope to change the impact that they have on the people in them.[46] This milieu, which Sarason called the "culture of the school," is not necessarily planned or deliberately created; it tends, instead, to be a phenomenon that is generated from (1) the activities of people in the school (for example, lecturing, listening, moving about according to schedule), (2) the physical objects in the environment (for example, walls, furniture, chalkboard, playground), and (3) the temporal regularities observed (for example, the length of classes, the pattern of the daily schedule, the pattern of the school calendar).

The influence of this interaction among activities, physical environment, and temporal regularities is seen as not only pervasive and relatively stable, but also as having very great power to mold the behavior of the people in the organization.

Sarason has extended this insight to attempts to plan and create settings in newly created organizations that presumably would elicit kinds of behaviors thought to be functional and productive in terms of the organization's mission.[47]

The Interaction-Influence System

A central concept in organizational behavior is that of the interaction-influence system of an organization. We should keep in mind that the basic function of organizational structure is to establish patterns of human interaction to get the tasks accomplished (who deals with whom, in what ways, and about what). Thus, departments, teams, schools, and divisions are typical formal structures, whereas friendship groups, people who work in close proximity to one another, and coffee-klatch groups are typical informal structures. The interactions between and among people thus put into contact with each other in conducting the day-to-day business of the organization establish the norms that are so powerful in shaping organizational behavior.

The interaction-influence system of the organization deals simultaneously with both structure and the processes of interaction. The two are mutually interdependent in such a dynamic way that they cannot be considered independently. In this sense, the interaction-influence patterns in shaping the organizational behavior of work groups are roughly the counterparts of person and environment in eliciting and shaping the behavior of individuals.

The interaction processes in the interaction-influence system include communication, motivation, leadership, goal setting, decision making, coordination, control, and evaluation. The ways in which these interactions are effected in the organization (their characteristics and quality) exercise an important influence on eliciting and shaping human behavior. Efforts to describe the organizational culture of educative organizations are, therefore, efforts to describe the characteristics of the organization's interaction-influence system.

Describing and Assessing Organizational Culture in Schools

The study of organizational culture presents nettlesome problems to the traditional researcher primarily because important elements of culture are subtle, unseen, and so familiar to persons inside the organization as to be considered self-evident and, in effect, invisible. Collecting, sorting, and summarizing data such as the significant historical events in the organization and their implications for present-day behavior, the impact of organizational heroes on contemporary thinking, and the influence of traditions and organizational myths is a task that does not lend itself to the tidiness of a printed questionnaire and statistical analysis of the responses to it. As the work of Ouchi, Peters and Waterman, Kanter, and Deal and Kennedy demonstrated, it is necessary to get inside the organization: to talk at length with people; to find out what they think is important to talk about; to hear the language they use; and to discover the symbols that reveal their assumptions, their beliefs, and the values to which they subscribe. For that reason, students of organizational culture tend to use qualitative research methods rather than traditional questionnaire-type studies. This has raised vigorous debate in many schools of education as to the epistemological value of qualitative research methods as contrasted with the more traditional statistical studies (of the experimental or quasi-experimental type) that have long been the stock-in-trade of educational researchers.

RELATIONSHIP BETWEEN ORGANIZATIONAL CULTURE AND ORGANIZATIONAL EFFECTIVENESS

Do various organizational cultures produce different outcomes, in terms of effectiveness, in the organization achieving its goals? The issue is far from simple: measuring organizational effectiveness is, in itself, a complex undertaking, and the traditional need felt by many people in management to control and direct subordinates in the *command* sense of the term tends to tinge with emotion discussion of the issue.

To a large extent, accepted conventions of research and rules of evidence, discussed above, form the heart of this controversy. It has long been accepted in the logic of science that cause-and-effect relationships are best established by such rationalistic research designs as the controlled experiment. Experimental research, of course, requires that one can control the relevant variables under study.

A substantial body of carefully controlled experimental research conducted in laboratory settings strongly undergirds the psychological concepts from which students of organizations draw in conceptualizing organizational behavior.[48] However, studies of actual organizations in the real world often must be conducted under conditions wherein such control is not possible. There is an analogous situation here with the extensive research literature on the possibility that "cigarette smoking causes cancer in humans," which is not a body of controlled experimental research that *proves* that cigarette smoking is the single causative factor. Research evidence *suggesting* (however strongly) a causal link between cigarette smoking and the incidence of cancer in humans is generally derived from such nonexperimental research as survey studies (many of which are longitudinal in design) or controlled research conducted on animals. Generally, there is such a strong *association* between the incidence of smoking and the incidence of cancer that many people accept that a cause-and-effect relationship exists. In terms of scientific rules of evidence, however, this is not *proof* and one can argue that, until evidence from fully controlled experiments is produced, the cause-and-effect relationship cannot be accepted as conclusive.

So it is with the link between organizational culture and organizational effectiveness: no significant body of *experimental* research in which the variables are fully controlled exists, and, therefore, discussion of the issue must be in the realm of *association* of significant variables. There is little question that many students of organizational behavior have ducked this issue by contenting themselves with refining techniques for defining and describing the variables of organizational culture or, in some cases, cautiously suggesting a possible relationship.

Cause and Effect

Rensis Likert sought to link organizational performance to the internal characteristics of the organization. His analysis is that the performance of an organization is determined by a three-link chain of causes and effects.

The first link in the chain is composed of the *causal variables,* which are under the control of the administration. Thus, administration (management) can *choose* the design of the organization's structure (mechanistic or organic, bureaucratic or flexible). Similarly, administration can *choose* the leadership style (for example, authoritarian or participative); it can *choose* a philosophy of operation (for example, teamwork or directive, problem-solving or rule-following). The choices that administration makes in selecting the options available are critical to and powerful in determining the nature of the management system in the organization (namely, Systems 1, 2, 3, or 4). These are seen as causing the interaction-influence system of the organization—in other words, its culture—to have the characteristics that it does have.

Intervening variables flow directly from (are caused largely by) these causal variables (that is, the choices that administration makes). Thus, the nature of motivation, communication, and other critical aspects of organizational functioning is determined.

End-result variables, the measures of an organization's success, depend heavily, of course, on the nature and quality of the internal functioning of the organization.

This analysis fits nicely with recent reports of qualitative research in U.S. public schools—such as Theodore Sizer's *Horace's Compromise,*[49] Ernest Boyer's *High School,*[50] and John Goodlad's *A Place Called School*[51]—and their counterparts from the corporate world—such as *In Search of Excellence, Theory Z, Corporate Cultures,* and *The Change Masters.* For, as Rosabeth Moss Kanter pointed out in the latter work and I discussed earlier, innovative companies are marked by a culture of pride and a climate of success in which the organizational norms support success-oriented effort—and that depends upon the values which the leaders enact in the daily life of the organization.

The Problem of Measuring School Effectiveness

Any effort to relate organizational culture (however described and measured) to the effectiveness of educative organizations squarely confronts the difficulties of assessing the effectiveness dimension. This problem requires that we identify indicators of organizational effectiveness for schools and ways of measuring them. Needless to say, this problem has been receiving markedly increased attention over the years.

In research parlance, we are dealing with sets of variables. Organizational climate and other internal characteristics of the school (for example, style of leadership, communication processes, motivational forces) are examples of *independent* variables. Other independent variables are characteristics of the situation in which the school, as an organization, is embedded. This, of course, would include such characteristics of the community as its wealth, its social-cultural traditions, its political power structure, and demography. Very often it seems clear that these two independent variables are highly interactive, but little has been done to explore this possibility. For example, we have scant firm evidence of what impact the situational variables with which a school contends have on shaping the characteristics of the interaction-influence system of the school. We must remember that the school is an open system, interactive with and responsive to its external environment. Though organizational culture focuses on the internal arrangements of schools, those always reflect, to some degree, the larger environment of the school's situation.

Dependent variables are indicators of organizational effectiveness. These can be grouped roughly as objective indicators and subjective indicators. Measures of achievement (such as test scores) and measures of some behaviors (for example, dropouts, absences) often can be quantified objectively. Very often we use subjective measures of school effectiveness, too. These could include performance ratings by various of the school's publics, as well as surveys of attitudes toward the school's performance.

One recent, sophisticated attempt to "get at" the complexities of this problem was a study by Wilbur Brookover and his associates of a random sample of 2,226 Michigan elementary schools. The dependent variable, by which effectiveness was measured, was the mean achievement scores of fourth-grade pupils in the standardized Michigan Assessment Program.

The key independent variable was a measure of school climate that was developed from the following definition:

> The school climate encompasses a composite of variables as defined and perceived by members of this group. These factors may be broadly conceived as the norms of the social system and expectations held for various members as perceived by the members of the group and communicated to members of the group.[52]

The investigators noted that a good deal of the previous research of this kind had used the socioeconomic status (SES) of the children or the racial composition of the school as a proxy for organizational climate. Among such studies that are well known to educators are the famous "Coleman report"[53] and the work of Christopher Jencks on inequality of schooling.[54] In this case, however, the researchers chose to devise an instrument to measure climate directly in the schools under study. The climate variable was essentially a measure of the norms and expectations in the school. Appropriately enough, the researchers called this the Student Sense of Academic Futility. Thus, the principal independent variables in the study were (1) mean school-level SES, (2) racial composition of the school (that is, percent of students who were white), and (3) climate of the school.

In commenting on their findings, the investigators said, "The first and foremost conclusion derived from this research is that some aspects of school social environment clearly make a difference in the academic achievement of schools."[55] Although large differences existed between the achievement levels in various schools, the socioeconomic and racial composition of the student bodies in those schools accounted for only a small percentage of the variance. The crucial variable, strongly associated with objective measures of student achievement, was the social climate of the school (measured, in this case, by the student's sense of academic futility).

The researchers concluded that this concept of climate, at least, is clearly related to school achievement:

> If we apply these findings to the school desegregation issue, it seems safe to conclude that neither racial nor socioeconomic desegregation of schools automatically produces higher school achievement. If the unfavorable social-psychological climate which typically characterizes segregated black and lower SES schools continues to prevail for the poor or minority students in the desegregated schools, desegregation is not likely to materially affect achievement of the students. If the social-psychological climate relevant to the poor and minority [students] is improved in conjunction with desegregation, higher achievement is likely to result.[56]

Strong research support for a close relationship between the culture of the school and outcomes also comes from a study of twelve inner-city London schools,[57] which posed the following research questions:

1. Do a child's experiences at school have any effect?
2. Does it matter which school a child attends?
3. If so, which are the features of the school that matter?

The first question was prompted, of course, by a number of U.S. studies that raise serious questions as to what effect attendance at school actually has (for example, Coleman's and Jencks's work). The second and third questions deal specifically with the cause-and-effect problem under discussion here.

To measure school outcomes the researchers used the following dependent variables: (1) pupil behavior, (2) pupil attendance, and (3) regularly scheduled public school examinations. The study showed, first, that there was a marked difference in the behavior, attendance, and achievement of the students in various secondary schools. Second, these differences between schools was not accounted for by the socioeconomic or ethnic differences of their students: clearly, students were likely to behave better and achieve more in some schools than in others. Third, these differences in student behavior and performance

> were *not* due to such physical factors as the size of the school, the age of the buildings or the space available; nor were they due to broad differences in administrative status or organization [for example, structure]. It was entirely possible for schools to obtain good outcomes in spite of initially rather unpromising and unprepossessing school premises, and within the context of somewhat differing administrative arrangements . . . the differences between schools in outcome *were* systematically related to their characteristics as social institutions.[58]

Key among these latter characteristics (that is, the independent variables) were (1) the behavior of teachers at work, (2) the emphasis placed on academic performance, (3) the provision for students to be rewarded for succeeding, and (4) the extent to which students were able to take responsibility. All these factors, the researchers pointed out, were open to modification by the staff, rather than fixed by external constraints. In short, this research strongly suggests that organizational culture (which they call "ethos") is a critical factor in student behavior and achievement. Moreover, much as Likert did, they pointed out that organizational culture is in the control of the people who manage the organization.

Joyce Epstein reported studies in schools which describe the perceptions of students' satisfaction with school in general, their commitment to school work, and their attitudes toward teachers.[59] Taken together, these are thought by Epstein to describe the quality of school life as the students perceive it. Further, this perception is described as, of course, being related to the behaviors of the students as participants in the organization. To conduct such studies, Epstein developed and validated a 27-item questionnaire designed to be used across school levels (that is, elementary, middle, and high school).

Rudolf Moos reported large-scale research in the United States, in both secondary school and college settings, that supports the mounting evidence in the literature that the learning and development of students are significantly influenced by characteristics of organizational culture.[60] After studying some 10,000 secondary school students in more than 500 classrooms, he was able to identify characteristics of classroom organizational culture that facilitate academic achievement, on the one hand, and those that induce stress, alienate students, and thereby inhibit learning, on the other hand. He measured the variances from classroom to classroom in such contextual influences as (1) stress on competition, (2) emphasis on rules, (3) supportive behavior by the teacher, and (4) extent of innovative activities. They were the independent variables. Moos then correlated these measures with measures of dependent variables, such as (1) student rate of absence, (2) grades earned, (3) student satisfaction with learning, and (4) student satisfaction with the teacher.

In college settings Moos studied 225 living groups (for example, coed and single-sex residence halls, fraternities and sororities), involving about 10,000 students. Using questionnaires, he measured distinctive characteristics of these various groups such as (1) emphasis on intellectuality, (2) social activities, and (3) group unity. He then sought to assess the effects of these variables on such dependent variables as (1) students' concepts of themselves, (2) personal interests and values, (3) aspirations, and (4) achievement.

Essentially, Moos found that students' learning and development are strongly influenced by the nature and qualities of the person-environment interaction in such educational settings as secondary school classrooms and college residence arrangements. An interesting aspect of his research is his attempt to demonstrate how organizational culture and human behavior are influenced, not only by the interaction-influence system of the group but also by other factors in the environment such as room design, schedule of activities, and layout of building. In his view, our knowledge of the causes and effects of organizational culture enables us to create and manage specified learning environments by controlling critical variables (such as competition, intellectuality, and formal structure). This, in turn, improves our ability to place students in the settings best suited to their needs—settings in which they will feel most comfortable and be most successful. This, he contends, is highly practical knowledge that can be used to develop administrative policies and pedagogical practices that are effective in dealing with student apathy, alienation, absenteeism, and dropouts.

Describing and Assessing Organizational Climate in Schools

To describe and assess the climate of a school requires (1) the development of a clear concept of what the key factors are in the interaction-influence system that determines climate, (2) the creation of some method of collecting data that describes these factors (usually a paper-and-pencil questionnaire), and (3) a procedure by which the data may be analyzed and, ultimately, displayed in a way that informs us.

Literally scores of ways of describing and assessing organizational climates of various kinds of organizations have been proffered in the literature. The great bulk of these can be dismissed because they are largely intuitive in nature, giving little attention to a clear, systematic concept of the nature of climate itself on which to develop data-gathering and data-analysis procedures. This leaves at least a dozen well-developed scientific approaches that have been used in many kinds of organizational settings, ranging from the crews of space capsules to universities, from prisoner-of-war camps to the employees of large offices. Because our focus here is on education, only climate-assessment techniques that deal specifically with educational organizations are discussed. Criteria for selecting the three climate-assessment techniques included in the discussion were as follows:

1. The contribution that the theoretic construct on which the technique is based can make to our understanding of the organizational climate itself.

2. The relative frequency with which the technique actually has been used in studies of *education.*

3. The scientific quality of the technique.

Organizational Climate Description Questionnaire (OCDQ)

With the publication in 1962 of a research report titled *The Organizational Climate of Schools,*[61] Andrew W. Halpin and Don B. Croft introduced the notion of organizational climate to educators. Because, by definition, organizational climate is experienced by people in the organization, they assumed that the *perceptions* of these people are a valid source of data. Though one may argue that perceptions themselves are not objective reflections of "reality" (but may be influenced by subjective factors), the point is that whatever people in the organization *perceive* as their experience is the reality to be described. The purpose of an assessment of organizational climate is to obtain an objective description of those perceptions. Therefore, Halpin and Croft sought to elicit from teachers the critical factors that they generally agreed were central to describing the climate of a school. It should be remembered that at the time of the Halpin and Croft research the concept of organizational cultures was unknown. It is now understood that climate is the study of the perceptions of participants of factors in the organizational environment that are likely to reflect the culture of the organization.

Eventually they identified two clusters of factors. One cluster consisted of four factors that describe the teachers' perceptions of the teachers as a human group:

Intimacy: the degree of social cohesiveness among teachers in the school.

Disengagement: the degree to which teachers are involved and committed to achieving the goals of the school.

Espirit: the apparent morale of the group.

Hindrance: the extent to which teachers see rules, paperwork, and "administrivia" as impeding their work.

The other cluster of climate factors was the collective perception of teachers concerning the principal:

Thrust: the dynamic behavior with which the principal sets a hard-working example.

Consideration: the extent to which the principal is seen as treating teachers with dignity and human concern.

Aloofness: the extent to which the principal is described as maintaining social distance (for example, cold and distant or warm and friendly).

Production emphasis: the extent to which the principal tries to get teachers to work harder (for example, supervising closely, being directive, demanding results).

Halpin and Croft's central finding (based on initial data obtained in seventy-one suburban elementary schools) was that descriptions of the teachers as a human social group tend to be associated with the teachers' perceptions of the principal in relatively consistent patterns. For example, some schools—said to have a *closed climate*—appear thus in the perceptions of teachers: teachers tend not to be highly engaged in their work, they do not work well together, and their achievement as a group is minimal. The principal in such a school is seen by the teachers as ineffective in leading them, as creating a great deal of hindrance to their work, and as not inclined to be concerned about their personal welfare. Teachers get little satisfaction from their work, morale is low, and there is likely to be a high turnover of teachers. The principal is seen as aloof and impersonal, and tends to urge teachers to work harder. Such a principal tends to emphasize rules, is often arbitrary, and generally "goes by the book"—keeping good records and getting reports out punctiliously. Such a principal is viewed by teachers as working with little personal drive, as being not terribly inventive or creative in reducing the obstacles and annoyances that teachers encounter, and as often philosophically ascribing problems in the school to outside forces over which he or she has no control.

Using the OCDQ, Halpin and Croft identified a range of types of climates that ran from the "closed" (as just described) to the *open climate* school which is, of course, quite different. The teachers of a school with an open climate tend to see the principal's behavior as an easy, authentic integration of the official role and his or her own personality. Such a principal works energetically, shows concern and even compassion for teachers, and yet is well able to lead, control, and direct them; he or she is not especially aloof or distant, seems to know how to follow rules and regulations with minimum hindrance to teachers, and does not feel the need to monitor teachers and supervise them closely, yet is in full control. Under such leadership, teachers obtain considerable satisfaction from their work and are sufficiently motivated to overcome most difficulties and frustrations. The teachers are proud to be part of the school, do not feel burdened by busywork, regulations, and "administrivia," and have enough incentive to solve their own problems and keep the organization moving.

Comments on OCDQ

The OCDQ concept of organizational climate produced some useful ways of viewing and describing aspects of the interaction-influence systems of schools (especially elementary schools with their simpler organizational structure). Its factor structure was, however, developed from a strictly deductive process (rather than from an empirical study of schools), and, indeed, little has been done since the instrument was originally developed to validate it or modify it as a result of experience. Its usefulness for measurement purposes is now somewhat limited, and more recent approaches—which have been under constant processes of testing and revision—are being used increasingly.

Organizational Climate Index (OCI)

George C. Stern developed a different approach to the description and measurement of organizational climate. The basic rationale that underlies Stern's understanding of climate emanates directly from the Lewinian view that individuals and groups in organizations must be understood in the context of their interaction with the environment $B = f(p \cdot e)$. In this view, behavior is related to *both* person and environment. Efforts to assess the climate of a given organization must, therefore, measure *both* characteristics of individuals and characteristics of the environment.

Stern, a psychologist, saw an analogy between human personality and the personality of the institution, and he drew on the much earlier work of Henry A. Murray, who had developed the concept of *need-press* as it shaped human personality.[62] Murray postulated that personality is the product of dynamic interplay between need, both internal and external, and press, which is roughly equivalent to the environmental pressures that lead to adaptive behavior.[63] Two questionnaire instruments were devised to determine the need-press factors Stern felt influenced the development of climate in institutions of higher education: the Activities Index (AI), which assessed the need structure of individuals, and the College Characteristics Index (CCI), which probed the organizational press as experienced by persons in the organization.[64]

Over the years, these two questionnaires have been used on a number of campuses, where they have helped researchers assess organizational climate in higher education settings. Differences among various institutions of higher learning—denominational colleges, state universities, liberal arts colleges, and teachers colleges, among others—are observable for measurable factors such as staff and facilities, achievement standards, aspirations of students, extent of student freedom and responsibility, academic climate, and social life on the campus. The level of intellectual press seems to be particularly valuable in explaining important differences among collegiate institutions.

George Stern and Carl Steinhoff developed an adaptation of the CCI, applicable to schools and other organizations, called the Organizational Climate Index (OCI), which was first used in 1965 in a study of the public schools in Syracuse, New York.[65] The OCI presents teachers with statements that could apply to their schools; the teachers then are asked to mark these statements true or false as applicable to their schools. Analysis of the data from studies of a number of schools has led to the formulation of the six OCI Factors:

Factor 1: Intellectual Climate. Schools with high scores on this factor have environments that are perceived as being conducive to scholarly interests in the humanities, arts, and sciences. The staff and the physical plant are seen to be facilitative of these interests and the general work atmosphere is characterized by intellectual activities and pursuits.

Factor 2: Achievement Standards. Environments with high scores on this factor are perceived to stress high standards of personal achievement. Tasks are successfully completed and high levels of motivation and energy are maintained. Recognition is given for work of good quality and quantity and the staff is expected to achieve at the highest levels.

Factor 3: Personal Dignity (Supportiveness). Organizational climates scoring high on this factor respect the integrity of the individual and provide a supportive environment that would closely approximate the needs of more dependent teachers. The working environment conveys a sense of fair play and openness.

Factor 4: Organizational Effectiveness. Schools with high scores on this factor have work environments that encourage and facilitate the effective performance of tasks. Work programs are planned and well organized, and people work together effectively to meet organizational objectives.

Factor 5: Orderliness. High scores on this factor are indicative of a press for organizational structure and procedural orderliness. Neatness counts and teachers are pressured to conform to a defined norm of personal appearance and institutional image. There are set procedures and teachers are expected to follow them.

Factor 6: Impulse Control. High scores on this factor imply a great deal of constraint and organizational restrictiveness in the work environment. Teachers have little opportunity for personal expression or for any form of impulsive behavior.

Schools with high scores on the development press dimension are characterized by organizational environments that emphasize intellectual and interpersonal activities. In general, these environments are intellectually stimulating, maintain high standards for achievement, and are supportive of personal expression. Such schools characteristically tend to motivate people, are concerned about their personal needs, and accept (indeed, encourage) a wide range of behavior styles among participants.

A school's score on control-press (task effectiveness) dimension is computed by adding together the scores for Factors 4 and 5. Schools high in control press are characterized by internal environments that emphasize orderliness and structure. Rules and going through channels are important in such schools, and concepts of what constitutes appropriate behavior tend to be clear-cut, narrow, and emphasized. In short, schools with such environments tend to be task oriented rather than people oriented.

In sum, the two key dimensions that describe the organizational climate of a school, using the Stern-Steinhoff Organizational Climate Index, are development press and control press which combine to describe its organizational climate. As the OCI has been applied to a number of schools, normative data have been developed that are useful for interpreting the score of an individual school. Obviously, schools with high development press (that is, meeting the intellectual-cognitive needs of teachers and also their social-emotional needs) are associated with a good deal of freedom to exercise initiative and to fulfill their motivational needs. Schools that emphasize control (for example, rules, close supervision, directive leadership), on the other hand, provide an environment that offers less opportunity for teachers to grow and develop as mature professional people.

Comments on the OCI

Though the Stern need-press theory of the psychological environments in educative organizations has not enjoyed the popularity among those concerned with public schools that the OCDQ has, it has been used in a number of studies. A deterrent to early popularity was the length and complexity of the questionnaires (the full OCI once having 300 items). Another deterrent was the relative complexity of the data analysis and interpretation procedures. A short form of the OCI that is simple to use has been available since 1975, however. This can be scored by hand, and school norms for elementary, junior high, senior high, rural, suburban, and urban, which also are simple to use, have been published.

Among the many strengths of the need-press approach are that (1) it is based upon a strong (if not simple) concept of organizational climate that has held up well and (2) it has a long history of meticulous research that has yielded assessment instruments that have been carefully scrutinized for validity and reliability. Consequently, the OCI is a powerful assessment tool that yields relatively rich and fine-grained data suited to the analysis of climates of individual schools. It is, at the same time, capable of producing the kinds of normative data needed to study groups of schools (for example, the schools in a given district or the schools involved in an experimental project).

In addition, the OCI appears to be applicable to a wide variety of educative organizations—elementary, secondary, and college,[66] urban or suburban. Various forms of the questionnaire instruments make it possible, also, to obtain data from pupils and students, as well as from adults such as teachers.

Four Management Systems

Having studied organizational climates extensively, Rensis Likert identified four management systems. Each is describable in terms of organizational climate and leadership behavior, as measured in terms of the organization's characteristics. System 1 is called *exploitive-authoritative* (or punitive-authoritarian) and, as is shown in Figure 5–3, is based on classical management concepts, a Theory *X* view of motivation, and a directive leadership style. System 2 is *benevolent-authoritative* (or paternalistic-authoritarian). It emphasizes a one-to-one relationship between subordinate and leader in an environment in which the subordinate is relatively isolated from others in work-related matters. System 3, called *consultative,* employs more of a participative leadership style in which the leader tends to consult with people *individually* in the process of making decisions. System 4, the *participative* (or group interactive) model of an organizational system, uses Theory *Y* concepts of human functioning and emphasizes team interaction in all of the critical organizational processes.

As Likert observed:

> The interaction-influence networks of our schools all too often are proving to be incapable of dealing constructively even with the internal school problems and conflicts, not to mention the conflicts impinging from the outside. Moreover, the present decision-making structure of the schools requires patterns of interaction that often aggravate conflict rather than resolving it constructively.
>
> Faculty meetings, for example, almost always employ parliamentary procedures that force a System 2 win-lose confrontation. The systematic, orderly problem solving that small groups can use does not and cannot occur in large meetings. . . . [I]t is distressing to observe the extraordinary capacity of *Robert's Rules of Order* to turn the interaction of sincere, intelligent persons into bitter, emotional, win-lose confrontation.[67]

He went on to point out that in meetings of fifty to one hundred faculty members there is little likelihood of creative problem solving, as factions of members joust through parliamentary maneuvering, and, in the end, few emerge with anything like genuine commitment to the actions that are finally taken.

SYSTEM 1: EXPLOITIVE AUTHORITATIVE

Motivational Forces

Taps fear, need for money and status. Ignores other motives, which cancel out those tapped. Attitudes are hostile, subservient upward, contemptuous downward. Mistrust prevalent. Little feeling of responsibility except at high levels. Dissatisfaction with job, peers, supervisor, and organization.

Communication Pattern

Little upward communication. Little lateral communication. Some downward communication, viewed suspicion by subordinates. Much distortion and deception.

Interaction-Influence Process

No cooperative teamwork, little mutual influence. Only moderate downward influence, usually overestimated.

Decision-Making Process

Decision made at top, based on partial and inaccurate information. Contributes little motivational value. Made on person-to-person basis, discouraging teamwork.

Goal-Setting Process

Orders issued. Overt acceptance. Covert resistance.

Control Process

Control at top only. Control data often distorted and falsified. Informal organizations exists, which works counter to the formal, reducing real control.

SYSTEM 2: BENEVOLENT AUTHORITATIVE

Motivational Forces

Taps need for money, ego motives such as desire for status and for power, sometimes fear. Untapped motives often cancel out those tapped, sometimes reinforce them. Attitudes are sometimes hostile, sometimes favorable toward organization, subservient upward, condescending downward, competitively hostile toward peers. Managers usually feel responsible for attaining goals, but rank and file do not. Dissatisfaction to moderate satisfaction with job, peers, supervisor, and organization.

Communication Pattern

Little upward communication. Little lateral communication. Great deal of downward communication, viewed with mixed feelings by subordinates. Some distortion and filtering.

Interaction-Influence Process

Very little cooperative teamwork, little upward influence except by informal means. Moderate downward influence.

Decision-Making Process

Policy decided at top, some implementation decisions made at lower levels, based on moderately accurate and adequate information. Contributes little motivational value. Made largely on person-to-person basis, discouraging teamwork.

Goal-Setting Process

Orders issued, perhaps with some chance to comment. Overt acceptance, but often covert resistance.

Control Process

Control largely at top. Control data often incomplete and inaccurate. Informal organization usually exists, working counter to the formal, partially reducing real control.

FIGURE 5–3   Likert's four management systems. From David G. Bowers, *Systems of Organization: Management of the Human Resource* (Ann Arbor: University of Michigan Press, 1976), pp. 104–5.

SYSTEM 3: CONSULTATIVE

Motivational Forces

Taps need for money, ego motives, and other major motives within the individual. Motivational forces usually reinforce each other. Attitudes usually favorable. Most persons feel responsible. Moderately high satisfaction with job, peers, supervisor, and organization.

Communication Pattern

Upward and downward communication is usually good. Lateral communication is fair to good. Slight tendency to filter or distort.

Interaction-Influence Process

Moderate amount of cooperation teamwork. Moderate upward influence. Moderate to substantial downward influence.

Decision-Making Process

Broad policy decided at top, more specific decisions made at lower levels, based on reasonably accurate and adequate information. Some contribution to motivation. Some group-based decision making.

Goal-Setting Process

Goals are set or orders issued after discussion with subordinates. Usually acceptance both overtly and covertly, but some occasional covert resistance.

Control Process

Control primarily at top, but some delegation to lower levels. Informal organization may exist and partially resist formal organization, partially reducing real control.

SYSTEM 4: PARTICIPATIVE GROUP

Motivational Forces

Taps all major motives except fear, including motivational forces coming from group processes. Motivational forces reinforce one another. Attitudes quite favorable. Trust prevalent. Persons at all levels feel quite responsible. Relatively high satisfaction throughout.

Communication Pattern

Information flows freely and accurately in all directions. Practically no forces to distort or filter.

Interaction-Influence Process

A great deal of cooperative teamwork. Substantial real influence upward, downward, and laterally.

Decision-Making Process

Decision making done throughout the organization, linked by overlapping groups and based on full and accurate information. Make largely on group basis encouraging teamwork.

Goal-Setting Process

Goals established by group participation, except in emergencies. Full goal acceptance, both overtly and covertly.

Control Process

Widespread real and felt responsibility for control function, informal and formal organizations are identical, with no reduction in real control.

FIGURE 5–3   Continued

In discussing Likert's approach to this problem, David Bowers pointed out that a place to begin is to understand what an organization is and what it is not. Bowers observed:

> An organization is not simply a physical plant or its equipment. It is not an army of positions, nor a collection of persons who fill these positions. It is not a sequence of work tasks or technical operations. It is all of these things, to be sure, but it is fundamentally something more. The basic building block of the organization is the face-to-face group, consisting of the supervisor and those subordinates immediately responsible to him [sic]. *The organization consists most basically of a structure of groups, linked together by overlapping memberships* into a pyramid through which the work flows.[68]

Thus, the organization is conceptualized as a roughly pyramidal structure whose basic unit is the face-to-face work group: people who regularly interact (communicate, influence, motivate) at work, together with their supervisor. Examples are department chairpersons and teachers in the departments, head librarians plus librarians and library aides, grade chairpersons and homeroom teachers, and so on. Such groups are (1) small enough to permit the development of effective group process that facilitates individual participation and (2) close enough to the task to be performed to make effective, creative decisions. To keep such groups coordinated requires effective communication between and among them: the primary work groups must be effectively linked together. Especially, Likert pointed out, it is essential that groups be linked *upward* in the organization, so that the groups lower in the organizational pyramid have the capability of interacting with and influencing higher levels of the organization.

> The capacity to exert influence upward is essential if a supervisor (or manager) is to perform his supervisory functions successfully. To be effective in leading his own work group, a superior must be able to influence his own boss, that is he needs to be skilled both as a supervisor and as a subordinate.[69]

Essentially, then, every supervisor or every administrator is a member of two face-to-face work groups: the group *for which* he or she is responsible and the group *to which* he or she is responsible. The total organization is composed of a planned system of such work groups that *overlap* and that are linked together by individuals who have roles in both of the overlapping groups. These individuals serve as "linking pins" between the groups—a role that requires them to facilitate communication, decision making, and other influence processes between levels of the organization and, also, across the organization.

Such a structure is not totally new in U.S. schooling, of course. The traditional high school principal's cabinet, for instance, generally includes chairpersons who link the departments to the cabinet. In turn, the principal is usually a member of a districtwide group (often also called a cabinet) comprising other principals, central office people, and the superintendent. The superintendent, in turn links the superintendent's cabinet to the school board (see Figure 5–4). However, Likert has

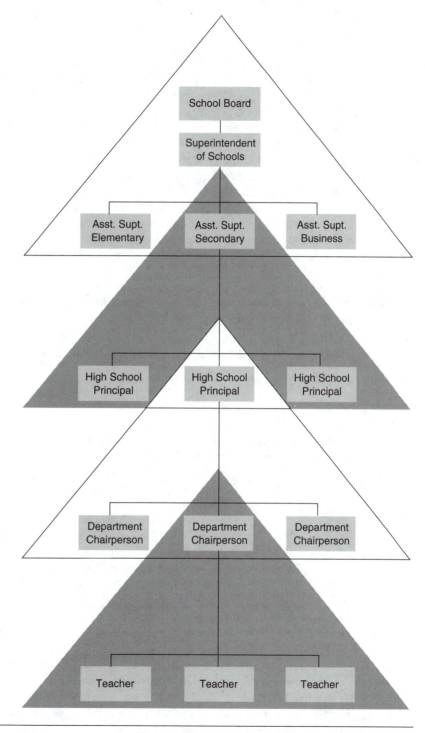

FIGURE 5–4 The linking-pin concept as applied to the decision-making structure of a medium-sized school district.

suggested that, *first,* such an organizational system can be extended and elaborated to include all facets of the school district organization (including elementary schools).[70] *Second*—and more important—Likert has described how such an arrangement can facilitate the development of a more functional interaction-influence system: one that is not characterized by the traditional, directive, downward-oriented concepts of line-and-staff organization but instead is characterized by free communication and influence, up, down, and across the organization, featuring a teamwork approach to problems at all levels.

In sum, "the effectiveness of the interaction-influence system of an organization and the capacity of this system to deal with difficult problems depend upon the effectiveness of the work groups of which the structure consists and upon the extent to which multiple linkage is provided."[71] Considering, therefore, the dynamic interdependence between structure (for example, linked, overlapping groups) and the influence system (for example, directive or collaborative) brings us to the issue of participation in making decisions. One seeking to develop a collaborative interaction-influence system must attend to developing a leadership or administrative style that will develop the skills and motivation of subordinates that support such an approach. In other words, one would seek to move from System 1 to System 4. This conforms to the major approaches to motivation (that is, the ideas of Maslow, Porter and Lawler, Herzberg, and others) discussed in Chapter 4.

CONCLUSION

The concept of organizational culture has emerged as central in the analysis of organizational behavior and organizational effectiveness. Organizational culture is the body of solutions to problems that has worked consistently for a group and that is therefore taught to new members as the correct way to perceive, think about, and feel in relation to those problems. Over time, organizational culture takes on meaning so deep that it defines the assumptions, values, beliefs, norms, and even the perceptions of participants in the organization. Though culture tends to drop from the conscious thoughts of participants over time, it continues to powerfully create meaning for them in their work and becomes "the rules of the game."

Studies of schools, have strongly supported the belief that organizational culture is a fundamental factor in determining the quality of educational organizations. Culture cannot be studied directly but is inferred from observed behavior such as language, use of artifacts, rituals, and symbolism commonly encountered in the workplace.

Organizational climate, which is the study of the perceptions of participants of certain intangible aspects of the environment, reflects the culture. Studies of organizational climate ordinarily use questionnaires to elicit perceptions from participants. The trend in the study of organizational climate in schools has been away from the study of the perceptions of adults toward the study of those of pupils and students.

As the study of organizational culture moved to a central position in organizational behavior in education, it was accompanied by increasing use of such qualitative research methods as participant observation and open-ended unstructured interviews to replace traditional statistical research methods. The use of qualitative research methods makes it possible to produce richly detailed "thick" descriptions of the organizational culture of schools, which are necessary in order to explain what is happening in them. Although the use of such methods is relatively recent in the study of organizational behavior in comparison with traditional statistical methods, they are derived from a long and respected research tradition in anthropology and sociology as well as educational administration. Qualitative research methods, such as ethnography, are based on very clear concepts of the nature of inquiry that are quite different from conventional rationalistic concepts and observe rules of procedure and rigor that are equally clear and different from those of conventional quantitative methods.

Much of the research on organizational culture, in both corporate and educational organizations, is related to the effectiveness of the organizations. Many studies describe relationships between performance of the company (in such terms as market share, sales, and profitability) and the organizational culture within the company. Comparable support exists for a similar thesis in education. In large measure, clearly establishing such causal connections in schooling is hampered by the extraordinary complexity of the organization and the confusion and ambiguity among and between various constituencies of schooling as to the criteria for determining what high performance is in a school.

A substantial and growing body of empirical evidence, derived from vigorous research in schools and other educative organizations, indicates that the effectiveness of these organizations, in terms of student learning and development, is significantly influenced by the quality and characteristics of the organizational culture. Not surprisingly, the research clearly suggests that schools that emphasize supportiveness, open communication, collaboration, intellectuality, and that reward achievement and success outperform (in terms of achievement, attendance, dropout rate, frustration, and alienation) those that emphasize competition, constraint and restrictiveness, rules and standard operating procedures, and that reward conformity. Further, by delineating the critical factors involved, the concepts arising from this body of research make it possible and practicable to plan and manage organizational culture purposefully. It would be difficult to overemphasize the implications arising from this research for administrative practice in the era marked by declining confidence in schools and school systems and by increasing demands for accountability for performance.

SUGGESTED READING

Deal, Terrence E., and Kent D. Peterson, *The Principal's Role in Shaping School Culture*. Washington, DC: U.S. Department of Education, Office of Educational Research and Improvement, 1990.
   Although some academics still debate whether one can or should deliberately change the culture of schools, the pragmatic practitioner, in view of the mounting evidence of the importance

of culture in evoking organizational behavior, tends to conclude that the issue is not whether one can or should, but how to do it. This little publication addresses the how-to-do-it in simple terms and provides the reader with a ten-point program on "how to build an effective culture."

Levine, Sarah L., *Promoting Adult Growth in Schools: The Promise of Professional Development.* Boston: Allyn and Bacon, 1989.

This book starts with an examination of the professional lives of school teachers and finds what many have found before: that teaching is isolating, inhibiting of personal growth and development and for these reasons is unsatisfying and rewarding. Moreover, this is inevitably reflected in the effectiveness of the schools. Levine goes on, however, to discuss what can be done by school principals and others to change all this so as to develop schools as growth-enhancing environments for the adults who work in them. Contains a great deal of useful, practical advice.

Lieberman, Ann, ed., *Building a Professional Culture in Schools.* New York: Teachers College Press, 1988.

Note that the title of this book uses the term "professional culture" rather than "organizational culture." This is not by chance: it reflects the belief that schools should be developing a very definite kind of culture. It is an interesting book of readings in which a number of currently popular writers, including activists, researchers, academics, and unionists, advocate various aspects of developing schools which are more collegial and in which teachers enact greater leadership than in the past.

Lutz, Frank W., and Laurence Iannaccone, *Understanding Educational Organizations: A Field Study Approach.* Columbus, OH: Charles E. Merrill Publishing Company, 1969.

Two pioneers in the long history of qualitative research in educational administration—known particularly for their study of the exercise of power in schools—describe their theory, their research methods, and procedures to use in the field. A sound introduction for the reader inexperienced in using field methods in the study of school culture.

Ott, J. Steven, *The Organizational Culture Perspective.* Pacific Grove, CA: Brooks/Cole Publishing Company, 1989.

A comprehensive textbook that provides a readable survey of contemporary organizational culture theory and research. Although it primarily deals with corporate culture, and includes numerous examples from business and industry, educators will find it a useful source for illuminating concepts of organizational culture that are readily applicable to educational settings.

Sarason, Seymour B., *The Culture of the School and the Problem of Change.* Boston: Allyn and Bacon, 1971.

Based on his own extensive experiences in schools, this classic small volume presents a sensitive, insightful description of schools, how they are "really" organized, and what this means for developing effective ways of facilitating change in them. An easy-to-read book that endures as an exceptional example of the use of the concept of culture as an organizer for the analysis of the school as an organization.

NOTES

1. Alfred J. Marrow, David G. Bowers, and Stanley E. Seashore, *Management by Participation* (New York: Harper & Row, Publishers, 1967).
2. Terrence E. Deal, "Cultural Change: Opportunity, Silent Killer or Metamorphosis?" (unpublished paper, no date).
3. Chester I. Barnard, *Functions of the Executive* (Boston: Harvard University Press, 1938).
4. Philip Selznick, *TVA and the Grass Roots* (Berkeley: University of California Press, 1949).
5. Marshall W. Meyer and associates, eds., *Environments and Organizations* (San Francisco: Jossey-Bass, 1978).
6. Andrew W. Halpin and Don B. Croft, *The Organizational Climate of Schools* (Chicago: Midwest Administration Center, The University of Chicago, 1962).

7. Bernard Clark, "The Organizational Saga in Higher Education," in *Managing Change in Educational Organizations,* J. Victor Baldridge and Terrence E. Deal, eds. (Berkeley, CA: McCutchan, 1975).

8. Michael Rutter, Barbara Maughan, Peter Mortimore, and Jane Ouston, with Alan Smith, *Fifteen Thousand Hours: Secondary Schools and Their Effects on Children* (Cambridge, MA: Harvard University Press, 1979).

9. Deal, "Cultural Change," p. 6.

10. Renato Tagiuri, "The Concept of Organizational Climate," in Renato Tagiuri and George H. Litwin, eds., *Organizational Climate: Exploration of a Concept* (Boston: Harvard University, Division of Research, Graduate School of Business Administration, 1968). See also, Carolyn S. Anderson, "The Search for School Climate: A Review of the Research." *Review of Educational Research,* 52 (Fall 1982), 368–420, and Cecil Miskel and Rodney Ogawa, "Work Motivation, Job Satisfaction, and Climate," in Norman J. Boyan, ed., *Handbook of Research on Educational Administration* (New York: Longman, 1988).

11. William Ouchi, *Theory Z: How American Business Can Meet the Japanese Challenge* (Reading, MA: Addison-Wesley, 1981).

12 Ibid., p. 165.

13. Thomas J. Peters and Robert H. Waterman, Jr., *In Search of Excellence: Lessons from America's Best-Run Companies* (New York: Harper & Row, Publishers, 1982).

14. Ibid., p. 282.

15. Terrence E. Deal and Allan A. Kennedy, *Corporate Cultures: The Rites and Rituals of Corporate Life* (Reading, MA: Addison-Wesley, 1982).

16. Peters and Waterman, *In Search of Excellence,* p. 319.

17. Edgar H. Schein, "How Culture Forms, Develops, and Changes," in *Gaining Control of the Corporate Culture,* Ralph H. Kilmann, Mary J. Saxton, Roy Serpa, and associates (San Francisco: Jossey-Bass, 1985), pp. 19–20.

18. Ibid., p. 20.

19. Ralph H. Kilmann, Mary J. Saxton, and Roy Serpa, "Five Key Issues in Understanding and Changing Culture," in Kilmann and others, *Gaining Control of the Corporate Culture,* p. 5.

20. Ibid.

21. Terrence E. Deal, "Cultural Change: Opportunity, Silent Killer, or Metamorphosis?" in *Gaining Control of the Corporate Culture* (revision of previously unpublished paper), p. 301.

22. Ibid.

23. Ralph H. Kilmann, "Five Steps for Closing Culture-Gaps," in Kilmann and others, *Gaining Control of the Corporate Culture,* p. 352.

24. Alan L. Wilkins and Kerry J. Patterson, "You Can't Get There from Here: What Will Make Culture Projects Fail," in Kilmann and others, *Gaining Control of the Corporate Culture,* p. 267.

25. George C. Homans, *The Human Group* (New York: Harcourt, Brace, & World, 1950), p. 123.

26. A. Paul Haire, *Handbook of Small Group Research* (New York: The Free Press, 1962), p. 24.

27. A. R. Cohen and others, *Effective Behavior in Organizations,* 3rd ed. (Homewood, IL: Richard D. Irwin, 1984), p. 62.

28. Schein, "How Culture Forms, Develops, and Changes," in Kilmann and others, *Gaining Control of the Corporate Culture,* p. 21.

29. Ibid., pp. 19–20.

30. Ralph H. Kilmann, Mary J. Saxton, and Roy Serpa, "Five Key Issues in Understanding and Changing Culture," in Kilmann and others, *Gaining Control of the Corporate Culture,* p. 5.

31. Ibid.

32. Terrence E. Deal, "Cultural Change: Opportunity, Silent Killer, or Metamorphosis?" in Kilmann and others, *Gaining Control of the Corporate Culture,* p. 301.

33. Halpin and Croft, *The Organizational Climate of Schools.*

34. Rosabeth Moss Kanter, *The Change Masters: Innovation and Entrepreneurship in the American Corporation* (New York: Simon & Schuster, 1983), p. 149.

35. George C. Homans, *The Human Group* (New York: Harcourt, Brace, & World, 1950), p. 123.

36. Haire, *Handbook of Small Group Research*, p. 24.

37. Kurt Lewin, *Principles of Topological Psychology* (New York: McGraw-Hill Book Company, 1936).

38. Garlie A. Forehand and B. Von Haller Gilmer, "Environmental Variations in Studies of Organizational Behavior," Psychological Bulletin, 62, no. 6 (December 1964), 361–82.
39. James G. March and Herbert A. Simon, *Organizations* (New York: John Wiley & Sons, 1959).
40. Renato Tagiuri, ed., *Research Needs in Executive Selection* (Boston: Harvard University, Graduate School of Business Administration, 1961).
41. Roger G. Barker describes the theory of behavior settings and ways of studying them in *Ecological Psychology: Concepts and Methods for Studying the Environment of Human Behavior* (Stanford, CA: Stanford University Press, 1968).
42. Roger G. Barker and Paul V. Gump, eds., *Big School, Small School* (Stanford, CA: Stanford University Press, 1964).
43. Leonard L. Baird, "Big School, Small School: A Critical Examination of the Hypothesis," *Journal of Educational Psychology,* 60 (1969), 253–60.
44. Leonard L. Baird, "The Relation of Vocational Interests to Life Goals, Self-Ratings of Ability and Personality Traits, and Potential for Achievement," *Journal of Educational Measurement,* 7 (1970), 233–39.
45. Susan Chira, "Is Smaller Better? Educators Now Say Yes for High School," *New York Times,* Wednesday, July 14, 1993, p. A1.
46. Seymour B. Sarason, *The Culture of the School and the Problem of Change* (Boston: Allyn and Bacon, 1971).
47. Seymour B. Sarason, *The Creation of Settings and Future Societies* (San Francisco: Jossey-Bass, 1972).
48. This field is well surveyed in Marvin D. Dunnette, ed., *Handbook of Industrial and Organizational Psychology* (Chicago: Rand McNally & Company, 1976).
49. Theodore R. Sizer, *Horace's Compromise: The Dilemma of the American High School* (Boston: Houghton Mifflin, 1984).
50. Ernest L. Boyer, *High School: A Report on Secondary Education in America* (New York: Harper & Row, Publishers, 1983).
51. John I. Goodlad, *A Place Called School: Prospects for the Future* (St. Louis: McGraw-Hill, 1983).
52. Wilbur B. Brookover and others, "Elementary School Social Climate and School Achievement," *American Educational Research Journal,* 15, no. 2 (Spring 1978), 302.
53. James S. Coleman and others, *Equality of Educational Opportunity* (Washington, DC: Government Printing Office, 1966).
54. Christopher Jencks and others, *Inequality* (New York: Basic Books, Publishers, 1972).
55. Brookover and others, "Elementary School Social Climate and School Achievement," p. 316.
56. Ibid., p. 317.
57. Rutter and others, *Fifteen Thousand Hours.*
58. Ibid., p. 178.
59. Joyce L. Epstein, ed., *The Quality of School Life* (Lexington, MA: D.C. Heath and Company, 1984).
60. Rudolf H. Moos, *Evaluating Educational Environments* (Palo Alto, CA: Consulting Psychologists Press, 1979).
61. Andrew W. Halpin and Don B. Croft, *The Organizational Climate of Schools* (U.S.O.E. Research Project, Contract no. SAE 543–8639, August 1962).
62. Henry A. Murray and others, *Explorations in Personality* (New York: Oxford University Press, 1938), p. 124.
63. For a full description of Stern's extensive research in this field, see George G. Stern, *People in Context: Measuring Person-Environment Congruence in Education and Industry* (New York: John Wiley & Sons, 1970).
64. George G. Stern, "Characteristics of Intellectual Climate in College Environments," *Harvard Educational Review,* 31 (Winter 1963), 5–41.
65. Carl R. Steinhoff, *Organizational Climate in a Public School System* (U.S.O.E. Cooperative Research Program, Contract no. OE-4–255, Project no. S-083, Syracuse University, New York, 1965).
66. See, for example, Carl R. Steinhoff and Lloyd Bishop, "Factors Differentiating Preparation Programs in Educational Administration: U.C.E.A. Study of Student Organizational Environment," *Educational Administration Quarterly,* 10 (1974), 35–50; and Lloyd Bishop and Carl R. Stein-

hoff, "Organizational Characteristics of Administrative Training Programs: Professors and Their Work Environments," *Journal of Educational Administration,* 13 (1975), 54–61.

67. Rensis Likert and Jane Gibson Likert, *New Ways of Managing Conflict* (New York: McGraw-Hill Book Company, 1976), pp. 218–19.

68. David G. Bowers, *Systems of Organization: Management of the Human Resource* (Ann Arbor: University of Michigan Press, 1976), pp. 2–3.

69. Rensis Likert, *New Patterns of Management* (New York: McGraw-Hill Book Company, 1961), p. 144.

70. Likert and Likert, *New Ways of Managing Conflict,* Chapter 12.

71. Likert, *New Patterns of Management,* p. 181.

Leadership

ABOUT THIS CHAPTER

Leadership is one of the most fascinating topics in organizational behavior and, at the same time, a notoriously slippery concept that has produced literally hundreds of definitions. One survey reported more than 350 definitions of leadership in the literature.[1] Clearly no one of them will satisfy everyone. However, the many definitions of leadership generally agree on two things:

1. Leadership is a group function: it occurs only in the processes of two or more people interacting.
2. Leaders intentionally seek to influence the behavior of other people.

Thus, any concept of leadership deals with exercising influence on others through social interaction. To understand leadership, we must examine the nature and quality of the social interactions involved. The heart of the matter is power: what kind of power is involved and how is it exercised?

THE POWER OF LEADERS

In an era when single-issue groups—such as racial, ethnic, and gender groups—that are part of the social mosaic in the United States view educational organizations as oppressive and those in the organizational hierarchy as minions of an oppressive system, many cringe from even acknowledging power as an aspect of leadership in other than pejorative terms. Indeed, the subtext of discussions of power in educational organizations is that power is, by definition, a form of oppression of those in the lower levels of the organization. For example, the authors of one set of case studies of leadership in schools attempted simply to eschew the use of the word "leadership" because they perceived it as tainted with their strongly negative view of hierarchy as pernicious oppression. Thereupon they tried to substitute the term "distributive leadership" because in their view it "emphasizes process over power."[2]

However, one must understand that those who lead are necessarily powerful people because power is the basic energy for initiating and sustaining action that translates intention into reality when people try to work collaboratively.[3] One cannot lead and be powerless. But the exercise of power is not necessarily oppression, indeed cannot be oppressive, in the exercise of leadership as it is being discussed here. Let me explain.

There are different kinds of power through which one may attempt to influence others, and they come from different sources. Understanding leadership requires one to understand the difference between the power of those who lead and the power of those who command. The two are frequently confused with one another. The difference between leadership and command lies in the sources from which power is derived.

Leadership Different from Command

Those who occupy official positions in the hierarchy of an organization exercise vested authority, which is the legitimate right to command. Vested authority rests on legal power that is customarily granted to official positions in the hierarchy such as dean, superintendent, or principal. Because the legal power of office is granted by those higher in the hierarchy, subordinates, in theory at least, have no control over it and must yield to it. In practice, of course, such absolute power is rarely found in U.S. educational organizations. When it is exercised, it is often viewed as oppression. Teachers' unions, for example, were created expressly to mediate and limit the arbitrary exercise of power of school boards and school district administrators over teachers; there is no doubt that they have generally been highly effective.

The power of leaders, on the other hand, is voluntarily granted by followers who accept the leader's influence and direction by shared agreement, no matter how informally the agreement is arrived at. Leaders do not wield legal power vested in an official office; rather, they exercise power that followers have willingly entrusted to them. Why do followers entrust power to leaders? Often, and perhaps at the highest level, because the followers are drawn to the ideas of the leader, because they share in the values and beliefs of the leader, and because they are convinced that the leader can represent the followers well in the inevitable conflict with others for control of resources to achieve what the leader and the followers are bound in mutual commitment to achieve.

The key to understanding the difference between the power of officeholders and the power of leaders lies in who controls the power. Followers can, and often do, withdraw the support that they have voluntarily entrusted to the leader. They can also voluntarily increase their grant of support, which increases the power of the leader. The Rev. Dr. Martin Luther King, Jr., for example, is generally acknowledged as one of the great and powerful leaders of the twentieth century, yet he had little in the way of legal authority to make his followers do anything. Nevertheless, Dr. King had extraordinary power to influence the behavior of followers and, ultimately, the course of the nation.

What Dr. King did have was ideas, a set of values and beliefs, and a clear vision of a better, more just, more morally perfect future that embodied all of these ideas and values. It was the intense wish of his followers to share in achieving these that motivated them to empower him with their strong active support. Thus, Dr. King was a very powerful man who could mobilize vast numbers of people in common purpose and set in train momentous events, yet he was no oppressor. He had learned much about leadership from studying Mohandas Gandhi who was, of course, a master of the art. Gandhi's lifework stands as a monument to the effectiveness of leadership, since he emerged victorious in 1947 from head-to-head confrontation with the determined oppression of seemingly invincible forces of entrenched colonialism.

Position power, such as that of a superintendent of schools or a school principal, provides the incumbent in an office in the hierarchy with legal authority for at least the potential for forcible domination and coercion. This is not leadership. It is superordination. We must distinguish between superordination and leadership:

> The source of superordination is *vested authority* [while] the source of leadership is *entrusted authority*. Authority is vested in a superordinate when power resides in the institution, and obedience is owed the superordinate by the subordinate in virtue of the role each occupies, roles the subordinate cannot alter.

> Authority is entrusted to a leader when power resides in the followers themselves, and cooperation is *granted* the leader by the follower . . . a judgment . . . the follower can alter. The superordinate may legitimately *compel* subordination; the leader can legitimately only *elicit* followership. The relationship between subordinate and superordinate is *compulsory,* between follower and leader *voluntary*.[4]

Power Defined

Power is commonly considered to be the capacity to influence others,[5] and different kinds of power can be used to exercise the influence. The classic, generally accepted description of power identifies five kinds, or sources, of power:[6]

- ✦ *Reward power.* Controlling rewards that will induce others to comply with the power wielder's wishes.
- ✦ *Coercive power.* Having control of potentially punishing resources that will induce others to avoid them.
- ✦ *Expert power.* Having knowledge that others want for themselves so much that they will be induced to comply with the power wielder so as to acquire the knowledge or benefit from it.
- ✦ *Legitimate power.* Having authority conferred by holding a position in an organization that is recognized by others as having a legitimate right to obedience.
- ✦ *Referent power.* When a power holder has personal charisma, or ideas and beliefs so admired by others that they are induced by the opportunity to be not only associated with the power holder but, insofar as possible, to become more like him or her.

Thus, the exercise of power is a reciprocal relationship between the power holder and others. One has power not only when he or she controls resources that can reward or punish people, for example, money and access to more power for the followers themselves (such as participation in making decisions),[7] but also when he or she has ideas about the future of the organization that people find exciting and want to "buy into."

The strength of the leader's power depends on the range of the sources of power drawn on. Leaders who draw on one source of power are inherently weaker than those who draw on multiple sources of power. Especially since the advent of teacher unions and the broadening judicial interpretations of the constitutional rights of teachers, many school principals perceive that their power to lead has been undercut because the official power inherent in the office to coerce teachers into compliance has waned markedly, as has the power to control their compensation. Actually the degradation of the coercive power of principals has *increased* the need for leadership. Strong school leaders still have access to significant sources of power:

+ Although the power of principals to control the appointment, assignment, compensation, tenure, and promotion of teachers has been sharply curbed, those represent only one aspect of reward power, and, as I shall discuss, they have little to do with the power to lead. Many teachers find helping behavior from principals to be highly rewarding, if it is nonjudgmental, supportive, collaborative, and caring in the tradition of self-development.[8] When they find such behavior by the principal rewarding enough, their support for the principal increases and the principal's power to lead increases as a result.

+ Teachers continue to recognize the authority of official positions in the organization because they value the organization. They largely defer to the legitimate power of those occupying official positions in the hierarchy of the organization.

+ Teachers generally resent and reject principals who pose as pedagogical experts by demanding that lesson plans be submitted for prior approval and principals who conduct critiques of observed teaching in the paternalistic judgmental manner that they may think appropriate for technical experts. However, teachers view favorably support from principals for fresh ideas. Teachers tend to recognize and see as powerful those principals who are expert in using collaborative, collegial methods of working together to identify and solve mutual problems. Such methods are personally rewarding to teachers at the higher levels of Maslow's concept of motivation and facilitate continuing personal self-growth.

+ Principals who have fresh, exciting ideas—who have a vision of the future—that others embrace and want to share are building referent power. Teachers tend to admire principals who express their vision coherently and vividly, who inspire enthusiasm, and who involve others in dialogue intended to mold and develop the ideas, and who cause them to see a connection between the "vision" and their own personal desires to achieve something meaningful, to be part of a new and better future that is unfolding. This is an important source of power for principals who would be leaders.

Leadership Defined

Although they do exercise various kinds of power, *leaders engage with followers* in seeking to achieve not only the goals of the leader but also significant goals of the followers. Thus "Leadership over human beings . . . is exercised when persons with certain purposes mobilize, in competition or in conflict with others, institutional, political, psychological and other resources so as to arouse and satisfy the motives of followers." That is as good a definition of leadership as we have at this time.[9]

These two kinds of power, position power and the authority voluntarily granted to leaders by followers, are not necessarily mutually exclusive. A university dean may have considerable legal clout in decisions regarding reappointment and tenure, yet at the same time have power that comes from strong support of a leader by the faculty. The litmus test is who controls the grant of power: a dean who loses the support of the faculty will also have lost considerable power to influence followers and get things done even though official position power remains undiminished. Presidents of the United States combine the official power of office with the power from supporters who willingly accord them great power. For example, the collapse of Richard Nixon's presidency after Watergate had little to do with the official legal power of the office of the president, but without the support of followers, his position in office was untenable.

TWO-FACTOR LEADERSHIP THEORY ABANDONED

Most of the formalistic theorizing that dominated the study of leadership only a few years ago has been largely abandoned. Instead, the seminal insights of Burns, which I have been discussing, gave rise to a new understanding of leadership and have gained ascendancy. The approach prior to Burns's work, which was studied by most present-day practicing educational administrators, generally defined the behavior of leaders in two dimensions:

✦ One dimension was the emphasis that the leader gives to getting the job done. This was often called *initiating structure* because it often involves structuring the work: delineating the relationship between the leader and the members of the work group, specifying the tasks to be performed, and endeavoring to establish well-defined patterns of organization, channels of communication, and methods of procedure, scheduling, and designating responsibilities. It was also often called *production emphasis* or *task emphasis,* for obvious reasons.

✦ The other dimension was the emphasis that the leader gives to developing friendship, mutual trust, respect, and warmth in relationships between the leader and followers.[10] These behaviors were usually labeled *consideration* or *concern for people.*

Bernard Bass spoke of leaders as tending to be either "follower focused" (i.e., emphasizing concern for people) or "task focused" (i.e., emphasizing rules and procedures for getting the task done):

A task-focused leader initiates structure, provides the information, determines what is to be done, issues the rules, promises rewards for compliance, and threatens punishments for disobedience. The follower-focused leader solicits advice, opinions, and information from followers and checks decisions or shares decision making with followers. The . . . task-focused leader uses his or her power to obtain compliance with what the leader has decided. The follower-focused leader uses his or her power to set the constraints within which followers are encouraged to join in deciding what is to be done.[11]

This two-dimensional theory held that leadership consisted of a mix of these two kinds of behaviors and that effectiveness as a leader depended on choosing the right blend in various kinds of situations. The general tendency is for individuals to favor one or the other of these behavioral orientations while placing less emphasis on the other dimension. It would be virtually impossible, in U.S. schools at least, for a leader to be totally absent in either one of the two behavioral dimensions of leadership. Students of leadership who wish to denigrate this concept of leader behavior, which has fallen into disrepute in academic circles, often achieve their purposes by reporting that they do not find leaders who are *always* task oriented or *always* people oriented.

In the two-dimensional approach to understanding leadership, great emphasis was given to leadership style. For example, one commonly hears complaints that educational leaders in the past emphasized the task, or managerial, dimension of leader behavior—which is often called autocratic leadership style—and few emphasized the consideration dimension—which defines the democratic style of leadership. Thus, individual styles of various leaders were described as tending to be autocratic or democratic, task oriented or people oriented, directive or collegial, and one may adopt a leadership style thought to be appropriate to the leader's personality, on the one hand, and the situation in which the leader works, on the other hand. All of this emanated from efforts to reduce the study of leadership to a science, and therein lay its weakness. In education today, recognition is rapidly growing that leadership cannot be reduced to formulas and prescriptions but must be attuned to the human variables and confusions that normally abound in busy, complex, and contradictory—that is, messy—human organizations.

It will help if you bear two things in mind:

+ Understanding of leadership is now undergoing great upheaval in all fields of human endeavor, not just in schools, and we have much to learn from enlightened leaders of business, industry, and the military, as well as from enlightened educational leaders.

+ The direction of change in this upheaval is away from the old concepts of leadership as the downward exercise of power and authority and toward developing respect and concern for the followers and the ability to see them as powerful sources of knowledge, creativity, and energy for improving the organization—sources heretofore largely untapped by administrators whose focus tended to be on hierarchical control.

LEADERSHIP AS A RELATIONSHIP WITH FOLLOWERS

Whenever we try to lead people we become part of their environment and, therefore, part of their "equation" for organizational behavior, $B = f(p \bullet e)$. Leaders are therefore not merely concerned with the leadership style and techniques that they intend to use but also with the quality and kinds of relationships that they have with followers. Leadership is not something that one does to people, nor is it a manner of behaving toward people: it is working with and through other people to achieve organizational goals.

What distinguishes leaders from other authority figures is the unique relationship between leaders and followers. Leaders relate to followers in ways that

+ Motivate them to unite with others in sharing a vision of where the organization should be going and how to get it there.

+ Arouse their personal commitment to the effort to bring the vision of a better future into being.

+ Organize the working environment so that the envisioned goals become central values in the organization.

+ Facilitate the work that followers need to do to achieve the vision.

How do leaders do these things? That depends, first, on what they think leadership is, and that is defined in terms of the character and quality of the relationship between leader and follower. This arises from the bedrock assumptions that the would-be leader holds about people and the world in which they work, the world from which all our cultural beliefs and values arise.

Using Douglas McGregor's concepts, one who accepts Theory *X* assumptions about followers tends to think about leadership pretty much as the stereotype of the traditional boss overseeing a gang in the field or on the shop floor: issuing orders, checking up, and prodding to keep things moving. One who accepts Theory *Y* assumptions about people at work tends to think about leadership more in terms of collaborating with others to reach organizational goals and achieve the organization's mission, sharing enthusiasm for the work to be done, providing help in solving problems, and supporting and encouraging. In the United States today, people working in education who subscribe to Theory *X* assumptions commonly mask them behind the kind of Theory *X* Soft behavior that was discussed in Chapter 2 (on motivation), so as not to appear insensitive and undemocratic. Theory *X* Soft behavior by the leader poses some serious moral and ethical problems, which I will discuss later in this chapter.

The key to understanding leadership, then, lies in understanding your own concept of the human nature of followers and how leaders relate to them. For example, Niccolo Machiavelli's assumptions about human nature were set forth in his advice to a young man of the ruling class in the fifteenth century. Machiavelli's treatise, *The Prince,* once was required reading for students in educational administration and is still widely admired today. It taught that the exercise of leadership by those who inherit positions of power as a privilege of membership in a dominant elite social class required the ruthless exercise of position power, the use of guile and deception when expedient to achieve the leader's personal agenda, and indifference to the concerns of others.

This Machiavellian view of leadership is still very prevalent, though of course it usually is expressed obliquely in cautious terms, and is usually disguised in Theory *X* Soft behavior so as to appear reasonably adapted to the democratic demands of our time. The central idea is that leadership consists largely of commanding and controlling other people. Consider, for example, this observation intended for a mass audience of readers from the management ranks of corporations:

> A leader is a leader only insofar as he [sic] has followers. If we want our subordinates to do something and they do not do it, then, plainly, they have not followed our lead. Likewise, if we want our charges to accomplish something, quite apart from how they go about it, and they do not accomplish it, then, again they have not followed our lead. Now these are the only two ways that we can be leaders: we can want certain *actions* and we can want certain *results. The degree in which we get what we want is the measure of our leadership.*

> A follower is a follower only insofar as he [sic] does what a leader wants in order to please the leader . . . we are all social creatures, and so we want to please the boss. . . . Work is done for the boss. We grow for our parents, learn for our teacher, win for our coach. Even the most independent of us presents his [sic] work as a gift for the boss.[12]

This statement says a great deal about the writers' assumptions about the human nature of followers and how leaders relate to them. On the other hand, consider this statement of assumptions about leadership from a modern military perspective:

> When you lead in battle you are leading people, human beings. I have seen competent leaders who stood in front of a platoon and all they saw was a platoon. But great leaders stand in front of a platoon and see it as 44 individuals, each of whom has hopes, each of whom has aspirations, each of whom wants to live, each of whom wants to do good.[13]

This expresses a very different view of human nature than was embodied in Max Weber's now classic work on bureaucracy. Weber's work first appeared in the early years of the twentieth century and became known in the United States only after World War II, when translations from the German were published in English.

Your Understanding of Human Nature Is Critical

At the turn of the century, the emergence of giant industrial corporations was transforming society in Europe. Max Weber saw that the old aristocracies could not provide the new kinds of leadership required in the expanding government, business, and industrial organizations of the day. To replace the absolute power inherited by privileged social classes, which was enjoyed by members of the German Junkers of

Weber's day and *The Prince* of Machiavelli's day, and to reject the exercise of traditional autocratic rule in modern industrial, commercial, and government organizations that were then emerging around the world, Weber supported the rise of a disciplined and orderly organization composed of official offices arranged hierarchically, with legally assigned power and authority descending from the top to the bottom. Weber approvingly gave this kind of organization a name: bureaucracy.[14]

In contrast to autocratic rule, the "law" of the bureaucratic organization lies in its written rules and regulations, official standard operating procedures, written memos, chain of command, and acceptance of the concepts of hierarchical superordination and subordination. It is a vision of organization that is rational, logical, impersonal, formal, predictable, and systematic, and it reflects beliefs about the nature and needs of the human beings who populate the organization: bureaucratic theory generally holds that people tend pretty much to be motivated by the lower levels of Maslow's hierarchy of needs, with emphasis on pay and benefits, job security, and advancement in rank.

Weber's work has had enormous influence in establishing and maintaining bureaucracy as the most pervasive and credible organizational concept in the world. Yet few who are taught the virtues of bureaucratic organization in their universities understand or even know that it was the same Max Weber, sociologist and theologian, who also wrote powerfully on the Protestant work ethic as a defining characteristic of human nature. Weber was convinced, and convinced many other people at the time, that Protestantism was undergirded by certain fundamental moral and ethical imperatives that were played out in the world of work, the so-called Protestant work ethic, in ways that were superior to those of non-Protestant cultures. Thus, in reality, Weber viewed bureaucracy as embodying and codifying in the world of work certain views of human nature that he believed were inherent in Protestant theology. The two were, in his mind, closely linked.

Let me return the theme of this discussion of leadership to the concept of organizational behavior that B = f(p • e). In exercising leadership, the leader has an array of options from which to choose in influencing the nature and quality of the organizational environment with which members interact in the course of their daily work. How one chooses depends on one's understanding of what kinds of behaviors are desirable and sought, on the one hand, and how they are likely to be elicited in the organization's environment, on the other hand. If, for example, you think that Machiavelli understood the realities of modern educational organizations, then his advice on leadership will be appealing and appear practical. If, on the other hand, you think that schools are best understood as bureaucracies, then you will do your best to create a bureaucratic environment for people to work in.

However, if you think of people in Theory Y terms, then you will try to create the organizational environment likely to elicit and support the high motivation and high levels of effort that they will find satisfying in their work. Such an environment is growth enhancing and engages the members of the organization in personal growth and development as well as in organizational growth and development—that is, a healthy state of increasing ability to identify and solve its own problems in an ever-changing world. An important part of such an organizational environment is leadership. It is precisely because bureaucratic organizations lack this internal dynamic for organization development in the context of constant change in the world, as do autocratic organizations, that they are such poor exemplars for the study of leadership.

Bureaucratic View of Leadership

Commonly the traditional bureaucratic officeholder tends to emulate the Lone Ranger when attempting leadership:

> The Lone Ranger, an imposing masked figure, rides up on a white horse to overcome great odds in solving the problems of the day. The model of the vanquishing leader— a bit mysterious, generous, but aloof—is a very common theme. Think of the setting: helpless, disorganized townsfolk are being threatened by some bad guys. The Lone Ranger, helped just by his trusty and loyal sidekick, arrives in the nick of time, with the right blend of courage and cunning, faces down the bad guys by being just a little quicker, smarter, and tougher, leaves a silver bullet as a symbol of his having solved the problem, and at the end, rides stoically off into the sunset. The grateful townspeople wonder who that masked man is—and wish he could stay—but are left to go about their mundane tasks no wiser or better prepared to deal with the next big problem. When again faced with a major crisis, they'll just have to hope for a return of the thundering hoofbeats and another last-minute rescue by the daring hero.[15]

Thus the townsfolk or, in our case, the faculty of the school or department, learn nothing from their experience that leaves them better prepared to continue the process of solving problems in the future, nor have they been motivated by the Lone Ranger to improve their problem-solving skills: the problem has been solved for the moment but the school has not increased its ability to solve problems as a result of the experience. For all the good work that he achieved, one must fault the Lone Ranger's performance as a leader because he did not leave the townsfolk functioning at a higher level than when he encountered them.

In contrast, contemporary thinking about leadership contends that leaders, unlike mere power wielders and bureaucratic managers, work with followers in ways that change both leaders and followers so that over time they are performing at increasingly higher levels of functioning than they were initially. This view of leadership is called "transforming" leadership.[16]

TRANSFORMING LEADERSHIP

The idea of "transforming" leadership was conceptualized by James MacGregor Burns[17] in his seminal Pulitzer prize–winning work and has directly influenced the thinking of scholars ever since. Burns's insights were later developed and elaborated by Bernard Bass.[18] They have subsequently been used as the basis of research, such as that of, for example, Warren Bennis,[19] Rosabeth Moss Kanter,[20] and Judy B. Rosener,[21] each of whom studied corporate leaders. More recently, the ideas of transforming leadership were used by Thomas Sergiovanni to organize a critique of school reform.[22]

Transforming Leadership Compared and Contrasted with Transactional Leadership

The heart of Burns's analysis was to compare and contrast traditional "transactional" leadership with the newer idea of "transforming" leadership. Having explained that leadership is different and distinct from simply wielding power over people, Burns went on to explain that there are two different basic types of leadership. In the most commonly used type of leadership, the relationship between leader and followers is based on quid pro quo transactions between leaders and followers. Transactional educational leaders can and do offer jobs, security, tenure, favorable ratings, and more in exchange for support, cooperation, and compliance of followers.

In contrast "the transformational leader looks for potential motives in followers, seeks to satisfy higher needs, and engages the full person of the follower. The result of transforming leadership is a relationship of mutual stimulation and elevation that converts followers into leaders and may convert leaders into moral agents."[23] This evokes a third, and higher level, of leadership: that is, the concept of "moral leadership" that began to receive so much attention in education in the 1990s.

Moral Leadership

The concept of moral leadership comprises three related ideas:

+ First, that the relationship between the leader and the led is not one merely of power but is a genuine sharing of mutual needs, aspirations, and values. The genuineness of this sharing is tested by whether or not the participation of followers is a matter of choice that is controlled by the follower.

+ Second, that the followers have latitude in responding to the initiatives of leaders: they have the ability to make informed choices as to who they will follow and why. As I shall explain more fully in a moment, the concept of transforming leadership means that followers voluntarily involve themselves in the leadership process. Among other things, followers voluntarily grant power and authority to leaders and are free to withdraw that grant. Therefore, in the highest level of transforming leadership, which is moral leadership, the followers must have access to alternative leaders from whom to choose and they must have knowledge of alternative plans and programs that they might embrace.

+ Third, that leaders take responsibility for delivering on the commitments and representations made to followers in negotiating the compact between leader and followers. "Thus, moral leadership is not mere preaching, or the uttering of pieties, or the insistence on social conformity. Moral leadership emerges from, and always returns to, the fundamental wants and needs, aspirations, and values of followers."[24] In this sense, moral leadership is very different from the thin veneer of participation that administrators frequently use to give their relationships with followers some patina of genuine involvement while control remains firmly in the administrators' hands.

A Progression

A progression is clearly inherent in the concept of transforming leadership:

+ At the lowest level of functioning is the exercise of power to exact the compliance of followers, which is not leadership at all.

+ At the entry level of leadership is transactional leadership, wherein the leader and followers bargain with each other to establish a "contract" for working together.

+ At a higher level of functioning is transforming leadership, in which the leaders and followers mutually engage in common cause cohered by their shared aspirations and values.

+ At the highest level is moral leadership, which demands motivating emotional stimuli, such as a shared mission, a sense of mutual purpose, and a covenant of shared values interwoven with the daily life and practices of ordinary people so as to inspire new and higher levels of commitment and involvement.

A Process of Growth and Development

The levels in this progression in transforming leadership increasingly draw on the higher levels of the inner motivations of followers and, in return, offer increasing opportunities for followers and leaders to grow and develop increasing capacities for effective organizational behavior. Thus transforming leaders engage the aspirations of followers, tap their inner motivations, energize their mental and emotional resources, and involve them enthusiastically in the work to be done. This kind of leadership does not merely obtain the compliance of followers, it evokes their personal commitment as they embrace the goals to be achieved as their very own, seeing them as an opportunity for a willing investment of their effort. It transforms the roles of both followers and leaders so that they become virtually interdependent,[25] their aspirations, motives, and values merged in mutual commitment to achieve the shared goals. Burns's focus was political leadership, not educational leadership, and he used Gandhi as one well-known exemplar of both transforming and moral leadership. One also thinks of the leadership of Martin Luther King, Jr. But such leadership is not limited to those who appear larger than life on the world stage. Many coaches, in various sports ranging from football to tennis, illustrate effective leadership in their work. Indeed, the metaphor of the coach is popular in speaking of leadership in many kinds of organizations. Many who have followed Burns's scholarly lead have described how readily his concepts of transforming leadership apply to realms other than politics, such as education and business. Increasingly one finds literature that describes the behavior of people in high-performing schools as being consistent with transformational leadership.

We know that members of educational organizations thrive on the experience of being part of an organization that is constantly growing in its internal capacity to detect and solve its own problems. A school having such characteristics is seen by teachers as a successful and effective place in which to work. For example, a substantial body of research, such as Dan Lortie's classic *Schoolteacher*,[26] tells us that teachers are highly motivated by feeling successful and effective in their teaching. From this, one can conclude that an educational leader in a school might seek to foster a culture that facilitates teaching and enhances the likelihood that one will be successful at it, that energizes and enthuses the efforts of teachers, that rewards and supports success in teaching, that celebrates teaching as a central value in the life of the school. Such a school is likely to have a history that stresses the importance of teaching, heros who epitomize achievement in teaching, and rituals and ceremonies that celebrate teaching and the successes of teachers. These are likely to be very prominent characteristics of the school that are emphasized daily at all levels of the organization. Thus, one can exercise leadership by working with and through teachers to transform the culture of the school and, in the process, transform the very ways in which the leader and the teachers relate to one another. It is widely believed that the vehicle for bringing about such a transformation is a vision of the future that is better, more desirable, more compelling, and more personally fulfilling than the reality of the present time.

Leadership and Vision

The vision that leaders seek to share with followers is a protean thing, continually being revised and annotated by changing values, emerging developments, and events that vindicate or repudiate aspects of the worldview previously held by either leader and followers, or both. Indeed, one of the pivotal activities of leaders is to engage constantly in the dynamic process of stating a vision of things to come; then revising in light of emerging events, ideas, and beliefs; and restating the vision of "where we are and where we are going" that coheres the members of the organization in mutual purpose and resolve. But in all its iterations, the vision of a leader is always uplifting, pointing to new directions, calling for progress from where we are to where we want to be, and describing how we will get there. Dramatic examples abound in the realm of politics and social movements: one thinks of Churchill's magnificent rallying cry to the British facing almost certain defeat in World War II, "We shall fight on," the stirring inspiration of Lincoln's low-key Gettysburg Address, and the immortal vision of King's revelation that "I have a dream." Educational leaders rarely have opportunities to exercise such dramatic flair and personal charisma, yet they must always be prepared to articulate their own personal vision for the organization as a rallying cry for the daily work to be done.

The purpose of the ongoing process of stating and discussing the vision is to buttress and develop the most critical factors in the development of organizational culture: the web of shared assumptions, beliefs, and values that unites the group in mutual solidarity. In the ordinary, bureaucratic organization these things are rarely examined and discussed, rarely made explicit and public, rarely challenged. Indeed, in ordinary organizations there is little even in the way of vocabulary for talking about such things, and the time-consuming minutiae of professional meetings usually drives such conversation out, so that the norm in the organization's culture is to avoid such discussion altogether.

The goal of forging agreement on the vision or mission of the organization is, ideally, to seek consensus as nearly as it can be practically achieved, but always consensus on a new and better state in the future. In one iteration the statement may not be as clear as it might be, and it must be restated in a hopefully clearer way. Sometimes even the nuance of a word or phrase can rouse unanticipated effect, and the statement must be rephrased more sensitively. Sometimes aspects of the stated vision are unacceptable to some members of the organization and an accommodation must be worked out. But throughout the process, the leader strives always to marshall consensus in support of something better: a higher plane of functioning, an elevated sense of motivation and commitment, an organization that is constantly metamorphosing into something better than it was. The point to remember is that the ongoing discussion of the organizational vision is a crucial dialogue through which the leader and the followers mutually engage in the process of forging the destiny that unites them in common cause. It is therefore a powerful engine for the empowerment of teachers. By participating in the never-ending process of creating, maintaining, and evolving a vision of the future of the school, teachers are themselves involved in a process of self-development and growth. Moreover, because the process is open, ongoing, and collaborative, the principal is also engaged in personal self-development and growth: the process engages the leader as much as anyone and in the end helps to forge and refine the leader's own vision.

Engaging in the give-and-take of the ongoing colloquy required to forge and maintain an evolving vision of the organization requires one to rethink assumptions, beliefs, and values that previously guided behavior at work and either reaffirm them or modify them in the light of this reflection as well as in the light of newly emerging realities. The process has a name—reflective practice—and many believe that it is essential if one is to continue to develop and improve one's professional practice over the years rather than to stagnate and become increasingly irrelevant.

Whose Vision Is It, Anyway?

At a time when school reform cries out for leadership, rather than bureaucratic command, schools should be evolving from top-down hierarchical management toward a more collaborative, collegial, participative form of leadership. Because the new form of organization facilitates and encourages the active participation of people who are on the lower rungs of the organizational hierarchy, it is sometimes popularly referred to as bottom-up organization. In such an organization the glue that binds the organization's participants together, that motivates them to unite in common purpose, is a vision of a different school, new and better, in the future. But whose vision is it, anyway?

Bureaucrats assume that experts high in the hierarchy are especially qualified to set the goals of the organization and determine how to reach them. The experts may or may not consult those on the lower levels of the organization in so doing. Leaders, on the other hand, assume that those on the lower levels of the organization have valuable knowledge, good ideas, and insights as to what the organization is about that must be an integral part of the mix that we call a vision of the organization.

Leaders assume that the ability to lead is widely distributed throughout the organization and often manifests itself when participants express new ideas, challenge traditional practices, and synthesize and express the ideas of a collegial group. That is why it is important for leaders to empower others to participate fully in the unending processes of creating and refining a vision of the mission of the school. But leadership is not a spectator sport: leaders do not stand passively on the sidelines hoping that others will lead the way and shape the future.

Leaders are not merely catalysts of the ideas of others, much as they encourage and facilitate participation, but have their own clearly thought-out vision of the future, their own sense of direction. Leaders have something important to say in the dialogue about "where we are and where we are going," something that engages the aspirations of others and raises their sights as to what can and should be achieved in their work, moves them forward to engage vigorously with others in building a new and better future in the organization. But leadership is not a solo performance, either. The leader's role in the process of developing a vision of the school, in addition to offering ideas and participating in discussion, emphasizes facilitating the involvement of others in an ongoing dialogue about the direction for the future.

One must remember that by definition transformational leadership involves mobilizing resources, including human and intellectual resources, *in conflict with others* so as to "arouse, engage, and satisy the motives of others."[27] Therefore, vision building is not always a placid process but often requires engagement with different worldviews of people in the group, different temperaments, different personal agendas, different levels of understanding, different hopes and aspirations, and different pedagogical approaches to the future. Therefore, whereas the school principal, for example, must avoid imposing a prepared mission statement on the teachers for ratification by them, he or she must have developed a clearly thought-out position from which to contribute, unhesitatingly and convincingly, to the discussion.

Perhaps the leader can do nothing more important in empowering teachers to create a process for forging and reworking the vision, or mission, of the school than to signal that it is not only important to do but it is okay to do. Traditionally, schools have not been places where adults can easily share the collegial relationships that are essential to leadership, as different from management, and teacher empowerment. The school leader, then, must demonstrate convincingly an interest in promoting collegiality and shared leadership, an interest in shifting the norms of the school's culture from the traditional to more collaborative ways of working together. Making this shift in the cultural norms of the school, translating the intent into daily practices that reduce the sense of isolation that is typical of teaching, will more than likely be gradual because teachers have learned, through experience, to be cautious in talking about their work. In traditional schools, teachers rarely see one another practice their craft, rarely discuss pedagogy in a serious way, and almost never deal with such matters in staff meetings, which are ordinarily filled with minor routine matters.

MANIPULATION AND EMPOWERMENT

One of the most common criticisms of educational administrators that is emerging in the literature on school reform is the charge that they tend to manipulate followers, often by using a veneer of seemingly participative involvement. By indirection these administrators get followers to pursue ends that the administrators seek, while seeming to be acting on the followers' intentions. Through this manipulation those who are in power maintain their power, whereas followers are induced to believe that the arrangement is appropriate and legitimate, if not inevitable. Teachers, for example, deeply socialized into the traditional ways of schools—having participated in them since they were five years old—generally accept the hierarchical power of principals and superintendents as a reality of life that is both inevitable and legitimate. It is commonplace for teachers who have had their views brushed aside to say to the principal, "Well, just tell me what you want me to do and I'll try my best to do it."

Critical Theory

A group of educational academicians who subscribe to a form of social criticism known as critical theory have been especially sensitive to and vociferous about this perceived shortcoming. Critical theory is a form of social criticism that holds that institutionalized oppression of groups of people in a society—cultural, ethnic, racial, and gender groups—is often supported by the oppressed peoples themselves, who believe the system to actually be in their own best interests. This, critical theorists contend, is achieved by the manipulation of meaning by those in power so as to legitimate the values and beliefs of the power elite. In that view, some critical theorists in the Marxian tradition would say, indeed have said, that workers in capitalist societies are oppressed by the powerful capitalist class but don't perceive it because through control of the press, education, organized religion, and other social institutions those in power systematically induce workers to believe that the values and beliefs of the capitalist class are legitimate and in the workers' best interests.

Critical theory is often applied to the analysis of the perceived oppression of nondominant races, women, the poor, and other social classes in present-day U.S. education.[28] The approach has also been applied to the study of relationships between official school leaders, such as principals, and teachers. Some school leaders mandate that teachers comply with organizational goals or that they embrace particular notions of organizational culture, whereas others induce compliance through more subtle, more manipulative, means. Nevertheless, by the mid-1980s recognition began to grow that bona fide participation by teachers in school affairs is highly desirable yet has traditionally been rare. However, with the recommendation in 1986 by the Carnegie Forum on Education and the Economy that teachers be given "a greater voice in the decisions that affect the school,"[29] the term *teacher empowerment* has been one of the most recurrent buzzwords in school educational circles.

An important aspect of empowerment is that it provides opportunities for teachers to participate actively, openly, and without fear in the endless process of shaping and molding the vision of the school and its culture through iterative discussion. By doing so, at least three things happen that Burns described as essential to transforming leadership:

+ Teachers participate actively in the dynamic ongoing processes of leadership by contributing their knowledge, insights, and ideas to the development of the vision for the school.

+ They acquire greater personal ownership, and thus a greater sense of personal commitment to, the values for which the school stands and that shape its vision for the future.

+ By their active personal engagement in the process, and by being personally committed its outcomes, teachers are stimulated to increase their awareness of both the larger mission of the school and the connection of their own daily mundane work to the achievement of that mission.

This process of leadership is very different from the manipulation of followers, guileful or otherwise, by power-wielding leaders that once passed for leadership. It taps the inner motivations of teachers—their aspirations, beliefs, and values—and enriches the significance of what they do by better connecting their daily work to the larger mission of the enterprise. Thus, transforming leadership inevitably empowers teachers.

LEADERSHIP AND MANAGEMENT

The rhetoric of reform chic contends that U.S. schools require leadership, not "mere management." This suggests that there is not only a difference between management and leadership but that, moreover, they are mutually exclusive. This view correctly derives from the fact that one manages things, not people, and one leads people, not things. We manage finances, inventories, and programs, for example, but we lead people. Moreover, there is a qualitative difference between managing and leading and, some contend, they are mutually exclusive. Warren Bennis and Burt Nanus, for example, have told us that "managers are people who do things right and leaders are people who do the right thing."[30] Some blame much of our present dearth of educational leadership on the existence of a managerial mystique, long promoted by schools of business as well as schools of education, that taught managers to pay attention to structures, roles, and indirect forms of communications and to ignore the ideas of people, their emotions, and to avoid direct involvement of others in leadership. The result has been a professionalization of management that deflected attention from the real business of schools, which is teaching, and conceptualized leadership as emphasis on rules, plans, management controls, and operating procedures.

This often manifests itself in the language of those who confuse schooling and teaching with "the delivery of educational services," and who do so with the cool detachment that a merchant might use to speak of the distribution of goods or the manager of a fast-food restaurant might describe the essence of the business. Thus, in schools we too often see

> an emphasis on doing things right, at the expense of doing the right things. In schools, improvement plans become substitutes for improvement outcomes. Scores on teacher-appraisal systems become substitutes for good teaching. Accumulation of credits in courses and inservice workshops become a substitute for changes in practice. Discipline plans become substitutes for student control. Leadership styles become substitutes for purpose and substance. Congeniality becomes a substitute for collegiality. Cooperation becomes a substitute for commitment. Compliance becomes a substitute for results.[31]

There is little question that as the U.S. public school enterprise became markedly more bureaucratized in the decades from 1945 to 1985, emphasis was focused on the bureaucratic concept of leadership, which we now call management. There is also little question that this myopic focus needs to be corrected, that leadership is badly needed in educational institutions at all levels. But we must be cautious about substituting management-bashing for leadership.

Educational leaders must—as must all leaders—be able to manage. John Gardner rightly pointed out that leaders often must allocate resources, deal with budgets, and organize the enterprise in order to enable people to do the work necessary to move the organization toward its vision.[32] He concluded, therefore, that leaders need to be skilled managers well able to deal with the mundane inner workings of organizational life that must be attended to if the vision is to be realized.

It is unarguable that schools have been, and still largely are, organized and administered as bureaucracies or, as the contemporary pejorative has it, using the factory as a model. There is little question that most educational administrators conceptualize their work largely in terms of management of operational routines. Clearly this emphasis has tended to thwart the development of leadership in schools while emphasizing management. Therefore, it is unarguable that U.S. schools are generally in need of more and better leadership. But it is false to argue that, therefore, principals should be leaders, not managers, because they need to be both.

Empowerment and Leadership

Recent research and writing on leadership[33] has sharpened the difference between managing and leading. Whereas managers may, and often do, involve other people in various ways in making decisions, leaders go beyond that: leaders are able "to create and communicate a vision that inspires followers."[34] Thus, whereas the main concern of educational administration once was viewed as controlling the behavior of teachers, with planning and decision making closely held in the hands of the hierarchy, the emerging concept is focused on developing a vision that involves followers, inspires them, and motivates their efforts. It is the shared vision of a better school in the future that has the power to transform the relationships between the teachers and the principal, for example, uniting them in mutually sharing the work required to achieve the vision. This is the reason that one hears so much today about the vision of the future as a key element in school leadership.

Creating this mutually shared vision cannot be done without sharing some of the power that was traditionally closely held by those in the administrative hierarchy with the rank and file of the organization: power, for example, in the form of information about the organization, authority to participate freely in making decisions, recognition of the legitimacy of followers as stakeholders in the enterprise, and creating an environment that facilitates the development of trust and open communication that is essential to collaborative group effort. This is the basis for the empowerment of teachers, parents, students, and others who were formerly shut out of the decision making of the organization.

A Moral or Ethical Problem

The notion of empowerment to improve organizational performance is not a new one, having been widely discussed and, to a limited extent, practiced in the 1970s under the banner of organization development, which used the term "power sharing" instead of today's "empowerment." Indeed, the organization development experience provided us with a wealth of knowledge about techniques that can be used to implement the concept of empowerment by training organization members in such techniques as shared decision making and developing trust and openness so as to create a growth-enhancing culture in the organization. But the failure of the organization development movement was anchored in the entrenched resistance of those who held position power to share their power with others. This resulted in many people holding position power playing Theory *X* Soft games with their subordinates in which they used various forms of participative methods—holding meetings, calling on people to be open and honest, using the language of participation—while guilefully making sure that no significant power was shared with subordinates.

Today this sort of Machiavellian manipulation is understood as constituting a serious moral or ethical problem, and concern about it is widespread, especially in educational settings. The quality of organizational life in the United States has dwindled over the last two or three decades while those in position power steadfastly ducked the issue of empowerment. Many hope that we have now entered a different era in which it is clear that empowerment methods of leadership are all that remain as we attempt to revitalize our schools. Efforts by people with position power to finesse the new imperative for collaboration, to use guile and Machiavellian subterfuge so as to manipulate appearances without changing realities in power relationships can, in the long run, only impede leadership and threaten our educational organizations even further.

A PRAGMATIC GUIDE TO LEADER BEHAVIOR

In the long-overdue shift away from bureaucratic management as the dominant organizational concept of schools toward a transforming leadership concept, what should leaders do differently? If, in bureaucratic organization, people in authority tend to direct others and make decisions for others to implement, what do leaders in nonbureaucratic organizations do? To answer these practical questions, we must first look to ourselves and face squarely what we assume about the nature of those whom we would lead.

A Pragmatic View of Leadership

Two major trends in understanding leadership have been expanding and accelerating with the passage of time in twentieth-century America:

- ✦ Growing recognition of and acceptance of the perception that the members of an organization constitute extremely valuable resources—rich in ideas, knowledge, creativity, and an astonishing level of human energy—that are available to the organization in the pursuit of goals and purposes that the members accept as their own.

- ✦ Growing recognition of the relative ineffectiveness of command and coercion as forms of leadership, in contrast to the development of organizational environments that are motivating, caring, inclusionary, and empowering of members as forms of leadership.

As I described earlier, in discussing the Western Electric researches, for example, these ideas were not born in the academic world, nor are they of recent vintage. What is new about them is that, in the face of increasing failure of traditional leadership methods, the "new" ideas are being embraced today as central to improving leadership so as to improve organizational performance. The ideas that undergird transforming leadership have been well known for decades, but they were largely denied, ignored, or subverted by managers and administrators seeking to preserve their hegemony. It is only recently, as the deleterious effects of traditional management and administration by power wielding have become increasingly understood and found unacceptable in the "real world" of everyday organizational life, that the traditional methods of the management mystique have been seriously challenged.

The Scanlon Plan

An early example of applying the "new" ideas to industrial organizations was the Scanlon Plan, which is now enjoying a resurgence after being widely ignored by managers since its development in the 1930s. In the hard, practical world of U.S. steel mills, Joseph N. Scanlon is widely credited with being a pioneer in reshaping organizational practice in industrial organizations to implement these "new" ideas. Today there is a "Scanlon Plan" that has been widely used in industrial organizations for that purpose. The story of how that plan came into being is fascinating, and is worth telling briefly here because of a strong parallel with the situation in U.S. education today.

The Scanlon Plan had its origins in the 1930s in the gritty rust-belt steel mill where Joe Scanlon worked and was a union official. Times were hard: the Great Depression was in full swing, the equipment in the plant was outmoded, competition for the shrinking market was fierce, profits were down, and the workers were seeking better wages and improved working conditions. As a result, the corporation was giving serious thought to getting out of the steel business. Scanlon realized that if the company and the union kept on with their traditional adversarial tactics, the plant would be closed and everybody would lose.

Joe Scanlon must have been a great negotiator, because he convinced the corporation, the international union, and his fellow workers to try a new, bold, cooperative effort to solve the problem. The plan was simple: the union would not press its wage demands immediately, management would pay the wage increases when improved productivity made it possible, and in the meantime there would be a cooperative all-out effort to improve productivity. "Once the workers' cooperation had been enlisted, their knowledge of the processes and suggestions for improving the operation were successful in reducing costs, decreasing waste, improving efficiency, and improving quality. After a few months the cooperation between workers and management paid off. The survival of the company was assured, and the employees received increased wages and improved working conditions."[35]

This was a great success story, of course, and Scanlon soon went with a small staff to the United Steelworkers Union, where he worked for a few years trying to perfect and promulgate the notion of union-management cooperation instead of traditional union-management conflict. Eventually he joined the faculty of the Massachusetts Institute of Technology. During his long tenure there, the Scanlon Plan was initiated in many companies, especially in the Midwest, and the rationale for the plan was honed and perfected.

When applied to specific organizations, the Scanlon Plan takes different forms in different organizations, but always

> the Scanlon Plan rests on the assumptions that people prefer to express themselves fully in all situations including work situations and that, when they do express themselves, they can be constructive and supportive of other people and the groups to which they belong. . . . [what] follows from this position [is] that the basic philosophy is best served when all members of the organization participate as fully as they can in the activities of the organization and when they are equitably rewarded for their participation. All principles of management that encourage people to identify with their work group, that encourage people to participate as much as they can, and that continually focus on equitably rewarding all members of the organization are seen as ways of applying the Scanlon Plan philosophy.[36]

Sadly, most corporate executives, as well as most educational administrators, have given little more than lip service, if that, to these ideas about leadership. Many have actively resisted them, preferring to hold onto their privileged positions of organizational power and enact the "great man" theory of leadership. "How can education learn from business?" some ask, "The institution that gave us the savings and loan scandal, junk bonds, unbridled greed, all the malodorous military contracts, and the infamous 'lobbying' of government officials." Others ask, "What has business to teach schools? Businesses are failing all around us, firing people in droves, sending jobs overseas, closing plants and stores rather than make them profitable, selling off assets so as to appear profitable. None of these things have anything to do with schools." True enough, yet many businesses are successful and often owe much of their success to using enlightened forms of leadership.

Servant Leadership

Consider this statement of assumptions about leadership from a successful Connecticut industrialist:

> The role of a leader is the servant's role. It's supporting his [sic] people, running interference for them. It's coming out with an atmosphere of understanding and love. You want people to feel they have complete control over their destiny at every level. Tyranny is not tolerated here. People who want to manage in the traditional sense are cast off by their peers like dandruff.[37]

That is, admittedly, a far cry from the ruthless image of, say, John "Neutron Jack" Welch of General Electric. He acquired his nickname in the admiring business press, such as the *Wall Street Journal,* who respected the cost-cutting toughness evidenced by his mass firings of employees, leaving, as the story goes, the buildings of the corporation standing but no employees in them. Yet we can learn a great deal that is useful from thoughtful corporate leaders if we are selective in choosing our mentors.

On the long road to the presidency, Bill Clinton contemplated the meaning of leadership and who he thought had something useful to say about it. He had been influenced by Max De Pree, a second-generation scion of a profitable company that is noted for producing fine office furniture. Many years ago, De Pree's company had implemented a Scanlon Plan, which sought, as Scanlon Plans always do, to develop trust, collegiality, and a culture of caring and empowerment as essentials of a profitable corporation. Because the company is so successful, it is frequently studied by business school faculty seeking to discover its "secrets." Finally, De Pree wrote a couple of small books telling all. They are rather plain, simple, straightforward books that set forth his ideas on leadership as he practices it on the job.

De Pree's thinking revolves around the belief that a leader is one who serves.[38] He summed up his views this way: "In a day when so much energy seems to be spent on maintenance and manuals, on bureaucracy and meaningless quantification, to be a leader is to enjoy the special privileges of complexity, of ambiguity, of diversity. But to be a leader means, especially, having the opportunity to make a meaningful difference in the lives of those who permit leaders to lead."[39]

LEADERSHIP AND LA DIFFÉRENCE

Since about 1990,[40] there has been a rapidly growing debate about whether successful women leaders behave in the same ways as successful men leaders. Conventional wisdom has long held that they do: that while in lower ranks in the organization women may acceptably behave "like a woman," in order to be successful in leadership positions it is necessary for women to emulate the ways of thinking and the behaviors of their male counterparts. In a study of 456 women corporate executives, political scientist Judy B. Rosener reported that such is not the case, that women in fact use very different leadership styles from men.

To conduct the survey on which her findings are based, Rosener not only sent questionnaires to women executives, but also asked each informant to identify a man in a similar position in a similar company. She then sent identical eight-page questionnaires to each of those men. Men, she reported, tend to use a "command style"—relishing personal power, thinking and making decisions in logical linear fashion, issuing orders, assuming that people are motivated by their personal self-interest (that is, acquiring money and power); however, women were more personal in their style, sharing information, sensitive to the feelings of others, promoting empowerment of followers, and motivating people by appealing to their commitment to the organization's ideals. At about the same time that Rosener's work appeared, Sally Helgesen wrote a book, *The Female Advantage,* asserting similar observations and further claiming that the behavior of women was not only different from that of men but more effective as well. Similar reports from both research and speculation have become prominent in the literature in the field of education as well.[41] The debate about whether it is individual personality or gender from which leader behavior style arises has been boiling and expanding ever since.

The genesis of the feminist approach to this debate is found by many in Carol Gilligan's influential 1982 book, *In a Different Voice: Psychological Theory and Women's Development.*[42] Based on a systematic program of research which gathered data from structured interviews, Gilligan's book has widely influenced the subsequent development of women's psychology and the contemporary feminist perspective on organizational behavior. Among the individuals who appear prominently in Gilligan's book is a group of children, including Jake and Amy, who are bright, articulate 11-year-olds.

Gilligan presented Amy and Jake with the well-known Heinz dilemma, which is one of the moral dilemmas that psychologists commonly use to reveal how people think and reason. The dilemma is this: What should Heinz, who is a poor man, do when he finds out that he cannot afford to buy the medicine that would save the life of his dying wife? The two children gave very different answers. Jake thought that Heinz should steal the medicine and gamble that, if caught, he could convince the judge that he had done the right thing. Amy, on the other hand, thought that he should try to borrow the money or, perhaps, talk about his problem with the druggist to see if something could be worked out. Drawing upon many examples such as this from her interviews and observations, Gilligan concluded that males and females tend to view and think about the world in different ways: that there are psychological differences related to gender, that there is a psychology of women. The important inference is, of course, that gender is the most influential factor in determining one's view of the world and how one responds to what is perceived.

This view contrasts sharply with, and seeks to compete with, the more widely accepted idea that was discussed earlier, that one's behavior is basically influenced by one's temperament. That concept rests on the research of Carl Jung and Katheryn Briggs and posits that temperament arises from four dimensions of characteristics that are as inborn and unchangeable as one's body build.[43] They are (1) introversion-extraversion, (2) sensation-intuition, (3) thinking-feeling, and (4) perceiving-judging. These characteristics combine in various patterns in individuals to produce temperament types that are unrelated to gender.

The literature on leadership, in the corporate world as well as in the education world, has recently experienced a surge of descriptions of how women leaders behave differently from men. The reason for the difference is ascribed to gender, rather than personality type. For example, Rosener described women corporate leaders as using "interactive leadership," encouraging the participation of others, sharing power and information with them, facilitating their inclusion in the group, making then feel important, evoking in them high levels of enthusiasm and excitement for the work. She reported that, in contrast, the male counterparts of these women tended to rely on "the traditional command-and-control leadership" style that has served them well in the past.[44] Rosener's report was eagerly seized upon by those who want to believe that women intuitively exercise the participative, empowering leader behavior required in many kinds of organizations today whereas men do not. However, one should not overlook the observations in the next-to-last paragraph of her widely influential article:

> Linking [participative, empowering] leadership directly to being female is a mistake. We know that women are capable of making their way through corporations by adhering the traditional corporate model and that they can wield power in ways similar to men. Indeed, some women may prefer that style. We also know from survey findings that some men use the transformational leadership style.[45]

Thus, Rosener stopped short of claiming that women possess some "natural" abilities to lead in participative, empowering ways that men do not possess. She contented herself with reaffirming that participative, empowering leadership style can be highly effective in corporations, and documenting that many women reported it as a style that they intuitively prefer to use. Acknowledging that "some" men use transformational leadership style, Rosener actually sidestepped the question of whether the differences between the behaviors of men and women that she reports are "the natural and inevitable consequences of the intrinsic biological natures of women and men."[46] In other words, to the extent to which gender differences exist in leadership style, they may be due to nonbiological factors such as the different ways in which men and boys and women and girls are socialized in our culture.

Undoubtedly, the issue of understanding the role of gender in leadership had emerged as a "hot" topic by the 1990s and will continue to be so in the future.

Feminist scholarship has already contributed richly to a better understanding of the different ways that men and women approach leading. Feminist scholarship also has illuminated the appropriateness of transformational leader behavior in educational organizations at a time when it was needed as never before to replace traditional command-and-control behavior.

CONCLUSION

The goal of leadership is to build human capital in the organization: to transform the relationship between leader and followers so that participants are energized and motivated by unity of purpose and mutually shared values. Transformative leadership is based on the conviction that the people in the organization constitute a resource rich in ideas, knowledge, creativity, and energy whose power can be fully tapped only by creating organizational environments that are motivating, inclusionary, caring, and empowering. The transformative leader is well aware that leadership involves not command and coercion, but encouraging the constant growth and development of followers. It is a teaching-learning process.

Adult learners, such as teachers, are motivated to learn new ways when they are active participants in their own learning, forging new ideas about the future of their lives at work and participating actively as team members in making the central decisions regarding their work. To move an organization from traditional transactional leadership to transformative leadership requires the development of a new process that is pursued steadfastly over time through which teachers can learn new roles and new skills required for active participation in teamwork and collaboration. This transformative team-building process must include constant attention to the building of greater levels of trust not only between the leader and the followers but among the collaborating followers as well. Thus, transformative leaders understand that leadership is a never-ending process of growth and development—a process of building human capital in the organization.

SUGGESTED READING

Bennis, Warren, and Burt Nanus, *Leaders: The Strategies for Taking Charge.* New York: Harper & Row, 1985.
> Bennis and Nanus identified some notably successful leaders in American business, studied their careers, and talked with them and their colleagues. The result is a small but rich trove of insight into leadership. If you are one of those in education who have a knee-jerk antipathy for trying to learn from private enterprise, you should try this book; it has a lot to say to educators who would be leaders. Bennis brings a remarkable background of achievement as scholar, university teacher and administrator, and corporate consultant to this small, lucid research-based book.

Burns, James MacGregor, *Leadership.* New York: Harper & Row, 1978.
> This highly readable Pulitzer prize–winning volume vividly interprets contemporary understanding of leadership. The aim of the book is to illuminate the dilemmas of political leadership; hence, it draws many of its examples from great political leaders. However, the lessons for educators are clear and readily understandable. Highly recommended not only for its impeccable

scholarship but also for the intellectual quality that is revealed by the open, straightforward writing that makes its ideas easily accessible.

Deal, Terrence E. and Kent D. Peterson, *The Leadership Paradox: Balancing Logic and Artistry in Schools.* San Francisco: Jossey-Bass, 1994.

> This small book suggests an approach to school leadership that combines the need for management and the need for leadership in the process of developing a powerful organizational culture that supports teaching and learning.

De Pree, Max, *Leadership Is an Art.* New York: Doubleday, 1989.

> This, for good or ill, is the slim volume that Bill Clinton found so inspiring when he was governor of Arkansas and candidate for the presidency. De Pree heads Herman Miller, Inc., a much-admired *Fortune* 500 manufacturer of upscale office furniture in Zeeland, Michigan. This corporation adopted the Scanlon Plan in 1952 and continues to use it with great success. The art of leadership, De Pree says, is liberating people to do what is required of them in the most effective and humane way possible. Thus, the leader is "servant" of followers in that leaders remove obstacles that prevent followers from doing their jobs. In short, the true leader enables followers to realize their full potential. The concept of "servant leadership," which is generally credited to Robert Greenleaf, was picked up not only by President Clinton but also by Ross Perot, who popularized it vigorously.

Gardner, John W., *On Leadership.* New York: The Free Press, 1990.

> Gardner is an extraordinary person and this is an extraordinary book that is highly recommended. Gardner's uncommonly broad and varied background ranges from an academic career in distinguished colleges, to positions of influence and responsibility in the White House (including a stint as U.S. Secretary of Health, Education, and Welfare), to the boardrooms of numerous major corporations. Gardner brings keen insight blended of pragmatic experience and scholarly knowledge to the problems and opportunities of leadership. Unlike the inaccessible psychobabble so common in the academic literature on leadership, Gardner's writing reveals his deep intellect in its simplicity, practicality, and straightforwardness.

Helgesen, Sally, *The Female Advantage: Women's Ways of Leadership.* New York: Doubleday Currency, 1990.

> This widely read book argues that men tend to think in linear fashion, lean toward hierarchical organization, emphasize logic, seek power for themselves, are uncomfortable with ambiguity, and are goal oriented, whereas women tend to think in more global connections rather than in straight lines, emphasize human interaction processes rather than hierarchy, have no great interest in personal power, are easily able to tolerate ambiguity, and are process oriented. The result, she believes, is a marked difference in thinking and organizational behavior between men and women—a difference that Helgesen firmly believes gives women a decided advantage as organizational leaders.

Houzes, James M., and Barry Z. Posner, *Credibility: How Leaders Gain and Lose It, Why People Demand It.* San Francisco: Jossey-Bass, 1993.

> After years of studying leaders (using surveys, case studies, and interviews) and consulting with leaders of major corporations, these experienced practical scholars conclude that the cornerstone of the relationship that defines leadership is credibility, and the essence of credibility is trust between the leader and followers. In this book, they describe how successful leaders develop trust in their relationships with followers by focusing on human issues such as honesty, sensitivity to diversity, the need for community, and developing and nurturing hope.

Powell, Gary, *Women and Men in Management.* Newbury Park, CA: Sage Publications, 1988.

> This entry in the literature on the gender wars in leadership concludes, after closely examining the published research on the subject, that there are few gender differences in the organizational behavior of men and women in similar jobs. Powell believes that faulty research methods account for much of the difference that feminist scholars have been claiming, and that innate differences in the leader behavior of men and women simply do not exist.

Rosener, Judy B., The Ways Women Lead. *Harvard Business Review,* 68(6), November-December 1990, pp. 119–25.

> Having studied 456 women business executives, Rosener reports that they behave very differently from male leaders in similar positions. She found that men emphasized a command-and-control

style (rational decision making, giving orders, appealing to the self-interest of followers), whereas women tended to work more "interactively" (sharing information and power, promoting empowerment, motivating people by appeals to organizational ideals and a shared vision of the future). Many women have found this article appealing, yet it remains highly controversial because the quality of the research design and methods have repeatedly been criticized.

Sergiovanni, Thomas J., *Moral Leadership: Getting to the Heart of School Improvement.* San Francisco: Jossey-Bass, 1992.

In this book, veteran writer Sergiovanni breaks away from the theorists of the modern era and tries to "reinvent leadership," emphasizing the roles of intuition, emotion, values, personal dreams, and what he insists on calling "mindscapes." For him, "The heart of leadership has to do with what a person believes, values, dreams about, and is committed to—the person's *personal dream*" (p. 7). It has to do, in other words, with what motivates individuals and commits them to sharing a vision of a better future with others. And that, Sergiovanni argues in this book, must be deontology—which, my dictionary suggests, is moral commitment to the vision and the work rather than seeking merely to satisfy one's own self-interests.

NOTES

1. Warren Bennis and Burt Nanus, *Leaders: The Strategies for Taking Charge* (New York: Harper & Row, 1985).
2. Paul Thurston, Renee Clift, and Marshall Schacht, "Preparing Leaders for Change-Oriented Schools," *Phi Delta Kappan,* 75 (November 1993), 262.
3. Bennis and Nanus, *Leaders: The Strategies for Taking Charge,* p. 15.
4. Jacob W. Getzels, "Theory and Research on Leadership: Some Comments and Some Alternatives," in *Leadership: The Science and the Art Today,* eds. Luvern L. Cunningham and William J. Gephart (Itasca, IL: F.E. Peacock, 1973), pp. 40–41. Emphasis in the original.
5. Meryl Reis Louis, "Putting Executive Action in Context: An Alternative View of Power," in *Executive Power,* eds. Suresh Srivastva and others (San Francisco: Jossey-Bass, 1986), p. 111.
6. This section is adapted from John R. P. French and Bertram Raven, "The Bases of Social Power," in *Studies in Social Power,* ed. Dorwin Cartwright (Ann Arbor: Institute for Social Research, University of Michigan, 1959). Many later writers have sought to extend the list for their own purposes, but the French and Raven work is still definitive.
7. W. Warner Burke, "Leadership as Empowering Others," in *Executive Power,* eds. Suresh Srivastva and others (San Francisco: Jossey-Bass, 1986), pp. 56–57.
8. David C. McClelland, *Power: The Inner Experience* (New York: Irvington, 1975), p. 18.
9. James MacGregor Burns, *Leadership* (New York: Harper & Row, 1978), p. 18.
10. Andrew W. Halpin, *Theory and Research in Administration* (New York: Macmillan, 1966), p. 86.
11. Bernard M. Bass, ed., *Stogdill's Handbook of Leadership: A Survey of Theory and Research,* rev. & exp. ed. (New York: Free Press, 1981).
12. David Keirsey and Marilyn Bates, *Please Understand Me: Character and Temperament Types* (Del Mar, CA: Prometheus Nemesis Book Company, 1984), p. 129. Emphasis in the original.
13. General H. Norman Schwartzkopf quoted in *U.S. News and World Report,* Vol. 110, May 27, 1991 (20), p. 36.
14. The English word "bureaucracy" is taken from the French *bureaucratie.* In French, *bureau* means *office.* The ending comes from the Greek, *kratie,* meaning *rule.* Literally, then, bureaucracy is the rule of offices.
15. David Bradford and Allan Cohen, *Managing for Excellence: Developing High Performance in Contemporary Organizations* (New York: John Wiley & Sons, 1984), p. 26.
16. Burns's original term, *transforming,* has been transmogrified by followers in the literature to include such variations as *transformational* and *transformative.*
17. Burns, *Leadership.*
18. Bernard Bass, *Leadership and Performance Beyond Expectations* (New York: Free Press, 1985).
19. Bennis and Nanus, *Leaders: The Strategies for Taking Charge.*

20. Rosabeth Moss Kanter, *The Change Masters: Innovation and Entrepreneurship in the American Corporation* (New York: Simon & Schuster, 1983).

21. Judy B. Rosener, "Ways Women Lead," *Harvard Business Review,* November–December 1990, 119–25.

22. Thomas J. Sergiovanni, *Moral Leadership: Getting to the Heart of School Reform* (San Francisco: Jossey-Bass, 1992).

23. Burns, *Leadership,* p. 4.

24. Ibid.

25. Op. cit., p. 21.

26. Dan C. Lortie, *Schoolteacher: A Sociological Study* (Chicago: University of Chicago Press, 1975).

27. Burns, *Leadership,* p. 18.

28. The literature on critical theory in education is large, and growing. See, for example, Gary L. Anderson, "Toward a Critical Constructivist Approach to School Administration: Invisibility, Legitimacy, and the Study of Non-Events," *Educational Administration Quarterly,* 26 (1990), 1, 38–59; William Foster, *Paradigms and Promises: New Approaches to Educational Administration* (Buffalo: Prometheus Books, 1986); Peter Watkins, "Leadership, Power, and Symbols in Educational Administration," in *Critical Perspectives on Educational Leadership,* ed. John Smyth (Philadelphia: The Falmer Press, 1989), pp. 9–37.

29. Carnegie Forum on Education and the Economy, *A Nation Prepared: Teachers for the 21st Century* (New York: The Forum, 1986), p. 24.

30. Bennis and Nanus, *Leaders: The Strategies for Taking Charge.*

31. Sergiovanni, *Moral Leadership: Getting to the Heart of School Improvement,* p. 4.

32. John W. Gardner, *On Leadership* (New York: The Free Press, 1989).

33. Notably the work of James MacGregor Burns, *Leadership* (New York: Harper & Row, 1978) and Bennis and Nanus, *Leaders: The Strategies for Taking Charge.*

34. Warren H. Schmidt and Jerome P. Finnegan, *The Race Without a Finish Line: America's Quest for Total Quality* (San Francisco: Jossey-Bass, 1992), p. 22.

35. Carl R. Frost, John H. Wakeley, and Robert A. Ruh, *The Scanlon Plan for Organization Development: Identity, Participation, and Equity* (East Lansing, MI: Michigan State University Press, 1974), p. 2.

36. Ibid., p. 1.

37. John Naisbett and Patricia Aburdene, *Re-inventing the Corporation* (New York: Warner, 1985).

38. Max De Pree, *Leadership Is an Art* (New York: Doubleday, 1989), p. 10.

39. Ibid., pp. 18–19.

40. Many regard the publication of an article by Judy B. Rosener in the *Harvard Business Review* in 1990 as marking the end of traditional belief that successful women leaders tend to emulate the behavior of men, and the beginning of a new realization that, in fact, successful women leaders behave in ways quite different from men.

41. See, for example, Charol Shakeshaft, *Women in Educational Administration* (Newbury Park: Sage Press, 1987).

42. Carol Gilligan, *In a Different Voice: Psychological Theory and Women's Development* (Cambridge, MA: Harvard University Press, 1982).

43. Keirsey and Bates, *Please Understand Me,* p. 2.

44. Rosener, "Ways Women Lead," p. 125.

45. Ibid.

46. Sandra Lipsitz Bem, *The Lenses of Gender: Transforming the Debate on Sexual Inequality* (New Haven, CT: Yale University Press, 1993), p. 2.

CHAPTER **7**

Conflict in Organizations

ABOUT THIS CHAPTER

Because educational organizations exist only to foster cooperative human endeavor in order to achieve goals that cannot be achieved individually, their organizational ideals normatively emphasize cooperation, harmony, and collaboration. Contemporary literature on schools ordinarily stresses such perceived virtues as empowerment, participation, and collaboration with little mention of competition and conflict. Yet "The potential for conflict permeates the relations of humankind, and that potential is a force for health and growth as well as destruction. . . . No group can be wholly harmonious . . . for such a group would be empty of process and structure."[1] Thus, because conflict is pervasive in all human experience, it is an important aspect of organizational behavior in education.

Conflict can occur even within a single individual (so-called intrapersonal conflict), typified by approach-avoidance conflict, the common situation in which the person feels torn between the desire to achieve two goals that are incompatible. This leads to feelings of stress and—not infrequently—behavior manifestations (for example, indecisiveness) and even physiological symptoms (for example, hypertension, ulcers). Moreover, conflict runs the gamut of social experience—between individuals, between groups, and between whole societies and cultures.

Conflict can occur *within* persons or social units; it is *intra*personal or *intra*group (or, of course, *intra*national). Conflict can also be experienced *between* two or more people or social units: so-called *inter*personal, *inter*group, or *inter*national conflict. In this chapter, I am not attempting to deal with the broad, general phenomenon of conflict; I will confine the discussion to conflict in organizational life—*organizational conflict* (that is, *intra*organizational conflict). Most commonly, this involves interpersonal conflict and intergroup conflict.

THE NATURE OF CONFLICT IN ORGANIZATIONS

In bureaucratic theory, the existence of conflict is viewed as evidence of breakdown in the organization: failure on the part of management to plan adequately and/or to exercise sufficient control. In human relations views, conflict is seen in an especially negative light as evidence of failure to develop appropriate norms in the group.

Traditional administrative theory has, therefore, been strongly biased in favor of the ideal of a smooth-running organization characterized by harmony, unity, co-ordination, efficiency, and order. Human relations adherents might seek to achieve this through happy, congenial work groups, whereas classical adherents would seek to achieve it through control and strong organizational structure. Both, however, tend to agree that conflict is disruptive: something to be avoided.

One of the more dramatic developments in the literature on organizations has been a reexamination of these positions, resulting in some more useful views.

Definition of Conflict

In the vast body of scientific literature, there is no consensus on a specific definition of "conflict."[2] There is general concurrence, however, that two things are essential to any conflict: (1) divergent (or apparently divergent) views and (2) incompatibility of those views.

Thus, Morton Deutsch said simply that "a conflict exists whenever incompatible activities occur."[3] But this incompatibility produces a dilemma—conflict becomes "the pursuit of incompatible, or at least seemingly incompatible, goals, such that gains to one side come out at the expense of the other."[4] We are confronted with the classic, zero-sum, win-lose situation that is potentially so dysfunctional to organizational life; everyone strives to avoid losing and losers seek to become winners. Though a conflict may originate as substantive (that is, "conflict rooted in the substance of the task"[5]), it readily can become affective (that is, "conflict deriving from the emotional, affective aspects of the . . . interpersonal relations").[6] This affective involvement is a central characteristic of conflict in organizations, which may be defined as "the active striving for one's own preferred outcome which, if attained, precludes the attainment by others of their own preferred outcome, *thereby producing hostility.*"[7]

The focus of contemporary application of behavioral science to organizations is precisely this: to manage conflict in the organization so that hostility can be either avoided or minimized. This is *not* the management of hostility; it is the management of conflict so as to reduce or eliminate hostility emanating from it.

Conflict Different from Attacks

There is a distinct difference between organizational conflict and its attendant hostility, on the one hand, and destructive attacks, on the other hand; to treat them alike can be a serious mistake. Kenneth Boulding suggested that we distinguish between malevolent hostility and nonmalevolent hostility.[8] Malevolent hostility is aimed at hurting, or worsening the position of, another individual or group, with scant regard for anything else, including consequences for the attacker. Nonmalevolent hostility, on the other hand, may well worsen the position of others but is acted out for the purpose of improving the position of the attacker. Malevolent hostility is often characterized by the use of issues as the basis for attack, which are, in reality, not important to the attacker except as a vehicle for damaging the opposition.

Malevolent hostility can, in turn, give rise to "nefarious attacks."[9] These are characterized by (1) the focus on persons rather than on issues, (2) the use of hateful language, (3) the use of dogmatic statements rather than questions, (4) the maintenance of fixed views regardless of new information or argument, and (5) the use of emotional terms.

The key difference between such attacks (whether malevolent, nefarious, or otherwise) and legitimate expressions of conflict lies in the motivation behind them, often not easily discernible. Although considerable (and often vigorous) conflict may erupt over such issues as improving school performance, ways of desegregating a school system, or how to group children for instruction, the parties to the conflict may well be motivated by essentially constructive goals. The key is whether the parties involved want to work with the system or are motivated by a wish to destroy it.

Warren Bennis has described, for example, how—in a period of student disruption at the State University of New York at Buffalo—he labored hard and long to deal with a student takeover of the campus, using his not inconsiderable skills as a third-party facilitator. But it was all to little avail. Looking back, Bennis came to realize that he really had not been in a two-party conflict-management situation at all.[10] The students—to the extent that they were organized—were committed to a set of political goals that had little to do with the educational goals that the university administrators embraced. In this case, the conflict was largely a device being used to achieve carefully masked goals. The student confrontations and rhetoric often were, in fact, malevolent with little intention of coming to agreement.

Any public education administrator needs to be sensitive to this problem and to be aware of the significant difference between attacks for the sake of destruction[11] and vigorous expression of essentially constructive—though sharply divergent and perhaps unwelcome—views.

Contemporary Views of Conflict

Conflict in organizations is now seen as inevitable, endemic, and often legitimate. This is because the individuals and groups within the human social system are interdependent and constantly engaged in the dynamic processes of defining and redefining the nature and extent of their interdependence. Important to the dynamics of this social process is the fact that the environment in which it occurs is, itself, constantly changing. Thus, as Chester Barnard pointed out, "inherent in the conception of free will in a changing environment"[12] are social patterns characterized by negotiating, stress, and conflict.

Moreover, there will be conflict in any well-led organization for, as we saw in the last chapter, leaders marshal and organize resources *in conflict with others*. By definition, leaders marshal resources (people, money, time, facilities, material) so as to achieve new goals. Given the finite resources available in an educational organization, there will invariably be competing ideas of what to do with them: how to use the time, how to involve people, where to spend the money, how to schedule facilities, and so on. Thus, when leadership is present, people in the organization must experience conflict as a normal part of organizational life. The central issue, then, is neither whether organizational conflict is present nor the degree to which it is present. The central issue is how well conflict is managed in the organization.

Effects of Organizational Conflict

This is an important issue because frequent and powerful hostility arising from conflict can have a devastating impact on the behavior of people in organizations. Psychological withdrawal from the hostility—such as alienation, apathy, and indifference—is a common symptom that keenly affects the functioning of the organization. Physical withdrawal—such as absence, tardiness, and turnover—is a widely occurring response to conflict in schools that is often written off as laziness on the part of teachers who have been spoiled by "soft" administrative practices. Outright hostile or aggressive behaviors—including job actions, property damage, and minor theft of property—are far from unknown responses by teachers to conflict situations that appear to be "too hot to handle" or totally frustrating.

Indeed, the behavioral consequences of conflict in educative organizations can be, to put it mildly, undesirable. Ineffective management of conflict (for example, a hard-nosed policy of punishment for "offenses," get-tough practices in the name of administering the negotiated contract, emphasizing the adversarial relationship between teachers and administration) can—and frequently does—create a climate that exacerbates the situation and is likely to develop a downward spiral of mounting frustration, deteriorating organizational climate, and increasing destructiveness, as shown in Figure 7–1. Obviously, the health of an organization caught in this syndrome tends to decline. Effective management of conflict, on the other hand (for example, treating it as a problem to be solved, emphasizing the collaborative essence of organizational life), can lead to outcomes that are productive and enhance the health of the organization over time, as shown in Figure 7–2.

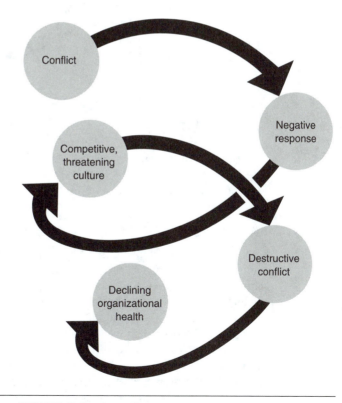

FIGURE 7–1 An ineffective conflict-response-climate syndrome leads to a lower state of organizational health.

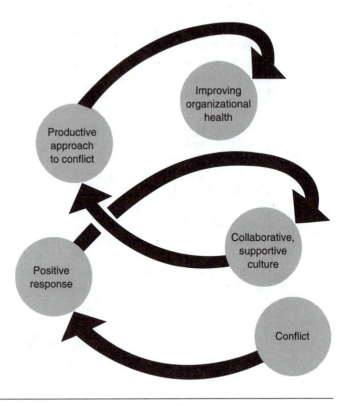

FIGURE 7–2   An effective conflict-response-climate syndrome leads to an improved state of organizational health.

The point to be emphasized is that conflict in itself is neither good nor bad; it is (in value terms) neutral. Its impact on the organization and the behavior of people largely depends on the way conflict is treated.

The Criterion: Organizational Performance

To speak of organizational conflict as good or bad, or as functional or dysfunctional, requires one to specify the criteria used in judging. Some people—many with a "humanistic" bias—simply find conflict repugnant and seek to abolish it wherever it may be found. Others are concerned about the internal stress that conflict often imposes on individuals. These, in themselves, are not of central concern in *organizational* terms. One would do well to keep in mind that, after all, there also are people who relish conflict, find it zestful, and seek it out. The issue, then, is the impact of conflict on the performance capability of the organization as a system.

Again, the problems of measuring the productivity of educational organizations and the discussion of the relevance of the school system's or school's internal conditions (that is, organizational culture, interaction-influence system) come to the fore. Thus, the functional or dysfunctional consequences of conflict on educative organizations are understood best in terms of organizational health, adaptability, and stability.

As has been seen, modern motivation theory makes clear that challenge, significance, and the need to solve problems are important attributes of work that people find interesting, enjoyable and, in a word, motivating. Also, as has been seen, concepts of participative leadership rest on the conviction that many people in the organization have good ideas and quality information to contribute to making better decisions in the organization. In this view, Kenneth Thomas observed that

> the confrontation of divergent views often produces ideas of superior quality. Divergent views are apt to be based upon different evidence, different considerations, different insights, different frames of reference. Disagreements may thus confront an individual with factors which he had previously ignored, and help him to arrive at a more comprehensive view which synthesizes elements of his own and other's positions.[13]

Finally, there is growing reason to believe (based on both research and expert opinion) that conflict causes people to seek effective ways of dealing with it, resulting in improved organizational functioning (for example, cohesiveness, clarified relationships, clearer problem-solving procedures).[14] Speaking of society in general, Deutsch observed that

> conflict within a group frequently helps to revitalize existent norms; or it contributes to the emergence of new norms. In this sense, social conflict is a mechanism for adjustment of norms adequate to new conditions. A flexible society benefits from conflict because such behavior, by helping to create and modify norms, assures its continuance under changed conditions.[15]

He went on to caution that rigid systems that suppress conflict smother a useful warning signal, thereby maximizing the danger of catastrophic breakdown.

We all have witnessed repeatedly the wisdom of these observations in national and international events of great and small magnitude. Educators in the United States also have seen it closer to home, where fearful explosions of pent-up hostility have, not infrequently, followed long periods of frustration brought on by organizations that thought they had either crushed or nimbly avoided impending conflict.

Although few who really understand conflict would advocate its deliberate use in organizational life, fewer still would advocate seeking its elimination or avoidance. Rather, by applying concepts of conflict management, the intent is to minimize the destructive potential, on the one hand, and make conflict as productive, creative, and useful as possible, on the other hand.

THE DYNAMICS OF ORGANIZATIONAL CONFLICT

Hostility

Many people say that they do not like conflict, avoid it whenever they can, and may even fear it. This is important to recognize because it leads to one of the least productive and most common approaches to conflict management: denial and avoidance. Therefore, it is not splitting hairs to point out that the aftermath to an episode of conflict is ordinarily more troubling than the conflict itself. Badly managed organizational conflict can generate hostility between the parties, and this can lead to hate, retribution, and antagonism.

A key goal of any approach to the management of conflict is to eliminate or reduce—to manage—the hostility arising from the conflict. But the time and place to intervene is before conflict can arise, rather than after. It is important for members of the organization to learn to talk openly about conflict long before the need arises and to discuss what conflict is and strategies and tactics that may be used to encourage it (yes, encourage it) in ways that will be productive and helpful to everyone.

Although numerous writers have compiled a long list of the causes of organizational conflict, Louis Pondy has classified most of them into three basic types of *latent* conflict:

1. When the organization's resources are insufficient to meet the requirements of the subunits to do their work, there is *competition for scarce resources* (for example, budget allocations, assigned teaching positions, space or facilities).

2. When one party seeks to control the activities "belonging" to another unit (and the second unit seeks to fend off such "interference"), the issue is *autonomy* (for example, protecting one's "turf").

3. When two parties in the organization must work together but cannot agree on how to do so, the source of conflict is *goal divergence* (for example, the school principal and the director of special education have differing views as to how mainstreaming issues are to be settled).[16]

A Contingency View

These latent sources of conflict are unlikely to disappear from organizational life. It is, therefore, important to develop a culture that supports productive approaches to conflict management.[17] Because there are a number of causes of conflict—even when classified or grouped, as above—it is obvious that there is no one best way of managing conflict. As John Thomas and Warren Bennis put it:

> An effective paradigm incorporates what might be termed a "situational" or "contingency" framework, a point of view reflected in much of the current theoretical and empirical work in organizational theory. There is a primary emphasis upon diagnosis and the assumption that it is self-defeating to adopt a "universally" applicable set of principles and guidelines for effecting change or managing conflict.[18]

As a basis for the necessary organizational diagnosis, two concepts concerning conflict are often used: one seeks to understand the internal dynamics of the events that occur in the process of conflict; the other seeks to analyze the external influences that tend to structure the conflict.

A Process View of Conflict

Conflict between two parties appears to unfold in a relatively orderly sequence of events and—unless something intervenes—the sequence tends to be repeated in episodes. Each episode is highly dynamic, with each party's behavior serving as a stimulus to evoke a response from the other. Further, each new episode is shaped in part by previous episodes.

One model of such a process is suggested by Thomas (see Figure 7–3), in which an episode is triggered by the *frustration* of one party by the act of another (for example, denial of a request, diminishment of status, disagreement, or an insult). This causes the participants to *conceptualize* the nature of the conflict—often a highly subjective process that suggests ways of defining and dealing with perceived issues in the conflict. Indeed—as experimental research reported by Robert Blake, Herbert Shepard, and Jane Mouton makes clear—this step of defining the issues and seeking alternative responses is frequently viewed by the parties to the conflict as a simple matter of victory or defeat. Alternatives other than winning or losing are easily overlooked.[19] This is followed by *behavior* intended to deal with the conflict. As Kenneth Thomas explained, understanding the bases for this behavior is a complex matter; but key elements surely include a mix of (1) a participant's desire to satisfy the other's concern (cooperative-uncooperative) and (2) the participant's desire to satisfy his or her own concern (assertive-unassertive).[20] *Interaction* of the parties follows, of course; this is a highly dynamic phase of the process. It can involve escalation or deescalation of the conflict, depending on such factors as the trust level that is established, biases and self-fulfilling prophesies that

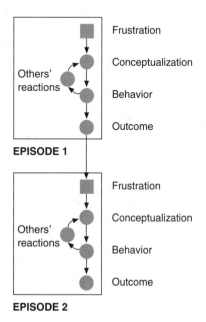

FIGURE 7–3

Process model of conflict episodes between two parties. Kenneth Thomas, "Conflict and Conflict Management," in *Handbook of Industrial and Organizational Psychology,* ed. Marvin D. Dunnette (Chicago: Rand McNally & Company, 1976), p. 895.

get in the way, the level of competition between the participants, and the openness and sensitivity each has to the other. The *outcome* of all this—the last stage in an episode of conflict—is not merely some agreement on substantive issues but includes residual emotions (for example, frustration, hostility, trust—either increased or decreased). These outcomes have potentially long-term effects on the aftermath of a conflict episode, particularly as they set the stage for ensuing episodes.

In commenting on the aftermath as part of a sequence of episodes, Louis Pondy pointed out that

> If the conflict is genuinely resolved to the satisfaction of all participants, the basis for a more cooperative relationship may be laid; or the participants, in their drive for a more ordered relationship may focus on latent conflicts not previously perceived and dealt with. On the other hand, if conflict is merely suppressed but not resolved, the latent conditions of conflict may be aggravated and explode in more serious form. . . . This legacy of a conflict episode is . . . called "conflict aftermath."[21]

A Structural View of Conflict

Although a process approach to conflict sees it as a *sequence of events,* a structural view tends to see conflict in terms of the *conditions that influence behavior.* For example, every organization has rules and procedures (written and unwritten, formal and informal) that regulate behavior (for example, who talks with whom about what). Rules and procedures often serve to avoid or manage conflict by clarifying such issues as how to proceed, when, and who has what responsibility. Of course, they also can cause or exacerbate conflict by becoming dysfunctional, such as when they lead to rigid, repetitious behavior that does not readily allow for exceptions (the typical bureaucratic "hardening of the categories").

Not infrequently, rules and procedures so complicate the processes of working out a relatively simple conflict through direct negotiation that they in fact create conflict. For example, in one school district an elementary school principal discovered that an order for a certain kind of paper had been cut sharply by an administrative assistant in the office of the assistant superintendent for business. When the principal contacted the administrative assistant to straighten out the matter, she was reminded that her complaint should be routed through the assistant superintendent for elementary education, who could take it up with the assistant superintendent of business, and so on. Needless to say, considerable conflict ensued, much time was lost, and the needed paper finally arrived at the school—in time for *next* year. The point is that simple rearrangements in the way that even minor decisions are made and differences are negotiated can influence the course of conflict in organizations.

Another structural factor lies in the kinds of people found in the organization, with particular reference to their personality predispositions, such as their attitudes toward authority and the extent and flexibility of their responses to others. In selecting new personnel, for example, many school districts and schools are attracted to candidates who seem to "fit in" over candidates who might add diversity to the staff.

A further structural factor influencing the incidence and nature of conflict in an organization is the social norms of the organization: the social pressures, for example, "to stand up and fight" or "not to rock the boat." The creation of organizational cultures that smooth over friction and frown on open challenge and questioning can make it very difficult to identify and confront conflict at all. Similarly, when secretiveness and restricted communication represent the organizational norm, it is difficult to know if a latent conflict exists, let alone to plan ways of dealing with it. Many administrators of educational organizations instinctively understand this and make it a rule to put as little communication in writing as possible, to assemble people for meetings as infrequently as possible, and—when meetings *must* be held—to be sure to control the proceedings tightly so as to minimize the "risk" of opening up issues that might "cause trouble."

Thus, the structural factors that shape conflict in organizations are strongly influenced by structural factors in the organization itself. In the words of the Likerts:

> The success of [an organization] is influenced greatly by its capacity to achieve cooperative coordination rather than hostile conflict among its functional departments and also to stimulate differences and then to capitalize on them by productive problem-solving leading to creative and acceptable solutions. . . . Institutions based on traditional organizational theory . . . lack the capacity to deal successfully with the conflicts created by the new demands which recently legitimized values are placing on them. . . . Repressive action brings costly backlash.[22]

They, of course, advocate developing a more responsive interaction-influence system through System 4 leadership, developing a supportive climate, de-emphasizing hierarchical status, and using consensus for productive (win-win) problem solving.

An Open-Systems View

Thus far I have been discussing organizational conflict entirely in terms of the internal functioning of educative organizations, and this will continue to be the focus of the chapter as a whole. It is, however, vital that one never loses the perspective that these organizations are open systems; they are interactive with their environments, and much that goes on within them reflects changes in the external environment.

In terms of conflict, a good case in point is P.L. 94–142, which was passed by Congress and signed into law on November 29, 1975. It is a classic example of power-coercive change strategy and probably set the stage for more widespread conflict in U.S. public schooling—at all levels—than anything since the *Brown* school desegregation decision of some two decades earlier. At the highest levels it raised conflicting constitutional issues: the interpretation of the Tenth Amendment that education is a state responsibility and a matter of local control *versus* the view that P.L. 94–142 is an exercise of federal responsibility to assure full civil rights to equal opportunity for the unserved (and inadequately served) handicapped.

However, the law also raised conflicts all along the line, from Washington, D.C., to the most remote school classroom in the land. For example, it sought to redefine the prerogatives of teachers to control instruction and related decision making by mandating the inclusion of parents in a participatory role in planning individualized instruction and in a formalized appeal process. The parent—formerly an outsider confined to an advisory role—suddenly became one of the insiders with new authority in relationship to the teacher.

The ability of schools to deal productively with this conflict thrust on them from the larger environment was unclear even as late as 1990 because external initiatives to mandate increasing control of the classroom decisions of teachers were still increasing in number and scope. It is, however, a clear and unambiguous illustration of how conflict—very much involving the internal functioning of schools and school systems—can be imposed on them by rapid change in the external system.

Gerald Griffin and David Rostetter have speculated as to whether Randall Collins's five hypotheses on coercive efforts to deal with coercion and conflict might apply.[23] As they pointed out:

1. Coercion leads to strong efforts to avoid being coerced.
2. If resources for fighting back are available, the greater the coercion applied the more counter aggression is called forth.
3. If resources are not available but opportunities to escape are, the greater the tendency to leave the situation.
4. If resources for fighting back and opportunities to escape are not available, or if there are other strong incentives for staying in the situation (material rewards or potential power), the greater coercion that is applied the greater the tendency to comply with exactly those demands that are necessary to avoid being coerced.
5. If resources for fighting back and opportunities for escape are not available, the . . . tendency to dull compliance and passive resistance [is increased].[24]

In this view, coercion leads to a conflict-hostility-resistance syndrome *within* the organization, very unlike the synergistic, creative, problem-solving culture that characterizes effective organizations. Only time will tell what effect this federal initiative, based on traditional concepts of schools as organizations, will ultimately have.

APPROACHES TO ORGANIZATIONAL CONFLICT

When conflict arises, the almost instinctive response of the parties involved is to adopt a strategy—backed by determination—to *win*. To most people that means, *ipso facto,* that the other party will *lose.*

> Confrontation, non-negotiable demands, and ultimatums have become the order of the day as *the* way of dealing with deep-seated differences. One party marshals all its forces to compel the other party to do what the first has decided it wants. Confrontation is from a fixed position and seeks to mobilize the power to win. Win-lose strategy is used in a variety of situations, such as struggles for civil rights; urban riots; student demonstrations and sit-ins; international conflicts; union-management disagreements; a hearing on next year's budget; a controversy between departments . . . or a controversy between professional staff and the lay board.[25]

The focal point of conflict management is the win-lose orientation and how to deal with it. It is important, *first,* to understand the dynamics and consequences of win-lose approaches to conflict and, *second,* to see what alternatives are available.

The Win-Lose Orientation to Conflict

The dynamics of win-lose conflict and their consequences for organizational behavior are well known. Group dynamicists in the 1950s and 1960s conducted extensive research on the phenomena of group conflict—including both experimental work and field observation studies (see the discussion of group dynamics and human relations in Chapter 1).[26]

"A win-lose orientation to conflict is characterized by one basic element," Blake, Shepard, and Mouton observe. "The contesting parties see their interests to be mutually exclusive. No compromise is possible. One must fail at the price of the other's success . . . [and] hope is abandoned of being able to appeal to each other on the basis of reason."[27] The parties to the conflict come to believe that the issues can be settled in one of three ways: (1) a power struggle, (2) intervention by a third party who possesses some sort of power greater than either of them (and this can include public opinion or moral suasion), or (3) fate.

The consequences of this approach are twofold:

1. *Between the parties to the conflict.* Antagonisms deepen, hostility rises, hope of finding a mutually acceptable solution fades, and as it does the search for such a solution ceases.

2. *Within the groups involved.* Spirits soar as members close ranks in preparation for battle. Differences of opinion, skepticism, and challenge of leadership or the "party line" are frowned on: members are pressured to support the decisions taken, to conform, to "go along," to be loyal to the group or get out. Leadership gravitates rapidly to a very small number of people, who are usually forceful and aggressive. Thus diversity of opinion, the search for quality ideas, and the broad involvement of members in developing creative responses are snuffed out in the group. This not only hardens the group's position in the conflict itself but, more importantly, sets the stage for ineffective functioning of the group after the conflict eases.[28]

Experimental studies of conflict[29] make it clear that the perception of individuals and groups is very much involved in conflict—often becoming distorted as the episode unfolds. And, of course, "perception is the key to behavior. The way people see things determines the way they will act. If their perceptions are distorted, the distortions are reflected in their behavior."[30] Thus, judgment is adversely affected by the conflict experience: one tends to become blindly loyal, to become hostile to members of the other group, and to denigrate not only their ideas but their worth as persons. Leaders of the opposition—formerly seen as mature, able people—are now seen as irresponsible and incapable. Indeed, even cognition is affected: in studying proposed solutions to the conflict, it becomes difficult or impossible to see merit in proposals put forth by "the other side," even though they may be in substantial agreement with one's own ideas. Thus, agreement becomes elusive. *Any* sign of questioning the position of one's group or any approval of proposals put forth from the other side is viewed by associates as backing down. Winning becomes everything. The ability to "see" alternatives, to be objective, and to suspend judgment while seeking to understand all are badly distorted as one increasingly shares the gung-ho drive of the group for "victory."

In terms of the process model of conflict (described earlier), win-lose is a way of conceptualizing the conflict and gives rise to predictable patterns of behavior in the interaction between parties to the conflict as the episode unfolds. But the consequences, it should be clear, are not limited to the shape and character of the conflict itself. Each of the groups involved in the conflict is powerfully affected in the aftermath. Usually, hostility between the winning group and the losing group is intensified, and subsequent episodes may be expected.

Commonly, the losing group will reject its leaders; very likely it will, in time, begin reappraising what went wrong and start preparing to do better next time. Powerful emotional reactions (resentment—even hatred—and anxiety) are likely to continue to distort the group's functioning, reducing the likelihood that it will develop a climate supportive of self-renewal and creative problem solving. Thus, win-lose solutions to conflict tend to build long-term, dysfunctional behaviors that result in a downward spiral of organizational climate, performance, and overall organizational health. A central concern of conflict management, then, is to seek more effective ways of conceptualizing conflict as a basis for more effective behavior.

A Contingency Approach to Conflict

Contingency approaches to management are predicated on the concept that diagnosis of the situation is necessary as a basis for action. In dealing with conflict, the contingency view holds that there is not one best way of managing it under all conditions, but that there are optimal ways of managing conflict under certain conditions. An important aspect of conflict management, then, is to consider (1) alternative ways of managing conflict and (2) the kinds of situations in which each of these various alternatives might be expected to be the most effective, not only in dealing with the critical issues but also in doing so in a way that strengthens the organization.

Diagnosing Conflict

In the first place, it is helpful to ascertain whether conflict *does* exist between the parties or whether a conflict only *appears* (to the parties) to exist. The criterion is whether the two parties seek goals that are actually incompatible.

Frequently, what appears to be a brewing conflict between two parties is, in fact, a misunderstanding. Recognizing the problems of distorted perception as discussed above, it is probable that a misunderstanding can be dealt with through explicit goal setting and improved communication. This often requires training individuals and groups in such skills as group goal setting and prioritizing, as well as in communication skills (for example, active listening, seeking feedback to check receiver's perceptions, using multiple channels).

If a conflict *does* exist, however (that is, the parties do have goals that are mutually incompatible), then it is necessary to select a method of dealing with it as productively as possible from among the many options available. *The general principle is that a win-lose approach tends to be the least productive, while a win-win approach—in which both parties win something (though not necessarily equally)—tends to be the most productive.*

Collaboration is a process in which the parties work together to define their problems and then engage in mutual problem solving. As a mode of dealing with conflict, this process requires, first, that the parties involved must want, actively, to try to use it (will give time and effort to participating). The process also requires that the people involved possess (1) the necessary skills for communicating and working in groups, effectively coupled with (2) attitudes that support a climate of openness, trust, and frankness in which to identify and work through problems.

In situations in which the *will* to do this exists but the skills are not well developed, a facilitator can be brought in to help the groups to learn the necessary skills and engage in the collaborative processes (though the facilitator does not get involved in the substance of decisions, merely the processes for making them). This is the highest level of win-win conflict management because it leaves the groups with new skills and new understandings that they can use in dealing with future problems. It is, of course, a form of organization development (organizational self-renewal). Not the least attribute of collaborative approaches to problem solving is the healthy sense of "ownership" or commitment to the solution arrived at that is unmatched by other approaches. In Likert and Likert's terms it is System 4 management; Blake, Shepard, and Mouton would call it 9, 9 style.

Bargaining, compromise, and other forms of splitting the difference have some elements in common with collaborative problem solving: (1) the parties must be willing to engage in the process (though sometimes they are legally required to do so); (2) there is some move toward collaboration (though usually this is restricted to the negotiators); and (3) the process is basically conciliatory and not in flagrant conflict with the organization's well-being. If the bargaining escalates to mediation and/or arbitration, the outside "third party" plays a role quite different from that of the group-process facilitator in a collaborative process: he or she *does* have the power to make judgments and impose decisions on the parties in conflict. Bargaining does seek to develop a long-term relationship between the parties and provides them with a mechanism for dealing with future problems. But bargaining is not a collaborative approach: it recognizes that the two parties are essentially adversaries and may use information as a form of power for strategic purposes.

Neither party wins in the typical bargaining/compromise situation, but then neither party is the loser. Although the term "bargaining" is readily associated with labor-management relations, negotiation processes are, in fact, widely employed within organizational settings to settle conflicts. For example, when two administrators confer to work out some problems between their divisions, it is not uncommon for them to use negotiating and compromise techniques systematically. If the negotiations do bog down, they may take the problem to their immediate superordinate for mediation (a common feature of the so-called bureaucratic mode of conflict management).

Avoidance (withdrawal, peaceful coexistence, indifference) is often employed when dealing with conflict. Avoidance is useful (1) when it is not likely that the latent conflict really can be resolved ("live with it") or (2) when the issues are not so important to the parties as to require the time and resources to work them out. As Blake and his colleagues pointed out, avoidance can be in the form of a "cease-fire," wherein two groups engaged in a long-term struggle decide to keep in contact, still entrenched in their positions, but not to get locked into combat with each other.[31] An interesting outcome of various avoidance responses to latent conflict is that, although conflict is not inevitable, neither is agreement possible. Thus, though hostile aftermath is avoided, the underlying problems are not dealt with; the latent conflict—with all its hazardous potential—remains, ready to become manifest at any time.

Power struggle is, of course, the effort by each party to win, regardless of the consequences for the other party. Although conflict, in itself, may be seen as having some beneficial potential for organizations (or, at least, as being nondestructive), this mode of dealing with it is viewed almost universally as being destructive. It is the classic win-lose situation.

A CONTINGENCY APPROACH TO DIAGNOSIS OF CONFLICT

An important aspect of diagnosis for the conflict manager is to ascertain the way *each party* to the conflict has conceptualized the situation.

Kenneth Thomas contended that it is common, in a conflict situation, to emphasize the extent to which a party is willing to cooperate with another party but to overlook a second critical factor: the party's desire to satisfy his or her own concerns.[32] Thus, in his view, two critical behavioral dimensions shape the way one conceptualizes conflict:

1. *Cooperativeness,* which is the extent to which one wishes to satisfy the concerns of the other.
2. *Assertiveness,* which is the extent to which one wishes to satisfy her or his own concerns.

These are seen as independent dimensions, as shown in Figure 7–4. Thus, in diagnosing conflict *as conceptualized by the parties involved,* the issue becomes more than merely a matter of cooperating or "acting professionally": cooperation can be viewed as literally a sacrifice of one's own needs.

From this analysis, Thomas identified five principal perspectives that may be used in conceptualizing conflict and behaviors commonly associated with those perspectives:

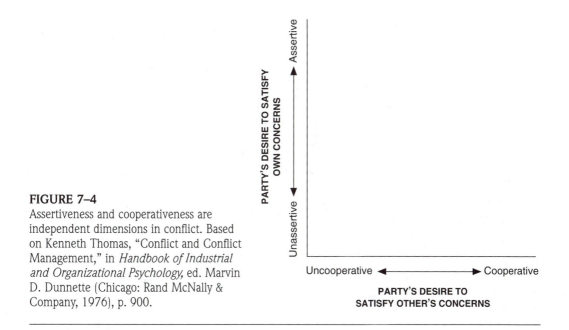

FIGURE 7–4

Assertiveness and cooperativeness are independent dimensions in conflict. Based on Kenneth Thomas, "Conflict and Conflict Management," in *Handbook of Industrial and Organizational Psychology,* ed. Marvin D. Dunnette (Chicago: Rand McNally & Company, 1976), p. 900.

1. *Competitive* behavior is the search to satisfy one's own concerns at the expense of others if need be. As shown in Figure 7–5, it is a high competitive-high uncooperative orientation. The effect is domination of the situation (as, for example, in hard-nosed contract negotiations in which nothing is yielded and every advantage is exploited). It is the classic win-lose view of conflict.

2. *Avoidant* (unassertive-uncooperative) behavior is usually expressed by apathy, withdrawal, and indifference. This does *not* mean that there is an absence of conflict but that it has been conceptualized as something not to deal with. Hence, the latent conflict remains and may be viewed differently at another time.

3. *Accommodation* (high cooperativeness-low assertiveness) is typified by appeasement: one attends to the other's concerns while neglecting his or her own. This orientation may be associated with a desire to maintain a working relationship even at some sacrifice of one's own interests.

4. *Sharing* orientation (moderate assertiveness-moderate cooperativeness) often leads to compromise (trade-offs, splitting the difference, horse-trading).

5. *Collaborative* orientation to conflict (high assertive-high cooperative) leads to efforts to satisfy fully the concerns of both parties through mutual problem solving. The solution to the conflict is a genuine integration of the desires of both sides. The concept is win-win.

This approach to the analysis of conflict helps to assess the kinds of strategies that might be most usefully employed in managing it (for example, bargaining,

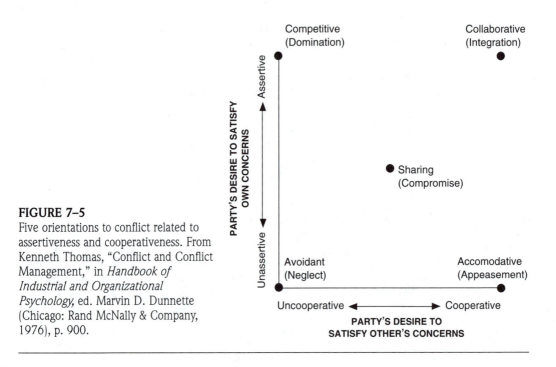

FIGURE 7–5

Five orientations to conflict related to assertiveness and cooperativeness. From Kenneth Thomas, "Conflict and Conflict Management," in *Handbook of Industrial and Organizational Psychology,* ed. Marvin D. Dunnette (Chicago: Rand McNally & Company, 1976), p. 900.

power, or collaboration). The goal, of course, is to manage the conflict in such a way that it will be as productive as possible for the organization while minimizing destructive consequences. It is important, therefore, to *consider the potential long-run consequences resulting from the aftermath of conflict.*

For example, avoidance or appeasement can be appealing responses because—in the short run—they are likely to head off the difficulties of seeking genuine solutions and have the added advantage of requiring the least in terms of organizational energy, time, and resources. But they do not solve the problem that triggered the conflict, nor do they develop the organization's capacity to deal productively with conflict.

Bargaining does help to develop the internal capacity of the organization to deal with conflict. But bargaining is not designed to produce optimal solutions: in the processes of horse-trading, neither side emerges completely satisfied, and quite likely the more skilled, hard-nosed negotiator will walk away with more than his or her opponent does. Bargaining is essentially an adversarial procedure—if not downright underhanded—using "dirty tricks" and wily ploys to gain advantage. These often engender resentment and mistrust, both dysfunctional attitudes in organizational life.

Competitive win-lose power plays and collaborative problem solving require the most energy, time, and resources. The essentially different consequences of each mode already have been described. Because the aftermath and long-term consequences of win-lose power struggles are well known to be dysfunctional and those of collaboration functional, few who are concerned about enhancing the organization's performance would fail to choose collaboration—whenever practicable—as the most desirable conceptualization of conflict, and competition as least desirable.

Because avoidance and appeasement are really *non*management of conflict, we are left with three basic general strategies for dealing with it: collaboration, bargaining, or power. Figure 7–6, which summarizes the essential characteristics of each of these strategies, also shows how bargaining incorporates certain features of *both* collaboration and power strategies. In this sense, bargaining serves as a bridge between power strategies and collaboration, making it *possible*—though far from inevitable—to move, over time, organizational processes from win-lose power struggles to win-win collaborative problem solving.

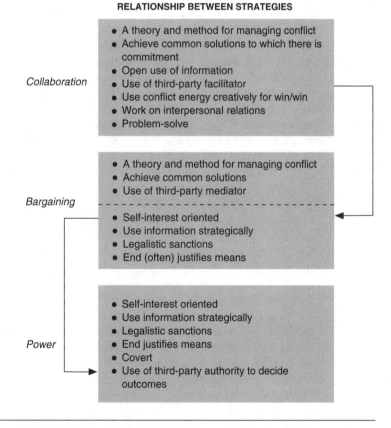

RELATIONSHIP BETWEEN STRATEGIES

Collaboration
- A theory and method for managing conflict
- Achieve common solutions to which there is commitment
- Open use of information
- Use of third-party facilitator
- Use conflict energy creatively for win/win
- Work on interpersonal relations
- Problem-solve

Bargaining
- A theory and method for managing conflict
- Achieve common solutions
- Use of third-party mediator
- -
- Self-interest oriented
- Use information strategically
- Legalistic sanctions
- End (often) justifies means

Power
- Self-interest oriented
- Use information strategically
- Legalistic sanctions
- End justifies means
- Covert
- Use of third-party authority to decide outcomes

FIGURE 7–6 Relationship between conflict management strategies. From C. Brooklyn Derr, *Managing Organizational Conflict: When to Use Collaboration, Bargaining and Power Approaches* (Monterey, CA: Naval Postgraduate School, 1975), p. 12.

CONCLUSION

Organizational conflict has been discussed in this chapter chiefly in terms of two-party clashes within the organization. Whereas conflict was once thought to signal a failure of the organization, it is being increasingly recognized as a normal and legitimate aspect of human social systems. Thus, conflict is not only inevitable but, contrary to earlier views, it can serve a useful function by stimulating creative solutions to problems.

Whether organizational conflict is destructive or constructive depends to a large extent on how it is managed. The day is over for the wily school administrator who could head off or terminate conflict with deft tricks or a swift exercise of power. Healthy organizations—characterized by well-developed problem-solving mechanisms and a collaborative climate—are able to identify conflict and deal with it in a collaborative way that leaves the organization stronger and more well-developed rather than weakened and wracked with hostility.

Ways of handling conflict in school districts and schools have been heavily influenced by the people who have been consulted for advice or by third-party intervention. Especially with the spread of collective bargaining, school districts have turned increasingly for advice to people trained and conditioned to view conflict in adversarial, combative terms (lawyers and, not infrequently, professional negotiators and mediators), rather than to people trained and conditioned to view it as a phenomenon of organizational behavior (applied social scientists, organizational psychologists). Too often this has produced essentially destructive, win-lose strategies and tactics. All too often it has been associated with the denigration of proposals to seek more productive approaches as being "unrealistic."

This chapter has proposed a way of diagnosing conflict in a given situation as a basis for choosing an appropriate management strategy. Clearly, there is no one best way of managing conflict in organizations. There are a number of ways, each suited to circumstances in a particular situation. The basic principle in choosing a way of managing conflict, however, is to use the approach most likely to minimize the destructive aspects (for example, hostility) and to maximize the opportunities for organizational growth and development (for example, to develop greater trust, to improve problem solving).

Finally, no phase in conflict management is more critical than diagnosis of the situation. Frequently the processes of conceptualizing, or analyzing, conflict confuses effects with causes. For example, a superintendent of schools asked a consultant, "What are some of the ways that I can deal with conflict in this school district?" When asked what kind of conflict he was talking about, the superintendent replied, "Well, you know, we had that teachers strike and it was pretty bad here. Now the teachers are back at work, but we have a lot of bad feeling everywhere. You know—hostility. We have to do something about it. What can we do?" Although, as I have explained, hostility is an important aspect of conflict, it is important to bear in mind that hostility does not describe a conflict, itself. Hostility is an emotional reaction that is all too often part of the outcome or aftermath of an episode of conflict. But trying to ameliorate hostile feelings is, perhaps, dealing with a symptom rather than a cause. If we fail to diagnose the conflict correctly and deal with the causes, then the conflict will continue in latent form ready to manifest itself at a later time.

SUGGESTED READING

Beckhard, Richard, "The Confrontation Meeting," *Harvard Business Review,* 45 (March-April 1967), 149–55.

> Description of "an activity that allows a total management group, drawn from all levels of the organization. to take a quick reading on its own health, and—*within a matter of hours*—to set action plans for improving it" (p. 149). Provides a specific design for a one-day meeting that can be used to deal with the stress of a crisis that helps the group (1) diagnose the situation, (2) set goals and priorities collaboratively, (3) develop a plan of action, and (4) implement the plan on both a short-range and a long-range basis.

Blake, Robert R., Herbert A. Shepard, and Jane S. Mouton, *Managing Intergroup Conflict in Industry.* Houston, TX: Gulf Publishing Company, 1964.

> This small, readable book has become a classic in the literature of conflict. It explains many of the insights into organizational conflict that now are widely accepted, and draws on experimental research as well as on the authors' own practical experience. Includes a straightforward contingency analysis.

Derr, C. Brooklyn, *Managing Organizational Conflict: When to Use Collaboration, Bargaining and Power Approaches.* Monterey, CA: Naval Postgraduate School, 1975.

> Proposes a contingency approach. Pointing out that collaboration, bargaining, and power approaches all are appropriate in the management of organizational conflict under certain conditions, the author explains how to diagnose the contingencies in different situations. Benefits and drawbacks for each strategy, under varying conditions, are discussed.

Likert, Rensis, and Jane Gibson Likert, *New Ways of Managing Conflict.* New York: McGraw-Hill Book Company, 1976.

> After analyzing the causes of increasing organizational conflict, this book describes procedures for substituting System 4 ("win-win") problem-solving strategies for the "win-lose" approach that usually leaves one party to a conflict frustrated and embittered. A highly specific, practical, how-to book with some explicit applications to schools that should be helpful to practitioners.

Wynn, Richard, *Administrative Response to Conflict.* Pittsburgh: Tri-State Area School Study Council, School of Education, University of Pittsburgh, 1972.

> In this twenty-three-page monograph the author attempts to distill contemporary concepts of organizational conflict into practical advice for school superintendents, school board members, and other public school practitioners. Emphasizes that organizational climate appears to predispose an organization toward either productive conflict or destructive conflict and that the administrator influences this climate by his or her administrative style and values.

NOTES

1. James MacGregor Burns, *Leadership* (New York: Harper & Row, 1978), p. 37.
2. Kenneth Thomas, "Conflict and Conflict Management," in *Handbook of Industrial and Organizational Psychology,* ed. Marvin D. Dunnette (Chicago: Rand McNally & Company, 1976), p. 890.
3. Morton Deutsch, *The Resolution of Conflict: Constructive and Destructive Processes* (New Haven: Yale University Press, 1973), p. 10.
4. Bernard Berelson and Gary A. Steiner, *Human Behavior: An Inventory of Scientific Findings* (New York: Harcourt Brace Jovanovich, Inc., 1964), p. 588.
5. H. Guetzkow and J. Cyr, "An Analysis of Conflict in Decision-making Groups," *Human Relations,* 7 (1954), 369.

6. Ibid.

7. Rensis Likert and Jane Gibson Likert, *New Ways of Managing Conflict* (New York: McGraw-Hill Book Company, 1976), p. 7. Emphasis added.

8. Kenneth E. Boulding, *Conflict and Defense: A General Theory* (New York: Harper & Brothers, Publishers, 1962), pp. 152–53.

9. Richard Wynn, *Administrative Response to Conflict* (Pittsburgh: Tri-State Area School Study Council, 1972), pp. 7–8.

10. Warren G. Bennis, *The Leaning Ivory Tower* (San Francisco: Jossey-Bass, 1973).

11. For advice on how to deal with "nefarious attacks," see Wynn, *Administrative Response to Conflict.*

12. Chester I. Barnard, *The Functions of the Executive* (Cambridge, MA: Harvard University Press, 1938), p. 36.

13. Thomas, "Conflict and Conflict Management," p. 891.

14. The research (none of it in schools) has been summarized by Thomas, "Conflict and Conflict Management."

15. Deutsch, *The Resolution of Conflict,* p. 9.

16. Louis R. Pondy, "Organizational Conflict: Concepts and Models," *Administrative Science Quarterly,* 12 (September 1967), 296–320.

17. Most writers in this field today use the term conflict *management,* connoting an ongoing organizational process that is heuristic and supportive of organization development over time. To many, the term conflict *resolution* carries the connotation of seeking final, conclusive solutions that will terminate even latent conflict—an unlikely event.

18. John M. Thomas and Warren G. Bennis, *Management of Change and Conflict* (Baltimore: Penguin Books, 1972), p. 20.

19. Robert R. Blake, Herbert A. Shepard, and Jane S. Mouton, *Managing Intergroup Conflict in Industry* (Houston, TX: Gulf Publishing Company, 1964).

20. Thomas, "Conflict and Conflict Management," p. 900.

21. Pondy, "Organizational Conflict."

22. Likert and Likert, *New Ways of Managing Conflict,* p. 7.

23. Randall Collins, *Conflict Sociology: Toward an Explanatory Science* (New York: Academic Press, 1975).

24. Gerald Griffin and David Rostetter, "A Conflict Theory Perspective for Viewing Certain Problems Associated with Public Law 94–142" (paper presented at the American Educational Research Association, Atlanta, GA, March 1978), p. 4.

25. Likert and Likert, *New Ways of Managing Conflict,* p. 59.

26. The research literature is rich and fascinating. See, for example, Muzafir Sherif and Carolyn W. Sherif, *Groups in Harmony and Tension* (New York: Harper & Brothers, Publishers, 1953); Muzafir Sherif and others, *Intergroup Conflict and Cooperation: The Robbers Cave Experiment* (Norman: Institute of Group Relations, University of Oklahoma Book Exchange, 1961); Morton Deutsch, "The Effects of Cooperation and Competition upon Group Process: An Experimental Study," *American Psychologist,* 4 (1949), 263–64; and—also by Deutsch—*The Resolution of Conflict.*

27. Blake, Shepard, and Mouton, *Managing Intergroup Conflict,* p. 18.

28. Likert and Likert, *New Ways of Managing Conflict,* p. 61.

29. Such as the work of Deutsch, Blake, and Sherif mentioned above.

30. Likert and Likert, *New Ways of Managing Conflict.*

31. Blake, Shepard, and Mouton, *Managing Intergroup Conflict,* p. 63.

32. Thomas, "Conflict and Conflict Management."

Decision Making

ABOUT THIS CHAPTER

Since mid-century, decision making has been widely recognized as being at the heart of organization and administration. For example, in a landmark book published in 1950, Herbert Simon observed that "a general theory of administration must include principles of organization that will insure correct decision-making."[1] By 1959 Daniel E. Griffiths had proposed a theory that administration *was* decision making.[2] He maintained that first, the structure of an organization is determined by the nature of its decision-making processes; second, an individual's rank in an organization is directly related to the control exerted over the decision process; and third that the effectiveness of an administrator is inversely proportional to the number of decisions that he or she must personally make.

Griffiths's theory, which was highly influential in educational circles for many years, highlights two important concepts: (1) that the administrator's task is to see to it that an adequate decision-making process is in place in the organization, and (2) that, because such a process is in place, the effective administrator makes relatively few decisions personally, although those few may be particularly potent in their impact on the organization. In this view, the administrator's influence resides more firmly in creating and monitoring the processes through which decisions shall be made by the organization than in personally making large numbers of the many decisions that are required in any busy complex organization.

However, Simon and Griffiths and their colleagues at that time envisioned that decision making could be rationalized, made logical, systematized, and optimized by applying logico-mathematico methods to the solution of educational problems. Many people believed them then, and many still would like to. With the passage of time, however, it has become apparent that many of our most trenchant educational problems are so ambiguous, multifaceted, and complex that they simply cannot be reduced to algorithms into which various quantitative data can be plugged so as to yield optimum educational decisions. Indeed, since mid-century there has been growing understanding that the human complexities of organizational life in commerce as well as in education sharply limit the usefulness of such decision-making approaches in many kinds of organizations. Certainly, since the dramatic rise of awareness by Americans in the 1970s that both their industrial and educational organizations were faltering in competition with others in the world, there has been a marked trend toward the more effective use of participative decision-making methods.

INDIVIDUAL VERSUS ORGANIZATIONAL DECISION MAKING

An important issue that enters many discussions of decision making is being raised here: the question of individual versus organizational decision making. On the one hand, there is the widely held expectation that persons in administrative positions will personally "be decisive." What that means is far from clear but it is often taken to mean making decisions swiftly, without delay or temporizing, and clearly, with minimum ambiguity. It often also implies that the individual tends to make decisions that conform to certain accepted qualitative standards: that, for example, decisions are well informed and ethically acceptable. Thus, discussions of administrative decision making often focus on the personal behaviors of individuals who are construed to be "decision makers."

On the other hand, because administration is defined as working with and through other people to achieve organizational goals, it is important to consider the mechanisms by which the organization (and not merely the individual) deals with decision making. In this perspective, the issue begins to turn on the ways in which the *organization* "acts" (or "behaves") in the process of making and implementing *organizational* decisions, rather than on the idiosyncratic behavior of the person in administrative office. For many of the clients of organizations (students and parents, for example), the individual roles of administrators in decision-making processes are obscure and perhaps irrelevant, whereas the "behavior" of the organization is highly proximate and relevant. In this view—although administrators may be seen as implicated—the vital decision-making functions are organizational.

This was illustrated by the situation in one university in which the heating system was constantly malfunctioning, classrooms were chronically unkempt, and student seating typically in disrepair. Students were astounded when, in the spring, an ambitious project was undertaken to beautify the campus by planting flowers and shrubs and setting sculptures among the trees. This, of course, prompted outcries from students, such as "What is wrong with this university? It obviously doesn't care what happens in the classrooms. All that matters is what visitors see on the outside!" The implication was, of course, that regardless of the persons who might be involved, somehow the decision-making processes of the university, as an organization, had gone awry.

The discussion of decision making in this chapter recognizes that the personal decision-making style of the administrator is important insofar as it gives rise to the ways in which the organization, as an entity, goes about the unending processes of identifying problems, conceptualizing them, and finding ways of dealing with them. The individual decision making of persons in administrative office takes on significance as organizational behavior chiefly because of its inevitable impact on the behavior of others as it affects the decision-making processes of the organization itself.

This emphasis on the responsibility of the administrator for the nature and quality of the decision-making processes used in an organization is compatible with the contemporary view that the administrator is a key actor in the development of the culture of the organization. That is, that decision-making practices are not so much the result of circumstances inherent in a given organization ("the kind of place a school is") as they are the choices of those in authority (namely administrators) as to how decisions *ought* to be made. These choices are closely tied to assumptions held by administrators on issues that are now familiar to the reader, such as

+ what motivates people at work.
+ the relative values of collaboration versus directiveness in the exercise of leadership in the workplace.
+ the desirability of a full flow of information up, down, and across the organization.
+ the best ways of maintaining organizational control and discipline.
+ the value of involving people throughout all levels of the organization in decision making.

RATIONALITY IN DECISION MAKING

Even an elementary understanding of contemporary approaches to decision making in organizations requires brief consideration of some of the ways in which we have learned to think about such things. We who live in the Western world tend to use and accept logic, rationality, and science when thinking about concepts such as decision making. This reflects generally held assumptions in our culture about the ways in which we "ought" to go about making decisions. These assumptions have formed the central core of our thinking about such matters.

During the three centuries since the Reformation, the history of Western thought and culture has been dominated by the rise of science, technology, and industry. Scientific thought, with its strong emphasis on logical rationality, has become virtually ingrained in the institutions of our culture. Thus, in seeking explanations of our experiences, we are accustomed to respect the rationality of logical positivism—in short, we have strongly tended to see the solution to all sorts of problems as requiring the application of "engineering" approaches.

This was reflected in Max Weber's analysis of bureaucratic organization. It was epitomized by the work of Frederick Taylor who, adapting the principles and methods of science to a form of "human engineering" in the workplace, sought to create a science of management which could be applied to everyday problems in the organization. Taylor called it "scientific management" and, as Donald Schön pointed out, "Taylor saw the . . . manager as a designer of work, a controller and monitor of performance . . . [seeking through these roles] to yield optimally efficient production."[3]

The concept of management as a science grew steadily during the first half of the century, but World War II stimulated its development enormously. This was due to three factors associated with the war:

+ The great emphasis on the roles of science and technology in winning the war.
+ The development of operations research and systems theory. These involved the application of the rational logic of mathematics modeling to the solution

of complex problems ranging from how to reduce the loss of shipping to submarine attack to how to increase the effectiveness of aerial bombing.

✦ The unprecedentedly vast scale of organizing that was required to manage the global dimensions of the conflict.

The post–World War II era was one of great optimism and energy as industry and business moved rapidly to exploit the ready markets that abounded as a result of the years of wartime shortages everywhere. Confidence in science and technology boomed and the rational, logical methods associated with science soared in acceptance and prestige. It was commonplace to refer to the wartime Manhattan Project as a model for conceptualizing and solving problems: "After all, if we could build an atomic bomb we ought to be able to solve this problem." Government expenditures for research surged to new heights on the "basis of the proposition that the production of new scientific knowledge could be used to create wealth, achieve national goals, improve human life, and solve social problems."[4]

As though to be sure that attention to the importance of the message did not lag, Russia launched Sputnik I in the fall of 1957. The United States reacted with another spasm of emphasis on the logic of applying mathematics and science to the solution of problems. Under the leadership of President Kennedy, the United States began a large-scale effort to develop new space technology. Before long, the educational infrastructure of the nation found itself involved in meeting the demands of the space program for scientists and mathematicians, as well as managers trained to apply the concepts of those disciplines to complex organizational challenges. The new rallying cry became, "If we can put a man on the moon, why can't we solve this problem?" The implication was, of course, that the National Aeronautics and Space Administration (NASA) had—since its inception under the presidency of Dwight Eisenhower—developed and demonstrated the effectiveness of a model for complex decision making that was applicable to all sorts of problems, social as well as technological.

During the post–World War II era, another similar model—widely admired and emulated—was proferred by medicine. It emphasized clinical-experimental research as the basis of knowledge.

The medical research center, with its medical school and its teaching hospital, became the institutional model to which other professions aspired. Here was a solid base of fundamental science, and a profession which had geared itself to implement the ever-changing products of research. Other professions, hoping to achieve some of medicine's effectiveness and prestige, sought to emulate its linkage of research and teaching institutions, its hierarchy of research and clinical roles, and its system for connecting basic and applied research to practice. The prestige and apparent success of the medical and engineering models exerted great attraction for the social sciences. In such fields as education . . . the very language . . . rich in references to measurement, controlled experiment, applied science, laboratories and clinics, was striking in its reverence for those models.[5]

Rational Decision-Making Models

It is not surprising, therefore, that students of decision making tried to develop, and assist administrators to master, a *science* of making better-quality decisions through the analysis of decision-making processes. An early and very major contributor in this effort was Herbert Simon.

Simon's analysis identified three major phases in the process of making decisions. First, there is *intelligence activity.* Not surprisingly, in view of the influence of World War II on postwar thought, Simon used the term "intelligence" much as military people do: the search of the environment that reveals circumstances that call for a decision. The second phase is *design activity:* the processes by which alternative courses of action are envisioned, developed, and analyzed. The third phase in Simon's analysis is *choice activity:* that is, the process of actually selecting a course of action from among the options under consideration.[6]

Simon's great stature as a scholar and his popularity as a consultant to numerous prestigious corporations enhanced wide acceptance of his pioneering approach to decision making, which now stands as classic work. Many who were to follow would create a substantial literature devoted to efforts to improve upon his conceptualization, usually by elaborating the number of steps to be found in the process. Thus, one finds numerous models proferred in the extensive literature on decision making. Two basic assumptions incorporated in virtually all of them are based on Simon's work: the assumption that decision making is an orderly, rational process that possesses an inherent logic; and the assumption that the steps in the process follow one another in an orderly, logical, sequential flow (which some refer to as "linear logic"). Such models, and the assumptions on which they are based, became important in the training of administrators and have been widely applied in planned, systematic ways to "real-world" organizations in the hope of improving their performance.

Peter F. Drucker, a leading organizational scholar whose thinking was very influential in corporate circles from the 1960s into the 1980s, listed the following steps in decision making:

1. Define the problem.
2. Analyze the problem.
3. Develop alternative solutions.
4. Decide on the best solution.
5. Convert decisions into effective actions.[7]

Such a formulation was seen as helping the administrator to organize decision making, make it more systematic, as an alternative to intuitive, perhaps haphazard, "knee-jerk responses" to the flow of events in the busy environment of organizational life. Drucker's model, much elaborated and detailed, was widely applied in corporate and governmental organizations throughout the United States, and it was accepted by many as the essential logic of administrative thought.

Nevertheless, even as the number of models proliferated and efforts to install them in organizations intensified, a widespread disparity between the theoretic notions of the scholars and actual practices of administrators was also apparent. Therefore, further work to improve decision-making models went forward. It was noted, for example, that decision making usually does not terminate with either a decision or the action to implement a decision. In the "real world," decision making is usually an iterative, ongoing process whereby the results of one decision provide new information on which to base yet other decisions. Thus, "feedback loops" were added to some process models to ensure that the outcomes of decisions would be considered as future decisions were pondered.

Eventually recognition of this cyclic nature of decision-making processes caused some students of the subject to abandon conventional lists of steps and linear flowcharts in favor of circular depictions. Both the feedback loop concept and the circular concept of decision-making processes illustrate two further assumptions commonly found in the literature on decision making: (1) decision making is an iterative cyclical process that proceeds over time to provide successive approximations of optimal action, and (2) reaching optimal decisions is the central goal of decision making.

However, it has long been obvious that people in an organization do not tend to search endlessly and relentlessly for the best way of achieving goals. They engage in decision-making procedures to seek alternative ways of doing things only when the organization's performance seems to be falling below some acceptable level. This "acceptable level" of performance is usually not the highest level of performance possible; rather, it is one that is good enough to fit the organization's perception of reality and values.[8] Moreover, once those in the organization sense the need to seek some alternative way of doing things, they tend to seek a course of action that is perceived as sufficient to alleviate the need for action. That is, they tend to make a decision that will relieve the proximate problem but are unlikely to seize the moment as occasion for moving to some optimal level of performance. This widespread tendency in organizations is called *satisficing*.

LIMITS ON RATIONALITY IN DECISION MAKING

As I have explained, much of the scholarly literature on decision making—both organizational and individual—represents the efforts of academicians to uncover and describe the logic assumed by them to be inherent in decision-making processes. Based upon these efforts, a number of "models" of decision-making processes have been developed. These models, it has often been assumed, can be useful in facilitating the learning of this logic by administrators so that it may be applied in their work. Many people—including practicing educational administrators, legislators, and school board members trained at a time when these assumptions were essentially unchallenged—persist in the belief that more rigorous application of these efforts to practice is essential to improving organizational performance.

However, ambiguity and uncertainty are dominant characteristics of the "real world" of the educational administrator. Organizations, their goals, their technologies, and their environments have become so complex that it is difficult to connect causes with effects, actions with outcomes. For example, the volatile nature of the economic, social, and political environments of the educational organization makes it difficult to predict the course of future events with any certitude. This condition is not limited to educational organizations by any means: it is of pressing importance in all forms of organizational life. This has caused researchers to reexamine organizational life more carefully in recent years and, in the process, to question old assumptions concerning the logic and rationality of decision making.

The Gap Between Theory and Practice

Scholars commonly seek to improve the performance of administrators by instructing them in the application of rational, logical models of decision making to their work. One of the better examples in the field of education is found in a training manual called *Deciding How to Decide: Decision Making in Schools.*[9] Intended to be the basis for organizing and presenting an in-service workshop to teach administrators when and how to involve others in decision making, the manual is essentially an orderly presentation of Victor Vroom and Philip Yetton's contingency model, which points up with remarkable clarity that the central issue in contemporary leadership is participation in the process of making decisions. The issue is often confused by value-laden arguments over the relative merits of hard-nosed, directive administrative style, as contrasted with a more consultative style. Even the eminent Peter Drucker lapses occasionally into contrasting "democratic management," "participatory democracy," and "permissiveness" with the supposed successes of autocratic, tyrannical management that makes decisions by fiat.[10] Clearly, the complexities of modern organizations require decision-making processes carefully selected with an eye to the probability of effectiveness in view of the contingencies in the situation. There may be situations in which an autocratic style is most effective and other situations that call for highly participatory methods for greatest effectiveness. As Vroom and Yetton see it, the problem for the leader is to analyze the contingencies in each situation and then behave in the most effective manner.

Vroom and Yetton tried to specify how leaders "ought" to behave in order to be effective in view of specific contingencies. The Vroom and Yetton model is not prescriptive, but it can be described as a normative model because it tries to tie appropriate leader behavior to specific contingencies.[11]

Five Leadership Styles

Vroom and Yetton have developed a taxonomy of five leadership styles, as follows:

AUTOCRATIC PROCESS

AI. Leader (manager, administrator) makes the decision using whatever information is available.

AII. Leader secures necessary information from members of the group, then makes the decision. In obtaining the information, the leader may or may not tell followers what the problem is.

CONSULTATIVE PROCESS

CI. Leader shares the problem with relevant members of the group on a one-to-one basis, getting their ideas and suggestions individually without bringing them together as a group; then the leader makes the decision.

CII. Leader shares the problem with members as a group at a meeting, then decides.

GROUP PROCESS

GII. Leader, acting as chairperson at a meeting of the group, shares the problem with the group and facilitates efforts of the group to reach consensus on a group decision. Leader may give information and express opinion but does not try to "sell" a particular decision or manipulate the group through covert means.

Notice that Vroom and Yetton have described these leadership styles in behavioral terms (for example, "leader decides" or "leader shares the problem with the group") rather than in general terms (for example, "directive style" or "participative style"). They do not imply that one style is more highly valued than others; that issue must be addressed in terms of which behavior "works" in the specific situation.

Seven Situation Issues

Analysis of the situation begins with "yes" or "no" answers to the following questions:

A. *Does the problem possess a quality requirement?* One quality might be time: is this a decision that must be made now, with no time to consult others? Other quality factors might be the desirability of stimulating team development or keeping people informed through participation.

B. *Does the leader have sufficient information to make a good decision?*

C. *Is the problem structured?*

D. *Is it necessary for others to accept the decision in order for it to be implemented?*

E. *If the leader makes the decision alone, how certain is it that others will accept it?*

F. *Do others share the organizational goals that will be attained by solving this problem?*

G. *Are the preferred solutions to the problem likely to create conflict among others in the group?*

Decision-Process Flowchart

The leader can quickly diagnose the situation contingencies by answering yes or no to each of these seven questions as they are arrayed on the decision-process flow-chart (Figure 8–1). As the flowchart shows, it is possible to identify fourteen types of problems in this way, and the preferred way of dealing with each becomes evident as one follows the chart from left to right.

Given a problem, the first question is, "Does the problem possess a quality requirement?" In effect the question is, "Is one decision preferable to or more rational than another?" If not, then questions B and C are irrelevant, and one follows the flowchart to question D, "Is acceptance of the decision by others important to implementing it?" If not, then it makes little difference as to which of the five leadership styles is utilized: AI, AII, CI, CII, or GII. However, the flowchart clearly suggests that there is a logical basis for utilizing various leadership styles for maximum effectiveness under specific, describable circumstances.

However, research conducted in a variety of organizations makes it clear that practicing managers and administrators rarely actually use such models in their work. Henry Mintzberg, Duru Raisinghani, and Andre Theoret have reported that normative decision-making models have no influence on the behavior of middle- and upper-level corporate managers.[12] James G. March found that decision makers, in fact, tend to make sense of problems not by applying logical models to them but by assessing what kinds of options are actually available to be used in solving them.[13] Paul C. Nutt, after examining seventy-eight different organizations, concluded that

> Nothing remotely resembling the normative methods described in the literature was carried out. Not even hybrid variations were observed. . . . The sequence of problem definition, alternative generation, refinement, and selection, called for by nearly every theorist seems rooted in rational arguments, not behavior. Executives do not use this process.[14]

The findings of a national survey of senior high school principals indicates a similar situation among that group of administrators.[15]

Thus we have an obvious gap between theory and practice. What does it mean? It could suggest that the administrators and managers whose behavior was studied by the researchers were ill trained and therefore unable to use the decision-making models available to them. An equally plausible explanation is that the decision-making models espoused in the scholarly literature arise from assumptions about the nature of administrative work that do not reflect the conditions that the administrator on the job actually encounters. This leads us to consider research that describes the behavior of managers and administrators as it actually occurs on the job.

The Nature of Managerial and Administrative Work

In 1973, Henry Mintzberg reported research that documented detailed descriptions of the activities of the chief executives of five organizations as they were observed

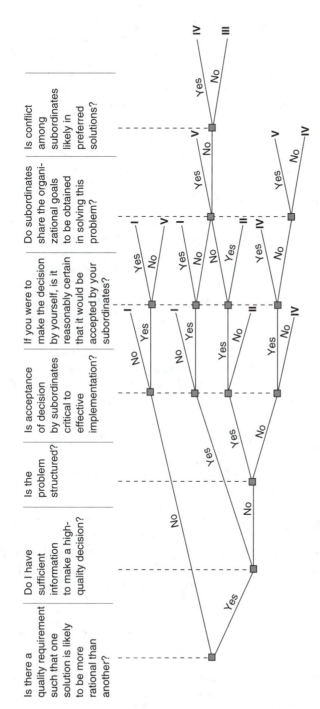

FIGURE 8–1 Vroom-Yetton normative leadership model. From Fred Luthans, *Organizational Behavior,* 2nd ed. (New York: McGraw-Hill Book Company, 1977), p. 458.

I. You solve the problem or make the decision yourself, using information available to you at the time. II. You obtain the necessary information from your subordinate(s), then decide on the solution to the problem yourself. You may or may not tell your subordinates what the problem is in getting the necessary information from them. The role played by your subordinates in making the decision is clearly one of providing the necessary information to you, rather than generating or evaluating alternative solutions. III. You share the problem with relevant subordinates individually, getting their ideas and suggestions without bringing them together as a group. Then *you* make the decision that may or may not reflect your subordinates' influence. IV. You share the problem with your subordinates as a group, collectively obtaining their ideas and suggestions. Then *you* make the decision that may of may not reflect your subordinates' influence. V. You share a problem with your subordinates as a group. Together you generate and evaluate alternatives and attempt to reach agreement (consensus) on a solution. Your role is much like that of a chairperson. You do not try to influence the group to adopt "your" solution and you are willing to accept and implement any solution that has the support of the entire group.

in their daily work.[16] The executives whose behaviors were thus recorded were (1) the manager of a consulting firm, (2) the president of an industrial company, (3) the manager of a hospital, (4) a manager of a consumer goods concern, and (5) the superintendent of a suburban school district. This research strikingly reveals, first, that the executive's work is very diverse and requires a broad range of skills, and, second, the pressure that appears to be inherent in the work. More specifically, Mintzberg developed five propositions from his observations:

1. Administrators and managers do a great deal of work, and do it at an unrelenting pace. Each day they attend a number of previously arranged meetings as well as a number of unplanned conferences and interactions, deal with a substantial volume of mail and paperwork, handle numerous phone calls. There are seldom any real breaks in the work.

2. In doing their work, administrators characteristically devote a brief time to each of a large number of decisions and these tend to center around specific, well-defined issues and problems. Important and trivial activities arise in juxtaposition to one another in an unplanned, random way, requiring quick mental shifts from topic to topic. There are many brief contacts with people interspersed with planned meetings of prolonged duration and other activities (such as desk work, telephone calls, unscheduled meetings, and tours) worked into the daily schedule.

3. Administrators prefer to deal with active problems that are well defined and nonroutine. Routine information (such as recurring reports) is given low priority whereas "fresh" information (even if of uncertain quality) is given high priority.

4. Verbal communication is much preferred. (In Mintzberg's original study, it accounted for over three-fourths of the executives' time and two-thirds of their activities.)

5. Managers maintain working relationships with three principal groups: superiors, subordinates, and outsiders.[17]

This research suggests a great deal about the ways in which administrators go about making decisions, particularly about why few seem to use formal decision-making models in their work. The rhythm of the administrator's workday comprises a driving force that evokes behavior in ways that are not likely to enter the mind of the contemplative scholar pondering the logic he or she seeks to find in the situation. As Mintzberg noted,

> The work of managing an organization may be described as taxing. The quantity of work to be done, or that the manager chooses to do, during the day is substantial and the pace is unrelenting. After hours, the chief executive (and probably many other managers as well) appears to be able to escape neither from an environment that recognizes the power and status of his position nor from his own mind, which has been well trained to search continually for new information.[18]

Why do managers maintain such a pace and such a workload? Mintzberg thinks it is because the job is inherently open-ended and ambiguous:

> The manager must always keep going, never sure when he has succeeded, never sure when his whole organization may come down around him because of some miscalculation. As a result, the manager is a person with perceptual preoccupation. He can never be free to forget his job, and he never has the pleasure of knowing, even temporarily, that there is nothing else he can do. No matter what kind of managerial job he has, he always carries the nagging suspicion that he might be able to contribute just a little bit more.[19]

In conducting his observations of the administrators he studied, Mintzberg developed a technique that required the frequent recording of code symbols that described behaviors being observed during numerous small time frames during the day. Eventually, these coded entries are reduced and arrayed statistically so as to produce a detailed quantified description of the observable behaviors that occurred over the total period of time during which observations were carried out.

A number of studies using the "Mintzberg technique" have examined the on-the-job behavior of such educational administrators as superintendents of schools and school principals.[20] These have substantially confirmed that Mintzberg's propositions apply to the work of school administrators. These administrators work long hours at an unrelenting pace. Their work is characterized by many brief interactions, mostly verbal. Meetings, phone calls, and paperwork account for almost every minute from the moment they enter the office in the morning until they leave in the afternoon or evening.

Mintzberg's use of the term "unrelenting pace" needs a little clarification here. One could conjure up the image of an assembly-line worker being driven at his or her task by the inexorable onrush of work coming down the line, never stopping, never varying. This is not what Mintzberg appeared to mean in describing the work of managers. In the manager's work situation, time becomes an important resource. Unlike the situation of the teacher, however, time for the administrator is a fluid resource rather than a constraining one.

For the teacher, critical time constraints (such as the school year, the school day, the bell schedule, and fixed constraints such as bus schedules and lunch schedules) sharply limit what he or she can or cannot do. Administrators, on the other hand, can—and often do—have considerable latitude to vary the pace of their work as seems appropriate to them. They can take extra time to carefully consider some even unimportant issues at length, if they wish, and seek to save time by making a series of rapid decisions on other matters. Or the administrator who wishes to do so can vary the use of time resources by stretching the workday into the evening, or the workweek into the weekend, and the workyear into the summer and holidays. This is, of course, what many educational administrators commonly do. Thus, the "unrelenting pace" is not at all necessarily an unvarying pace; it is one in which characteristically the work to be done is never completed, and there is always more to be done. One never knows when the task is finished.

These characteristics of administrative work combine with the ambiguity inherent in the educational system—an ambiguity arising from the unclear goals and priorities of schools and school systems, uncertain methods of evaluating administrative performance, and problematic preferences exercised by various constituency groups—to put considerable pressure on educational administrators. One result, and an additional source of pressure, is that they—like administrators in other fields—seldom stop thinking about their work.[21]

How Administrators Think

Recent research suggests that a source of confusion in the minds of scholars who study organizations and the behavior of administrators in them may be the fact that academic people and administrators tend to think about administrative work in different ways. The models for decision making described in the beginning of this chapter are the products of persons conditioned in the belief that highly logical, linear thinking, sometimes called "scientific thinking," is the single most appropriate way of exploring problems and seeking alternatives in the decision-making process. Largely academics, such observers tend to expect to see administrators behave in much the same ways that they, themselves, do. They maintain, that is, "that thinking is visible in the form of long reflective episodes during which managers sit alone, away from the action, trying to make logical inferences from facts. Since observers do not see many episodes that look like this, they conclude that managers do not do much thinking."[22] Indeed, much of the in-service training for administrators that emphasizes the so-called models for decision making is little more than an effort to train administrators in formal methods of reflective thought. The assumption underlying such training is that one can improve the decision-making behavior of administrators by improving their skills in logical, reflective thought.

But why is it that researchers report so few occasions in which administrators are observed, as scientists frequently are, thinking reflectively—cogitating, mulling over a problem, considering alternatives in the dispassionate calm of a quiet retreat? Karl Weick proposes three possible explanations. First, they do think but not while they are on the job: "they think at home, on airplanes, in the john, on weekends. . . . Thus, the reason researchers do not see managers think is that managers do not think when the observers are around."[23] The second possibility is that, essentially, managers don't think because they have reduced uncertainty to such an extent and anticipate the future so very well that they are confronted by few situations in which they are perplexed or bewildered. The third possibility proposed by Weick (and the one he considers most likely) is that managers think all the time but researchers have missed that fact because, while researchers look for episodes evidencing reflective thinking, managers go at the thinking process quite differently. That is, thinking is inseparably woven into, and occurs simultaneously with, managerial and administrative action.

Thus, when administrators tour, read, talk, supervise, and meet with others, all of those actions contain thought and, indeed, they *are* the ways in which administrators do their thinking. "Connected ideas, which are the essence of thought," Weick explains, "can be formed and managed *outside* the mind, with relatively little assistance from the mind. This is how managers work, and this is why we are misled when we use reflection as an index of how much their work involves thinking."[24] Thus, most of the thinking that administrators do is woven into their actions when their actions are taken with attention, intention, and control; that is, they pay attention to what is happening, impose order on their actions, and correct their performance when it strays from accepted standards.[25]

In considering the ways in which administrators think about their work, it is important to bear in mind that the organizational environment in which the work is done is characterized by ambiguity, uncertainty, and disorder: it is, in a word, messy. Situations that require decisions are often fluid and, therefore, difficult to analyze even after the fact; they are subject to a number of interpretations, often conflicting; and (as will be explained more fully below) they are often not clearly bounded and labeled. In the daily flow of action, administrators typically engage in brief, spontaneous, face-to-face, verbal interaction with others. They are, in other words, constantly "fighting fires." But

> fighting fires, which managers do all the time, is not necessarily thick-headed or slow witted. Firefighting has seemed like mindless activity because we have used scientific activity as the ideal case for comparison, because we have thought of thinking as a separate activity that stops when people put out fires, because we have presumed that the only time people think is when they make distinct decisions or solve clearcut problems . . . and because we keep examining things as if they occurred in sequences rather than simultaneously.[26]

A crucial issue is implied in this view: whether administration is, or can be, a science in the traditional sense or whether it is, instead, an art or a craft. Many continue to pursue the notion of administration as the application of management science to organizational problems (much as engineering is the application of physics and mathematics to other sorts of real-world problems), as envisioned earlier in this century. Those holding this view tend, of course, to emphasize the development of technical rationality in organizational decision making. Others, however—cognizant of the great complexities of human organizations and the uncertainty, instability, and uniqueness that are commonly found in them—recognize the importance of intuitive judgment and skill, the sense of proportion and appropriateness in the context of the traditions and values of the organization's culture. Schön, like Weick, found the thinking of managers closely entwined with the action demanded in their work. He observed:

> Managers do reflect in action. Sometimes, when reflection is triggered by uncertainty, the manager says, in effect, "This is puzzling; how can I understand it?" Sometimes, when a sense of opportunity provokes reflection, the manager asks, "What can I make of this?" And sometimes, when a manager is surprised by the success of his own intuitive knowing, he asks himself, "What have I really been doing?"[27]

Thus Schön makes clear that the term "art" has a twofold meaning in describing administration: intuitive approaches to understanding situations and also one's reflection, in a context of action, when one encounters events that are incongruent with his or her intuitive understandings.

The reader should note carefully that, in this discussion, we are talking about *trained* intuition.[28] The point is that we can learn—through both formal education and socialization into the organization's culture—to "see" a complex system as an organic whole as well as we can be trained (as we commonly are) to see individual parts of the whole. This crucial point is difficult for some observers to accept perhaps for two main reasons. One is that, in the strong tradition of technical rationality that has long been so emphasized in Western culture, the logic of breaking complex phenomena down into relatively simple, quantifiable parts has been thoroughly ingrained in many of us. It seems so sensible, so "right," that holistic approaches to complex problems are suspect. It is also probable that recent research on right- and left-hemisphere brain functioning is important to our understanding here. One mode of consciousness, associated with the left hemisphere, is generally described as analytic, rational, sequential, convergent, logical, objective, and linear. The other, associated with the right hemisphere, is characterized as intuitive, holistic, pattern-recognizing, artistic, subjective, and nonlogical. Unquestionably, emphasis has been placed on training left-brain functions in education that stresses logical-positivistic approaches to decision making. If we are to improve the way we apply right-hemisphere functioning to our decision making, it is likely that we will also have to improve our training strategies.[29]

Thus, it is argued that administrators are thinking all the time, that their thinking is closely intertwined with the actions (decisions) they take, and that everyday thinking almost never represents a sequence of steps. This suggests that formal models for decision making have little relevance to everyday administrative thinking and that to try to implement them would run counter to the "real world" as administrators experience it. In that world, problem situations are experienced holistically and the steps found in usual decision-making models are considered simultaneously rather than serially. This view suggests that emphasis on holistic thought—which seeks understanding of the complexities, interconnections, ambiguities and uncertainties of educational organizations—might be more fruitful in decision making than the linear-and-step models proffered in the past.

The Influence of Organizational Culture on Decision Making

Earlier in this book, the concept of organizational culture was discussed as being at the core of understanding organizational behavior, such as decision making. Organizational culture involves the norms that develop in a work group, the dominant values advocated by the organization, the philosophy that guides the organization's policies concerning employees and client groups, and the feeling that is evident in the ways in which people interact with one another. Thus, it clearly deals with basic assumptions and beliefs that are shared by those who are members of the organization. Taken together, these define the organization itself in crucial ways: why it exists, how it has survived, what it is about. In the process of developing and becoming part of the way of life in the organization, these values and basic beliefs tend to become solidly—almost unquestioningly—established as "the way we do things here." In this way, they shape the very view of the world that members bring to problems and decision making. We speak of "intuition" in the processes of thinking; organizational culture plays a large role in shaping that intuition in that the assumptions and beliefs that compose the essence of organizational culture are largely taken for granted by participants. This is especially so in educational organizations inasmuch as those who work in them are generally highly socialized to the values and central beliefs of the organization through long years of commitment to them.

Consider the educational and work history of professionals in schools and institutions of higher education. Most of these people entered school at the age of five or (at the most) six years and have remained in educational organizations with only brief absences (such as for military service or child rearing) virtually continuously throughout their formative years and the later years in which they established themselves as full adult members of society. As a result, they strongly tend to have "bought into" the values of education and educational organizations and, as professionals in these organizations, are highly committed to their core values, central beliefs, and goals. In the long process of being so thoroughly socialized into the organization—first as pupil, then as student, and, ultimately, as professional—those who work in educational organizations tend strongly to accept the "rules of the game" for getting along and "the ropes" that must be learned in order to become accepted as a member.[30]

In other words, these individuals become members of a set of persons who have a long history of sharing common experiences. These shared experiences have, over time, led to the creation of a shared view of the world and their place in it.[31] This shared view enables people in the organization to make sense of commonplace as well as unusual events, ascribe meaning to symbols and rituals, and share in a common understanding of how to deal with unfolding action in appropriate ways. Such sense making is described by Karl Weick as being central to understanding how people in organizations attribute credibility to interpretations that they have made of their experience.[32] Such a shared view is developed over a period of time during which the participants engage in a great deal of communicating, testing, and refinement of the shared view until it is eventually perceived to have been so effective for so long that it is rarely thought about or talked about any more: it is taken for granted.[33] This constitutes the development of an *organizational culture*. And it is culture that largely determines how one literally perceives and understands the world; it is the concept that captures the subtle, elusive, intangible, largely unconscious forces that shape thought in a workplace.[34]

Mintzberg's analysis, which is supported by a number of studies in educational organizations, makes clear that administrators spend little time in reflective thought: they are active, they spend much of their time communicating, interruptions are frequent, and they have little opportunity to be alone in peace and quiet.

But, as Schön and Weick have pointed out, that does not necessarily mean that administrators do not think: it means that their thinking is closely intertwined with their action on the job.

But, is their thinking merely random, perhaps geared to the last person that they talked with or the latest crisis that has emerged? Probably not. Organizational culture is a powerful environment that reflects past experiences, summarizes them, and distills them into simplifications that help to explain the enormously complex world of the organization. In this sense, the organization—the school, the university—may be understood as a body of thought[35] that has evolved over time and that guides the administrator in understanding what is going on and how to deal with it. This body of thought embodies a highly complex array of subtleties, inconsistencies, and competing truths: it reflects the complexities and delicate balances of the administrator's world. Efforts to reduce this complexity through such simplification processes as imposing decision-making models on it are not likely to be very workable. In this view, therefore, the culture of the organization represents significant thinking prior to action and is implicit in the decision-making behavior of administrators.

The role and power of organizational culture to shape and mold the thinking and, therefore, the decision making of people in organizations is not a new concept by any means. However, only in relatively recent years has it received widespread serious attention from organizational analysts and administrative practitioners alike as an approach to improving the decision making of organizations.

Closing the Gap Between Theory and Practice

What guidance does the theoretic and research literature offer for practicing administrators attempting to implement these newer concepts in decision making? One answer is that in selecting an administrative style to use in practice, one needs to examine one's assumptions as to what is the most effective approach to administrative practice. Let us consider briefly how some of the important points of this book come together at this juncture to see where they lead us in administrative decision making.

Administration has been defined as *working with and through people to achieve organizational goals.* It has long been accepted that the functions of administration are planning, organizing, leading, coordinating, and controlling. But the persistent puzzling issue throughout this century has been, what are the most effective ways of performing these functions? As I have described, there are conflicting ways to approach administrative practice: classical approaches and human resources approaches being the leading contenders among the currently competing systems of analysis through which administrative practice is interpreted. Except for those administrators who choose to pursue a mindless eclectic course in their professional work, the administrator must choose between these competing systems of analysis in deciding how to go about his or her professional work. The choice that the administrator chooses to embrace rests largely on the assumptions about the nature of organizations and the people in them.

THEORY OF PRACTICE

The assumptions that form the foundations of one's professional practice constitute, in the language of Chris Argyris and Donald Schön, a theory of practice. But we do not always practice what we preach: the actual theory of practice that one uses in deciding what to do is not always explicit, clear, and well reasoned. Indeed, given human frailty, we often espouse one theory and actually act on the basis of another, perhaps conflicting, theory. Therefore we commonly witness administrators verbalizing their commitment to values that support improving the quality of work life in educational organizations while engaging in actions that are perceived by role referents to be antithetical to such improvement. Thus as individuals—often enlightened and well intended—we act out the conflict between opposing ideas about organizations and people that has characterized organizational theory for decades.

Human Resources Development

There is a pattern in the history of the competition between the two major conflicting systems of analysis. Over the course of this century, the classical (or bureaucratic) approach has gradually lost credibility in the analysis of *educational* organizations, at least, as the organizational problems of schools and universities have deepened even as the application of bureaucratic attempts at solution grew and multiplied. Simultaneously, as more sophisticated research was pushed forward, the credibility and usefulness of human resources approaches grew steadily and that pattern seems likely to continue into the foreseeable future. This pattern is clearly evident in the body of research literature that is being discussed in this book. It is called human resources development (HRD). HRD is based on the overlapping theories and concepts of such scholars as Douglas McGregor, Abraham Maslow, Frederick Herzberg, Chris Argyris, Rensis Likert, James March, Karl Weick, and William Ouchi.

McGregor described two sets of conflicting assumptions that administrators tend to hold about people and their attitudes toward work: Theory *X*, the belief that people are lazy and will avoid work if they can, and Theory *Y*, the belief that people seek responsibility and want to perform satisfying work. These concepts are now well understood by many administrators.

Maslow's concept of motivation is based on a hierarchy of prepotent needs in which satisfied needs are seen as not motivating people but in which yet unsatisfied needs can be motivators.

Herzberg's work identified "maintenance" factors, such as compensation and working conditions, as not being motivators but as being essential in order for such motivating factors as satisfaction arising from achievement in the work itself and a sense of autonomy on the job to be effective.

Likert conceptualized four management styles (System 1–System 4), each using different styles of leadership, motivation, and conflict management that have predictable outcomes in terms of organizational culture as well as end results in terms of organizational effectiveness. Further, and perhaps more important, Likert pointed out that it is the administrator—who has options from which to choose in deciding what the philosophy of management is to be, how communication is to be carried out, and how decisions shall be made in the organization—who bears major responsibility for the culture that develops in an organization.

Vroom and Yetton lent strong support to Likert's views by demonstrating that administrators are key actors in controlling decision making in the organization, and that this control is exercised by the decision-making style that administrators choose to use.

Argyris's work emphasized the need to develop greater harmony and consistency between the goals of organizations and the human needs of people who work in them, and that this requires replacing directive administrative styles with more participative styles.

James March pointed out that ambiguity and uncertainty characterize the natural state of affairs in organizations, rather than the patterns of predictability and order that administrators have traditionally sought to find in them. Thus, streams of problems, solutions, participants, and opportunities for making choices swirl around, occasionally resulting in decisions, though rarely arrived at in the orderly sequential fashion usually envisioned by formal rational decision-making models.

Karl Weick made clear that, instead of the close hierarchical cause-and-effect linkages that classical theory assumes to be present in organizations, the instructional activities of schools are characteristically loosely coupled. This loose coupling not only calls traditional assumptions about management methods into question, but opens new visions as to how schools can be managed so as to reduce the rigidity and ineffectiveness so frequently observed in them.

William Ouchi and others—including Terrence Deal, Rosabeth Moss Kanter, Edgar Schein, and Marshall W. Meyer—have explained that there are various ways of exercising administrative control in organizations. Although traditional bureaucratic hierarchy is one way, and often thought to be the only way, in fact, the norms of the culture of an organization evolving through its history are an exceedingly powerful means through which administrators exercise influence over others. Further, they explain, the cultures of some organizations are more effective than others in implementing HRD concepts of motivation, leadership, conflict management, decision making, and change.

These HRD perspectives on organization provide a set of assumptions on which to base the practice of administration that are clear alternatives to classical perspectives. Whereas those who choose to use classical bureaucratic perspectives on organization continue to push hard for reducing ambiguity through increasing use of rules and close surveillance, striving for greater logic and predictability through more planning, increased specification of objectives, and tighter hierarchical control, contemporary best thinking in management emphasizes tapping the inner motivations and abilities of participants while recognizing that disorder and illogic are often ordinary characteristics of effective organizations. Taken together, the assumptions of HRD constitute a theory of decision making, the centerpiece of which is participative methods. Lately, it has been increasingly called the empowerment of others.

PARTICIPATIVE DECISION MAKING

Much of decision making revolves around issues of participation in solving problems and making decisions. Participation is defined as the mental and emotional involvement of a person in a group situation that encourages the individual to contribute to group goals and to share responsibility for them.[36]

Participation in this sense is "mental and emotional involvement"; this is the notion of "ownership" of (or "buying into") decisions. It is genuine ego involvement, not merely being present and "going through the motions." Such involvement is motivating to the participant, and thus it releases his or her own energy, creativity, and initiative. This is what distinguishes participation from *consent,* which is the major feature of voting on issues or approving proposals.[37] This ego involvement, this sense of "ownership," also encourages people to accept greater responsibility for the organizations's effectiveness. Having "bought into" the goals and the decisions of the group, the individual sees himself or herself as having a stake in seeing them work out well. This, in turn, stimulates the development of teamwork so characteristic of effective organizations.

The use of participative decision making has two major potential benefits: (1) arriving at better decisions and (2) enhancing the growth and development of the organization's participants (for example, greater sharing of goals, improved motivation, improved communication, better-developed group-process skills). As a practical guide for implementing participative processes in educative organizations, three factors in particular should be borne in mind: (1) the need for an explicit decision-making process, (2) the nature of the problem to be solved or the issue to be decided, and (3) criteria for including people in the process.

Participative Decision Making and Empowerment

Participative decision making requires the interaction of power and influence from two sources: the power and influence of the administrator and the power and influence of others in the organization. In educational organizations these "others" are generally faculty members, students, and/or community members. When the organization is conceptualized as a traditional bureaucracy, which emphasizes the top-downward exercise of hierarchical power, the power of administrators is ordinarily viewed as being in conflict with that of others. Indeed, in such a view the administrator tends to consider it important to husband power, expand it if possible, and limit the power and influence of others. Unionized teachers, on the other hand, consider it important to resist the expansion of administrator power and seek to enlarge their own power. These are important elements in establishing and maintaining control of decision making in the organization when the participants are responding to traditional values and beliefs.

Administrators who embrace these traditional views of organization and administration may view the management of participative decision making in the organization as requiring a conflict management approach. In the traditional organization, characterized by boss-worker relationships that we now tend to associate with the stereotypic "factory model," the power and influence of the administrator dominates the decision-making process and the followers have little ability to influence the course of events. As Tannenbaum and Schmidt depict in Figure 8–2, this is the situation in which the administrator decides what is to be done and communicates the decision to others to be carried out. But you will notice that this is only the starting point in a dimension of possible behaviors along which the administrator may choose to recognize the power of others to exercise influence on the process. This is the basis for the concept of empowering others in the school.

As Tannenbaum and Schmidt see it, a next step that increases the freedom of followers to influence decision making may occur when the administrator seeks to have followers approve and "buy into" the decision when it is announced to be implemented. This often requires some "selling" of the new idea to the followers. As Figure 8–2 shows, the administrator has a range of other options by which the role of followers in the process may be expanded and their power in decision making increased. For example, referring to the diagram, we can see a possible progression:

- ✦ First, permit followers to ask questions after a decision is taken.
- ✦ Then, offer a tentative decision subject to possible change after discussion with followers, before the administrator finalizes the decision.
- ✦ Next, present the problem to followers, and make a decision only after discussion with them to get their opinions.
- ✦ And so on, until, finally, the organization has the possibility of making many of its most important decisions in a highly collegial and collaborative way.

In traditional organizations, which are markedly hierarchical, the process of deciding how to make decisions is largely controlled by the administrator, not the followers. In such a case, the progress of the organization from autocratic decision making toward collaborative decision making resides largely in the extent to which the administrator sees power-sharing as a win-win proposition, a desirable state of affairs, rather than a threat to administrative hegemony. Many present-day educational organizations, though still hierarchical, have developed collaborative cultures to such an extent that reverting to the more primitive autocratic model would be difficult: the administrator is not so much confronted with the issue of whether or not others will be involved in decision making but, rather, how and to what extent they will be involved.

An Explicit Decision-Making Process

Participation can mean many things. All too often, the process, when not properly attended to, can be seen by participants as vague and ill defined. Under such conditions people are not sure when to participate or what their proper role is in the process.

The most important decision that a group makes is to *decide how it will make decisions.* This is often one of the most inexplicit facts of organizational life: not uncommonly, people literally do not know who makes decisions or how they are

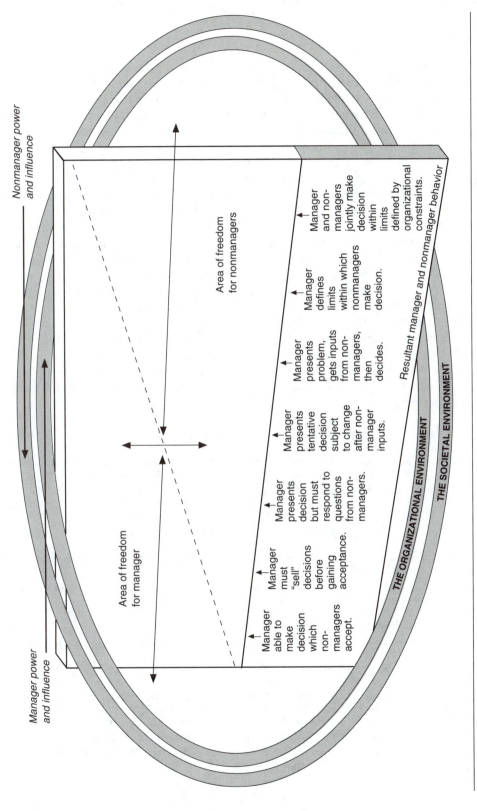

FIGURE 8–2 Leadership style is evident in a range of possible behaviors. From Robert Tannenbaum and Warren H. Schmidt, "How to Choose a Leadership Pattern." *Harvard Business Review*, 51 (May-June 1973), p. 167. Copyright © 1973 by the President and Fellows of Harvard College; all rights reserved.

Nonmanager power and influence

Manager power and influence

Area of freedom for manager

Area of freedom for nonmanagers

Manager able to make decision which non-managers accept.

Manager must "sell" decisions before gaining acceptance.

Manager presents decision but must respond to questions from non-managers.

Manager presents tentative decision subject to change after non-manager inputs.

Manager presents problem, gets inputs from non-managers, then decides.

Manager defines limits within which nonmanagers make decision.

Manager and non-managers jointly make decision within limits defined by organizational constraints.

Resultant manager and nonmanager behavior

THE ORGANIZATIONAL ENVIRONMENT

THE SOCIETAL ENVIRONMENT

made, let alone know how they individually may participate in the process. It is important, therefore, for the organization to develop an *explicit, publicly known* set of processes for making decisions that is *acceptable to its participants.*

The best time to grapple with this problem is before it is necessary to make a decision. One illustrative way of initiating this process is to convene a meeting of a school faculty (or other work group) for the purpose of reviewing the recent performance of the group. After selecting a few, *specific,* recent, decision-making episodes, the group can assess its experience by asking a few questions, such as these: What were the processes by which this decision was reached? Do we all agree that we know how the decision was reached? How do we feel about that way of solving this problem? Should we use similar procedures next time, or should we make some changes? What suggestions are there for (1) identifying and defining problems, (2) deciding how to deal with them (and who should be involved), and (3) keeping everyone informed as to what is going on?

Simple steps such as these can begin to focus on the importance attached to the *way* that problems are defined and dealt with—a focus on group process. To be successful it must be accompanied by an emphasis on developing a climate in the group that supports open communication and stresses the skills required for revealing and working through differences among members of the group.

Readers who seek more specific suggestions and advice on developing explicit decision-making processes in the organization may find it useful to consult the following:

Bradford, Leland P., *Making Meetings Work: A Guide for Leaders and Group Members.* La Jolla, CA: University Associates, 1976.
>   The old master shows—among other things—how to turn apathy and indifference into involvement and concern, how to use conflict constructively, and how to arrive at a decision.

Doyle, Michael, and David Straus, *How to Make Meetings Work.* Chicago: Playboy Press, 1976.
>   Explicit do-it-yourself manual shows how to make meetings more productive by applying concepts of participative decision making. Excellent for staff development.

Dunsing, Richard J., *You and I Have Simply Got to Stop Meeting This Way.* New York: AMACOM, 1977.
>   Emphasizes the need to tailor your approach to meetings, based on careful analysis of specific needs in your situation.

Likert, Rensis, and Jane Gibson Likert, "Integrative Goals and Consensus in Problem Solving," in *New Ways of Managing Conflict.* New York: McGraw-Hill Book Company, 1976.
>   Excellent short chapter clearly discusses the nature of consensus and its importance to group problem solving.

Schindler-Rainman, Eva, and Ronald Lippitt, with Jack Cole, *Taking Your Meetings out of the Doldrums.* La Jolla, CA: University Associates, 1975.
>   A treasure-trove of detailed suggestions for making sure that meetings are productive and stimulating.

Schmuck, Richard A., "Developing Collaborative Decision-Making: The Importance of Trusting, Strong and Skillful Leaders," *Educational Technology,* 12, no. 10 (October 1972), 43–47.
>   The entire issue of this journal is devoted to organization development in schools.

Schmuck, Richard A., Philip J. Runkel, Janet H. Arends, and Richard I. Arends, *The Second Handbook of Organizational Development in Schools.* Palo Alto, CA: Mayfield Publishing Company, 1977.
>   (See annotation under Suggested Reading in Chapter 9.)

Smith, Carole E., *Better Meetings: A Handbook for Trainers of Policy Councils and Other Decision-Making Groups.* Atlanta: Humanics Press, 1975.

> A "must" for those meetings that bring school staff members and community people together for joint decision making.

Who Identifies the Problem?

Many would contend that as one contemplates involving others in creating an explicit group decision-making process, an even more fundamental question must be confronted—who decides what problem it is that requires collaborative solution or decision? For, as has been said many times, the most important step in making a decision is to define the problem. Whoever defines the problem literally controls the decision-making process.

With this in mind, if you look again at the Schmidt and Tannenbaum model, you will notice that at the lowest levels of group involvement, it is the administrator who decides not only what the problem is but what the solution is. However, as one increases the area of freedom for others to participate in the decision-making process—that is, as one increases the empowerment of the group—a central factor is, who defines the problem? At the lowest levels of participation, the administrator tends to define not only the problem but the solution as well. The trend toward greater empowerment of others is marked by the administrator tending to identify the problem but leaving the options for solving the problem somewhat open to others. At the highest levels of participation, the administrator and the other participants become involved in a more genuine collaborative process of, first, mutually agreeing on the definition of the problem itself and, second, of jointly deciding how to deal with it.

Emergent and Discrete Problems

Participative decision making has salience primarily because it tends to produce decisions of better quality than those reached by even highly capable individuals. But some kinds of problems are best solved by expert individuals, whereas other kinds of problems are best solved by groups. To achieve the highest possible quality of decisions, therefore, it is necessary to analyze the situation. Indeed, one of the indicators of a highly skilled group is that its members are able to make such analyses, thereby knowing what problems the group should try to work through and what problems it should refer to appropriate experts.

Some problems have the following characteristics: (1) the elements of the problem are relatively unambiguous, clear-cut, and often quantifiable; (2) the elements of the problem are readily separable; (3) the solution to the problem requires a logical sequence of acts that may be readily performed by one person; and (4) the boundaries of the whole problem are relatively easy to discern. Problems of this kind may be called *discrete,* and they may well be solved best by an expert individual.

Some problems are quite different: (1) the elements of the problem are ambiguous, uncertain, and not readily quantifiable; (2) the elements of the problem are so dynamically intertwined that it is difficult to separate them on the basis of objective criteria (in fact, obtaining measurements may be difficult); (3) the solution to the problem requires the continued coordination and interaction of a number of people; and (4) the dimensions and nature of the problem cannot be fully known at the time of decision but will come into better view as iterative processes of dealing with the problem cause it to unfold over time. Such problems may be called *emergent*. The highest-quality solution to problems of this kind are likely to come from a group of people who (a) are in the best position to possess among them the knowledge necessary to solve the problem and (b) will be involved in implementing the decision after it is made.

A typical discrete problem in a school district is handling school supplies. The myriad problems involved in consolidated purchasing, warehousing, and distributing supplies to schools are relatively clear-cut and can be ordered into a logical sequence by an expert. Indeed, as compared with the skilled business manager—with his or her intimate knowledge of the budget, contract law, purchasing procedures, and the vagaries of the school supply market—a group of school district administrators trying to deal with the problem of getting the right supplies at the right price to the right places on time could well be a matter of the blind leading the blind. Similarly, laying out school bus routes for maximum economy and efficiency is normally a discrete problem. The use of mathematical models and computer simulations, now relatively common in larger districts, requires the use of experts who have the requisite technical skills and the techniques for grasping the full dimensions of the problem.

Policy issues in public education, on the other hand, are very often emergent problems. The matter of implementing competency-based education, for example, clearly meets the description of an emergent problem. Often the issue confronts school district administrators on the level of "How shall we implement the decision that has been handed down to us?" rather than in terms of "Should we do it?"

As every educator knows, concepts of competency-based education involve many facets of the school enterprise in dynamic interrelationship, and certainly the specialized knowledge of many individuals in the system must be brought to bear on the problem in highly coordinated fashion even to understand the problem. Therefore a decision to undertake such an endeavor will require commitment to the program by many people, continuous close collaboration and free flow of communication, and recognition that success depends upon an iterative process of decision making as the extent and implications of the problem become apparent.

Many of the problems encountered in the course of day-to-day administrative practice are, such as is this, emergent. Indeed, as education grows more complex there appears to be less and less certitude that many important issues can be resolved by experts who pass their solutions on to others to implement. Appropriate solutions require free and open communication among a number of individuals who pool and share information. Close collaboration is necessary to weigh and evaluate information in the process of developing an informed judgment as to which of several alternatives might be best. Commitment to the implementation of the solution is essential in order to maintain the collaboration that is the basis of the iterative processes of decision making.

Who Should Participate?

A commonly held erroneous assumption that is often made about participative decision making is that its intent is to involve everyone in every decision. Clearly, this is neither practical nor desirable. Edwin Bridges has suggested two rules for identifying decisions in which it is appropriate for teachers to participate:

1. *The test of relevance.* "[W]hen the teacher's personal stakes in the decision are high," Bridges has stated, "their interest in participation should also be high."[38] Problems that clearly meet this test concern teaching methods and materials, discipline, curriculum, and organizing for instruction.

2. *The test of expertise.* It is not enough for the teacher to have a stake in the decision; if his or her participation is to be significant, the teacher must be competent to contribute effectively. In dealing with the physical education department's program schedule, for example, English teachers may be fitted by training and experience to contribute little or nothing.

I would add that there is a significant third test to use in deciding about which problems the teachers should be consulted:

3. *The test of jurisdiction.* Schools are organized on a hierarchical basis; the individual school and staff have jurisdiction only over those decision-making areas that are assigned to them, either by design or omission. Problems may be *relevant* to teachers, and the teachers may have the requisite *expertise,* but—right or wrong—they may not have *jurisdiction.* Participation in the making of decisions that the group cannot implement can lead to frustration at least as great as simple nonparticipation.

Desire of Individuals to Participate

Another practical consideration is whether or not individuals themselves wish to be involved in the making of a decision. The demands of time and personal interest inevitably require each person in the organization to establish (albeit imprecisely, perhaps) some priorities for his or her own time and energies. Chester Barnard pointed out that there are some things in which some individuals simply are not interested: he spoke of such matters as falling within the individuals's *Zone of Indifference.*[39] To seek active involvement of teachers in matters to which they are essentially indifferent is, of course, to court resistance in various forms. It is common, for example, for school principals to seek involvement of teachers, either on a limited basis (for example, limiting participation to expressing views and opinions) or on low-level problems (reserving important decisions for themselves). There is little wonder that teachers are often indifferent to such participation.

There are areas of decision making in which teachers take great personal interest over a sustained period of time; in effect, this area may be described as a *Zone of Sensitivity.*[40] These matters represent "personal stakes," as it were, and could include such things as teaching assignments and evaluation of professional performance. When dealing with problems that fall within a staff's Zone of Sensitivity, a high degree of participation in a group-process mode of decision making would, of course, be indicated. The principal would enhance his or her authority with such involvement.

There is a third category of problems in which teachers have something at stake but not enough to make them especially concerned as individuals. These fall in the *Zone of Ambivalence.*[41] For example, it may be difficult for everyone on the staff to become concerned about preparing the agenda for a professional conference day or scheduling an assembly program. Thus, to avoid needless negative feelings from teachers who feel that they are already overburdened by the unnecessary bureaucratic demands of administrators, involvement of teachers with problems of this sort has to be selective. To be effective, such involvement should be restricted (for example, have a small representative group deal with the problem or simply be sure to keep everyone informed as the problem is processed to a decision).

Although there are undoubtedly clusters of issues to which teachers may be sensitive, ambivalent, or indifferent, it is not possible simply to assume these generalizations: some assessment should be part of the diagnosis in each situation. When the group is small it is possible to do this through discussion. In dealing with larger groups, it may be useful to employ a paper-and-pencil inventory as a diagnostic aid. One such technique used by Robert Owens and Edward Lewis in a large senior high school reveals that interest in participating in certain issues may be associated with certain characteristics of teachers. For example, experienced teachers and inexperienced teachers on the same school staff may have dissimilar views toward participation in dealing with specific issues.[42] Thus, Owens and Lewis reported that probationary teachers had much higher interest in learning about such things as the policies and rules of the school, the curriculum that they were to teach, and procedures for supervisory evaluation of their work. Older teachers were more concerned about maintaining traditions of the school and issues pertaining to their involvement in key decisions in the school.

TEAM ADMINISTRATION

While much attention has recently been given to collaborative behavior within schools, it has also been seen as important in the administration of school districts, where it is usually called team administration. A defining concept of team administration is participative decision making. Robert Duncan stated it succinctly: "Team administration simply refers to genuine involvement—before the fact—of all levels of administration in goal-setting, decision-making, and problem-solving processes."[43] Similarly, a state association of school principals said:

> In place of the unilateral decisions which were made by the superintendent and passed down through the ranks to the level of final implementation, this new format would

require a team approach to decision-making, providing an opportunity for all administrative and supervisory personnel to contribute . . . to the process. . . . In return for this participation on the part of . . . principals, the superintendent must be willing to demonstrate his confidence in group processes; he must involve individuals so that they may feel a part of the decisions which are made . . . he must understand that this type of involvement is imperative if the principal is to consider himself a member of an administrative team.[44]

Harold McNally concluded: "The administrative team is a group formally constituted by the board of education and the superintendent, comprising both central office and middle echelon administrative-supervisory personnel, with expressly stated responsibility and authority for participation in school system decision making."[45]

Administrative teams vary considerably in the techniques used for participation in making decisions. Five techniques are commonly found. Ranging from the least participation to the maximum, they are[46]

1. *Discussion.* Perhaps the simplest level of participation, the discussion of a problem is widely used to ascertain that team members are aware of the problem and that a decision about this problem must be made. When participation is limited to discussion, the administrator makes the decision, but he or she hopes that the others will accept the decision more readily than if he or she were to communicate the decision to them *before* discussion.

2. *Information seeking.* This technique of participation is more than mere discussion; it also involves the administrator's obtaining information so as to facilitate making a more rational, logical decision.

These types of participation are most useful for decisions that fall within the participants' zone of indifference; presumably, the decisions involved would not be of vital interest to them, and each actual decision would be made by the administrator. The essential purposes of involving others at these levels would be (1) to help the administrator make a better decision and (2) to enhance the likelihood that the decision will be accepted by the group when it is made. To decide matters outside the members' zone of indifference—and to allow them to participate actively—other forms of involvement will be used:

3. *Democratic-centralist.* Undoubtedly the most commonly used procedure, this method consists of the administrator's presenting the problem to the staff and asking for suggestions, reactions, and ideas. The administrator will make the decision, but he or she will try to reflect the staff's participation in the decision.

4. *Parliamentarian.* When the team members are actually to make a decision but it does not appear likely that unanimity or even consensus will prevail, the

parliamentarian technique is often used. It offers the great advantage of specifically providing for minority opinions, conflict of ideas and values, and shifting positions in time as issues, facts, and values change. It has the distinct disadvantage of creating winners and losers.

5. *Participant-determining.* The essential characteristic of this procedure is that consensus is required of the group. It is one that would be used when (1) the issues are considered very important to the team members and (2) when it appears that consensus probably can be reached. Because consensus can be looked upon as pressure, the participant-determining method would probably not be used frequently. However, when it is used successfully, it is a powerful decision-making procedure.

Participation Requires High Level of Skills

One of the persistently under-recognized problems in implementing participative decision-making methods is the need to provide participants with training in the group process skills that are needed to make collaboration work well. The intention to collaborate in making decisions is simply not sufficient in itself. Moreover, it is insufficient that only the administrator be skilled in participative methods: it is essential that all participants understand and know how to play their roles effectively.

All too often, it is assumed that every educated adult knows how to take part in a meeting, and do it well. That can be a mistake, especially if one seeks to develop collaborative, collegial participation in making decisions in the organization. The mistake becomes more serious as the importance of the decision increases and the consequences of the decision loom larger in the lives of the people involved. At its best, participative decision making in educational organizations uses collaborative group methods, whereas our larger society outside of the school generally emphasizes competitive group methods. For example, whenever we have a meeting, we often unthinkingly assume that the best way to make decisions is by voting, when, in fact, voting is a highly competitive process whereby some people become winners and others become losers. That may be highly appropriate in our democratic political system, but it is generally not appropriate in organizational decision making, wherein the goal is neither victory nor compromise but consensus and empowerment, not win-lose but win-win.

To date, the teaching and practice of collaborative group skills has been virtually absent from university programs of preparation for both teachers and administrators. Therefore, to engage in and develop participative decision making in education, it is important for decision-making groups to have adequate support in the form of access to on-the-job training and technical consultation to help members to hone and refine their skills as effective group members. Trust building, conflict management, problem solving, and open communication are among the important skill areas in which members of collaborative groups need ongoing support. Some training and skill development can be done through lectures and workshops, but third-party consultation, in which groups can get impartial feedback on the functioning of their group at work and reflect on their own experiences with the process, is essential.

A PARADIGM FOR DECISION MAKING

Confusion can be a very real hazard in organizational decision making. Unless participants know just what procedures the organization is using to arrive at decisions and what their own role and function will be in the procedures, the very advantages ascribed to "democratic" or participatory decision making may well be nullified. It would be difficult to find research support for the possible contention that ambiguity in the decision-making processes in a school is somehow a virtue. In addition to knowing *how* people are to participate in decision making, that is, what their role and functions will be, they must know *just when* they will participate.

It is also important that participants understand the orderly steps of the decision-making process as the organization moves toward a decision. These steps can be charted, and in so doing, some of the critical choices to be made can be seen more readily.

A skeleton of a proposed decision-making paradigm might resemble the one in Figure 8–3, which shows the four steps typically involved in reaching a decision: (1) defining the problem, (2) identifying possible alternatives, (3) predicting the consequences of each reasonable alternative, and (4) choosing the alternative to be followed.[47] In Figure 8–3 these four steps are identified by the numbers along the *time* dimension. In practice, individual administrators and their staffs might employ other series of steps, perhaps labeled differently; the suggested paradigm is readily adaptable to any sequence of decision-making behavior. Along the *behavior* dimension, a choice must be made as to who is going to perform each necessary decision-making function. Here, broken lines indicate choices of action that the administrator can elect to make: to involve the staff at any one step, at all of them, or, indeed, not to involve them at all.

In other words, when the administrator receives (or becomes aware of) information indicating the need for a decision, the choice is clear: he or she can either use or ignore the information. If the decision maker elects to act on the information, he or she can logically proceed either (1) by defining the problem or (2) by giving the information to the staff and asking them to define the problem. From then on, the process of decision making can comprise any combination of participation that the decision makers desire. The administrator can handle every phase of the process alone or can utilize any combination of participation by the staff. But we must bear in mind that the administrator has no monopoly on the initiation of participation. The concept of participative decision making requires that all members have access to means of initiating decision-making processes.

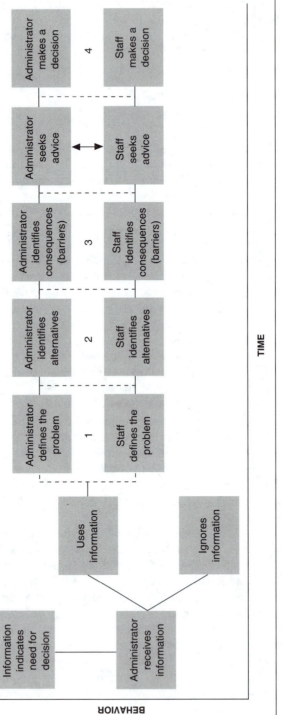

FIGURE 8–3 A paradigm for shared decision making in the school.

CONCLUSION

The wish to simplify organizational decision making and render it more rational has spawned a large number of decision-making models, each of which seeks to reveal the order and logic of organizational life. A commonplace puzzle, however, is that administrators are infrequently observed—even after training—using such models in their work or spending prolonged periods of time in episodes of reflective thinking. Recent research is giving rise to the understanding that (1) educational organizations and administrative work are far more complex than had formerly been believed and (2) administrators go about the thinking that precedes decision making in ways that differ significantly from that of scholars and researchers. Events in the organizational world rarely occur in neat sequence; more rarely still does one thing occur at a time. Rather, the administrator is typically confronted with ambiguous circumstances in which a number of events are unfolding simultaneously, various goals and values of the school may be in conflict, and truth may take several forms, yet the need for decisions presses inexorably on at a relentless pace.

Further, many organizational problems are ill understood at the time that decisions must be made. They may be described as being emergent problems. That is they tend to be ambiguous, difficult to define, and the information needed to solve them is scattered among a number of people. Moreover, dealing with emergent problems leads to an iteration of diagnosis and solution by a process of successive approximation over time.

Under these conditions of ambiguity and uncertainty, which are connate characteristics of educational organizations, the trend in organizational decision making in education has been in the direction of empowering teachers and others to participate more fully in making important decisions. This trend is not merely an organizational response intended to placate individuals who have long felt alienated and even oppressed by the traditional top-down decision-making processes of hierarchical organizations. It is primarily intended to improve the quality of decisions by more adequately drawing on the knowledge and experience of key people who are closest to the action in the core enterprise of the school: teaching. At the same time, empowerment through participation in decision making tends to more adequately meet intrinsic motivational needs of individuals and to strengthen the growth-enhancing qualities of the organization's culture in ways and to a degree that traditional decision-making methods simply cannot match.

Shifting from traditional methods to participative methods requires administrators to develop a new understanding of power, a new sense of administrative wisdom. Traditionally, it was believed that there was only so much power available in the organization and the wise administrator would garner and husband all that was possible. Thus, empowering teachers and others to participate in decision making would be viewed by the administrator as losing power by giving it away to others. Modern, empowering administrators, on the other hand, understand that one gains power by sharing it with others because in collaborative effort the power available to the group multiplies.

The intention to share power with others and increase participation in decision making is, in itself, insufficient to assure success. Such efforts must be accompanied by the support of ongoing technical training and consultation to help all participants, administrators and others alike, to master the group process skills that are essential to making empowerment succeed. They must also be accompanied by the development of concrete and publicly known processes through which one participates in the collaborative process.

SUGGESTED READING

Bolman, Lee G., and Terrence E. Deal, "Applying the Human Resource Approach," in *Modern Approaches to Understanding and Managing Organizations.* San Francisco: Jossey-Bass, 1984.

> Describes the basis for the HRM approach to decision making and practical considerations in applying it in practice. Includes discussions of participative methods, organizational democracy, and organization development.

Cunningham, William G., "Decision Making," in *Systematic Planning for Educational Change.* Palo Alto, CA: Mayfield Publishing Company, 1982.

> One of the better discussions of formal decision-making procedures based on conventional logical linear models. Features a description of decision tree analysis that can be very effective in dealing with discrete problems.

Kanter, Rosabeth Moss, "Dilemmas of Participation," in *The Change Masters: Innovation and Entrepreneurship in the American Corporation.* New York: Simon & Schuster, 1983.

> As the title suggests, this chapter explores problems and apparent dilemmas confronting administrators seeking to implement participative decision-making methods and suggests ways of dealing with them.

Wynn, Richard, and Charles W. Guditus, *Team Management: Leadership by Consensus.* Columbus, OH: Charles E. Merrill Publishing Company, 1984.

> An excellent resource for readers who want a detailed, practical guide for implementing participative management in educational organizations.

NOTES

1. Herbert A. Simon, *Administrative Behavior* (New York: Macmillan, 1950), p. 1.
2. Daniel E. Griffiths, *Administrative Theory* (New York: Appleton-Century-Crofts, 1959), p. 89.
3. Donald A. Schön, *The Reflective Practitioner: How Professionals Think in Action* (New York: Basic Books, 1983) p. 237.
4. Ibid., p. 39.
5. Ibid.
6. Herbert A. Simon, *The New Science of Management Decision* (New York: Harper & Row, 1960), p. 2.
7. Peter F. Drucker, *Management: Tasks, Responsibilities, and Practices* (New York: Harper & Row, 1974), pp. 19–20.
8. James G. March and Hebert A. Simon, *Organizations* (New York: John Wiley & Sons, 1958).
9. *Deciding How to Decide: Decision Making in Schools.* Project Leadership Presenter's Guide prepared by the Research-Based Training for School Administrators Project (Eugene: Center for Educational Policy and Management, College of Education, University of Oregon, 1983).
10. Drucker, *Management,* pp. 264–65.
11. Victor H. Vroom and Philip W. Yetton, *Leadership and Decisionmaking* (Pittsburgh: University of Pittsburgh Press, 1973).

12. Henry Mintzberg, Duru Raisinghani, and Andre Theoret, "The Structure of 'Unstructured' Decision Processes," *Administrative Science Quarterly,* 21 (June 1976), 246–75.

13. James G. March, "Footnotes to Organizational Change," *Administrative Science Quarterly,* 26 (December 1981), 563–77.

14. Paul C. Nutt, "Types of Organizational Decision Processes," *Administrative Science Quarterly,* 29 (September 1984), 446.

15. National Association of Secondary School Principals, *The Senior High School Principalship* (Reston, VA: National Association of Secondary School Principals, 1978).

16. Henry Mintzberg, *The Nature of Managerial Work* (New York: Harper & Row, 1973).

17. These five points are summarized from Mintzberg, *The Nature of Managerial Work,* pp. 28–48.

18. Ibid., p. 30.

19. Ibid.

20. For examples see Van Cleve Morris, Robert L Crowson, Emanuel Hurwitz, Jr., and Cynthia Porter-Gehrie, *The Urban Principal: Discretionary Decision-Making in a Large Educational Organization* (unpublished manuscript, University of Illinois at Chicago, 1981). This study was elaborated into a book by the same authors entitled *Principals in Action: The Reality of Managing Schools* (Columbus, OH: Charles E. Merrill Publishing Company, 1984). Also see Nancy J. Pitner, "Descriptive Study of the Everyday Activities of Suburban School Superintendents: The Management of Information" (unpublished doctoral dissertation, The Ohio State University, 1978).

21. Mintzberg. *The Nature of Managerial Work;* Sune Carlson, *Executive Behavior: A Study of the Work Load and the Working Methods of Managing Directors* (Stockholm: Strombergs, 1951); Pitner, "Descriptive Study of the Everyday Activities of Suburban School Superintendents"; William H. Whyte, Jr., "How Hard Do Executives Work?" *Fortune* (January 1948), 108–11.

22. Karl E. Weick, "Managerial Thought in the Context of Action," in *The Executive Mind,* ed. Suresh Srivastva (San Francisco: Jossey-Bass, 1983), p. 222.

23. Ibid., pp. 222–23.

24. Ibid., p. 222. Emphasis in the original.

25. Ibid., pp. 226–27.

26. Ibid., p. 236.

27. Schön, *The Reflective Practitioner,* pp. 240–41.

28. T. R. Blackburn, "Sensuous-Intellectual Complementarity in Science," *Science,* 172 (1971), 1003–1007.

29. Louis R. Pondy, "Union of Rationality and Intuition in Management Action," in *The Executive Mind,* ed. Suresh Srivasva (San Francisco: Jossey-Bass, 1983).

30. Edgar H. Schein, "Organizational Socialization and the Profession of Management," *Industrial Management Review,* 9 (1968), 115; John Van Manaan, "Breaking In: Socialization to Work," in *Handbook of Work, Organization and Society,* ed. Robert Dubin (Chicago: Rand McNally & Company, 1976); R. R. Ritti and G. R. Funkhouser, *The Ropes to Skip and the Ropes to Know* (Columbus, OH: Grid, 1982).

31. Edgar H. Schein, *Organizational Culture and Leadership* (San Francisco: Jossey-Bass, 1985), p. 6.

32. Weick, "Managerial Thought."

33. Schein, *Organizational Culture,* p. 7.

34. Terrence E. Deal, "Cultural Change: Opportunity, Silent Killer or Metamorphosis?" in *Gaining Control of the Corporate Culture,* eds. Ralph H. Kilmann, Mary J. Saxton, Roy Serpa, and Associates (San Francisco: Jossey-Bass, 1985).

35. Karl E. Weick, "Cognitive Processes in Organizations," in *Research in Organizational Behavior,* Vol. 1, ed. Barry M. Staw (Greenwich, CT: JAI Press, 1979), pp. 41–74.

36. Kenneth Davis, *Human Behavior at Work: Human Relations and Organizational Behavior,* 4th ed. (New York: McGraw-Hill Book Company, 1972), p. 136.

37. Mary Parker Follett, "The Psychology of Consent and Participation," in *Dynamic Administration: The Collected Papers of Mary Parker Follett,* ed. Henry C. Metcalf and Lyndall Urwick (New York: Harper & Row, Publishers, 1941), pp. 210–12.

38. Edwin M. Bridges, "A Model for Shared Decision Making in the School Principalship," *Educational Administration Quarterly,* 3, no. 1 (Winter 1967), 52.

39. Chester I. Barnard, *The Functions of the Executive* (Cambridge, MA: Harvard University Press, 1938).
40. Robert G. Owens and Edward Lewis, "Managing Participation in Organizational Decisions," *Group and Organization Studies,* 1 (1976), 56–66.
41. Ibid.
42. Ibid.
43. Robert Duncan, "Public Law 217 and the Administrative Team," *Indiana School Boards Association Journal,* 20 (1974), 10.
44. Ohio Department of Elementary School Principals, *The Administrative Team,* (1971), 2–3.
45. Harold J. McNally, "A Matter of Trust," *National Elementary Principal,* 53, no. 1 (November-December 1973), 23.
46. The five types of participation discussed here are from Edwin M. Bridges, "A Model for Shared Decision Making in the School Principalship," *Educational Administration Quarterly,* 3, no. 1 (Winter 1967), 52–59.
47. Ibid., p. 53.

Organizational Change

CHAPTER 9

ABOUT THIS CHAPTER

One of the dominant concepts to have emerged in the twentieth century is that of planned, controlled, and directed social change. It is a worldwide belief today that societies need not be confined to adaptive reaction to changing values and events as they unfold but that they can consciously direct the forces of change to suit predetermined goals and social values. A related and equally important trend, which has given impetus to the notion that social change can be successfully planned and managed, is the emphasis on the growing belief that planned and controlled change in *individual* lives is not only possible, but necessary if the long-range goals of each one of us are to be realized.

This dynamic concept of social change has been fueled and shaped by the theories and values from two principal sources: one is Marxist political and social theory, and the other is the empirically based social sciences largely as developed in the United States. The impact of this emerging concept on educational institutions and organizations has been extraordinary, for it implies that the processes of creating a desirable society require creating a compatible educational system. Although there is some debate about the power of educational systems to create societies, there is little argument that planned social change is supported by compatible educational systems.

Early in the century, prevailing views emphasized social change as flowing from economic and technological transformations in the world. Since mid-century, however, ever-increasing attention has been given to the centrality of social and cultural values as a dynamic in change processes. Clearly, in the second half of the twentieth century, for example, education has come to be viewed as a key to equality and equity in all societies. In this sense, education has been thrust into a central position in the political world, for deciding what equity is and what social values are crucial is clearly a political issue and not merely a technical educational issue. In order for an educational system to reflect the will of the political community, change in educational organizations cannot be planned and managed by educational policy makers alone: provision must be made for orchestrating the participation of all the social groups involved.

But educational organizations are expected not only to be vehicles for social change; they are expected also to preserve and transmit traditional values to younger members of society at the same time as they are expected to prepare them to deal with an ever-changing world. Thus, schools and other educational organizations must confront not merely change but, rather, the integration of stability *and* change. And, many observers, impatient to bring about change in schools, have pointed out again and again that the more things change in schools, the more they remain the same. Yet, as Matthew Miles has reminded us:

> many aspects of schools as organizations, and the value orientations of their inhabitants, are founded on history and constitute . . . genotypical properties. These are im-

portant to the schools; they help maintain continuity and balance in the face of the school's ambiguous mission and its vulnerability to external pressures from parents and others. Therefore, it is likely that, while rapid shifts in specific school practices are relatively more possible, changes touching on the central core of assumptions and structures will be far more difficult to achieve.[1]

SCHOOL REFORM AND CHANGE

Clearly, the school reform movement that was kicked off with publication of *A Nation at Risk* in 1983[2] has been the greatest and most sustained concerted national effort to change the central core of assumptions and structures of the public schools in the history of the Republic. Since its inception, "the country has been searching for some magical way to reform and restructure public schools. We have tried—and are still trying—all sorts of alchemical nostrums we hope will turn our educationally leaden schools into schools of educational gold."[3] Over the years the discourses on school reform have been well leavened with bold calls for sweeping changes such as restructuring education, reinventing schools, and recreating our educational goals for the year 2000. Yet so little had changed in U.S. schooling by 1990 that Seymour Sarason pondered the seeming intractability of the schools in face of years of reform effort and predicted the failure of educational reform[4] unless the strategies and tactics of change were, themselves, changed.

The essence of Sarason's analysis was that schools seemed to be intractable only because the strategies and tactics selected to carry out reform efforts had largely been ineffective in significantly altering the central core of assumptions and structures—that is to say, the organizational culture—of schools. He explained, as I discussed earlier in this book, that the nucleus of that core of organizational behavior is power, particularly the power of assumptions about power: especially whether power is assumed to be authority conferred or denied by one's position in the hierarchy or is assumed to arise from mutual collaboration among people of all levels and at every position in the organization. Thus, according to Sarason, if we want to bring about significant change in the schools, we must come to terms with the power of culture to shape the assumptions and beliefs of people in the school, the power that motivates, the power used in attempts to lead, the power to participate in making important decisions, the power that gives rise to organizational behavior in schools.

What is there about the strategies and tactics of the reform movement that have generally failed to make much progress in achieving reform? Sarason, one of the most astute observers of schools and change since 1971, thinks it is because school reform generally avoids dealing with power relationships in the school, which he sees as central to bringing about educational change.

Power Relationships and School Restructuring

School reform literally means to give new form to the school,[5] that is, to change the school in fundamental ways. This concept is popularly called restructuring. But the question is, how can schools be restructured? The key lies in changing power relationships in the school. How do we bring about such change? State legislatures and school boards usually try to change power relationships by mandate. For example, a legislature may mandate—as a number already have—that every school district in the state shall institute school site management by a certain date; legislators may say, "There, we've made a big change. We've changed the power relationships in every school district in this state." Or a school board may mandate, as was done in Chicago, that each school set up a community council, and the board members may think, "Now we've given the community greater power in deciding how things will be done in the schools. This will bring about great changes in the education of children." Clearly, then, those who wield legal hierarchical power can attempt to force change upon schools by altering the power relationships in them by fiat.

On the other hand, schools—like other organizations—can be changed from within. Sarason, for example, spoke approvingly about the Scanlon Plan, which was discussed in Chapter 6, as a way of altering power relationships voluntarily by involving everyone in the organization in the process of change. Noting that the Scanlon Plan has been used mostly in troubled industrial and business organizations, Sarason pointed out that the Scanlon Plan has made two major contributions to our thinking about bringing about organizational change in educational organizations:

+ It conceptualizes the organization as a whole, not this part or that part.

+ It is essentially and explicitly an educational rationale in that it seeks to promote the personal and vocational development of everyone. "I use the word *educational*," Sarason explained, "because it aims to expand people's knowledge of and commitment to their individual . . . growth."[6]

In short, Sarason pointed out that it is clearly possible to change educational organizations from the outside-in and from the top-down, and it is also possible to change them from the inside-out and from the bottom-up. If we are looking for changes in the central core of assumptions and structures of the school, rather than merely changes in the formal official aspects of the organization, the question becomes, which approach is the more effective of the two?

Aims of Educational Reform

For example, what kinds of changes does educational reform seek to bring about in the schools? What are the inner assumptions that we seek to change? From his analysis of the rhetoric, Sarason listed five aims that most agree would constitute major changes in the inner core of assumptions that are so difficult to bring about:

+ To reduce the wide gulf between the educational accomplishments of children of different social classes and racial backgrounds.

+ To get students to experience schooling as a process to which they are willingly attracted, not a compulsory one they see as confining and boring.

+ To enable students to acquire knowledge and skills that are not merely rote learning or memorized abstractions, but rather are acquired in ways that interrelate the learning and give personal purpose, now and in the future, to each student.

✦ To engender interest in and curiosity about human accomplishments, past and present. To get students to want to know how the present contains the past—that is, to want to know this as a way of enlarging their own identities: personal, social, and as citizens.

✦ To acquaint students with the domain of career options and how schooling relates to these options in a fast-changing world of work.[7]

If these encompass at least a substantial part of the aims of educational reform, what is there about the strategies and tactics of the reform movement that have generally failed to make much progress in achieving them? To answer that question, we turn to a brief discussion of the strategies and tactics of organizational change that are available to us.

THE TRADITION OF CHANGE IN AMERICAN EDUCATION

Historically, change in American education was viewed largely as a process of "natural diffusion." That is, new ideas and practices arose in some fashion and spread in some unplanned way from school to school and from district to district. The result was that schools generally changed very slowly: in the late 1950s Paul Mort observed that it then took about fifty years for a newly invented educational practice to be generally diffused and accepted in schools throughout the country and that the average school lagged some twenty-five years behind the best practice of the time.[8]

Natural Diffusion Processes

Mort observed a pattern to this unplanned process of diffusion:

> Educational change proceeds very slowly. After an invention which is destined to spread throughout the school appears, fifteen years typically elapse before it is found in three percent of the school systems. . . . After practices reach the three percent point of diffusion, their rate of spread accelerates. An additional 20 years usually suffices for an almost complete diffusion in an area the size of an average state. There are indications that the rate of spread throughout the nation is not much slower.[9]

This is well illustrated by the introduction and spread of kindergartens. In 1873—nearly twenty years after the introduction of private kindergartens to the United States from Germany—the city of St. Louis established the first public school kindergartens. By the mid-1950s, kindergarten education had been firmly established in the profession as a desirable educational practice, and, indeed, such federally funded projects as Head Start provided strong stimuli for spurring its development. However, as late as the 1967–1968 school year (ninety-four years after the introduction of kindergartens in St. Louis), only 46 percent of the nation's school districts provided kindergarten education for their children.[10]

For many years, Mort was considered the leading student of educational change in this country. The main thesis of his work was that adequacy of financial support is the key factor in determining how much lag a school system exhibits in adopting innovative practices. Vigorously active in his many years as a teacher and researcher at Teachers College, Columbia University, Mort left a storehouse of knowledge and a large number of devoted students who have heavily influenced the thinking of school administrators with regard to the factors that enhance change and innovation in schools. Largely because of this influence, per pupil expenditure has long been considered the most reliable predictor of a school's chances of adopting educational innovations.

The systematic underpinnings of the cost-quality relationship in education are generally felt to have been established in 1936 by Paul Mort and Francis Cornell's study of Pennsylvania schools.[11] Numerous studies dealing with the relationship between expenditure and measures of school output have followed, which generally support the not-too-surprising notion that high expenditure is generally associated with various indicators of superior school output. A troublesome fact was noted rather early in this research, however: it is possible for school districts to have high per pupil costs and still have inferior schools.[12] Considerable research has been undertaken since 1938 to explain this fact, much of it exploring the nature of the cost-quality relationship itself. Mort tended to think of this relationship as linear: more money would tend to assure higher educational quality, and there was no point of diminishing returns. Since 1965, however, increasing attention has been paid to the possibility that cost-quality relationships in education are actually curvilinear and have an optimum point beyond which additional expenditure fails to yield increased school output.[13]

Sociological Views of Diffusion

Although it would be absurd to say that penurious circumstances would enhance the schools' efforts to reduce the lag in change, more recent research tends to emphasize the influences of social structure on the amount and rate of change. For example, Richard O. Carlson studied the rate and pattern of the adoption of "new math" in a West Virginia county.[14] Carlson reported that the position that a superintendent of schools held in the social structure of the school superintendents of the county made it possible to make reasonable predictions about the amount and rate of innovation in that superintendent's school district. When the superintendent was looked on as a leader by his or her peers, as influential among other superintendents, and as being in communication with many of them, his or her district tended to adopt innovations early and thoroughly. Contrary to the bulk of existing research on cost-quality relationships, Carlson did not find a parallel between innovation and the financial support level of the school district. If nothing else, such studies—and Carlson's study represents only one of many sociological studies of organizational change and innovation—indicate that money spent is only one factor in the adaptability of schools, to use Mort's term. Within limits that are not yet clear, it is probably not even the major factor.

Planned, Managed Diffusion

The strategy by which money is spent may have a greater impact on change in schools than conventional indices such as per pupil expenditure may indicate. One of the more spectacular and better-known attempts to alter significantly the pattern of change in the public schools in the post-Sputnik era was undertaken by the Physical Science Study Committee (PSSC) in 1956, under the leadership of Professor J. R. Zacharias of the Massachusetts Institute of Technology.[15] Briefly, the PSSC group wanted to improve the teaching of physical science in U.S. high schools. Retraining thousands of teachers, developing new curricula for all sizes of school districts, and persuading the local school boards to buy the needed materials and equipment all might well have taken half a century to accomplish using traditional methods. Instead, within ten years after the project was inaugurated, high schools were considered to be behind the times if they did not offer a PSSC course.

This incredibly swift mass adoption was achieved by a strategy that involved three phases: (1) inventing the new curriculum, (2) diffusing knowledge of the new curriculum widely and rapidly among high school science teachers, and (3) getting the new curriculum adopted in local schools. This strategy involved the use of a number of new ideas. In addition to bypassing local school districts wherever possible, the PSSC group invested its money in novel and powerful ways. First, by spending $4.5 million in two and one-half years to hire a full-time professional "team," a portable, self-contained curriculum "package" was developed and tested in practice. This "package" included filmed lessons, textbooks, teachers' guides, tests, and laboratory guides and apparatus—a completely unified, integrated unit that could be moved *in toto* into almost any high school. Second, physics teachers were introduced to the new techniques by attending institutes, for which they received financial grants and stipends. Some forty institutes were made available each year throughout the country for this purpose. Third, by providing funds to be matched by the federal government (largely through the National Defense Education Act), the PSSC group persuaded local school boards to buy the package for their schools.

Three Strategies of Planned Change

Contemporary approaches to change are dominated by efforts to develop strategies and tactics that may enable us to plan, manage, and control change. In this book, the taxonomy suggested by Robert Chin is used as the basis for discussion.[16] As I shall explain, Chin posited that three major "strategic orientations" are useful in planning and managing change:

1. Empirical-rational strategies.
2. Power-coercive strategies.
3. Normative-reeducative strategies.

EMPIRICAL-RATIONAL STRATEGIES OF CHANGE

The traditional processes of unplanned dissemination of new ideas to schools have given way to strategies of planned, managed dissemination intended to spread new ideas and practices swiftly. Much research and study have been devoted to these strategies, which primarily focus on more closely linking the findings of research to the practices of education. This linkage requires improving communication between researchers and practitioners (users, consumers of research) so that the traditional, scornful distance between them will be replaced by a more productive, cooperative (if not collaborative) relationship.

This approach sees the scientific production of new knowledge and its use in daily activities as the key to planned change in education. It is referred to broadly as knowledge production and utilization (KPU). Numerous models for implementing the strategy have been proposed and tried; all of these attempt to develop an orderly process, with a clear sequence of related steps leading from the origination of new knowledge to its ultimate application in practice. The aim is to bridge the gap between theory and practice. To do this requires not only that the functions or activities of the process be described but also that someone (or some agency) be designated to carry them out.

Research, Development, and Diffusion (R, D, and D)

Various models for implementing KPU concepts of change appear under different appellations, depending on the number of steps that are seen as important. An R and D model, for example, suggests that someone ought to be conducting research and that someone ought to be developing some useful products from that research. As in all KPU models, research is meant here to be the invention or discovery of new knowledge, regardless of its applicability to immediate problems. In R and D work, the quality and validity of the research are of paramount importance. The model recognizes, however, that the research scientist is not always the person best equipped to translate research findings into useful products.

The *development* phase of R and D includes such things as solving design problems, considering feasibility in "real-world" conditions, and cost. Development essentially means translating research into products that are practical for use; these can range from school buildings to pupil seating, from textbooks to comprehensive packaged curricula, or from instructional techniques to new types of football helmets. In free enterprise societies this stage has been largely the province of profit-seeking firms that have the necessary financial resources and entrepreneurial skills.

The *diffusion* phase of R, D, and D is seen as a third and distinctive phase; it is, more or less, the "marketing" activities of R, D, and D. The aim is to make the new products readily available in attractive, easy-to-use form at reasonable cost to the adopter.

Of course, the ultimate goal is to get the new ideas into use. Some, therefore, treat *adoption* as a separate aspect of the process and may even call it research, development, dissemination, and adoption (R, D, D, A) to emphasize this point. As David Clark and Egon Guba have made clear,[17] the processes of adoption are not simple. They described a three-stage process: (1) *a trial,* during which the new product is tested in some limited way, (2) *installation,* a process of refinement and adaptation to local conditions if the trial appears promising, and finally—if all goes well—(3) *institutionalization,* which means that the innovation becomes an integral part of the system. A test of institutionalization is whether or not the invention continues in use if external support and encouragement are withdrawn. (See Figure 9–1.)

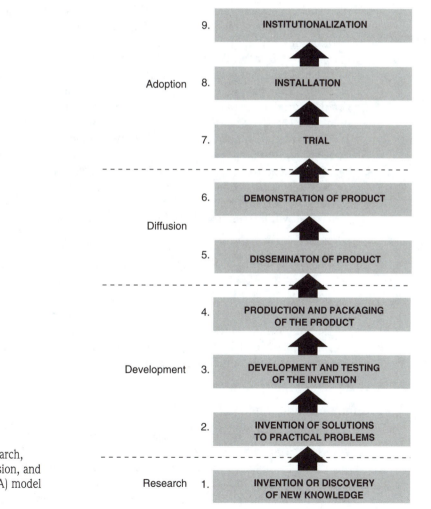

FIGURE 9–1

Concept of the Research, Development, Diffusion, and Adoption (R, D, D, A) model of change.

The "Agricultural Model"

It would be difficult to overemphasize the impact that the U.S. experience with planned, controlled change in agriculture has had on the thinking of those who advocate KPU strategies for education. Rural sociologists early discovered the processes and linkages that facilitated the rapid spread of new and better farming practices through the social system. The development of a network of land grant universities, agricultural experimentation stations, and the ubiquitous county agent are a few of the readily visible key parts of the extensive system that helps farmers to use new, yet proven, knowledge in the practical business of boosting production and lowering costs. When agriculture is compared to the public schools in terms of the speed with which new knowledge and techniques are put into widespread use, it is quickly apparent that agriculture has adopted innovations with far less lag than schools have. Thus, much of the model building and formalistic process development usually found in KPU approaches to change in education is based on efforts to replicate the "agricultural model" in terms appropriate to education.

Beginning in the late 1950s, federal activity was considerably increased in this direction. For example, the National Defense Education Act (NDEA) of 1958 triggered the production of the spate of innovative curriculum "packages" that appeared in the 1960s.[18] Title IV of the Elementary and Secondary Education Act (ESEA) of 1965 provided for the creation of twenty regional educational laboratories and ten Educational Research and Development Centers throughout the country. The Educational Resources Information Center (ERIC) also appeared, with federal support, in the 1960s. This nationwide network of twenty information clearinghouses seeks to facilitate the rapid communication of research and development activities in forms that will be useful to those in education. The National Institute of Education (NIE) was organized in 1972 expressly for the purpose of fostering research, experimentation, and dissemination of knowledge that could be applied to the improvement of public schooling. The creation of a cabinet-level Department of Education in the executive branch of the federal government in 1979 was strongly supported by many who believed that such an agency was needed to exercise greater order, system, and control in educational KPU. Thus, in a span of a quarter-century, the nation moved vigorously to systematize and stimulate planned KPU in education through federal leadership, in place of the traditional, relatively unplanned, scattered, local, and small-scale efforts of the past.

Assumptions and Implications of KPU Approaches to Change

KPU approaches to change are based on two critical assumptions: (1) that the new knowledge (product, technique) will be perceived by potential adopters as desirable and (2) that adopters—being rational and reasonable—will do what is desirable because it is in their own self-interest. In other words, "the belief is that good ideas will be used to improve education."[19] It typifies what Robert Chin has described as an *empirical-rational strategy of change:* that is, the new knowledge or practice is empirically demonstrated to be good, and, therefore, one rationally expects it to be adopted.[20] It is a strategy that fits neatly into the traditions and values of Western scientific-technological culture.

To facilitate adoption, new ideas have to reach the adopters in practicable form. Thus, the local physician uses a new "wonder drug" with patients in the office when it is available in convenient containers and when the directions permit easy application with familiar implements. Increasingly, schools are being offered relatively complete instructional "delivery systems" that seek to provide comprehensive "packages" for instruction that, in turn, are based on demonstrably effective concepts and are complete enough to meet a significant need of the school. These are often referred to as *innovations,* and much attention is given to the difficulties of "installing" innovations in schools.

The term "innovation" has been severely debased through misuse in the literature on organizational change and stability. Some people simply use it more or less as a synonym for "change." For example, H. G. Barnett posited that "innovation is any thought, behavior or thing that is new because it is qualitatively different from existing forms."[21] But such a broad generalization fails to convey the essence of innovation as it is used in organizational change. In fact, it fails to differentiate innovation from *organizational drift:* the inevitable, unplanned, incremental changes that pervade all organizations that exist in a culture whose dominant characteristic is change. Innovation has acquired a pejorative sense in educational circles owing to the frequency with which innovations have been introduced, tried, used, and abandoned.

In this book, the term *innovation* is used in referring to planned, novel, deliberate, specific change that is intended to help the organization (1) achieve existing goals more effectively or (2) achieve new goals. The concept of specificity is crucial: "innovations in education . . . ordinarily have a defined, particular, specified character."[22] Thus, one usually speaks of *an* innovation as something that can be specified in terms of (a) concepts, (b) a set of operating procedures, and (c) a relevant technology to which we attach a name (for example, magnet schools, alternative education, DISTAR reading program, individually prescribed instruction, and minimal competency testing). Thus, not all organizational change can be described as innovation; indeed, as I shall describe shortly, much desirable organizational change is not necessarily innovative in the sense that the term is used here.

The point to be emphasized, however, is that such empirical-rational strategies of change as KPU and R, D, and D tend to focus on innovation. The concept is that good ideas are developed outside the school and are, ultimately, *installed* in the school. Thus, there is much concern about problems of disseminating the innovation and of installing the innovation in adopting schools. At the installation level, those who favor the innovation see it as empirically proven and view adoption as rational; conversely, they tend to view barriers to installation at the school level as nonrational (if not irrational). It is at this point that the empirical rationalist becomes concerned, not with *educational* change in a broad sense, but with *organizational* change to facilitate the adoption process.

Other Empirical-Rational Strategies

To simplify this discussion, I have focused on one empirical-rational strategy, namely, linking basic research to practice by building diffusion networks and stimulating applied research. This typically involves creating research and development centers, linking state education departments to regional educational laboratories, and developing consortia of universities and school districts. Other empirical-rational strategies for change include the following.

Personnel Selection and Replacement

This strategy includes "clearing out the dead-wood" (through dismissal, early retirement, reorganization, transfers), as well as changing the criteria for the certification and employment of new people. Though many proponents of school reform advocated use of this strategy in the 1980s, many administrators confronted with a chronic shortage of teachers considered it of problematic value.

Utopian Thinking

Futurists seek to develop scientific techniques for improving forecasting of the future. Their efforts are, of course, based on the highly rational premise that skill in predicting the future can be helpful in making decisions at the present time. Their empirical rational attempts to project what *might* exist in the future, what the alternatives may be, and what *ought* to be can lead to planned efforts to direct the course of events toward some desired goal, rather than to accept whatever may occur.

POWER-COERCIVE STRATEGIES OF CHANGE

A power-coercive approach to change differs significantly from an empirical-rational one in its willingness to use (or threaten to use) *sanctions* in order to obtain compliance from adopters. Sanctions are usually political, financial, or moral. In the power-coercive point of view, rationality, reason, and human relations all are secondary to the ability to effect changes directly through the exercise of power.

One way of exercising political power is to gain control over the political institutions that pass legislation, issue executive orders, and hand down court decisions. These are commonly accompanied by financial sanctions to heighten their coercive effect. The popularity of this strategy in the United States is visible in the welter of legislation, judicial decisions, and governmental regulations—each with sanctions for noncompliance—that draw so much time and attention from educational policymakers and administrators.

Robert Chin and Kenneth Benne described the restructuring of power elites as another power-coercive strategy to bring about change.[23] It is well recognized that our society has a power structure in which relatively limited groups have extraordinary power to effect change, either to make things happen or to keep them from happening. Instead of accepting the existing power structure as fixed and inevitable, it is possible to change the power structure. If this is done—either by shifting power to new hands or by spreading power more equitably among more people—it is possible to achieve new goals.

This has, of course, been well illustrated by the efforts of minority groups and women to gain representation in the key decision-making groups concerning schools, such as school boards, administrative positions, and boards that control finances. It is illustrated, too, by teachers—long maintained in a powerless and dependent state—who have unionized in an effort to shift their power relationships with administrators and school boards so as to bring about change. A third illustration is the coalition of groups concerned about the education of the handicapped, which has resulted in a series of laws and judicial decisions that have sharply rearranged the power structure in some key areas of educational decision making.

A THIRD STRATEGY: ORGANIZATIONAL SELF-RENEWAL

Both empirical-rational and power-coercive strategies of change share two assumptions: (1) that good ideas are best developed outside of the organization and (2) that the organization is the target of external forces for change. Implicit in these strategies is the notion that organizations—when left to their own devices—generally emphasize stability over change and generally are resistant to change; they therefore must be *made* to change. There is little question that both of these strategic orientations are effective under certain conditions. But there also is little question that educational organizations have demonstrated remarkable resilience in dealing with these external forces for change by maintaining considerable stability over time and often frustrating even vigorous empirical-rational and power-coercive efforts. The nature and extent of this frustration are illustrated by research conducted by the Rand Corporation for the United States Office of Education between 1973 and 1977.

The Rand Study of Federal Programs Supporting Educational Change

The concerns that led to this research were well expressed in 1975, in a publication of the National Institute of Education, which reflected the then-prevailing mood of the Congress:

> Over the past decade and a half, the federal government has spent over a billion dollars on research and development on the country's educational problems, and billions more on categorical aid to schools and districts. Yet, the problems remain intractable, and the repeated research finding that innovations produce "no significant differences" has engendered such frustration that some have begun to despair of the schools' potential for improvement. A disturbingly familiar national behavior pattern is beginning to manifest itself in education. We are a "can-do," "quick-fix" society. The answer to a problem is a program. If the program fails, we try another one, and if a whole series of programs fails, we tire of that problem and go on to fresher ones.[24]

In an effort to understand this situation, Rand undertook a study of federally funded programs that had been designed to introduce and spread innovative practices in public schools. "These change agent programs," it was noted, "normally offer temporary federal funding to school districts as 'seed money.' If an innovation is successful, it is assumed that the district will incorporate and spread part or all of the project using other sources of funds."[25] (Recall the discussion earlier in this chapter concerning the adoption and institutionalization of innovations, and see again Figure 9–1.)

The study consisted of a series of related investigations of 293 projects in eighteen states sponsored under the following federal programs:

1. Elementary and Secondary Education Act (ESEA), Title III—Innovative Projects.
2. ESEA, Title VII—Bilingual Projects.
3. Vocational Education Act, 1968 amendments, Part D—Exemplary Programs.
4. Right to Read Program.

The research focused on two main issues: (1) the kinds of strategies and conditions that tend to promote change in the school and the kinds that do not and (2) the factors that promote or deter the institutionalization of innovation (which has been tried and adopted) after the federal "seed money" runs out.[26]

Although there is no pretense of summarizing this large and complex research here, the salient finding is clear: the differences among school districts in the extent to which they successfully adopted and implemented innovations are explained not so much by either (1) the nature of the innovation itself or (2) the amount of federal funding but, rather, are explained more by the *characteristics of the organization and the management of the local school districts and schools themselves.* For example:

> In cases of successful implementation, the districts were generally characterized by . . . a "problem-solving" orientation. That is, they had identified and frequently had already begun to attack the problem before federal money became available. By contrast, failures in implementation were associated with an "opportunistic" orientation. These districts simply supplemented their budgets with money that happened to be available.[27]

School districts that were successful in implementing innovative programs tended, also, to exhibit other characteristics:

+ They tended to reject rigidly packaged innovations that did not permit adaptation to local conditions.
+ They were strongly involved in developing their own local materials, rather than simply adopting materials that had been developed elsewhere.
+ They engaged in continuous planning and replanning rather than in "one-shot" planning at the beginning of a project.

✦ They engaged in ongoing training of people as needs arose in the projects and as defined by the participants (rather than in "one-shot" training at the outset or in having training needs identified by outside "experts").

✦ Consistent technical assistance was available locally for projects, rather than one or two-day visits from outside "experts."

✦ Innovative projects received strong support from key administrators at both the district and the school levels (for example, superintendent of schools and principal).

In sum, this research gives strong support to the view, long held by applied behavioral scientists, that organizational characteristics of the target school systems and schools at which empirical-rational and power-coercive strategies of change are aimed are crucial to determining the effectiveness of those schools *and* their capacity to change.

In the words of the NIE report, increasing of productivity is not primarily

> a problem which can be solved by installing new accountability systems, teaching administrators improved purchasing techniques, or utilizing superior technology, but is a problem of improving the organizational culture (problem-solving and decision-making structures, incentives to change, skills in managing collaborative planning and implementation, mutual support and communication, opportunities for relevant training, etc.) in which people work.[28]

This development at the local school district and school level is viewed as a necessary precondition to effective utilization of knowledge, no matter how it is produced, packaged, and disseminated:

> No matter how good the channels which transmit knowledge and products to practitioners, it appears that such products will spread slowly and see little effective use until schools and districts develop the capacity to engage in an active search for solutions to their own problems, to adapt solutions to the particulars of their own situation, and equally important, to adapt themselves as organizations to the requirements of the selected solutions.[29]

A Normative-Reeducative Strategy

These views express the essence of the third major strategy orientation to change identified by Chin: the normative-reeducative strategy. This orientation is based on an understanding of organizations and people in them that is quite different from the orientation usually held by the empirical-rational or power-coercive views, which are essentially classical or bureaucratic and tend to see the organization as a creation apart from people. Organization theory, in this view, "deals with human *response* to organization rather than with human activity in *creating* organizations."[30]

Normative-reeducative strategies of change, on the other hand, posit that the norms of the organization's interaction-influence system (attitudes, beliefs, and values—in other words, culture) can be deliberately shifted to more productive norms by collaborative action of the people who populate the organization. Andrew Halpin would describe this as shifting from a closed climate to a more open climate. In George Stern's terminology it would be enhancing development press of the organizational climate. Rensis Likert would speak of moving away from System 1 management style toward System 4 (see Chapter 5).

Organizational Health

To be effective, an organization must accomplish three essential core activities *over time:*

1. Achieve its goals.
2. Maintain itself internally.
3. Adapt to its environment.[31]

Thus, the organization must be effective, stable, yet capable of changing appropriately. Organizations differ in their abilities to accomplish these things; in other words, they exhibit different degrees of *organizational health.* A healthy organization "not only survives in its environment, but continues to cope adequately over the long haul, and continuously develops and extends its surviving and coping activities. Short-run operations on any particular day may be effective or ineffective, but continued survival, adequate coping, and growth are taking place."[32]

The unhealthy organization, on the other hand, is steadily ineffective. It may cope with its environment effectively on a short-term basis with a "crash program," a concentrated drive to meet a particularly threatening situation, or other "administration-by-crises" techniques, but in the long run the unhealthy organization becomes less and less able to cope with its environment. Rather than gaining in its ability to cope with a situation, it declines in this capacity over time and tends to become dysfunctional.

No single output measure or time slice of organizational performance can provide a reliable, accurate measure of organizational health: a central concern is the organization's continuing ability to cope with change and to adapt to the future. This ability is best viewed in the perspective of time. There are, however, some relatively specific indicators of organizational health:

1. *Goal focus.* This is the extent to which people in the organization understand and accept the achievable and appropriate goals of the organization.
2. *Communication adequacy.* This is vertical and horizontal internal communication and external communication with the environment, and the ease and facility of communication (as against the amount of "noise" and "distortion" that can inhibit and confuse communication).
3. *Optimal power equalization.* An important element of this dimension is the issue of collaboration versus coercion.

4. *Human resources utilization.* This is the effective use of personnel, so that they—as persons—feel that they are growing and developing in their jobs.

5. *Cohesiveness.* This is the extent to which participants like the organization and want to remain in it in order to influence the collaborative style.

6. *Morale.* This is exhibited as feelings of well-being and satisfaction.

7. *Innovativeness.* This is the tendency to devise new procedures and goals, to grow, to develop, and to become more differentiated over a period of time.

8. *Autonomy.* Rather than being merely a "tool of the environment" that responds passively to outside stimuli, the autonomous organization tends to determine its own behavior in harmony with external demands.

9. *Adaptation.* Healthy organizations should be able to change, correct, and adapt faster than the environment.

10. *Problem-solving adequacy.* This includes mechanisms for sensing and perceiving problems, as well as those for solving problems permanently and with minimum strain.[33]

Organization Self-Renewal

It is a commonplace observation, of course, that organizations have a tendency to atrophy over time, becoming obsessed with maintaining themselves, increasing bureaucratic rigidity, and seeking to shore up traditional practices. In a world characterized by rapid change, such organizations tend to be viewed as *un*healthy, emphasizing maintenance of the organization at the expense of the need for constant adaptability so as to keep pace with the change in the demands and expectations of its external environment.

The concept of organization self-renewal was first comprehensively described by Rensis Likert in 1961.[34] He described ways of managing the interaction-influence system of the organization in ways that would stimulate creativity, promote growth of people in the organization, and facilitate solution of the organization's problems. In 1969 Gordon Lippitt elaborated a well-developed approach to the processes of renewal based on the view that every organization has a life cycle (birth-youth-maturity) with different renewal needs at each stage of its existence.[35] As early as 1967, Matthew Miles and Dale Lake described an application of the concept to school systems in the Cooperative Project for Educational Development.[36]

Organization self-renewal postulates that effective change cannot be imposed on a school; rather, it seeks to develop an internal capacity for continuous problem solving. The processes of renewal include the increased capacity to (1) sense and identify emerging problems, (2) establish goals, objectives, and priorities, (3) generate valid alternative solutions, and (4) implement a selected alternative. An outcome of renewal processes is to shift the culture of the school from emphasis on traditional routines and bureaucratic rigidity toward a culture that actively supports the view that much of the knowledge needed to plan and carry out change in schools is possessed by people in the schools themselves.[37] Further, it recognizes that "the optimal unit for educational change is the single school with its pupils, teachers, principal—those who live there every day—as primary participants."[38]

The self-renewing school possesses three essential characteristics: *First,* a culture that supports adaptability and responsiveness to change. Such a culture is supportive of open communication, especially from the bottom upward, and values problem solving as a high priority. *Second,* a set of clear-cut, explicit, and well-known procedures through which participants can engage in the orderly processes of systematic, collaborative problem solving. *Third,* such a school is not a parochial institution relying solely on internal energy, ideas, and resources for solving problems. Rather, it is a school that knows when and how to reach out to seek appropriate ideas and resources for use in solving its problems.[39]

Organization Development (OD)

Organization development (OD) is the principal process for increasing the self-renewal capability of school districts and schools. OD has been defined in many ways because it is difficult to capture the full essence of such a complex approach to improving organizational performance. However, after a comprehensive study of OD in American and Canadian schools, Michael Fullan, Matthew Miles, and Gib Taylor offered this definition in 1978:

> Organization development in school districts is a coherent, systematically-planned, sustained effort at system self-study and improvement, focusing explicitly on change in formal and informal procedures, processes, norms or structures, using behavioral science concepts. The goals of OD include *both* the quality of life of individuals as well as improving organizational functioning and performance.[40]

In practice, OD involves a cluster of at least ten concepts that characterize the process:

1. The goal of OD.
2. System renewal.
3. A systems approach.
4. Focus on people.
5. An educational strategy.
6. Learning through experience.
7. Dealing with real problems.
8. A planned strategy.
9. Change agent.
10. Involvement of top-level administration.

Each of these ten OD concepts is briefly described as follows.[41]

1. The Goal of OD

The primary goal of OD is to improve the functioning of the organization itself. Improving the productivity and effectiveness of the organization is seen as largely dependent on developing the organization's capability to make better quality decisions about its affairs—decisions affecting its structure, its tasks, its use of technology, its use of human resources, and its goals. The primary approach to this is to develop a work-oriented culture in the organization that will maximize the involvement of the organization's people in more effective decision making regarding matters of importance to them and to the goals of the organization.

Although OD may very well lead to the adoption of a new program or curriculum, to a restructuring of the organization, or to a commitment to new goals, these are not considered to be first steps to improved effectiveness of schools and school systems. Neither does OD assume—as some have speculated—that significant organizational change will result from programs limited to improving the personal and interpersonal skills of individuals or groups, whether through counseling, sensitivity training, conventional education, or any other means. This is not likely to be enough to alter significantly established norms that shape the work-related behavior of the organization: rules, expectations, traditions, and habits.

2. System Renewal

Organization development rejects the notion that atrophy is inevitable in organizations. Stated positively, the view is that an organization can develop self-renewing characteristics, enabling it to increase its capability, to adapt to change, and to improve its record of goal achievement.

This concept of system self-renewal sees the organization not as being helplessly buffeted about by exigencies and changes thrust on it, but as growing in its ability to initiate change, to have an increasing impact on its environment, and to develop an increasing capability to adapt to new conditions and solve new problems over time. Perhaps more important is its ability to develop a growing sense of purpose and direction over time. The view is of an energized system marked by increasing vitality and imaginative creativity.

The self-renewal concept is at the center of the difference between organization development and organization improvement. The goal is not merely to overcome an immediate problem and arrive at a new "frozen" state of organizational functioning. The concept is one of building into the organizational system the conditions, the skills, the processes, and the culture that foster continual development of the organization over a sustained period of time. Although OD may be triggered by a specific event—such as initiating a new school or facing up to community criticism—the event itself merely provides an entry point for action.

If OD techniques are used to develop responses to the event and then are dropped, rather than continued and extended, then the project is not OD at all but another piecemeal change effort so characteristic of public schools. The concept of management by crisis is so firmly embedded in U.S. educational administration that developing planned, systematic, and sustained approaches has quite possibly become the central problem of administering change in schools.

3. A Systems Approach

Organization development is based on the concept of the organization as a complex sociotechnical system. Such a view of the organization, of course, emphasizes the wholeness of the organizational system and the dynamic interrelatedness of its component subsystems: human, structural, technological, and task.

The school, for example, is a sociotechnical system. It comprises subsystems, of course—departments, grade levels, informal groups, teams, and work groups—that are in a constant state of dynamic interrelationship. The school is also a subsystem of larger systems: the school district, for example, and the community in which it functions.

As we have described, such a view has fundamental implications for those concerned with administering organizational change; these are translated into certain fundamental assumptions:

1. To effect change that has long-range staying power one must change the whole system and not merely certain of its parts or subsystems.

2. Moreover, because of the dynamic interrelatedness and interdependency of the component subsystems, any significant change in a subsystem will produce compensatory or retaliatory changes in other subsystems.

3. Events very rarely occur in isolation or from single causes. Systems concepts of the organization emphasize the importance of dealing with events as manifestations of interrelated forces, issues, problems, causes, phenomena, and needs. The world of the organization is recognized as the complex system that it is, and ascribing single causation to phenomena or treating events as isolated incidents can mask our full understanding of them.

4. The organizational system is defined, not by walls or membranes, but by existing patterns of human behavior. These patterns are not static, but are in constant dynamic equilibrium—as Kurt Lewin's concept of force-field analysis illustrates. Therefore, the crucial information that the administrator requires comes from analyzing the specific field of forces at a particular time, rather than from analyzing generalized historical data from the past or from other organizations.

4. Focus on People

The main concern for OD is the human social system of the organization, rather than task, technology, or structure dimensions. Specifically, the focus is on the organizational culture that characterizes the climate of beliefs influencing behavior—such as the ways in which superordinates and subordinates deal with one another, the ways in which work groups relate to each other, and the extent to which people in the organization are involved in identifying organizational problems and seeking solutions to them. Attitudes, values, feelings, and openness of communication are typical concerns for OD. It matters what people think, how open their communication is, how they deal with conflict, and to what extent they feel involved in their jobs, because these kinds of human concerns help determine how much work gets done and how well. People who have learned to keep their thoughts to themselves, to be discreet in proffering a new idea or in voicing doubt or criticism, contribute little to the organization's ability to diagnose its problems and find solutions. The culture of many schools encourages this kind of behavior—leaving decisions to the upper echelons and frowning upon lower participants who "cause trouble" by raising questions.

Commonly, the school's culture carefully structures organizational behavior so as to minimize open, free, and vigorous participation in central decisions—witness the typical faculty meeting with its crowded agenda of minutiae or the superintendent's *pro forma* appearances before the staff, which are filled with routine platitudes. Organizations with such characteristics tend to be relatively inflexible, slow to change, and defensive in a fast-changing environment.

In the OD view, one of the great resources available to an organization trying to improve its effectiveness is its own people. By encouraging people to become involved, concerned participants, rather than making them feel powerless and manipulated by unseen and inscrutable forces, the organization can draw ever-increasing strength, vitality, and creativity from its people.

5. An Educational Strategy

Organization development seeks to stimulate organization self-renewal by changing the behavior of people in the organization in significant ways through education. In this sense, however, education has little relationship to conventional, in-service education concepts that usually (1) are chiefly concerned with the acquisition of cognitive knowledge and (2) take place in a typical classroom setting that emphasizes the learner as a dependent recipient of knowledge.

The educational strategy and processes of OD primarily focus on the elements important to shaping the organizational climate and culture of the organization: the complex web of dynamic organizational variables that so deeply influences the way that people feel about their role in the organization, the attitudes and expectations they develop toward their coworkers, and the quality of the relationships between individuals and groups within the organization. Conventionally, these kinds of problems— involving conflict, communication barriers, suspicion and fear, and questions of organizational effectiveness—have been skirted carefully in organizations: they are too "touchy," too sensitive to treat adequately. OD seeks ways not only to face such problems, which are central to the organization's functioning, but also to increase the participants' abilities to solve them in productive ways. Because it changes the norms of the organization through a strategy of study and learning the process is a normative-reeducative strategy.

6. Learning Through Experience

The concept of learning by doing applied to organizational life is the basis for learning in OD. Educative techniques strongly stress the building of knowledge and skill in organizational behavior through a two-step, experience-based process in which a work-related group of people (1) shares a common experience and then (2) examines that experience to see what it can learn from it.

This can be done in relatively controlled conditions of laboratory training, such as in a T-group. It also can be a study of real-life experiences that group members actually have shared in the organization. But the basis for learning is the group's actual experience, not hypothetical situations. The group members are encouraged to question and to raise issues concerning group functioning, drawing insights and learning directly from this experience.

One purpose of this insistence on examining experience in this way is to develop within the participants a long-lasting set of techniques and understandings that will enable them to learn and profit repeatedly from their own experiences over a sustained period of time. If this can be developed as a significant part of the group life of an organization, it can be a strong element of the desired self-renewal process.

7. Dealing with Real Problems

Organization development is applied to an organization in order to deal with existing, pressing problems. In some cases these problems may be serious enough to threaten the very survival of the organization, although they usually are not so dramatic. The educational processes do not involve learning about someone else's problem or discussing general cases but are directed to the specific organization under consideration—with its special conditions that make it unique.

What kind of problems might call for OD in a school? An attempt to catalogue such a wide range of possibilities would not be helpful, but it might be useful to mention a few typical situations:

1. Conditions of rapid change—such as a major school-district reorganization or the result of a sweeping court order—that might promote an "identity crisis" and organizational confusion of considerable magnitude.

2. A leadership crisis, such as when a new superintendent finds that there is little response to his or her initiatives.

3. Poor organizational effectiveness (however it is measured) that must be resolved in ways other than defensiveness or seeking excuses.

4. A high level of conflict, whether evidenced by excessive bickering and infighting or by the apathy characteristic of withdrawal from too painful a situation.

Often, of course, these kinds of problems are interrelated; opening up one for examination and solution may well lead to other problems that were not considered to be of great concern at the outset. This heuristic characteristic of OD concepts and processes has great power to penetrate to the central problems of the organization. Therefore, the major criterion in identifying the problem to be worked on in the initial stages is that it be of genuine concern to the organization's participants— something they feel is important to them, rather than something about which only someone else is concerned.

Organization development efforts should be viewed in the long-term sense suggested by the self-renewal concept, enabling the process to start from seemingly superficial problems and eventually reach the core. Thus, OD is not a one-shot approach to the alleviation of some limited, narrowly defined crisis, after which it will be abandoned. Indeed, as OD techniques become more popular and respectable in the eyes of administrators and managers, there is rising concern that the demand for such a "Band-Aid" approach (identifying OD with management by crisis rather than with the development of self-renewal) could discredit more ethical OD approaches.

8. A Planned Strategy

Another characteristic of OD—again in harmony with its overall systems approach— is that the effort must be planned systematically. The technology of OD embraces a wide range of possible activities and techniques. But they, in themselves, do not constitute OD. Indeed, a defining characteristic of OD is that it is a form of planned change: a strategy in which goals have been identified and a design for achieving them has been laid out. The plan must be specific: identifying target populations, establishing a timetable, and committing resources necessary to its fulfillment. The plan also must be specifically tailored to the particular circumstances of the organization.

Emphasizing the importance of a plan for OD should not imply rigidity. Indeed, if the effort is initially successful, it is probable that the increasing involvement of participants will require modifying and shaping the plan over time. It is important to provide for this in the planning stages, lest the effort turn into just another in-service program. Conversely, however, haphazard introduction of bits and pieces of OD technology, without clear purposive planning and the commitment to carry it through, can do more harm than good.

It has been noted, for example, that the decision to undertake OD in an organization can, in itself, produce some organizational improvement: it is often a signal to members involved that the culture is changing and that new ideas and new ways of doing things are becoming more of a possibility and reality. Obviously, a badly mounted OD program or the sudden termination of one that has been started following raised hopes (because, perhaps, of the administrator's timidity or the lack of sufficient resources for the program) can result in an understandable backlash of feeling.

An OD program is a complex and sophisticated undertaking; it involves a wide range of possible interventions that deal with potentially sensitive matters. A highly qualified OD specialist often can facilitate the planning and carrying out of such a program by helping the administrator develop a practical OD design tailored to the specific realities of his or her organization. The designing of an OD project offers both the administrator and the behavioral scientist the rare opportunity to collaborate in a common cause.

9. Change Agent

OD is characterized by the participation of a change agent who has a vital and very specific role to play, at least in the initial stages of the change effort. Indeed, OD—in the various forms currently known to us—is impossible without a competent change agent. This person may have various official titles in different organizations; regardless, the term "consultant" is almost always used among OD practitioners to refer to the specialist who helps an organization design and carry out an OD program.

The consultant is so vital to the success or failure of OD that a substantial part of the literature is devoted to descriptions of his or her role, function, and specialized competencies, the nature of his or her relationships to client organizations, and so forth.

Finding an appropriate consultant and establishing an effective working relationship with him or her may well be the administrator's most crucial role in establishing OD in his or her school. Indeed, the need for consultant help has been the source of some of the thorniest problems in implementing OD. There can be much confusion, under the best of circumstances, about the consultant: what his or her role is, from whom he or she takes orders, what impact his or her presence has on the usual relationships between administrators and teachers—these are some of the problem areas that commonly appear in OD work. They are the subject of considerable study and discussion among OD consultants themselves, as they attempt to shape their own roles in appropriate ways.

In general terms, consultants may be either from outside the organization (external consultants) or from within the organization (internal consultants). In its early history, OD efforts depended exclusively on external consultants. Of course, the relationship of the external consultant to the organization is temporary and requires that extra money be found to cover the consulting fees. One reaction to this has been efforts to train individuals appropriately so that they may function as internal consultants;[42] typically, once such a position has been budgeted, it tends to become a long-term, institutionalized arrangement. It appears likely that the role of internal change agents, or consultants, will become increasingly visible and formalized in school districts in the years ahead. However, the need for external consultants to deal with particularly complex and difficult problems of change will probably not be completely eliminated.

Some limited progress has been made in developing procedures for carrying out certain crucial aspects of OD activities without the direct assistance of behavioral science consultants.[43] At this stage of the development of OD, however, the consultant is a key individual. Policy and administration problems in dealing with OD consultants are discussed later in this book.

10. Involvement of Top-Level Administration

Inevitably, one must conclude from the social systems orientation of OD that one cannot change part of the system in constructive ways without affecting other parts of the system. For example, management cannot presume to change the organization without being part of the process. Organizational change is not a matter of "us" (the administration) changing "them" (the teachers and other subordinates) or even of changing "it" (the organization as some sort of entity detached from "us"). Administration must be an active partner involved in the development process to assure that all subsystems of the organizational system stay appropriately linked together in the dynamic, interactive way. This is one of the identifying characteristics of the increasingly effective organization.

In operational terms, OD recognizes that organizations are hierarchical and will continue to be so. When subordinates see that the administration is doing something to organizations in the name of improving their effectiveness—something in which administrators are not involved except as observers—the subordinates are very likely to be wary and less than fully committed. On the other hand, if the administration is already interested in the undertaking, committed to it, and involved in visible ways, subordinates are much more inclined to view the effort as valid and will be more highly motivated to involve themselves. In any organization, subordinates tend to develop highly sensitive antennae that pick up reliable indications of what is really important at higher levels through all the static and noise that may surround the issuance of official statements.

This was illustrated in the case of a large suburban school district. Located in a highly industrialized community, the district was undergoing the stresses and strains related to the social and ethnic problems that have become so commonplace in recent years. The new superintendent—who was young, bright, articulate, energetic, and had with an enviable record in other districts—moved early to bring the principals and other key administrators together and organize them as a team. With a new and greater opportunity to play a crucial role in establishing policy and dealing with districtwide problems, this group was soon involved in important, districtwide issues that had significant implications for each school. Unfortunately, the team quickly ran into difficulties: wrangling broke out, decisions arrived at in meetings were undercut by private deals made outside of the team (often involving school board members), and some members created an alliance to control voting on issues before the team on the basis of the self-interest of their departments or schools. A number of principals—who had enjoyed considerable autonomy under the previous superintendent to "wheel and deal" with school board members in behalf of their individual schools—felt that the whole team idea was simply a scheme to undermine them. The superintendent discussed these problems with the group and won easy agreement that a consultant should be brought in to help them find solutions.

During an exploratory meeting, the consultant was able to establish a basis for working with the group. In addition to agreeing on some goals and some modes of operating, the group agreed to certain ground rules. One, suggested by the consultant and quickly supported unanimously, was that all members of the group must attend each scheduled training session, if at all possible. This was a highly capable and sophisticated group, and within a few meetings with the consultant there was a general feeling that real progress was being made and that the training effort should be continued. At the session following that decision, the superintendent announced that—because of the eruption of an unforeseen crisis—he would have to rush off soon after the group convened.

At the next session, he strongly endorsed the training effort and expressed keen interest in it but had to hurry off to another emergency. At the subsequent session, three principals—after a decent interval—withdrew and hurried off to attend to "emergencies" at their schools. Needless to say, the superintendent's team members realized that, as soon as the original crisis had eased, the training program no longer was a high priority matter at the top, and they responded accordingly.

A Sociotechnical View

Those who are inexperienced in participative approaches to management often think of them as being "soft," "permissive," and incompatible with the structure, discipline, and power that characterize organizations. In fact, however, what is needed is a new, more effective, approach to management: an approach that stresses more functional administrative structures and seeks more effective organizational behavior. Although the new structures may well be more flexible and adaptable than those of the past, they will not be fuzzy or ill defined; neither will the more effective work-related behaviors be lacking in clear, exact description and definition.

When the administrator confronts the need for more involvement of staff in decision making or seeks to move the organization in a more "organic" or self-renewing direction, does it mean that system, orderly procedures, and control must be abandoned? The answer is, of course, negative. In fact, quite the opposite is true: the need is to provide organizational structures that will enhance and facilitate the development of more adaptive decision-making styles to replace the rigid hierarchical structures characteristic of the mechanistic organization.

The shift in organizational system development, then, is not away from the clarity, order, and control associated with traditional views of organizational structure toward an ill-defined, disorderly, laissez-faire administration. What is sought, administratively, is a new and more functional basis for *task* analysis, *structural* arrangements, selection and use of *technology,* and selection and professional development of individual *people* and groups of people on the staff.

The rationality of this view—which is a sociotechnical orientation—becomes increasingly apparent when we acknowledge that technological change and innovation are likely to play an increasingly important role in organizational change in schools in the future. The function of the administrator, then, is to develop organizational structures that—while providing clearly for such imperatives as coordination of effort toward goal attainment—assure the development of more adaptive ways of integrating people, technology, task, and structure in a dynamic, problem-solving fashion.

Force-Field Analysis

How can one analyze an organizational situation so as to better understand how to deal with it? Force-field analysis has proven to be a useful analytic approach for both the researcher and the administrator.[44]

Basically, this approach sees a social or organizational *status quo* as a state of equilibrium resulting from the balance between two opposing sets of forces. There are forces for change, sometimes called *driving forces,* and these are opposed by forces for remaining unchanged, sometimes called *restraining forces.* When these force fields are in balance, as in Figure 9–2, we have equilibrium—no change. Obviously, when one or another of these forces is removed or weakened, the equilibrium is upset and change occurs, as shown in Figure 9–3. On a very simple level, such an imbalance can be brought about by the introduction of a new work technique or the acquisition of new skills by participants. But an organization is essentially a stable entity generally characterized by equilibrium; an imbalance of equilibrium will bring about readjustments that will again lead to a new organizational equilibrium. This simple concept can become very complex when applied to a large-scale organization. But it also can be a practical aid to the administrator who seeks to understand his or her organization better so as to facilitate either change or stability in the organization. The analytic process of identifying restraining forces and driving forces ranges from a very simple approach at the rudimentary level to rather sophisticated techniques.

Force-field analysis eventually led its creator, Kurt Lewin, to a fundamental three-step change strategy that has come into increasingly popular use. It is predicated on the notion that in order to effect organizational change, it is first necessary to break the equilibrium of the force field: that is, the organization must be *unfrozen.* Once that is done, it is possible to introduce *change*—to move the organization to a new level. But no one knows better than educational administrators how fragile change can be, and how easily the organization can slip back into its old ways. Therefore, the third step in the three-step change process is *refreezing.* This is an

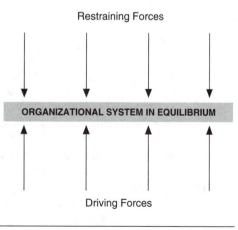

FIGURE 9–2
Force field in equilibrium.

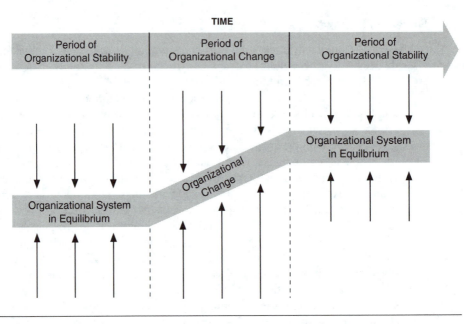

TIME

| Period of Organizational Stability | Period of Organizational Change | Period of Organizational Stability |

Organizational System in Equilibrium

Organizational Change

Organizational System in Equilbrium

FIGURE 9–3   Imbalance of force field causes organizational change until a new equilibrium is reached.

institutionalizing process that serves to protect and ensure the long-range retention of the change. Of course, refreezing smacks of a new *status quo;* in Lewin's view, the desired amount of flexibility could be built in by establishing "an organizational set up which is equivalent to a stable circular causal process."[45] Unfreezing can be a highly traumatic experience to a very rigid and resisting organization, But it can also be built in as a normal part of its life cycle, as suggested in Figure 9–4 in order to achieve greater organizational flexibility over time.

The value of a force-field analysis is diagnostic: it permits the preparation of plans for specific action designed to achieve the changes sought. The success of such a plan will depend in large measure on the clarity with which the likely consequences of proposed action are perceived. Of the four major organizational subsystems—task, technological, structure, and human—only the human subsystem has the capacity to react differentially to differing conditions.

Great art and literature teem with depictions of heroic achievements of people moved by such feelings as love, faith, courage, and duty. Much of the literature on organizations is concerned with apathy, anger, frustration, and apprehensions of people and their great power to inhibit the organization's goal achievement. Although administrators must be deeply concerned with the work to be performed in the school, the structure of the organization, and the technology that is used, none of these has the capability of resisting plans for action. It is only the human subsystem that has that capability.

But it is not productive for the administrator to view opposition to change in any form—whether as outright resistance, apathy, skepticism, or whatever—as obdurate

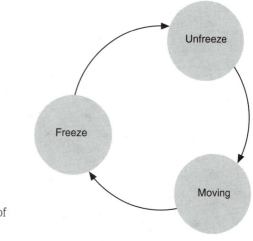

FIGURE 9–4
A three-step change process as an ongoing life cycle of
an organization.

behavior. If "increasing the driving forces" is interpreted by the administrator as meaning the stepped-up use of authority and power to get people behind the change effort, it is highly predictable that the result will be strong reactions against the change. Pressure generates counterpressure, and in the school setting, where the administrator's coercive power is sharply limited, it is not likely that the equilibrium of the force field can be broken by such an approach. At the very least, it is predictable that, as the pressure is relaxed—as it must be eventually—there will be a tendency for the organization to retreat to its old ways under the pressure of the restraining forces.

In school situations it is likely to be more effective to help bring the restraining forces into the open as legitimate in the process of change. By creating a culture in which feelings can be expressed instead of secretly harbored, by opening communication and valuing the right to question and challenge, and by helping those who would oppose the forces of change to examine and deal with the concerns that cause their resistance, it is likely that (1) unforeseen probable consequences of proposed actions would be brought into the planning process and, perhaps more important, (2) the level of resistance will be diminished.

As the opposition contributes to shape and mold decisions, its views are also shaped, molded, and modified in the process. *To obtain this kind of participation requires the existence of a developmental, or growth-enhancing, organizational culture that characteristically*

1. is intellectually, politically, and aesthetically stimulating.
2. emphasizes individual and group achievement.
3. places high value on the personal dignity of individuals.
4. accepts divergent feelings and views in a nonjudgmental way.
5. is oriented to problem solving rather than to winning or losing in intraorganizational skirmishes.

The establishment of orderly problem-solving processes that provide maximum participation for those who will be affected by the change is necessary to develop the collaborative approach suggested here. Although the point of view is important, it must be accompanied by effective specific procedures for making it work, creating the climate needed and assuring that the way in which decisions are reached is understood and workable. Development of a new organizational culture and building the group skills for open, collaborative decision making require definite training and practice. These things are not achieved through cognitive understanding and determination alone: they require the development of new insights, new values and commitments, and new group process skills that are best taught and learned in problem-solving situations.

It must be remembered that the creation of a new organizational culture—a new environment for working and solving problems—requires participants to develop new and more effective responses to events, to act differently than they have done in the past. As every educator is keenly aware, such changes in human functioning do not often occur as a result of learning *about* the new, more effective ways of doing things. Opportunities must be provided wherein the new behaviors may be developed in practice: in short, *learning by doing* is required. The goal is to develop new and more productive norms of work-oriented behavior through reeducation.

Change is likely to be stabilized and maintained in the organization over time, when the new, more effective level of performance can be maintained without coercion and without continuous expenditures of administrative energy and vigilance to keep it going. Indeed, this is one practical criterion by which the administrator may judge whether or not change has been "accomplished."

An appropriate plan for organizational change must take cognizance of these realities. It must also recognize that the goal of changing an organization in significant ways presents a challenge in terms of difficulty and in terms of the time span required. There are no quick and easy solutions, though there will probably never be a shortage of those who claim to possess such solutions. Hersey and Blanchard's admonition on this point is highly appropriate:

> Changes in knowledge are the easiest to make, followed by changes in attitudes. Attitude structures differ from knowledge structures in that they are emotionally charged in a positive or a negative way. Changes in behavior are significantly more difficult and time consuming than either of the two previous levels. But the implementation of group or organizational performance change is perhaps the most difficult and time consuming.[46]

RESEARCH ON THE EFFECTIVENESS OF OD

In reporting a major study of OD in schools, Fullan, Miles, and Taylor pointed out that a problem of assessing OD efforts to develop the self-renewal, problem-solving capacity of school systems and schools lies in the fact that many so-called OD projects are partial, incomplete, short-term activities lacking the planning, scope, and sustained effort required for success.[47] In many cases, for example, a few days of "human relations training" for teachers, or the use of an outside consultant for a few sessions, is incorrectly labeled an "OD project." Often the effort is limited to attempts to reduce conflict or otherwise to ameliorate unpleasant aspects of organizational culture, with little or no intention of significantly affecting organizational structure or processes of decision making. For reasons such as these, surveys of OD activities in education tend to show spotty success; yet those school districts that are successful with OD generally tend to institutionalize it and maintain it over time. Not a few school districts now have OD school renewal projects that have been functioning for a period of years.

Philip Runkel and Richard Schmuck, at the Center for Educational Policy and Management (CEPM) at the University of Oregon, have conducted the most comprehensive research and development work in this field. They began their work in 1967, and in 1974 they published the findings of their studies up to that time. In assessing whether or not OD has been successful in a district or school, they caution against accepting superficial claims about *any* effort at change:

> Our experience in looking for outcomes has taught us that they are not simple. . . . Editors of scientific journals and providers of funds should demand detailed documentation when a researcher claims that one or more schools have "installed" or "adopted" some particular new way of doing things. The depth and variety in the ways that a new structure such as team teaching can be installed or adopted in a school are stupefying, and so are the ways a principal can cover up with verbiage the fact that the innovation really has not taken hold in his school at all. Statements that go no farther than, "In a school that had adopted a team teaching the previous year, . . . " or "We shall install team teaching in X schools next year . . . ," should never be accepted without skepticism.[48]

Their findings regarding OD in schools include these:

+ Success is more likely when the school faculty senses a readiness to change and welcomes the OD project.
+ Entering into OD may be the most critical phase of the project and requires a skilled and experienced OD consultant to avoid hidden pitfalls.
+ Open, active support from administrators is critical to success.
+ OD is more likely to be helpful in a school in which the staff is in substantial agreement on goals.
+ An OD project can be thought of as consisting of four main phases: (1) entry, (2) diagnosis of organizational problems, (3) institutionalization, and (4) maintenance.

John Goodlad has been associated with studies of organizational change in public schools since the late 1940s. After witnessing the "continuing, frustrating failure of promising innovations to alter school practice in desired ways"[49] he undertook to lead a five-year research and development project addressing the prob-

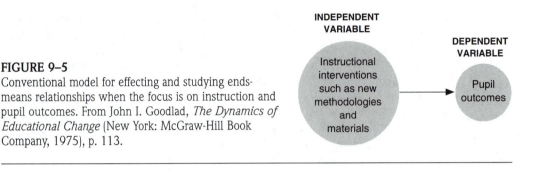

FIGURE 9–5

Conventional model for effecting and studying ends-means relationships when the focus is on instruction and pupil outcomes. From John I. Goodlad, *The Dynamics of Educational Change* (New York: McGraw-Hill Book Company, 1975), p. 113.

lems of personal and institutional renewal in education. Goodlad started by pointing out that the conventional model for studying educational change is to manipulate certain instructional interventions (such as class size or teaching method) and to look for changes in pupil outcomes. As shown in Figure 9–5, such a research design treats pupil outcomes as the dependent variable and instruction (for example, methods and materials) as the independent variable. However, Goodlad's long-term observation of the difficulty of installing and sustaining instructional reforms led him to realize that "the explanatory thesis for this difficulty . . . is that the regularities of the school sustain certain practices, through expectations, approval, and reward. Teachers, as individuals, usually are not able to run successfully against these regularities or to create the schoolwide structures and processes necessary to sustain new practices."[50] This suggested the need to focus on the entire culture of the school; further, "We see everything constituting the culture of the school—its operational curriculum, written and unwritten rules, verbal and nonverbal communication, physical properties, pedagogical regularities, principal's leadership behavior and so on."[51] This led to research design in which the school's culture is the independent variable, and *both* (1) the behavior of the teacher and (2) pupil outcomes are seen as dependent on that culture, whereas *at the same time* pupil outcomes are seen as dependent on teacher behavior (see Figure 9–6).

In practical terms, Goodlad judged that, although the relationships, as shown in Figure 9–7, probably correctly represent important elements of "reality" for

FIGURE 9–6

A paradigm for studying ends-means-effects relationships and for improving schooling and learning. From John I. Goodlad, *The Dynamics of Educational Change* (New York: McGraw-Hill Book Company, 1975), p. 117.

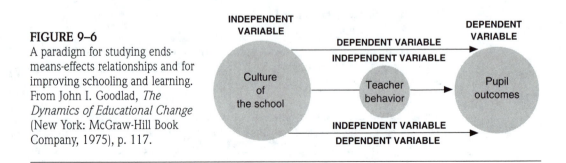

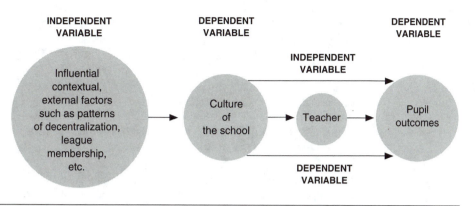

FIGURE 9–7   A paradigm for improving and studying educational practice with changes in the entire culture of a school the focus of attention. From John I. Goodlad, *The Dynamics of Educational Change* (New York: McGraw-Hill Book Company, 1975), p. 114.

schools, the design is much too complex for the practical study of schools in the "real world." He therefore settled on a study of the "causes" of the culture of the school, as shown in Figure 9–6.

The central proposition of Goodlad's research was "that entire schools can and should be regarded as malleable and capable of changing, and that, as schools change in their cultural characteristics, so do the people in them."[52] Further, a basic assumption was that in order to succeed, a client school must exhibit an internal sense of need, a desire to change. The principal experimental intervention was to train faculty members of schools to engage in a four-step process called DDAE (dialogue, decision making, action, and evaluation), which is essentially an OD intervention aimed at developing self-renewal in the schools. A significant additional feature of Goodlad's work was to join the participating schools in this five-year project into a "league" so that they could provide one another with a sense of mutual support and nurturance during the experimental period.

As Goodlad reported:

> In the high DDAE schools there were more cooperative teaching arrangements, more friendship networks among teachers, and more task-oriented communication among teachers. Teachers had more influence in decision-making, especially in areas affecting schools as total units. The quality of principal leadership was higher and principal influence depended more on competence. The principals in high DDAE schools were more apt to see teacher influence on schools as a desirable condition. These schools ranked higher on indices of school climate. By contrast, there were more self-contained classrooms in low DDAE schools. Teacher influence was more narrowly limited to areas affecting only a few people rather than the school as a whole and the principal was more apt to see teacher influence on schoolwide decisions as undesirable. The principal's influence was more likely to depend upon status and power to reward.[53]

The characteristics of high DDAE seemed to be associated in a school with significant potential for ongoing growth and self-renewal. But a visitor to such a school would have difficulty in isolating *an* innovation in that school because

> most of those being widely advocated were there: considerable use of audiovisual aids, especially by two or three children at a time and on their own; some of the new curricular materials, modified, flexible classroom space; multiage or non-graded groups and classes; use of parent volunteers in the instructional program; team planning, teaching, and evaluation.[54]

This kind of observation is characteristic of the self-renewing school: it is a growing and developing organization, not because of some agreement with an outside agency to employ a given innovation, but, rather, because it is continuously engaged in systematic problem solving and is able to select appropriate technology from all that is available.

W. EDWARDS DEMING AND TOTAL QUALITY MANAGEMENT

Contemporary thinking about organizational change is dominated by the work of W. Edwards Deming, whose ideas transformed Japanese industrial management from 1950 to 1980 while they were determinedly ignored and resisted in the United States. In the 1980s Deming's ideas began to transform management in the United States as well, and by the 1990s some U.S. educators were beginning to pay attention to them. Deming's story is truly spellbinding, and cannot be fully told in a book such as this. However, his ideas are essential knowledge for anyone who is interested in school reform.

To the student of organizational behavior in education, the most fascinating thing about Deming's work on organizational change is that most of it was not new. His genius was in weaving together into a coherent tapestry the threads of many ideas that had been discussed and advocated by a few students of organization, but strongly ignored and resisted by administrators, legislators, intellectual reformers, and school board members for decades. The most original aspect of his work, the ideas with which he began in Japan, had to do with the application of sophisticated statistical analysis of product quality in mass-production factories. But, as time went on, it became obvious to him that the knowledge about product defects that statistical analyses provided was in itself insufficient even in factories to bring about significant, lasting improvement in the functioning of the organization. He saw that, in order to transform Japanese industrial organizations from the joke that they were in the 1940s to the world-class powerhouses they became by the 1980s, it was necessary for them to embrace modern human resources ideas about organizational behavior. Deming soon came to devote most of his time and attention to propagating ideas about cooperation in the workplace: power-sharing, the motivating power of a shared organizational vision, transforming leadership, win-win conflict management, and growth-enhancing organizational culture that have already been dis-

cussed in this book. Thus he became a powerful advocate of participative management, empowerment, and transforming leadership as essential to the development
of organizations dedicated to high-quality work. These were the ideas that both industrial managers and educational administrators in the United States scoffed at and
parodied during the 1950s, 1960s, and 1970s, while their Japanese counterparts
seized on them eagerly and used them to build organizations that produced products whose quality became the new standard of the world.

Transforming Change

On June 24, 1980, NBC-TV aired a documentary "white paper" that explored the
question, *If Japan Can, Why Can't We?* In that year the imbalance of trade with
Japan made the United States look like a third-world country: while the United
States shipped $20.8 billion in raw materials such as lumber, coal, scrap metal, non-
ferrous metals, and seed grains and soybeans, it imported from Japan $30.7 billion
in such manufactured goods as automobiles, electronics, and finished steel.[55] The
implications for the future of U.S. business and industry were dismal indeed, and
most of the NBC show was devoted to the then-usual explanations to dismiss the
facts: the Japanese, so the explanation went, were able to market cheap copies of
American goods at low cost because they received unfair government subsidies,
copied American products instead of creating their own, and employed low-paid
"slave labor." But the last segment of the show introduced something very new that
was to prove astonishingly powerful: the ideas about quality management that W.
Edwards Deming had been teaching to Japanese managers since 1950. As an illustration, that segment showed how he had helped the management of the Nashua
Corporation, a small manufacturer of carbonless-paper products, apply those same
ideas in the United States with great success.

Some top executives of the Ford Motor Company, which by then was awash
in red ink and considering pulling out of its North American business because faltering sales were causing the company to lose hundreds of millions of dollars each
year, happened to be watching NBC that night. As early as 1978, a few who had
gone to Japan to learn the secret of their success had heard Japanese executives extolling the ideas that Deming had been teaching them. The Japanese were incredu-
lous that these educated, sophisticated, highly paid U.S. corporate executives had
not even heard of Deming until then. Desperate for a way out of Ford's downward
spiral in competition with Japan, they decided to look into these ideas. Ford's president, Donald E. Petersen, urgently appealed to a skeptical W. Edwards Deming to
work with his company.[56]

One February afternoon in 1981, Deming met with Ford leaders at their head-
quarters in Dearborn, Michigan. They fully expected him to suggest the installation
of some new inspection system or control processes. To their surprise, he talked to
them about the culture of the corporation and the vision of the future of the company
that its leaders shared. He went on to say that Ford's problems with low quality were
not the fault of the workers: he estimated that 85 percent of Ford's then-notorious
low product quality and undependability, which was hurting sales badly, rested on

the shoulders of the company's managers. This was a shock treatment for these powerful, wealthy corporate barons. However, Deming suggested that they talk with some people who had tried using his ideas in their business in the United States.

On May 15, 1981, twelve executives of the Ford Motor Company visited the Nashua Corporation. There William Conway, then Nashua's CEO, explained to them that total quality management (TQM), as Deming's concept had become known, is not merely some new inspection technique or added activity: it goes to the heart of an organization's culture and becomes the basic operating principle of every participant in the organization.[57] This was a whole new concept: that organizations are changed by being transformed from one kind of organization into a new and different kind of organization. TQM would be embraced by a few companies with whom Deming would work—Ford, Xerox, The New York Times, Dow Chemical, Procter & Gamble, and American Telephone & Telegraph notable among them. Their successes paved the way for wide acceptance of Deming's ideas.

Some educational critics, especially those who think of themselves as critical theorists—seeing that Deming had focused on industrial organizations and had used quantitative data and statistical analyses—have recoiled in horror at the thought of applying his ideas to educational organizations. These educational critics see Deming's ideas as merely the resurrection of the despised "factory model" in new guise, a neo form of Taylorism. Such stereotypic criticism misses the central idea that emerges from Deming's work, the idea of organizational transformation, which will probably endure as Deming's greatest legacy to thought on organizational change.

Simple Change Different from Transforming Change

Ordinarily, organizations are considered to be relatively stable systems that change by adapting to changing external demands. Indeed, a traditional measure of organizational excellence has been adaptability: how well and how quickly the organization recognizes and adapts to changes in its environment, thus retaining its long-term stability. In this sense, organizational change has heretofore been a relatively simple matter of adopting new technologies, adapting to new political realities, and conforming to new demands while the inner core remains relatively unchanged. Schools, for example, have made many adaptive changes over the years, yet their core activities have remained remarkably stable throughout.

This is illustrated by the way that schools have changed structurally over the years by reshuffling the clusters of grades: elementary school changed from grades 1–8 to K–6; the junior high school was invented, then became the middle school; high schools used to encompass grades 9–12, but now many are composed of grades 10–12. Usually such changes are occasioned in school districts by demographic shifts that put pressure on existing school facilities. These pressures can be eased most cheaply by redistributing class-groups of students between the buildings in new ways. This is usually accompanied by the creation of some educational rationale that makes it appear that the district is thoughtfully engaging in planned educational change. Through it all, the inner assumptions and structures—reflected in such things as teaching, classes, course credits, and schedules—changed very little, if at all.

Other efforts to change schools have been more genuinely motivated by educational philosophy and have sought to be more fundamental in changing the organization: one thinks of team teaching, open classrooms, revamping the curriculum and introducing new curricula, prolonged controversies over methods of teaching reading, and dozens of other changes that have occupied educators for decades and have resulted in slight change in schooling itself. That is because these are relatively simple changes, basically intended to help the school adapt to changes in the larger society. Deming's ideas (TQM), on the other hand, seek to transform the organization into something very different from what it was before.

> Unlike effecting simple change . . . *transforming* an organization into a TQManagement system is more fundamental . . . more like the caterpillar's metamorphosis than a chameleon's color change. Unlike the chameleon, the butterfly will maintain its hue despite new circumstances. What sets transformation apart from a single change, or a series of changes, is continuous movement in which all parts of the organization adjust toward the same end, at the same time.[58]

Brief Background on Deming

By 1939, when Deming joined the Census Bureau in Washington, he was already the acknowledged world expert on statistical sampling.[59] He soon became an international authority on techniques for designing and conducting census taking, as well. It was not surprising that in 1947, when the MacArthur administration* decided to conduct a census and assess the needs of war-torn Japan, Deming was chosen to oversee the project. By 1950, while in Japan, Deming became aware of the intense desire on the part of Japanese industrial managers to improve the quality of their products so that they could compete in world markets.

This was a subject that Deming knew a great deal about from his years of working on problems of quality for Western Electric, AT&T's manufacturing subsidiary, with Walter A. Shewart at the Bell Telephone Laboratories. Shewart was the senior of the two and Deming considered him to be a mentor as well as a friend and an associate. Deming edited Shewart's 1931 book, *Statistical Method from the Viewpoint of Quality.*[60] Thus it was not an accident that Western Electric telephones became the standard in the world for quality, reliability, and durability during the 1930s and 1940s.† However—and this is a point that should not be missed by educators—the Shewart-Deming collaboration on quality "was found to have great application not just in manufacturing but in the service end of the phone business. For years the American phone system was the envy of the world, providing a level of quality and of service unmatched anywhere else."[61]

---

*Harry S Truman was president of the United States, but Douglas MacArthur was in command in occupied Japan at the time.

†Coincidentally, their collaboration happened to occur at the Hawthorne works of Western Electric while the now-famed Western Electric studies were in progress there, though it seems unlikely that either Shewart or Deming was aware of those studies at the time.

Not surprisingly, astute Japanese industrial managers began to ask Deming to teach them how to improve the quality of their products. He began by teaching the Japanese some advanced techniques of statistical sampling, called "statistical process control," through which they could improve their procedures of inspecting for quality. Knowing only this much is sufficient to make many educators very wary of anything to do with Deming, especially those educators who are primarily concerned with the human dimensions of schooling. However, before long Deming realized that statistical sampling was only a part of managing for quality, and not the most important part. Deming quickly understood that what had been overlooked in the past was the human dimension of the problem, and it was here that he quickly focused his efforts and ultimately made his greatest contributions to understanding organizational change. It is in this area that educators can learn the most from W. Edwards Deming about planning and directing organizational change.

Lessons from Deming's Work

Transforming an organization is a near-total process that not only takes a great deal of effort and thought, it requires unswerving commitment from those in authority at the top of the organization. Fundamental to the process is a transformation of the organization's culture—the basic assumptions, beliefs, and values that give purpose to the behavior of everyone in the organization. Obviously, this is a complex and multifaceted undertaking. In simplified summary, such transformation of an organization is characterized by a cluster of concepts.

1. The Concept of Total Quality

The most difficult lesson from Deming for the educator to deal with is the way one thinks about quality. Deming was primarily concerned with manufactured products such as automobiles—a very different thing from educating children. At first glance, one might think that educators have little to learn from his industrial-oriented thinking. However, many believe that Deming's concepts of quality have, in fact, a great deal of relevance for schooling.

Traditionally, manufacturers had thought of quality in terms of the individual parts that, when finally assembled, made up the automobile. Quality was defined by establishing tolerances that were allowable in the dimensions of each part. For example, if a part was supposed to be 3 cm long, it might be considered acceptable if inspectors found that it actually measured within a range, say, from 2.988 cm to 3.002 cm. In factories around the world in 1950, it was usual practice to have inspectors check batches of finished parts after they came off the assembly line and accept those that were within the range of tolerances and reject the others. Rejected parts were either sent back to be fixed or scrapped, always an expensive process and usually with dubious results. Thus, as various parts were manufactured within their acceptable ranges of deviation and assembled into the final product, what ultimately emerged was, say, an automobile that was far from meeting the customer's expectations yet was deemed by the manufacturer to be "good enough."

Deming taught a different concept of quality to the Japanese, which came to be called "total quality." The goal was to make every part as right as possible, to do it the first time, and to strive constantly for perfection rather than to make things "good enough." This seems to be a simple enough idea, but in U.S. industry in 1950 it was literally unheard of, a revolutionary idea. In the 1950s and 1960s, when the American car buyer had little choice except to buy cars built to the traditional standard, the cars had to be considered good enough and they sold very well indeed because they were needed. However, by the 1970s, when Japanese cars reflecting the new concept of total quality became increasingly available as competitors in the U.S. marketplace, U.S manufacturers found themselves at a competitive disadvantage and their sales slumped while sales of Japanese cars soared. The Japanese were selling quality cars while the Americans were still trying to sell cars thought to be "good enough."

But Deming soon realized that this fundamental change in industrial practice could never be achieved by the traditional top-down boss-to-worker management practices that had given rise to the existing system in the first place. In fact, he realized, the central problem was traditional ways of doing things; these had to be changed if the fundamental shift to total quality concepts was to be possible at all. This realization led to the development of other interrelated ideas, which are described below. Together, they comprise the core of Deming's approach to total quality management.

2. Management Responsibility

Deming's entire approach rested on the premise that primary responsibility for the shortcomings of organizational performance result from management behavior and are not due to careless or inept workers. This is because managers control the ways in which decisions are made and how people work together. Though many organizational consultants in the United States had been making this same argument with scant effect since the results of the Western Electric studies had been published, Deming was able to demonstrate its simple truth by the unarguable success wrought by Japanese organizations with which he worked.

The argument is well known in U.S. schooling. Administrators, school board members, and others have long argued that disappointing educational performance is the fault of incompetent and uncaring teachers. The "fix" commonly prescribed has been to provide teachers with in-service training, nearly always narrowly delimited to instructional techniques; to more closely inspect and regulate their work; to require them to use "teacher proof" curricula and instructional materials. Rarely, in education as in industry, have administrators entertained the possibility that their managerial methods may well be a major part of the problem.

3. Testing Is Not the Answer

Deming made clear that the time-honored practice of inspecting for quality after the parts had been manufactured was inferior to designing a process that would produce better quality in the first instance. "Cease dependence on inspection to achieve quality," Deming exhorted. "Eliminate the need of inspection on a mass basis by building quality into the product in the first place."[62] The parallel in schooling is, of course, in relying on frequent testing to assess the quality of the educational process.

4. Intrinsic Motivation Is Best

Deming argued that enlisting the efforts of willing workers to do things properly the first time, and providing them with the proper tools to do the job, was more effective in improving organizational performance than either doing more testing or increasing the closeness of inspection by supervisors. To traditional U.S managers, weaned on top-down direction and control of workers, this was a difficult concept to take seriously. Their counterparts in educational organizations found it equally confounding, though it is an idea that has been advocated by organizational specialists for decades.

5. Emphasize Problem-Solving

Deming contended that workers possessed a great deal of expertise and knowledge that managers rarely enlisted in dealing with problems of organizational effectiveness. Thus, he urged greater cooperation between managers and workers in solving their mutual problems. This required that the fear and mistrust that workers ordinarily have of their superiors be driven out and replaced by trust and openness in the cooperative search for ways to improve organizational performance.

6. Eliminate Performance Ratings

To traditional managers, one of the more shocking and unbelievable of Deming's injunctions was that if the organization wants to maximize quality it will eliminate production quotas, performance ratings, and bonuses tied to productivity. The reasons are simple: quality is achieved through cooperation, not competition. This requires the development of an organizational culture in which openness, trust, and honesty in sharing information and ideas are prized, which is undermined by such practices as annual performance ratings. Deming put it this way:

> Evaluation of performance, merit rating, or annual review . . . nourishes short-term performance, annihilates long-term planning, builds fear, demolishes teamwork, nourishes rivalry and politics. It leaves people bitter, crushed, bruised, battered, desolate, despondent, dejected, feeling inferior, even some depressed . . . unable to comprehend why they are inferior. It is unfair, as it ascribes to the people in a group differences that may be caused totally by the system that they work in.[63]

7. Emphasize Sensitivity to the Needs of the Customer

Quality of organizational performance, Deming believed, lies in placing the needs of the customer foremost. Moreover, everyone—in every kind of organization—has a customer, Deming said, either inside or outside the organization, or both. Some educators, believing that it defiles teaching as a mere mercantile activity, are repelled by this idea. However, teachers have little problem with the proposition that schools should be sensitive to the needs of students and should strive to meet them. Yet one of the most common criticisms of schools is that they virtually ignore the real needs and expectations of students and persist in tailoring their efforts in harmony with tradition, custom, and the demands of various audiences rather than the needs of their "customers." In Deming's view, the customer's needs drive the entire organization.

8. Kaizen, *or the Principle of Continuous Improvement*

This is where Americans have the most to learn from the Japanese experience with Deming's ideas. It is also probably the most culturally influenced aspect of his work. Americans typically favor approaching a problem of change from the "silver bullet" perspective:

+ We look for a breakthrough invention, a "silver bullet" that represents a whole new approach to a problem.
+ We work very strenuously in short bursts of activity that we hope will "turn things around" quickly, so we think in terms of programs, projects, and task forces.
+ Like a ball game, we want a clear beginning to the process of change and an unambiguous final ending signal that leaves us the unambiguous winners.

School reform, itself, is often conceptualized in this way: something that can be achieved, put into place, and left to "run" while we turn to other interests in our lives. "Innovation" is an oft-repeated word in discussions on U.S. education. Discourses on school reform testify to the wish for bold new concepts, innovations if you will, such as reinventing schools, restructuring schools, turning top-down organizations into bottom-up organizations. We rattle on about a seemingly endless array of potential "breakthrough" programs of all sorts such as magnet schools, schools of choice, privatizing schools, Schools 2000, and school site management.

The Japanese, in contrast, think of organizational improvement as *kaizen,* or a continuous process: a patient day-by-day, week-by-week process of discovery that never ends, of taking small steps that make the functioning of the organization increasingly a little better all the time, over time. One thinks of the fable of the tortoise and the hare. Deming spoke of it as "constancy of purpose," and it was the first of fourteen points that he thought were basic to organizational change.[64]

William Lareau illuminated the differences between *kaizen* in Japan and innovation in the United States.[65] A key element of *kaizen,* he tells us, rests on the differences between American (or Western) and Japanese perceptions of job functions. In the West, employees are generally seen as having two types of duties:

1. *Maintenance*—keeping things running and doing the work.
2. *Innovation*—coming up with bold new ways of doing things, such as a new technology, new systems, and so on.

However, in the West a relatively few specialists have the task of innovating; most employees are expected to devote their energies almost exclusively to maintenance activities.

The Japanese view of job functions is much different. They believe that employees also have two job functions, but they are different functions:

1. *Maintenance*—as in the West, this is doing the work.

2. *Improvement*—making the process better.

There are two kinds of improvement, Lareau explained: *kaizen* and innovation. Rather than some bold new way of doing things, such as a new technology, *kaizen* is the ongoing pursuit of improvements *by every employee.* The latter point, that every employee is expected to pursue improvements, is a key difference between the approaches to change that Deming taught to the Japanese and the traditional top-down Western approach.

In practice, *kaizen* uses low technology which is inexpensive, involves everyone in collaborative group efforts, focuses on small improvements, and makes maximum use of conventional knowledge. Everyone is a player; administrators play the role of coaches rather than bosses; the focus is on adaptive, small, low-cost improvements; and employees are valued highly as knowledgeable and helpful partners.

Innovation, on the other hand, in practice emphasizes new, preferably high, technology, which is usually expensive, and turns first to the use of machines and systems; focuses on the creativity of a few heros to lead the way; and tends to start over with new stuff. A few specialists, who tend to work alone, create the system or technology; the role of everyone else is to adapt to it, playing, more or less, the role of robots. The goal is, ideally, to make relatively infrequent huge leaps by using technology and creating entire new systems.

A key element in the difference between *kaizen* and innovation is time. Those who practice *kaizen* must be patient, persistent, constant in purpose, to use Deming's phrase, and realize that it takes time to work out the vision that the group has for itself. Those who seek innovation tend to be impatient, seek a powerful one-shot opportunity, and expect to see clear results in short order.

CONCLUSION

Although many ways of classifying strategies for planned, managed organizational change have been devised, this chapter used Robert Chin's three-part typology:

1. *Empirical-rational strategies* are based on the concept that change can be fostered by systematically inventing or discovering better ideas and making them readily available in useful form to schools. Adherents of this strategy are often confounded by the difficulties usually encountered in the processes of "in-

stalling" new practices in the "target" schools. Typical difficulties are (1) ignoring the new ideas, (2) resisting or rejecting the new ideas, or (3) modifying the idea or practice in such ways that, when put into practice, it has been significantly changed.

2. *Power-coercive strategies* are based on the use (or potential use) of sanctions to compel the organization to change. For example, a state education department might require each school district to draw up and implement a program of competency-based instruction in accordance with specific guidelines. This could be accompanied by specific required timetables, forms of reporting, and other techniques for monitoring compliance. Problems often encountered with this strategy include the problem that public school systems (and, certainly, what are sometimes called "state public school systems") are—at best—composed of relatively loosely coupled components, through which it is difficult to transmit precise orders and from which it is difficult to extract compliance. As I have described, *satisficing* is commonplace in organizational decision making: that is, adopting workable responses to demands (sufficient to avoid sanctions) but not seeking maximally effective responses when faced with an array of conflicting demands.

3. *Normative-reeducative strategies* are based on the notion of bringing about change in schools by improving their problem-solving capabilities as organizations. This requires shifting the normative values of the school's culture (interaction-influence system) from those usually associated with hierarchical (bureaucratic, mechanistic, classical) organization to more creative, problem-solving norms. This process is widely referred to as *organizational self-renewal*. Techniques and processes for bringing about organizational self-renewal focus on developing increased skills among the staff members of individual schools in studying and diagnosing their own organizational problems systematically and in working out solutions to them. The term *organization development* (OD) is widely applied to these techniques for increasing the self-renewal capacity of schools.

The critical importance of helping schools to develop their own inner capacity for self-renewal was not widely understood (outside of the field of organizational behavior) until the failure of extensive applications of both empirical-rational and power-coercive strategies to achieve desired levels of success had produced widespread frustration and concern. By the 1980s, it was clear to thoughtful people concerned with education that the long-neglected area of developing self-renewal in schools would have to be addressed seriously if change in U.S. schooling were to move forward. By thus improving the organizational health of schools, it appears possible to make schools more proactive than defensive and to reach out responsively to adopt new ideas and implement changing goals of society.

Though schools are organizations and, therefore, share much with other kinds of organizations, it must be remembered that we know relatively little about their specific organizational characteristics. Although research on the organizational characteristics of schools is increasing, until very recently our assumptions about them have been derived largely from studies in other kinds of organizations (for example, business firms, military organizations, government agencies). But schools do possess special properties (not all, necessarily, unique) that may well affect the ways in which they should deal with issues of stability and change.

A common observation is, for example, that they are largely populated by a nonvoluntary clientele. Fullan, Miles, and Taylor pointed out six other special properties that undoubtedly must be considered in planning change.[66]

1. *Their goals are diffuse,* usually stated in general, even abstract terms with effectiveness measurement difficult and uncertain.

2. *Their technical capability* is low, with a weak specific scientific base underlying educational practice.

3. *They are loosely coupled systems,* which gives rise to coordination problems: activities are not always clearly connected to goals, and control (for example, accountability) is difficult to establish. (Recall the discussion in Chapter 3 that pointed out that this organizational feature of schools is not necessarily entirely negative: it also can be a source of flexibility and adaptability.)

4. *Boundary management is difficult* inasmuch as "the skin of the organization seems overly thin, over-permeable to dissatisfied stakeholders."[67]

5. *Schools are "domesticated" organizations,* noncompetitive, surviving in a relatively protected environment, and with little incentive for significant change.

6. *Schools are part of a constrained decentralized system:* fifteen thousand school districts in the United States with 89,000 buildings, each nominally autonomous, yet with many national constraints (for example, national textbook market, accreditation and certification requirements, statutes and case law).

In this organizational context, a legacy of study and practical experience that stretches back to the Western Electric studies and that has been brilliantly woven into a coherent tapestry by W. Edwards Deming, underscores the pragmatic necessity of developing and improving people-oriented change strategies in schools.

SUGGESTED READING

Argyris, Chris, *Knowledge for Action: A Guide to Overcoming Barriers to Organizational Change.* San Francisco: Jossey-Bass, 1993.

> One of the most respected students of organizational change offers practical guidance for improving the abilities of organizational members to solve the human problems of working together. Invaluable for the educational leader who wants to improve collegial behavior and implement empowerment on the job.

Bonstingl, John Jay, *Schools of Quality: An Introduction to Total Quality Management.* Washington, DC: Association for Supervision and Curriculum Development, 1992.

After taking one of Deming's famous four-day seminars in January 1992, this author undertook to translate Deming's ideas so that they could be applied specifically to schools. An early entry in the surge of interest in applying concepts of quality to educational organizations.

Deming, W. Edwards, *Out of the Crisis: Productivity and Competitive Position*. Cambridge: Cambridge University Press, 1982, 1986.

In addition to being awkwardly written, this book is problematic for educators because it addresses industrial organizations almost exclusively. Deming began to consider the problems of other kinds of organizations and how his approach to change could be applied to them only after it was written. Nevertheless, because there are so many interpretations of Deming's work around—including my own—the serious student will find it worthwhile to read the original work of the master.

Halberstam, David, *The Reckoning*. New York: William Morrow and Company, 1986.

Written at the height of the U.S. crisis, the same year in which Deming wrote his book, when there was fear for the very future of the United States in the face of Japanese success in the business and industrial world, Halberstam tried to demythologize the dramatic confrontation. He does it well, giving the reader a feeling for the dynamics and gritty details of who was involved and what actually happened. His portrayal of Deming's involvement with the Japanese is vivid and illuminating and, in itself, is reason enough to read this book.

Maeroff, Gene I., *The Empowerment of Teachers: Overcoming the Crisis of Confidence*. New York: Teachers College Press, 1988.

Written by a professional writer who is a Senior Fellow at the Carnegie Foundation and was a consultant for the Rockefeller Foundation, and under a grant from the Rockefeller Foundation, this book strongly argues the case for teacher empowerment, which is an idea supported by both foundations. It includes an incisive analysis of the professional circumstances of public school teachers today and shows how, by restructuring schools to provide greater autonomy to teachers, they may be significantly changed. Maeroff believes, of course, that these changes will result in marked improvement in the performance of schools.

Schmidt, Warren H. and Jerome P. Finnegan, *The Race Without a Finish Line: Lessons from the Malcolm Baldridge Winners*. San Francisco: Jossey-Bass, 1992.

Japan has the Deming Prize, which is funded by the royalties from Deming's writings, to recognize the companies that have done the most outstanding job of improving their products and organizations. Since 1988, the United States has had the Malcolm Baldridge Quality Award for the same purpose. This book describes what is meant by total quality and how the quality revolution has unfolded in the United States by recounting the experiences of such Baldridge award winners as the Commercial Nuclear Fuel Division of the Westinghouse Electric Corporation, Motorola Inc., Xerox Corporation Business Products and Systems, Cadillac Motor Car Division of the General Motors Corporation, Federal Express Corporation, and IBM.

Schmuck, Richard A., Philip J. Runkel, Jane H. Arends, and Richard I. Arends, *The Second Handbook of Organization Development in Schools*. Palo Alto, CA: Mayfield Publishing Company, 1977.

A classic, in its second edition, this is the bible for practitioners who want to know what organization development and organization self-renewal are all about. Filled with specific, practical, how-to help, aids, and advice for those who want to be involved in implementing the theory and concepts in a school or school system. Very strongly recommended.

Walton, Mary, *Deming Management at Work: Six Successful Companies That Use the Quality Principles of the World-Famous W. Edwards Deming*. New York: Perigee Books, 1991.

An excellent analysis of Deming's philosophy and methods and how they have been applied in transforming six U.S. businesses. Its description, for example, of how Florida Light & Power spent four years transforming itself until it won the prestigious Deming Award from the Japanese Union of Scientists and Engineers is highly illuminating and can help educators think through some of the parallels between schooling and business organizations. Walton also describes how some nonindustrial organizations have used quality concepts, including the Tri-Cities (Kingsport, Johnson City, and Bristol) of Tennessee, the Hospital Corporation of America, and the United States Navy.

NOTES

1. Matthew B. Miles, "Some Properties of Schools as Social Institutions," in *Change in School Systems,* ed. Goodwin Watson (Washington, DC: National Training Laboratories, NEA, 1967), p. 20.
2. National Commission on Excellence in Education, *A Nation at Risk* (Washington, DC: Government Printing Office, 1983).
3. Evans Clinchy, "Magnet Schools Matter," *Education Week,* December 8, 1993, p. 28.
4. Seymour B. Sarason, *The Predictable Failure of Educational Reform: Can We Change Before It's Too Late?* (San Francisco: Jossey-Bass, 1990).
5. Ibid., p. 73.
6. Ibid., p. 72.
7. Ibid.
8. Paul R. Mort and Donald H. Ross, *Principles of School Administration* (New York: McGraw-Hill Book Company, 1957), p. 181.
9. Paul R. Mort, "Educational Adaptability," in *Administration for Adaptability,* ed. Donald H. Ross (New York: Metropolitan School Study Council, 1958), pp. 32–33.
10. "Kindergarten Education, 1967–68." *NEA Research Bulletin,* 47, no. 1 (March 1969), 10.
11. Paul R. Mort and Francis G. Cornell, *American Schools in Transition* (New York: Teachers College, Columbia University, 1941).
12. A. G. Grace and G. A. Moe, *State Aid and School Costs* (New York: McGraw-Hill Book Company, 1938), p. 324.
13. Austin D. Swanson, "The Cost-Quality Relationship," in *The Challenge of Change in School Finance,* Proceedings of the Tenth Annual Conference on School Finance (Washington, DC: Committee on Educational Finance, National Education Association, 1967), pp. 151–65.
14. Richard O. Carlson, *Adoption of Educational Innovations* (Eugene: Center for the Advanced Study of Educational Administration, University of Oregon, 1965).
15. For a full description of PSSC, see Paul E. March, "The Physical Science Study Committee: A Case History of Nationwide Curriculum Development" (unpublished doctoral dissertation, Graduate School of Education, Harvard University, 1963).
16. Two other taxonomies that are widely used are those developed by (a) Daniel Katz and Robert L. Kahn, and (b) Ronald G. Havelock. There is substantial agreement among the three taxonomies. For a discussion, see Robert G. Owens and Carl R. Steinhoff, *Administering Change in Schools* (Englewood Cliffs, NJ: Prentice-Hall, 1976), Chapter 4.
17. David L. Clark and Egon G. Guba, "An Examination of Potential Change Roles in Education," in *Rational Planning in Curriculum and Instruction,* ed. Ole Sand (Washington, DC: National Education Association, 1967).
18. Such as the Biological Sciences Curriculum Study (BSCS), the Physical Sciences Study Committee (PSSC), the Chemical Bond Approach Project (Chem Bond or CBA), and the School Mathematics Study Group (SMSG).
19. Gerald Zaltman, David Florio, and Linda Sikorski, *Dynamic Educational Change: Models, Strategies, Tactics, and Management* (New York: The Free Press, 1977), p. 77.
20. Robert Chin, "Basic Strategies and Procedures in Effecting Change," in *Educational Organization and Administration Concepts, Practice and Issues,* ed. Edgar L. Morphet and others (Englewood Cliffs, NJ: Prentice-Hall, 1967).
21. Homer Garner Barnett, *Innovation: The Basis of Cultural Change* (New York: McGraw-Hill Book Company, 1953).
22. Matthew B. Miles, *Innovation in Education* (New York: Columbia University Press, 1964), p. 14.
23. Robert Chin and Kenneth D. Benne, "General Strategies for Effecting Changes in Human Systems," in *The Planning of Change,* 2nd. ed., ed. Warren G. Bennis, Kenneth D. Benne, and Robert Chin (New York: Holt, Rinehart & Winston, 1969).
24. Group on School Capacity for Problem Solving, *Program Plan* (Washington, DC: National Institute of Education, June 1975), p. 1.
25. Paul Berman and Milbrey Wallin McLaughlin, *Federal Programs Supporting Educational Change, Volume VIII: Implementing and Sustaining Innovations* (Santa Monica, CA: Rand Corporation, May 1978), p. iii.

26. This study is fully reported in eight volumes under the general title, *Federal Programs Supporting Educational Change* (Santa Monica, CA: Rand Corporation).
Volume I: *A Model of Educational Change* by Paul Berman and Milbrey Wallin McLaughlin (1975).
Volume II: *Factors Affecting Change Agent Projects* by Paul Berman and Edward Pauley (1975).
Volume III: *The Process of Change* by Peter W. Greenwood, Dale Mann, and Milbrey Wallin McLaughlin (1975).
Volume IV: *The Findings in Review* by Paul Berman and Milbrey Wallin McLaughlin (1975).
Volume V: *Executive Summary* by Paul Berman, Peter W. Greenwood, Milbrey Wallin McLaughlin, and John Pincus (1975).
Volume VI: *Implementing and Sustaining Title VII Bilingual Projects* by Gerald Sumner and Gail Zellman (1977).
Volume VII: *Factors Affecting Implementation and Continuation* by Paul Berman and others (1977).
Volume VIII: *Implementing and Sustaining Innovations* by Paul Berman and Milbrey Wallin McLaughlin (1978).
27. Group on School Capacity for Problem-Solving, p. 1.
28. Ibid., p. 4.
29. Ibid., p. 5.
30. T. Barr Greenfield, "Organizations as Social Inventions: Rethinking Assumptions about Change," *Journal of Applied Behavioral Science,* 9, no. 5 (1973), 551–74.
31. Chris Argyris, *Integrating the Individual and the Organization* (New York: John Wiley & Sons, 1964), p. 123.
32. Matthew B. Miles, "Planned Change and Organizational Health: Figure and Ground," in Richard O. Carlson and others, *Change Processes in the Public Schools* (Eugene: Center for the Advanced Study of Educational Administration, University of Oregon, 1965), p. 17.
33. Adapted from Miles, "Planned Change," pp. 18–21.
34. Rensis Likert, *New Patterns of Management* (New York: McGraw-Hill Book Company, 1961).
35. Gordon L. Lippitt, *Organizational Renewal: Achieving Viability in a Changing World* (New York: Appleton-Century-Crofts, 1969).
36. Matthew B. Miles and Dale G. Lake, "Self-Renewal in School Systems: A Strategy for Planned Change," in *Concepts for Social Change,* ed. Goodwin Watson (Washington, DC: National Training Laboratories, NEA, 1967).
37. Far West Laboratory, "A Statement of Organizational Qualification for Documentation and Analysis of Organizational Strategies for Sustained Improvement of Urban Schools" (paper submitted to Program on Local Problem-Solving, National Institute of Education, San Francisco, 1974).
38. John I. Goodlad, *The Dynamics of Educational Change: Toward Responsive Schools* (New York: McGraw-Hill Book Company, 1975), p. 175.
39. Gerald Zaltman, David H. Florio, and Linda A. Sikorski, *Dynamic Educational Change: Models, Strategies, Tactics, and Management* (New York: The Free Press, 1977), p. 89.
40. Michael Fullan, Matthew B. Miles, and Gib Taylor, *OD in Schools: The State of the Art, Volume I: Introduction and Executive Summary.* Final report to the National Institute of Education, Contract nos. 400-77-0051-0052 (Toronto: Ontario Institute for Studies in Education, August 1978), p. 14.
41. The following discussion of OD concepts and force-field analysis is from Robert G. Owens and Carl R. Steinhoff. *Administering Change in Schools* (Englewood Cliffs, NJ: Prentice-Hall, 1976), pp. 142–48.
42. See, for example, Spencer Wyant, *Organizational Development from the Inside: A Progress Report on the First Cadre of Organizational Specialists* (Eugene: Center for the Advanced Study of Educational Administration, University of Oregon, 1972).
43. Jack R. Gibb, "TORI Theory: Consultantless Team-building," *Journal of Contemporary Business,* 1 (Summer 1972), 33–34.
44. The concepts of force-field analysis and the three-step cycle of organizational change are generally credited to Kurt Lewin, "Frontiers in Group Dynamics," *Human Relations,* 1 (1947), 5–41. The definitive work in this field by Lewin is *Field Theory in Social Science* (New York: Harper & Row, Publishers, 1951).

45. Lewin, "Frontiers in Group Dynamics," p. 35.

46. Paul Hersey and Kenneth H. Blanchard, *Management of Organizational Behavior: Utilizing Human Resources,* 3rd ed. (Englewood Cliffs, NJ: Prentice-Hall, 1977), p. 2.

47. Michael Fullan, Matthew B. Miles, and Gib Taylor, *OD in Schools: The State of the Art* (Toronto, Ontario: Ontario Institute for Educational Studies, 1978), 4 volumes.

48. Philip J. Runkel and Richard A. Schmuck, *Findings from the Research and Development Program on Strategies of Organizational Change at CEPM-CASEA* (Eugene: Center for the Advanced Study of Educational Administration, Center for Educational Policy and Management, University of Oregon, 1974), p. 34.

49. John I. Goodlad, *The Dynamics of Educational Change: Toward Responsive Schools* (New York: McGraw-Hill Book Company, 1975), p. xi.

50. Ibid., p. 113.

51. Ibid.

52. Ibid., p. 115.

53. Ibid., p. 135.

54. Ibid., pp. 139–40.

55. Mary Walton, *Deming Management at Work: Six Successful Companies that Use the Quality Principles of the World-Famous W. Edwards Deming* (New York: Perigee Books, 1991), p. 13.

56. Andrea Gabor, *The Man Who Discovered Quality: How W. Edwards Deming Brought the Quality Revolution to America—The Stories of Ford, Xerox, and GM* (New York: Times Books, Random House, 1990), p. 3.

57. Warren H. Schmidt and Jerome P. Finnegan, *The Race Without a Finish Line: American's Quest for Total Quality* (San Francisco: Jossey-Bass, 1992), p. 196.

58. Schmidt and Finnegan, *The Race,* p. 90.

59. Rafael Aguayo, *Dr. Deming: The American Who Taught the Japanese About Quality* (New York: Carol Publishing Group, A Lyle Stuart Book, 1990), p. 7.

60. Walter A. Shewart, *Statistical Method from the Viewpoint of Quality* (New York: Van Nostrand, 1931).

61. Aguayo, *Dr. Deming,* p. 7.

62. W. Edwards Deming, *Out of the Crisis: Quality, Productivity and Competitive Position* (Cambridge: Cambridge University Press, 1982), p. 23.

63. Ibid., pp. 101–102.

64. Ibid., p. 23.

65. This section follows the ideas of William Lareau, *American Samurai: A Warrior for the Coming Dark Ages of American Business* (New York: Warner Books, 1991).

66. Fullan, Miles, and Taylor, *OD in Schools,* p. 2.

67. Ibid.

The Holographic Imperative and Qualitative Research

ABOUT THIS CHAPTER

There was a time when people believed that scientific thinking required us to extract phenomena from the real world, break them down into constituent parts and, after examining them closely, reassemble them, conceptually or actually, in order to understand how things happen. This is reductionist thinking and it derives from a rational model of thought: the belief that some rational order and system underlies the manifest confusion and ambiguities that are obvious in the world around us. Moreover, it has long been assumed that the most powerful scientific explanations would be those that could be proved by empirically testing theoretical propositions through mathematical algorithms.[1]

THE HOLOGRAPHIC IMPERATIVE

For a long time, students of organizational behavior believed the above statement. Indeed, much of the organizational theory that has been described in this book emerged from traditional rationalistic, reductionist thinking intended to produce mathematically demonstrable certitude. However, much of what has been described in this text came from a new and different kind of scientific thinking that is now emerging and that cuts across all of the scientific disciplines.

It has been called "the holographic imperative" because it emphasizes the need for holographic thinking, which entails "viewing the problem in three dimensions, at many different levels of detail and from every angle."[2] This new kind of thinking explains, in large part, the growing interest in organizational culture and organizational climate and how they help to explain the behavior of people at work. Through the examination of culture as an explanation of organizational behavior one views the organization in depth as a complex integrated whole for which there can be no single, simple explanation. Organizations and the behavior of people in them must be understood in different ways when viewed from different perspectives.

Importance of the New Scientific Thinking

The newer, holographic, kind of scientific thinking is essential and it is important. It is essential if we are to better understand the apparent disorder, ambiguities, and disjunctures in our organizational environments—both physical and social—that we have long ignored because they are difficult to study. James Gleick called this seeming inexplicable disorder that is so commonplace in human experience Chaos. In a remarkable 1987 best-selling book he described the new ways of thinking that scientists from all disciplines are using in the process of "making a new science."

They are doing this, he explained, by trying to understand the complexities of the world we live in, rather than to concentrate on the neat bits of that world that can be easily separated from the whole for convenient study.[3]

It is holistic thinking, rather than the traditional reductionist thinking of science, and it represents a major shift in science. "We find strong evidence that a number of the underpinnings of our basic beliefs are under challenge," noted James Ogilvy and Peter Schwartz. "That challenge is coming from a multifaceted revolution of the sort that we have experienced only a few times in the course of our civilization's history: the revolution that began more than a century ago and has gathered momentum ever since involves as great a change as the Copernican revolution or the emergence of the Enlightenment."[4]

We need not probe deeply into this new scientific revolution here. However, we must be aware that new ways of thinking about schools that reflect these major shifts in scientific thought are having great impact on the ways in which we study organizations and the behavior of people in them. In recent years, a new approach to organizational research that reflects the new way of thinking scientifically, called *naturalistic* research, has developed rapidly to challenge the traditional approaches to research that have been dominant in the study of educational organizations for generations.

In supplanting traditional rationalistic ways of thinking, naturalistic research methods have, in fact, made it possible for significant new knowledge of organizational behavior in education to develop. For example, the concepts of organizational culture have emerged as dominantly as they have in contemporary understanding of organizational behavior in schools precisely because reductionist views had become so unsatisfactory in explaining behavior in them that people sought more powerful holistic, holographic explanations.

Although a shift in ways of thinking that is as fundamental as this is not simple and easy to understand, its importance requires that we become aware of the ways in which it differs essentially from the old ways of scientific thinking that are now being challenged. Studies of organizational culture exemplify the use of this kind of thinking as it is used in research on organizational behavior.

DESCRIBING AND ASSESSING ORGANIZATIONAL CULTURE IN SCHOOLS

The study of organizational culture presents nettlesome problems to the traditional researcher primarily because important elements of culture are subtle, unseen, and so familiar to persons inside the organization as to be considered self-evident and unworthy of discussion. Collecting, sorting, and summarizing data such as the significant historical events in the organization and their implications for present-day behavior, the impact of organizational heroes on contemporary thinking, and the influence of traditions and organizational myths is a task that does not lend itself to the tidiness of a printed questionnaire and statistical analysis of the responses to it. As the work of Ouchi, Peters and Waterman, Kanter, and Deal and Kennedy demonstrated, it is necessary to get inside the organization: to talk at length with people; to find out what they think is important to talk about; to hear the language they use; and to discover the symbols that reveal their assumptions, their beliefs, and the values to which they subscribe. For that reason, students of organizational culture tend to use field research methods rather than traditional questionnaire-type studies. This has raised vigorous debate in many schools of education as to the epistemological value of field research methods as contrasted with the more traditional statistical studies (of the experimental or quasi-experimental type) that have long been the stock-in-trade of educational researchers. In order to understand contemporary issues in organizational culture in education, it is essential to have some grasp of the research problems involved.[5]

As Egon Guba[6] has pointed out, there are several paradigms[7] for discovering "truth" or for "understanding." There is, for example, a judicial paradigm that has well-established rules of procedure, rules of evidence, and criteria for judging the adequacy of a given judicial proceeding. The judicial paradigm provides guidelines for behavior in courtrooms, hearings, and other judicial approaches to discovering "facts," "truth," and "understanding." Until recently the judicial paradigm has had little utility in educational inquiry but is now gaining popularity as an approach to educational evaluation.[8]

Another widely used paradigm for gaining understanding or discovering meaning is that of expert judgment. This is, of course, commonly used in the accreditation of educational institutions in which the site visiting team is expected to exercise expert judgment. Such an approach is commonplace in judging athletic performances and artistic efforts of many kinds.[9]

Two Paradigms of Systematic Inquiry

At the present time, two other—and distinctly different—paradigms vie for dominance in systematic inquiry in educational administration. These paradigms gained prominence in the 1950s with the so-called theory movement in educational administration. A major factor in the theory movement was the recognition that the social and behavioral sciences had much to contribute to the study of administration—not only theory, concepts, and knowledge drawn from these sciences but also their research traditions. The history of the social and behavioral sciences, themselves, had been filled for over a century with epistemological issues related to the "two modes of thought,"[10] that is, deductive and inductive inquiry.

William James described the tender-minded and the tough-minded; others have spoken of the theoretical and the practical. "Hard versus soft," "natural versus social," "science versus criticism," "quantifiers versus describers," and "rigor versus intuition" are common clichés often used to describe the dichotomy between the "two modes of thought" in administrative and organizational research. Thus, in reducing the dialectic to simple and rigid polarities, and often coming close to moral judgments such as "good" or "bad," the complexities and nuances in these two approaches to "knowing," "understanding," and, not least important, thinking are obscured.

The Issue of Terminology

On the other hand, the lack of precision and clarity as to the essential characteristics of the two paradigms of administrative inquiry as well as their implications for methodology tends to obscure and confuse the criteria that are appropriate to use in judging methodological adequacy. How should these paradigms be described and what should they be called? This is not a simple issue. Indeed, it has generated increasing debate among inquirers and research methodologists in educational administration in recent years.[11]

In this discussion, the traditional, long-dominant paradigm is called *rationalistic* and is conceptualized as a paradigm that, while it embraces a number of research techniques, is essentially associated with deductive thinking and logical-positivist views of "knowing" and "understanding" social and organizational phenomena. The other major paradigm in administrative inquiry is labeled the *naturalistic* paradigm. It, too, includes a number of research techniques, but it is essentially based on inductive thinking and is associated with phenomenological views of "knowing" and "understanding" social and organizational phenomena.

It is neither possible nor desirable to examine here all of the "shades of gray" that may or may not describe various methodological views that may or may not lie on a possible continuum between these two paradigms. Indeed, it is likely that emphasis on blurring the essential differences between the paradigms makes it more difficult to establish well-recognized criteria by which to assess the methodological adequacy of research. Therefore, in the following discussion, the rationalistic and the naturalistic paradigms are described as a relatively simple dichotomy—as prototypes, somewhat in the sense that Weber discussed the characteristics of ideal bureaucratic organizations in his classic work.

One recognizes, of course, that in the "real world" such prototypes are rarely encountered. Indeed, it can be reasonably argued that the traditional "rules" that govern rationalistic administrative inquiry are so rarely followed as to give rise to frequent expressions of concern about the quality of research in the field of educational administration. The central point to be made is that there are legitimate ways of conducting administrative inquiry other than the traditional (rationalistic) way and that the use of other alternatives does not result in sloppy research.

It is recognized that both the naturalistic and the rationalistic paradigms represent legitimate modes of systematic inquiry. They are different paradigms arising from different perceptions of such things as the nature of social phenomena and ways of understanding them. Although the two paradigms often tend to compete for legitimacy and support, they are, in fact, complementary methods of investigation available for use in the knowledge-production process essential to informing educational administration.

The Rationalistic Paradigm

Of the two research paradigms, the rationalistic paradigm stands clearly as *the* dominant approach in educational administration. It is often called quantitative research though, as will be seen, this is a misnomer. It is commonly thought to be a methodology, which it really is not. However, this paradigm is more widely published, taught, accepted, and rewarded in educational research circles than any other approach,[12] and it has been well established as the dominant method of disciplined inquiry.

Clearly the epitome of the rationalistic paradigm is the controlled experiment, which Donald Campbell and Julian Stanley describe as

> the only means of settling disputes regarding educational practice, the only way of verifying educational improvements, and the only way of establishing a cumulative tradition in which improvements can be introduced without the danger of faddish discard of old wisdom in favor of inferior novelties.[13]

Little administrative research has used the controlled experimental research design, however.

In the rationalistic paradigm, nonexperimental research methods are considered inferior, but acceptable, methods if certain procedural safeguards to ensure the basic integrity of the study are adequate. Essentially, the view is that what exists can be extrapolated from its environment and, because it exists, it exists in some measure and, thus, can be quantified. Some basic assumptions that underlie this set of notions about "procedural safeguards" and "integrity" are the following:

1. That certain parts of the real world, which are called "variables," may be singled out (literally or through statistical manipulation) from reality for study or treatment while other parts of the setting are controlled. Ideally, therefore, laboratory experimentation is the epitome of method because of the greater control it affords the inquirer.

2. That the inquirer and the subject under study are, and should remain, independent of one another. Typically this is facilitated by interposing "objective" data-gathering instruments between the inquirer and the subjects under study.

3. That context-free generalizations are not only possible but also the essential goal of inquiry.

4. That quantitative methods are inherently preferable to nonquantitative methods—thus leading to the common confusion between the concept of quantitative methods and the rationalistic paradigm itself.

5. That the use of a priori theory and hypothetico-deductive methods (typically hypothesis-testing) is important to the design of studies and to the cumulation of knowledge itself.

6. That a preordinate design should specify each step of the inquiry in advance, from data collection through its analysis.[14]

Operationally, research organized by the tenets of the rationalistic paradigm begins with an existing theory, which is used to set up an articulated problem in advance of the inquiry. The next step is to convert the problem into dependent and independent variables. Having done this, the researcher proceeds to develop strategies and instruments in an attempt to control and uncover relationships between and among the naturally occurring variables through the design. Once the steps of the preordinate research design have been completed, the inquirer returns to the theory to interpret the results.[15]

Here, the term "rationalistic" will be used in referring to inquiries that (1) use formal instruments or other a priori techniques for categorizing as the primary basis for collecting data, (2) transform the data into quantitative expressions of one kind or another, and (3) attempt to generalize the findings in some formal way to some universe beyond that bounded by the inquiry. It is realized, of course, that this is not an exhaustive list of the characteristics of the "rationalistic" paradigm of inquiry, but they are viewed as the salient ones and, therefore, are regarded as modal characteristics.

The rationalistic paradigm is—by an awesome margin—the dominant, established tradition in systematic inquiry. Any competing paradigm must be compared and contrasted with this standard approach to inquiry in modern science.

The Naturalistic Paradigm

The second of the two inquiry paradigms in science is the naturalistic paradigm. What is not always clear is that naturalistic inquiry is based on two sets of concepts, which taken together provide a strong rationale for it as a research paradigm.[16] One set of concepts is the *naturalistic-ecological hypothesis,* which claims that human behavior is so significantly influenced by the context in which it occurs that regularities in those contexts are often more powerful in shaping behavior than differences among the individuals present. In this view, the behavior of people in schools is seen as powerfully influenced by the organizational context in which it occurs.[17] Thus, "if one wants to generalize research findings in schools, then the research is best conducted within school settings where all these forces are intact."[18]

The other set of concepts basic to naturalistic inquiry is the *qualitative-phenomenological hypothesis.* This essentially holds that one cannot understand human behavior without understanding the framework within which the individuals under study interpret their environment and that this, in turn, can best be understood through understanding their thoughts, feelings, values, perceptions, and actions.

The term "naturalistic" is appropriate as will be explained, but first it should be made clear that the naturalistic paradigm is a different way of "knowing" than the rationalistic paradigm. It emanates from a basically different view of the six assumptions discussed earlier. The naturalistic inquirer posits that

1. In the real world, events and phenomena cannot be teased out from the context in which they are inextricably embedded, and understanding involves the interrelationships among all of the many parts of the whole.

2. It is illusory to suppose that interaction between inquirer and subject might be eliminated. Indeed, this dynamic relationship can make it practicable for the inquirer, himself or herself, to become the data-gathering and processing "transducer."

3. Generalizations are suspect, at best, and knowledge inevitably relates to a particular context.

4. Qualitative methods—which emphasize both inner and outer knowledge of man in his world—are preferable. As William Filstead put it, "Qualitative methodology allows the researcher to get close to the data, thereby developing the analytical, conceptual, and categorical components of explanation from the data itself."[19]

5. Theory emerges from the data themselves in the sense that Glaser and Strauss describe "grounded theory."[20]

6. The naturalistic inquirer, believing in unfolding multiple realities (through interactions with respondents that will change both them and the inquirer over time) and in grounded theory, will insist on a design that unfolds over time and that is never complete until the inquiry is arbitrarily terminated as time, resources, and other logistical considerations may dictate.[21]

What Does "Naturalistic" Mean?

It is important to start with some clear notion as to exactly what the term "naturalistic" means when it is applied to inquiry. Partly because the term has complex meanings, but mainly because it is at odds with awesomely well-entrenched traditional concepts regarding inquiry, it helps to try to define the term in two ways: (1) what it essentially means to inquirers and (2) how it differs from what may be called "rationalistic" inquiry.

The term "naturalistic" expresses one view as to the nature of reality. It is the view that the real world that we encounter "out there" is a dynamic system all of whose "parts" are so interrelated that one part inevitably influences the other parts. To understand the reality of that world requires acceptance of the notion that the parts cannot be separated, bit by bit, for careful examination without distorting the system that one seeks to understand. The parts must be examined as best as possible in the context of the whole. It is, essentially, a phenomenological view—as differentiated from a logical-positivistic view—of reality of the world.

On the one hand, the logical-positivist approach to understanding the complex world emphasizes singling out various "variables" for study while attempting to control other variables in the situation. The naturalist, on the other hand, views this as altering the situation, resulting in distortions of our understanding of reality. Thus, if one seeks to understand the realities of human organizations and the behavior of people in them, the naturalistic view would hold that those organizations must be examined in all the rich confusion of their daily existence. Human behavior must be studied *in situ* if it is to be understood.

The term "naturalistic" is used here in referring to inquiries that (1) primarily employ direct contact between investigators and actors in the situation as a means of collecting data, (2) use emergent strategies to design the study rather than a priori specification, (3) develop data categories from examination of the data themselves after collection, and (4) do not attempt to generalize the findings to a universe beyond that bounded by the study. Again, it is realized that many other characteristics may properly be associated with naturalistic inquiry, but to me these are the salient—and therefore modal—characteristics of naturalistic inquiry.

Are "Naturalistic" and "Qualitative" Synonymous?

It is now possible to turn to the term "qualitative" in the context of the foregoing discussion. Although "naturalistic" alludes to *ways* in which one may seek to examine reality and these ways emphasize the wholeness and phenomenological interrelatedness of the real world, "qualitative" alludes to the *nature of the understanding* that is sought. Qualitative inquiry seeks to understand human behavior and human experience from the actor's own frame of reference, not the frame of reference of the investigator. Thus, naturalistic inquiry seeks to illuminate social realities, human perceptions, and organizational realities untainted by the intrusion of formal measurement procedures[22] or reordering the situation to fit the preconceived notions of the investigator. The qualitative nature of the resulting description enables the investigator to see the "real world" *as those under study see it.*

Thus, qualitative description is not necessarily the exclusive territory of the naturalistic inquirer. Positivists can, and do, use qualitative methods in their investigations. For example, data gathered through paper-and-pencil instruments can be (and often are) used as indicators of group norms or values or other social forces that influence behavior.[23] However, the *techniques* for uncovering and describing the qualities of these norms and values differ importantly between the two approaches. The naturalistic inquirer will in all likelihood regard gestures, language, and behavioral patterns of the subjects as significant descriptive data. The positivist, on the other hand, tends to search for understanding through data supplied by either the subjects or others using such standardized means as questionnaires and inventories or through analysis of demographic or other descriptive data. The *nature* of the quality of description yielded by these two approaches differs, however, in important ways: one yields lean, spare description stripped of the contextual references in which the data originated; the other yields what Clifford Geertz called *thick description.*[24]

Thick description provides meaning of human behavior in the real world in such terms as cultural norms, deep-seated values and motives arising from cherished tradition, and community values. "Believing, with Max Weber, that man is an animal suspended in webs of significance he himself has spun," commented Geertz, "I take culture to be those webs, and the analysis of it to be therefore not an experimental science in search of law but an interpretive one in search of meaning."[25] Thus, thick description conveys very much the sense of the web of interrelated contextual factors that is associated with the situation under study. Thick description is more than mere information or descriptive data: it conveys literal description that figuratively transports the readers into the situation with a sense of insight, understanding, and illumination not only of the facts or the events in the case, but also of the texture, the quality, and the power of the context *as the participants in the situation experienced it.*

This qualitative characteristic of inquiry is well illustrated by Philip Cusick, who spent six months in a high school as a participant observer. He noted, for example, that teachers in the school routinely spent ten to fifteen minutes of the forty-minute class period checking excuses and passes and on other actions intended to control students.[26] Further, when teachers finally did attend to the lesson for that class period, inattentiveness on the part of some students and numerous interruptions from others greatly reduced the amount of time devoted to teaching and learning activities. Thus, he estimated that the average student spent less than one and a half hours a day mentally engaged in the processes of learning.[27] But Cusick's observations go beyond this sort of informing, which is relatively objective and quantified, to take on the richer meaning associated with thick description.

He discovered, for example, that teachers and administrators often ignored gambling and stealing among the students and punished those who cut classes or violated school routine.[28] Students who did little work were reported to succeed academically as long as they paid strict attention to classroom routines and school rules.[29]

This sort of qualitative description of life in schools has been confirmed numerous times in a wide variety of sources such as those cited by Charles Silberman in "Education for Docility."[30] Such description "takes the reader there" and conveys a keen insight into the behavior of people in those schools. It is qualitatively "thick" in that much that is meaningful about the context-bound nature of the behavior under study is conveyed.

Judging the Adequacy of a Naturalistic Study

As the "domain assumptions"[31] that underlie rationalistic and naturalistic inquiry are basically different and essentially polar, so the criteria by which to judge the appropriateness of research design and methodological adequacy of studies representing the two domains are significantly different. The question arises as to which criteria are appropriate in judging the adequacy of a reported study.

In rationalistic inquiry, for example, the researcher seeks some slice of the "real world"[32] that is comprehensive enough to be generalizable. Therefore, in assessing the design of such a study one looks for representativeness of the sample, which is usually assured by either a random sample or a selected sample. If the response rate is adequate, it is possible to generalize the results to a large population which the sample represents. This is, of course, commonly referred to as external validity.

To minimize bias on the part of the investigator, the researcher seeks to eliminate subjectivity and maximize objectivity. At least a careful social distance is maintained between subject and investigator—often by interposing formal data-collecting instruments (such as paper-and-pencil questionnaires) between the two—in order to minimize affective bias (such as empathy) that arises from interactions. Normally the proximity of the investigator to the situation under study is minimized to assure maximum detachment from it.

In the rationalistic paradigm, the investigator seeks to control for the unknown and unknowable. For example, random procedures are normally used for selecting samples of subjects within the total population under study. Researchers may not even know what the differences are that they are seeking to cancel out: they need only to know that random distribution across groups should prevent any differences from making a difference.[33] If it is not feasible to select the sample of a population randomly, the investigator may seek to heighten control of unknown variables by matching population samples on the basis of "relevant variables." The remaining variables, having been declared irrelevant, are no longer considered to be intrusive in the realm under study.

One is concerned also in rationalistic inquiry with the need to be sure that the data-collection measures yield consistent results. If the tests are given again or if the interviews are replicated, will the same results be obtained or is there likely to be some drift leading to confounding interpretation?[34] Thus, researchers are concerned with the reliability of their data-gathering procedures such as instrument reliability, reliability between items, and reliability between and among raters and/or interviewers.

Certainly a preordinate research design is essential in rationalistic inquiry. It should specify in advance of initiating the study each step that will be taken to collect and analyze data in order to test the hypotheses or answer the research questions. Important in the design are the specified procedures by which the investigator will deal with issues of external validity, objectivity, internal validity, and reliability. When the preordinate design of research utilizing the rationalistic paradigm is evaluated, these are important criteria by which its adequacy is judged. In execution of the research and, finally, in examining the written research report, these are or ought to be important issues under consideration.

Because of the assumptions about the nature of reality and ways of understanding that reality in the naturalistic paradigm, the traditional concern for objectivity, validity, and reliability have little relevance for the design of naturalistic research. Michael Scriven's now-classic work on subjectivity and objectivity was a major contribution, pointing out that what have traditionally been called "objective" and "subjective" have commonly been confused with the quantification of data, often masking the matter of subjective bias.[35] In short, Scriven made clear that quantification in research, usually accompanied by statistical manipulation of data, has come to be confused with objectivity, which is the *sine qua non* of rationalistic research.

In order to avoid unreliable, biased, or opinionated data, the naturalistic inquirer seeks not some "objectivity" brought about through methodology but, rather, strives for validity through personalized, intimate understandings of phenomena stressing "close in" observations to achieve factual, reliable, and confirmable data.[36] Whereas the rationalistic methodologist might pursue confirmation through the use of data from a number of subjects, the naturalistic methodologist often seeks to confirm through the intensive study of a small group or even a single individual.

The striving for generalizability has had powerful impact on the canons of the rationalistic paradigm of inquiry. However, Lee Cronbach has brilliantly argued that generalizations are not enduring: they do, in fact, break down over time in all fields of science, the physical and biological as well as the social sciences.[37] If the stars shift their courses so as to render star maps obsolete, and DDT fails to control mosquitoes as genetic transformations make them resistant to the compound, and as protons are apparently found to degenerate, it becomes clear that every generalization is less scientific truth than it is history. Further, it may reasonably be argued, of course, that the processes of developing generalizations in the "hard sciences" are appropriately different from the case in educational administration. Often in the physical and biological sciences, investigators seek generalizations based on a large number of like events, which must necessarily be observed indirectly. Thus, statistical methods facilitate the building of models that may be explanatory. In educational organizations, in contrast, there are relatively few events that may be described as "alike" and, what is more, these events often may be best observed directly.

But more germane to the present discussion is the inescapable conclusion that, far from achieving generalizations, rationalistic inquiry used in the study of social systems reveals "truth" very much embedded in the context in which it is discovered. This concept is crucial in administrative and organizational inquiry for, as Guba and Lincoln have observed: "It is virtually impossible to imagine any human behavior that is not heavily mediated by the context in which it occurs."[38] Thus, the notion of discovering context-free generalizations in human social systems is seriously called into question by the naturalistic paradigm.

Characteristics of the Naturalistic Research Plan

The inquirer in the rationalistic paradigm views research design as a sequence of discrete procedures bounded by a predetermined time line. The naturalistic investigator views the design as providing an emergent plan for a highly interactive process of gathering data from which analysis will be developed. It is described here as an interactive process because data collection and analysis go on simultaneously, with the analysis giving direction to the data collection by suggesting what to check, when to seek confirmation, and how to extend the data collection itself. To be more specific, it is now in order to turn to a brief discussion of three elements that are ordinarily found in the plan of a naturalistic study: the research strategy, strategies for collecting data, and the audit trail. This is appropriate whether considering the proposal stage, the execution, or the reporting of naturalistic research.

The Research Strategy

Normally, the research strategy will provide for a rather broad-scale exploration at the outset that is simultaneously accompanied by checking for accuracy, seeking verification, testing, probing, and confirming as the data collection proceeds. Typically, the strategy will emphasize data gathering in the early phase of the project. Checking, verifying, testing, probing, and confirming activities will follow in a funnel-like design resulting in less data gathering in later phases of the study along with a concurrent increase in analysis—checking, verifying, and confirming (see Figure 10–1).

In the early stage of such a study, perhaps 80 percent of the time and effort will be spent in gathering data, whereas 20 percent will be devoted to analysis; in the latter stages of the study, this may be reversed with 80 percent devoted to analy-

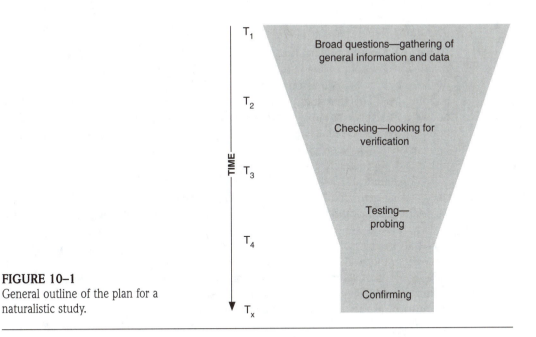

FIGURE 10–1
General outline of the plan for a naturalistic study.

sis and 20 percent devoted to data collection (see Figure 10–2). An important element in the design of naturalistic research is starting with questions of broad scope and proceeding through a conceptual funnel—working with data all the while, ever trying to more fully understand what the data mean—making decisions as to how to check and how to verify as the investigation unfolds. It is important in the design of such a study that the investigator be fully prepared to look for unanticipated perceptions arising from the data as he or she gets closer and closer to the data over time.

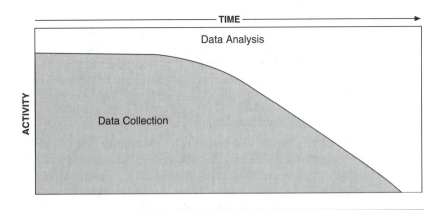

FIGURE 10–2 Typical pattern of data collection and data analysis in a naturalistic study.

The Audit Trail

Guba and Lincoln have proposed that an "audit trail" be carefully maintained throughout the course of a naturalistic study. This should consist of documentation of the nature of each decision in the research plan, the data on which it was based, and the reasoning that entered into it.[39] The existence of a carefully documented audit trail makes it possible to do two important things: (1) to examine the procedures of the study, either while it is in progress or after the fact, in order to verify its consistency and credibility by independent external auditors and (2) to make it possible to reproduce the study at another time.

An audit trail consists of deliberately leaving sufficient evidence so that someone external to the inquiry could review the processes and results of the inquiry and ascertain whether the processes were appropriate and the results were reasonable and credible. A basic component of the audit trail is the investigator's log. In this personal journal, the investigator meticulously records not only all contacts throughout the study from beginning to end, but also two other key kinds of information: (1) the reasoning and logic that entered into every decision as the investigation unfolded and (2) the hunches, guesses, feelings, and perceptions of the investigator as they occurred during the course of the investigation.

But a log is not an audit trail; at best it is an annotated index to the audit trail. The trail itself will consist of numerous documents that carefully preserve the record of the investigation. Among them may be the following:

1. Raw notes from interviews and observations.
2. Edited summary notes of interviews and observations.
3. Records of meetings about the research.
4. All documents used as data sources.
5. Guidelines and "rules" used for content analysis of documents.
6. Decision rules by which data were categorized.
7. Interview guidelines.
8. Completed documents that may have been commissioned as part of the study.

Guba has proposed that, particularly in the case of evaluation studies, an independent external auditor be employed to conduct an impartial audit and report on the reasonableness of the study's findings in light of the investigative procedures used.

Strategies for Collecting Data

It is important that the naturalistic research design (1) provide for multiple data sources and methods of collection and (2) describe the techniques that were used to check and validate analyses as the research proceeded. The procedures used to implement these strategies are important in determining the credibility of any naturalistic study. Six procedures relevant to data gathering in naturalistic inquiry are described in the next section.

Procedures to Enhance Credibility

When confronted with the bewildering, dynamic patterns of interrelated people, events, and contexts in organizations, investigators are necessarily called on to "make sense" of the confusion. At the same time, they are called upon to demonstrate that the steps they have taken in this sense-making process yield credible explanations. How, for example, does the researcher using the naturalistic approach sort out the complex patterns of behavior in an organization so as to discern what is "really" happening? And, having done so, how do researchers assure themselves and others that they understood what was "really" happening and were not misled by the intrusion of bias and various sources of error? How can the findings of such inquiry be accepted as credible interpretations of reality? Answers to questions such as these must be provided by the naturalistic inquirer, and these answers must be in harmony with the basic assumptions of the naturalistic paradigm—the holistic perspective on reality, the multiple factors of causation, the likelihood that truth may not be singular and that there may be many "truths" in a situation, and the certainty that the truths are all context-bound. Such a study, then, will utilize a number of techniques intended to enhance its credibility. Six of these techniques considered essential to the design of naturalistic inquiry will be briefly discussed.

Prolonged Data Gathering on Site

Time—an extended period of time—spent immersed in the situation is important. It provides for entry into the situation, "learning the language," and becoming accepted, trusted, and ultimately relatively unnoticed. Time permits the researcher to see the atypical in the situation against a backdrop of broad trends so that he or she can sort the significant from the passing event. Time also permits the researcher to check his or her deepening perceptions of what is happening and to examine his or her own biases and attitudes in terms of the situation under study. In short, time is essential to permit the researcher to shift from predispositions, through early impressions, to a deeper level of understanding. Throughout the period of prolonged data gathering, the inquirer's log should record a chronicle of the struggle to understand—the thickening of description and the deepening of insight into the situation under study.

Triangulation

The investigator uses a number of sources of information and data, not necessarily about different things but also perhaps about the same things. For example, as themes begin to arise from interviews or documents or observation, they are cross-checked with other sources so as to verify them, to check the accuracy of information, and to test different actors' perceptions of given events. Whenever possible, the researcher should use multiple data-gathering techniques including interviews, document analysis, self-reports, questionnaires, observation, and other approaches. This ensures the potential for cross-checking and verifying data.

Member Checks

The investigator continuously corroborates data, information, and perceptions with relevant others in the organization being studied. Quite literally he or she may go to an actor in the situation and say, "Some people say that [such and such] is typical of the way things get done here. What do you think?" The process of member checks is perhaps the single most important means available to the naturalistic inquirer for establishing the credibility of an inquiry. Again, the researcher's log and the audit trail should include careful documentation of member checks and how the feedback from them was used in the inquiry.

Referential Adequacy Materials

Wherever possible the investigator should create and maintain a file of materials from the site that relate to findings and interpretations. This can include all sorts of relevant documents (for example, handbooks, copies of memos, and other ephemeral materials). It might well also include videotapes, audiotapes, photographs, and films. These materials can help preserve over time some sense of the context in which observations were made and thus aid in recall of events. The investigator must make careful judgments, however, in balancing, on the one hand, the wish to have a complete videotaped record of the study with, on the other hand, the need not to intrude excessively into the setting under study, thereby changing the context.

Thick Description

In the course of prolonged observation, the investigator will be carefully triangulating, conducting member checks, corroborating information, and collecting referential adequacy materials *all for the purpose of developing thick description.* This calls for synthesizing, integrating, and relating observations in such a way as to "take the reader there." This is not an easy task and it will be treated further, below.

Peer Consultation

It is desirable, particularly in the case of lengthy observational studies, to be able to disengage from the setting and discuss the progress of the work and the nature of the experience with qualified peers who are interested.[40] For the graduate student investigator this might be a meeting with the thesis director or other members of the thesis committee who are skilled in naturalistic methods. Peer consultation provides opportunities while the inquiry is still in progress to check one's thinking, to raise questions and concerns, and to talk through problems of which the investigator may or may not be aware. Again, the investigator's log should record peer consultation, note the nature of the feedback received, and reveal how the study has been redirected as a result.

Characteristics of the Naturalistic Research Report

In reporting rationalistic research, language becomes important and words significant. For example, persons under study are routinely referred to as *subjects,* a term etymologically derived from the Latin word *subjectus,* meaning literally to place one under, put one under, another's authority.[41] Form also becomes important and is highly standardized. Speaking to this point, Eisner observed:

> the standardization of style is considered a virtue. One is supposed to identify the problem, review the literature, describe the instruments and population, report the treatment, present and discuss the results and, finally, project possible implications. If, in this format, any sense of the personality of the investigator shines through, it is to be neutralized. This is accomplished by requiring that writers use the third person singular or the first person plural instead of using the I form. The people studied are referred to as "subjects" or "S's" and whatever uniqueness particular individuals might have are [sic] to be disregarded.[42]

A distinctive characteristic of the naturalistic research report is that it is usually written in ordinary language. In contrast with research reports in the rationalistic paradigm, naturalistic inquirers rarely refer to "subjects" let alone "S's." More commonly they speak of *respondents*—from the Latin word *respondens,* meaning responding, answering.[43] The difference between this term and the rationalistic paradigm's use of *subject* is not inconsequential; the latter clearly reveals the intent of the rationalistic inquirer to control the subjects (or, at least, control what happens to them) as opposed to the naturalistic inquirer's intent to *understand* what the respondent experiences, knows, believes, feels, and values.

A second characteristic of the naturalistic research report is that it is trustworthy. It must be based on trustworthy data collection and analysis procedures, a few of which have been discussed. But the report itself must be plausible, carefully documented, and provide corroboration from multiple sources. In short, it is valid, meaning not only that it is accurate or based on well-corroborated evidence, but also that it provides rich, thick description. Judgments and conclusions in the report should be demonstrably reasonable, meaning that they are well connected to the evidence and supportable by a carefully maintained audit trail.

Third, as should all research reports, it should be well organized. Its parts should be well interconnected and follow a clear plan of exposition. The report should be as free of jargon as possible, but it should be lively and rich in thick description that "takes the reader there."

Fourth, the report should be fair and ethical. The evidence in it should not have been obtained under false pretenses and the report should scrupulously observe agreements as to confidentiality, either explicit or implied, that were entered into during the study. Certainly it is as important to safeguard the rights of respondents as it is to safeguard the rights of subjects in rationalistically designed research. The problem of defining and specifying ethical behavior, as all researchers know, grows more complex with time.

Among naturalistic inquirers there is some debate as to how much the investigator should interpret his or her observations for the reader. Some, such as Roger Barker,[44] contend that events and conditions should be described, leaving the reader to interpret the meaning; others, such as Louis Smith and W. Geoffrey,[45] attempt to provide thick description supplemented by interpretation. However, a basic purpose of the naturalistic research report is to "take the reader there"—to provide a report that yields a rich sense of understanding events and of having insight as to their meaning or, more likely, meanings. Therefore, an important factor in judging the adequacy of a naturalistic research report is the clarity with which the texture and quality of the findings are transmitted to the reader.

There are numerous classic examples in this regard that are instructive. One thinks, for example, of William Whyte's description of the bowling matches between the Norton Street gang and another young men's group.[46] In reading it, one comes to understand the social relationships that were played out between the groups and the individuals in them. By describing the bowling match in careful detail, Whyte enables the reader to "see" how this one incident portrayed behavior that he had seen many times before in the neighborhood in other contexts.

As an illustration, the following quotation from a section of a study of the schooling of hearing-impaired children is apropos. It is an example of thick description, portrayed in ordinary language in a lively manner—all important criteria in judging the adequacy of a naturalistic research report.

"SOUNDS IN A SILENT WORLD"

The silent world of the deaf can only be inferred by the hearing observer, he cannot fully know it. It is a world apart from the experience of that observer. It has a different language, different customs, and different values. Its inhabitants rely on different senses in interpreting their experiences. The citizens of the silent world think differently, linking concepts which have arisen from experience, rather than creating syntactical arrangements of language that describe experience. They seek associations among those who are like themselves and derive enjoyment from their companionship. They find it difficult to cope with the citizens of the hearing world, who speak a language foreign to them, who have values different from their own, who make demands on them which are often incomprehensible, and who, in turn, often fail to understand them when they strive to make themselves understood.

They and their hearing associates live in two distinctly different cultures. They have agreed on names for these cultures. One is called the deaf world. The other is called the hearing world. The symbolism of these conventional terms is not accidental.

Sometimes the relatives and the educators of the citizens of the silent world desperately desire for them to move into their world. Seldom is that their desire, and seldom is it possible. They are content, rather, to remain in the company of their deaf friends and to seek fulfillment in the world of silence.

The hearing individual who wishes to enter the silent world may get his passport in order and move among the natives. He may even go so far as to learn the language. It is a strange and foreign one. It also requires the use of a totally different communication system. No longer can he rely on speaking or writing but must learn a new alphabet and new concept-symbols which are expressed in an entirely different medium, manual signs. He may even develop considerable dexterity in the use of this strange language and "speech," but at best it will remain a second language. It is not his native tongue. He must be prepared to remain forever alien. He is not equipped to experience the reality of the deaf person's world. He can only infer that reality, handicapped as he is by his own cultural differences. To step into that world is a cultural shock.

Surprisingly, the silent world is a noisy place. Contrary to one's expectations, upon entering that world he is immediately struck by the volume of sound. But the sounds are not those normally encountered. The citizens of this world have been taught to accompany their use of the native sign language with the use of oral speech, even though they, themselves, cannot hear that speech. The result is striking. It is a speech the visitor is unprepared for.[47]

CONCLUSION

Scientific thinking has, for a long time, been dominated by rationalistic, positivistic, reductionist ideas. The traditional concept of scientific research, methodologically celebrated in the controlled laboratory experiment as the epitome of scientific method, has therefore long been established in the study of organizational behavior as the standard of scientific rigor.

Within the last century, however, a new approach to scientific thinking has been developing in all of the sciences, not merely in the social and behavioral sciences. The new scientific thinking emphasizes the need to take a *holographic* view of the phenomena that we wish to study, a view that is holistic, a view that examines the context as well as the parts. This has, of course, required the development of rigorous research methods that are compatible with the new view. Among these are qualitative, naturalistic methods of field research.

Qualitative, naturalistic research methods—such as ethnography—offer a way to study the behavior of people in educational organizations that use the newer, holographic, holistic approach to scientific understanding. Since about 1980 there has been an upsurge in the use of these methods in the study of organizational behavior in educational organizations.

Qualitative, naturalistic research methods have been described and discussed as a legitimate method of choice in the study, for example, of organizational culture. Qualitative, naturalistic research is viewed as a way of seeking "truth" or understanding in organizations that is different from "truth" or understanding as traditional scientists have conceptualized it. It is an alternative research method, well suited to certain kinds of research questions but not necessarily superior to or inferior to other research methods.

The essential theory of qualitative research has been described and the research procedures used to implement the theory have been discussed. Further, these have been compared and contrasted with traditional quasi-experimental research so as to differentiate clearly between the assumptions and the procedures properly used by the two approaches.

SUGGESTED READING

Bogdan, Robert C., and Sari Knopp Bicklen, *Qualitative Research for Education: An Introduction to Theory and Methods.* Boston: Allyn and Bacon, 1982.

This is an excellent introduction to qualitative research theory and methods. In 252 easy-to-read pages, Bogdan and Bicklen provide an authoritative, yet highly lucid, overview that conveys with considerable clarity what qualitative research is and why. A very useful book for those who want to get a clearer grasp of what qualitative research is and for those who want to plan and carry out a study.

Fetterman, David M., *Ethnography Step by Step*. Newbury Park, CA: Sage Publications, 1989.
This small book does just what its title promises. As is true of most how-to-do-it volumes, it shows only one way to do ethnography, which is the qualitative study of culture. It is a reliable guide to the basics of a standard approach to qualitative research. Its 7-page bibliography is superb.

Marshall, Catherine, and Gretchen B. Rossman, *Designing Qualitative Research*. Newbury Park, CA: Sage Publications, 1989.
As the title suggests, this book concentrates on the issues and procedures for designing the qualitative study. In addition to providing an excellent orientation to the research process, it is a mine of practical advice and suggestions. The 10-page bibliography overlooks some standard references; nevertheless, it is a good one. A fine book for anyone considering launching a qualitative study.

NOTES

1. See, for example, the classic work of Daniel E. Griffiths, *Administrative Theory* (New York: Appleton-Century-Crofts, 1959).
2. Richard F. Tucker, " 'Holographic' Science to Meet Energy Needs," *Scientific American* (March 1990), 128.
3. James Gleick, *Chaos: Making a New Science* (New York: The Viking Press, 1987).
4. Peter Schwartz and James Ogilvy, *The Emergent Paradigm: Changing Patterns of Thought and Belief* (Menlo Park, CA: SRI International, 1979) p. 1.
5. The following section is adapted from Robert G. Owens, "Methodological Rigor in Naturalistic Inquiry: Some Issues and Answers," *Educational Administration Quarterly*, 18, no. 2 (Spring 1982), 1–21.
6. Egon G. Guba, "ERIC/ECTJ Annual Review Paper: Criteria for Assessing the Trustworthiness of Naturalistic Inquiries," *Educational Communication and Technology Journal*, 29 (Summer 1981), 75–91.
7. Thomas S. Kuhn, *The Structure of Scientific Revolutions*, vol. 2, no. 2, *International Encyclopedia of Unified Science*, 2nd ed. (Chicago: University of Chicago Press, 1970).
8. Robert L. Wolf, "The Use of Judicial Methods in the Formulation of Educational Policy," *Educational Evaluation and Policy Analysis*, 1 (January-February 1979), 19–28.
9. Elliot W. Eisner, "On the Differences between Scientific and Artistic Approaches to Qualitative Research." *Educational Researcher*, 10 (April 1981), 5–9.
10. James B. Conant, *Two Modes of Thought: My Encounters with Science and Education* (New York: Trident, 1964).
11. See, for example, R. Lindgren and R. Kottkamp, "The Nature of Research: A Conference Report," *UCEA Review*, 22 (Winter 1981), 2–4; and A. L. Jefferson, "Qualitative Research: Implications for Educational Administration, a Conference Report," *UCEA Review*, 22 (Winter 1981), 5–6.
12. Ray C. Rist, "On the Relations among Educational Research Paradigms: From Disdain to Detente," *Anthropology and Education*, 8, no. 2 (May 1977), 42–48.
13. Donald T. Campbell and Julian C. Stanley, *Experimental and Quasi-Experimental Designs for Research* (Chicago: Rand McNally & Company, 1963), p. 2.
14. Robert E. Stake, *Evaluating the Arts in Education* (Columbus, OH: Charles E. Merrill Publishing Company, 1975).
15. Francis A. J. Ianni, "Field Research and Educational Administration," *UCEA Review*, 17 (February 1976).
16. Stephen Wilson, "The Use of Ethnographic Techniques in Educational Research," *Review of Educational Research*, 47, no. 1 (Winter 1977), 245–65.

17. For examples, see Roger G. Barker, *Ecological Psychology* (Stanford: California University Press, 1968); Dan C. Lortie, "Observations on Teaching as Work," in *Second Handbook on Research on Teaching,* R. M. Travers, ed. (Chicago: Rand McNally & Company, 1973); James G. March, "American Public School Administration: A Short Analysis," *School Review,* 86, no. 2 (February 1978), 217–49; and Seymour Sarason, *The Problem of Change and the Culture of the School* (Boston: Allyn and Bacon, 1971).

18. Wilson, "The Use of Ethnographic Techniques," p. 248.

19. William J. Filstead, *Qualitative Methodology* (Chicago: Markham, 1970), p. 6.

20. Barney G. Glaser and A. L. Strauss, *The Discovery of Grounded Theory* (Chicago: Aldine Publishing Co., 1967).

21. Guba, "ERIC/ECTJ Annual Review Paper," p. 8.

22. Robert L. Wolf and Barbara Tymitz, "Ethnography and Reading: Matching Inquiry Mode to Process," *Reading Research Quarterly,* 12 (1976–1977), 5–11.

23. Jack D. Douglas, ed., *Understanding Everyday Life: Toward Reconstruction of Sociological Knowledge* (Chicago: Aldine Publishing Co., 1970).

24. Clifford Geertz, "On the Nature of Anthropological Understanding," *American Scientist,* 63 (January-February 1975), 47–53.

25. Clifford Geertz, *The Interpretation of Cultures* (New York: Basic Books, Publishers, 1973), p. 5.

26. Philip Cusick, *Inside High School* (New York: Holt, Rinehart & Winston, 1973), p. 29.

27. Ibid., pp. 42–68.

28. Ibid., p. 160.

29. Ibid., p. 61.

30. Charles E. Silberman, *Crisis in the Classroom* (New York: Random House, 1970).

31. Alvin W. Gouldner, *The Coming Crisis in Western Sociology* (New York: Basic Books, Publishers, 1970).

32. Kenneth Carlson, "Ways in Which Research Methodology Distorts Policy Issues," *Urban Review,* 11 (Spring 1979), 3–14.

33. Ibid., p. 5.

34. Michael Q. Patton, *Alternative Evaluation Research Paradigm* (Grand Forks: University of North Dakota Press, 1975).

35. Michael Scriven, "Objectivity and Subjectivity in Educational Research," Chapter V, in *Philosophical Redirection of Educational Research,* 71st Yearbook, Part 1, National Society for the Study of Education, L. G. Thomas, ed. (Chicago: University of Chicago Press, 1972).

36. Rist, "On the Relations," p. 46.

37. Lee J. Cronbach, "Beyond the Two Disciplines of Scientific Psychology," *American Psychologist,* 30 (February 1975), 116–27.

38. Egon G. Guba and Yvonna S. Lincoln, *Effective Evaluation* (San Francisco: Jossey-Bass, 1981), p. 62.

39. Ibid., p. 122.

40. Jack T. Murphy, *Getting the Facts* (Santa Monica, CA: Goodyear Publishing Co. 1980), pp. 71–72.

41. Robert L. Wolf. "An Overview of Conceptual and Methodological Issues in Naturalistic Evaluation," (paper presented at the annual meeting of the American Educational Research Association, Boston, April 1980), p. 4.

42. Eisner, "On the Differences," p. 7.

43. Wolf, "An Overview of Conceptual and Methodological Issues," p. 3.

44. Barker, *Ecological Psychology.*

45. Louis M. Smith and W. Geoffrey, *The Complexities of an Urban Classroom* (New York: Holt, Rinehart & Winston, 1968).

46. William F. Whyte, *Street Corner Society,* 2nd ed. (Chicago: University of Chicago Press, 1955).

47. James R. Upchurch, "A Description of a School Culture by Teachers of Hearing Impaired Children" (unpublished doctoral dissertation, Indiana University, 1980), pp. 69–74.

Page numbers followed by an *f* indicate figures.